新时代背景下中企海外投资法律实务导航系列丛书　　总策划　李海容

共建"一带一路"中国投资者赴欧投资法律实务

李海容　主编

中国政法大学出版社

2024·北京

声　明　1. 版权所有，侵权必究。
　　　　　2. 如有缺页、倒装问题，由出版社负责退换。

图书在版编目（CIP）数据

共建"一带一路"：中国投资者赴欧投资法律实务 / 李海容主编. -- 北京：中国政法大学出版社，2024.7.
ISBN 978-7-5764-1610-7

Ⅰ．D922.295

中国国家版本馆 CIP 数据核字第 2024XW4085 号

书　名	共建"一带一路"：中国投资者赴欧投资法律实务 GONGJIAN "YIDAIYILU"：ZHONGGUO TOUZIZHE FUOU TOUZI FALÜ SHIWU
出版者	中国政法大学出版社
地　址	北京市海淀区西土城路 25 号
邮　箱	bianjishi07public@163.com
网　址	http://www.cuplpress.com（网络实名：中国政法大学出版社）
电　话	010-58908466(第七编辑部) 010-58908334(邮购部)
承　印	固安华明印业有限公司
开　本	720mm×960mm 1/16
印　张	23.75
字　数	376 千字
版　次	2024 年 7 月第 1 版
印　次	2024 年 7 月第 1 次印刷
定　价	120.00 元

编委会

总策划：李海容
主　编：李海容
编委会：吕　威　崔北婕　苏　兰　敖　翔
　　　　　岳虹君　王　钰　段皓文　赵丹丹

序 一

在全球经济一体化的大潮中，中国成长为世界第二大经济体，也是资本输出大国和资本输入大国。中国企业如璀璨星辰，境外投资的步伐愈发坚定且迅捷。随着"一带一路"倡议的深入推进，中国企业在国际舞台上展现出前所未有的活力与影响力。然而，境外投资之路并非坦途，交织着复杂多变的法律问题，风险与机遇并存。因此，对中国企业而言，系统地研究并熟练应对境外投资的法律实务问题，不仅是必要的，更是刻不容缓的。

"新时代背景下中企海外投资法律实务导航系列丛书"旨在为中国企业赴海外投资提供一份详尽的法律实务指南。编者在丛书中深入分析了投资目的地国家法律的最新发展动态，结合中国企业的实际需求，从投资前的尽职调查、投资协议的磋商与签署，到投资后的运营与管理等环节，全面系统地梳理了境外投资各环节可能面临的法律问题及应对策略。

在进行海外投资的过程中，中国企业既要应对东道国独特的法律环境，还需要适应境内外投资交易习惯差异带来的挑战。丛书特别强调了案例研究的重要性，旨在指导企业在遵守目的地国家法律、行业规则和交易习惯的同时，有效保护并促进自身的合法权益，从而在交易中占据有利地位，制定最佳应对策略。同时，编者也关注到了经营者集中审查、合规经营等热点话题，以期为中国企业提供全面而务实的法律支持。

法律实务的精髓在于实践与理论的结合。本丛书在阐述法律规则的同时，注重提供实务操作的指引。本丛书邀请国外著名的法律实务专家就其所在国的投资案例进行法律分析，使读者能够直观地感受到法律规则在实际操作中的应用，从而更好地理解和运用这些规则。该系列丛书的欧洲篇，介绍了各个国家的热门行业，如瑞士的工业投资，法国的医药行业投资，罗马尼亚、葡萄牙的新能源投资，斯洛文尼亚的家电投资，以及希腊、荷兰的物流领域投资，乃至通过开曼群岛和英属维尔京群岛构建的投资架构等，为读者提供了宝贵的实践经验和深刻的法律见解。

当我们在考虑对外投资时，首先，外资准入与国家安全审查是中国投资者必须跨越的第一道法律门槛。以《共建"一带一路"：中国投资者赴欧投资法律实务》为例，欧洲各国对外资的审查标准不一，且随着地缘政治形势的变化，审查力度日益加强。中国投资者在进入欧洲市场前，必须深入研究目标国家的外资政策和法律环境，确保投资活动符合相关法律法规的要求，避免触发国家安全审查机制。其次，环境保护与劳工权益保护是欧洲法律体系中的两大核心议题。欧洲各国对环境保护和劳工权益的重视程度远超许多其他地区，相关法律法规的制定和执行也更为严格。中国投资者在欧洲投资时，也需要遵守这些法律，确保生产经营活动不对环境造成破坏，同时保障员工的合法权益。这不仅是对法律的尊重，更是企业具有社会责任感的体现。再次，税务筹划与合规也是中国投资者在欧洲投资过程中必须面对的重要法律问题。欧洲的税收制度复杂多变，各国之间的税收政策也存在较大差异。中国投资者在享受欧洲市场带来的经济利益的同时，也必须妥善应对税务风险，制订合理的税务筹划方案，确保税务合规，避免不必要的法律纠纷和财务损失。最后，合同与争议解决机制也是法律实务领域需要重点关注的议题。在跨国投资过程中，合同的签订与执行是保障双方权益的关键环节。中国投资者在与欧洲合作伙伴签订合同时，需要注重合同条款的明确性和可执行性，确保自身权益得到充分保障。同时，在争议解决方面，了解并熟悉欧洲的争议解决机制，如仲裁、诉讼等，也是保障投资活动顺利进行的重要前提。我也非常高兴地看到，本系列丛书对这些法律关键问题都有所涉猎。此外，中国缔结的双边投资协定和区域贸易协定所提供的投资者保护、多边投资担保机构（MIGA）和中国出口信用保险公司提供的海外投资政治风险保险、解决投资争端国际中心（ICSID）提供的国际投资仲裁和调解服务等，也值得我国企业和法律专业人士进一步关注。

近年来，我国一些领先的律师事务所在推动我国企业"走出去"和共建"一带一路"中发挥的作用日益显著。他们借助与国外律师事务所的广泛合作关系，为我国企业的海外投资提供了专业和高效的法律服务。而且，一些律师将其工作经验进行总结，出版了不少理论和实务相结合的著作和论文，推动了我国国际投资法和国际经济法研究走向实务。本丛书即是一个典型的实例。在此，我向本丛书的编写团队由衷地致以祝贺。我相信，本丛书必将有助于中国企业更加自信地走向世界，更加从容地应对各种法律挑战。同时，我也期待本丛书能够激发更多学者和实务工作者对国际投资法律实务的深入研究，共同推动中国企业对外投资的稳健发展。

在全球化的时代浪潮下，中国企业的对外投资不仅是经济行为，更是文化交流和国际合作的重要桥梁。让我们携手并进，为中国企业的国际化之路添砖加瓦，为共同构建人类命运共同体贡献中国智慧和中国方案。

谨序于此，供诸君览之，或有所益，以之为鉴。

左海聪
对外经济贸易大学法学院教授
"一带一路"法治研究中心主任
涉外法治研究院首席专家
中国法学会国际经济法研究会副会长
于北京朝阳惠新里
2024 年 7 月 5 日

序 二

在全球化日益加速的今天，经济合作与文化交流也愈加紧密，中国企业在不断发展壮大的过程中在国际经济舞台上日渐崭露头角。与此同时，中国提出的"一带一路"倡议，作为中国对外开放政策中关键且重要的一环，不仅为中国企业提供了更广阔的发展空间，也为沿线各国注入了新的发展活力。本丛书致力于深入剖析中国企业在海外投资，特别是在"一带一路"沿线国家的投资现状，所面临的挑战以及未来的发展潜力，旨在为积极拓展国际市场的中国企业提供一份全面而实用的导航手册和策略指南。

为了积极推动中国企业"走出去"，中国政府精心制定并实施了一系列海外投资激励政策。其中，"一带一路"倡议便是有力的政策支持。该倡议以共商、共建、共享为核心理念，围绕政策沟通、设施联通、贸易畅通、资金融通和民心相通五大支柱，力求构建一个开放（open）、包容（inclusive）、平衡（balanced）、普惠（beneficial for all）的区域经济合作新体系。这一宏伟蓝图不仅极大地拓展了中国企业的国际化发展空间，更为沿线各国经济的蓬勃发展注入了强劲的新动力。欧洲，作为中国企业海外投资的重点区域，同时也是"一带一路"倡议中不可或缺的一环，以其成熟稳定的市场经济、尖端的技术以及先进的管理经验，成为众多中国企业争相投资的沃土。而亚洲，这个全球经济的蓬勃引擎，如今正以前所未有的活力与潜力展现在世界的面前。多元文化在这里交融，广袤的经济发展空间为中国企业的海外拓展提供了无数机遇与可能。在这样一个大背景下，中国企业正以勇于开拓的姿态，踏上世界舞台的拓展之路。

然而，中国企业在海外投资的征途上，亦面临重重挑战。文化差异横亘其中、法律环境错综复杂、市场准入规则重重，以及政治风险潜藏深处，而这些都要求企业在决策前进行详尽地研究与严谨地评估。这套关于中国企业海外投资的系列丛书，通过精选案例与深度解读，不仅展示了世界主要国家及地区独特的经济、政治风貌，更聚焦热门的投资领域，剖析了各国（地区）特有的法律框架。书中还详尽地探讨了外商投资审查、经营者集中申报、特殊行业的监管审批以及核心交易文件与条款等共性法律问题，分享了宝贵的成功经验，使这套丛书既具理论价值，又富实践意义，为读者提供了珍贵的参考与启示。

中国企业的"走出去"不仅是经济活动，更是文化与文明的交流融合。我们期待这套丛书能够助力中国企业更好地融入全球经济体系，实现互利共赢，共同推动构建人类命运共同体的宏伟蓝图。

在此，我要向这套丛书的总策划及主编李海容律师致以敬意。她深耕境外投资领域多年，承办了近百个境外上市及境外投资并购项目，足迹遍布数十个国家和地区。她独具匠心地策划了这套覆盖面广泛的系列丛书，并汇聚了各国一线且具有丰富海外投资交易经验的专业法律团队，致力于为中国企业提供全方位的前沿法律服务。感谢她以及所有参与本书撰写、翻译、编辑的团队，是他们的辛勤工作与密切合作，使这套丛书得以以中英双语形式完美呈现。

希望这套丛书能成为中国企业与读者了解海外投资的一手信息与指南，为中国企业的国际化征程提供有力的支持与帮助。

谨以此序，向所有积极"走出去"的中国企业和支持"走出去"的各方人士致以敬意。愿中国企业在国际舞台上绽放更加耀眼的光芒，共同书写人类命运共同体的新篇章！

是为序。

吴　鹏
北京市中伦律师事务所创始合伙人、管理合伙人
中伦公益基金会理事长
北京市市场监督管理局反垄断专家
中国国际经济贸易仲裁委仲裁员
北京大学兼职硕士导师
中国人民大学兼职硕士导师
中国法学会经济法研究会常务理事
中国社会科学院法学研究所私法研究中心研究员
ICC China 竞争委员会副主席
中日民商法学会副会长
中国世界贸易组织研究会竞争政策与法律专业委员会专家
大韩贸易投资振兴公社（KOTRA）韩国投资宣传大使
2024 年 7 月 1 日

自　序

作为本系列海外投资实务丛书的总策划，我已经在中国企业"走出去"的法律实务领域耕耘了整整17个年头。在这期间，我助力中国企业进行海外投资的足迹已遍及世界四十余个国家和地区，承办了近百个中国企业的海外上市及海外投资并购项目，也亲眼见证了中国企业从初出国门的懵懂探索，到跨国投资日臻成熟的发展历程。在这一过程中，我与中国企业并肩成长，在"走出去"的道路上为他们保驾护航，共同迎接每一个挑战与机遇。

在2017年，基于自己十余年的海外投资经验和心得，我撰写了个人专著《海外投资并购——实务操作及典型案例解析》，书中详尽剖析了近20个中国企业海外并购的实际案例，通过对成功案例的剖析，系统地阐述了中国企业海外并购成功的关键要素与常用策略。在撰写的过程中，我仔细研究了市面上的海外投资类书籍和此领域已公开发表的文章，发现其中直接来源于海外国家的一手信息和资料相对匮乏，这意味着中国本土企业在获取海外投资目标国家的直接信息方面，可能会遇到信息滞后和视角局限的问题。海外市场的一手信息对于中国企业"走出去"具有举足轻重的意义，能为企业海外拓展的调研和科学决策提供关键性支撑。若企业在进军海外市场前未能充分收集投资目标国的全面准确信息，其"走出去"的征程可能会面临更多的风险和不确定性。

近年来，我惊喜地发现市场上陆续涌现了诸如境外投资国别报告、境外投资环境报告等介绍海外当地信息的出版物和文章。这些资料为企业"走出去"提供了极为有益的参考。不得不说，海外投资在中国确实是一个新兴且充满活力的业务领域。这一趋势的出现，正是中国企业综合实力显著提升，寻求更广阔国际舞台的必然结果。在17年的职业生涯中，我亲身参与并见证了这一历程，从无数的海外投资项目中汲取经验，不断学习、探索、总结、提炼，逐步实现了自我成长与专业提升。多年来，我有幸为中国政法大学的研究生们讲授涉外法律实务课程。在教学的过程中，我欣喜地发现，法律实务界中那些拥有丰富海外实践经验的涉外法律从业者，他们所传授的涉外法律知识，对培养我国涉外法律专业人才起到了至关重要的作用。他们的经验与智慧，不仅丰富了课程内容，更为学生们提供了宝贵的实践指导和职业启示。这样的交流与传承，无疑将推动我国涉外法律领域的持续发展，助力培养出更多具备国际视野和专业技能的优秀人才。

因此，我坚定决心要为中国企业的海外投资策划一套投资实务丛书，力求覆盖中国企业"走出去"所涉足的尽可能多的国家和地区，旨在传递来自海外投资实务一线的信息和经验。这套丛书不仅会从中国法的视角审视世界，更会深度剖析海外各国的法律政策与实务案例，汇聚各国投资领域的第一手信息和前沿经验，为中国企业打造一套全面、实用的海外投资实务操作指南。希望中国企业能通过我们的系列丛书了解来自每一个收录国家的投资环境和信息。本丛书首册《共建"一带一路"：中国投资者赴欧投资法律实务》收录了10多个国家或地区的投资案例文章，亚洲卷也紧随其后，覆盖了10多个国家的投资文章。接下来，第三卷和第四卷也会陆续上线，不断扩展丛书的地域覆盖面和投资领域涵盖面。这套丛书并不侧重于海外投资的理论讲述，因为作者和编者均是各国法律实务领域的资深从业者，他们丰富的当地投资经验使丛书更具实践指导意义。本丛书从各国投资实务角度出发，分享和分析当地成功的投资案例，解读外国投资人在该国的投资策略，法律政策要求、实务操作要点，以及落地过程中可能面临的问题和挑战，并提供实务案例中的解决方案。通过这些案例，我们直观地展示了各国投资实务落地的核心要点。针对境外律师及法律从业者撰写的每一篇当地实务投资文章，我带领主策划团队也从中国企业海外投资业务的角度，进行了有针对性的逐篇点评，提炼和提示中国企业通过各篇文章关注该国投资的关键点。此外，本丛书以中英双语对照的形式呈现给中国读者，旨在为中国读者提供便捷、实用的参考，成为一本陪伴中国企业海外投资的实务导航"口袋书"。

本书的撰写历经了一段相当长的过程，因为我们需要与几十个境外国家的一线法律实务从业者进行联络，并协调他们撰稿、供稿、改稿、最终定稿。这些来自各国的撰稿者都是在繁忙的工作之余，无私地为本套丛书贡献了珍贵的稿件。在此，我们要向所有参与供稿的各国律师和实务从业者表示衷心的感谢。他们所提供的文稿汇集了各国一线的投资实战经验和海外一手信息，极具价值。尤其感谢他们，在经过疫情的挑战后，仍数次配合我们更新稿件。当然，也要向参与本丛书编写的团队小伙伴们表达诚挚的谢意，正是他们持续的辛勤付出，才使得本丛书得以顺利完成。

我衷心希望，通过阅读本系列丛书，读者能够获得来自各投资前沿国家的一线信息，从而助力中国企业更稳健、更成功地走向世界。在此，我想借用法治日报社对我的一句评价，以此寄语正走向国际市场的中国企业："深耕'一带一路'，跑出中国'加速度'，以赤子之心和专业能力展示中国自信，在世界舞台吟唱中国好声音。"

谨以此序，向所有关注和支持中国企业"走出去"的人士致以敬意。感谢你们的一路相伴与鼓励，正是有了你们的支持，中国企业才能在国际舞台上更加自信地展翅飞翔。

是为序。

李海容

2024 年 7 月 1 日

目　录

| 前　言　中国投资者赴欧投资概览 | 001 |

| 股权并购在奥地利：在高科技汽车行业开展投资
Equity in Austria
Investing in the High-tech Automotive Industry | 009 |

| 股权并购在法国：在制药行业开展投资
Equity in France
Investing in the Pharmaceutical Industry | 035 |

| 以芬兰为主导的项目投资：在房地产开发行业开展投资
Finnish-led Project Investment
Investing in the Real Estate Development Industry | 059 |

| 投资在罗马尼亚：光伏项目建设
Investments in Romania
the Construction of Photovoltaic Projects | 078 |

| 投资在挪威：在多种行业开展投资
Investments in Norway
Investing in Multiple Industries | 101 |

| 投资在葡萄牙：在风能领域开展投资
Investments in Portugal
Investing in the Wind Energy Industry | 136 |

| 股权并购在瑞士：在工业和服务领域开展投资 | 153 |

投资在塞尔维亚：绿地投资

Investments in Serbia
Green Field Investments   167

股权并购在斯洛文尼亚：在家电行业开展投资

Equity in Slovenia
Investing in the Home Appliance Industry   204

股权并购在希腊：在物流运输领域开展投资

Equity in Greece
Investing in the Logistics and Transportation Industry   227

投资在匈牙利：绿地投资

Investments in Hungary
Green Field Investments   255

股权并购在荷兰：在物流产业开展投资

Equity in Netherlands
Investing in the Logistics Industry   278

投资在德国：并购德国工程服务公司

Investments in Germany
Acquisition of a German engineering services company   304

在开曼群岛和英属维尔京群岛构建投资：通过开曼群岛和英属维尔京群岛拓展"一带一路"

Investments in the Cayman Islands and the BVI
Expanding the Belt and Road through the Cayman Islands and the BVI   340

前　言
中国投资者赴欧投资概览

2015年3月，国家发展改革委、外交部、商务部经国务院授权发布《推动共建丝绸之路经济带和21世纪海上丝绸之路的愿景与行动》，中国政府积极推动"一带一路"建设，加强与沿线国家的沟通、磋商和合作，并与部分国家签署了共建"一带一路"合作备忘录。"一带一路"沿线国家中，目前已与我国正式签订官方合作备忘录的欧洲国家包括奥地利、希腊、匈牙利、罗马尼亚、塞尔维亚、波兰、斯洛文尼亚等多个国家。

基于我国投资者对欧洲国家的投资规模及欧洲国家的经济发展水平、投资环境，我们选择了"一带一路"沿线国家中典型13个欧洲国家，具体包括奥地利、法国、芬兰、罗马尼亚、挪威、葡萄牙、德国、塞尔维亚、波兰、斯洛文尼亚、希腊、匈牙利、瑞士，为中国投资者赴欧投资提供指引。

欧盟（European Union，EU）是世界上第二大经济实体，是欧洲最为重要的区域国际组织，对欧盟国家的法律制度和投资环境带来至关重要的影响，本书选择的前述13个欧洲国家中，属于欧盟国家的有奥地利、法国、芬兰、罗马尼亚、葡萄牙、斯洛文尼亚、希腊、匈牙利、荷兰和德国10国，本书亦将提示欧盟相关规则对外国投资者带来的影响。

同时，由于开曼群岛和英属维尔京群岛（British Virgin Islands，BVI）通常作为中国投资者对外投资的路径企业所在地，本书中也予以介绍。

中国投资者赴欧投资情况

根据中国外交部的统计，2022年度中国企业对欧洲13个国家的投资情况

如表 1 所示：[1]

表 1　2022 年度中国企业对欧洲 13 个国家的投资情况

单位：万美元

序号	国别	2022 年流量	2022 年末存量
1	奥地利	−13 497	52 392
2	法国	4848	481 426
3	芬兰	4769	72 141
4	罗马尼亚	1159	22 022
5	挪威	107	1931
6	葡萄牙	144	2503
7	瑞士	13 368	826 909
8	塞尔维亚	15 939	55 746
9	斯洛文尼亚	−59	47 349
10	希腊	−137	12 522
11	匈牙利	26 046	58 066
12	荷兰	−104 980	2 830 170
13	德国	197 864	1 855 056

欧洲国家基本情况

总体而言，政治上，欧洲国家的对外关系较为开放，与世界大多数国家和地区建立了关系，并缔结了贸易、投资或经济合作协定，政治环境稳定透明，社会稳定；经济上，欧洲国家市场高度自由且发展成熟，基础设施完善，鼓励外国投资，为中国投资者赴欧洲投资营造了良好的投资环境。

欧洲经济发展水平居各大洲之首，根据世界银行的公开数据，我们选择的

---

[1] 数据来源：商务部、国家统计局和国家外汇管理局《2022 年度中国对外直接投资统计公报》，2023 年 9 月 28 日发布。

13 个欧洲国家 2022 年的人均 GDP 如表 2 所示：[1]

表 2 2022 年欧洲 13 国人均 GDP

单位：美元

序号	国别	人均 GDP
1	奥地利	52 084.7
2	法国	40 886.3
3	芬兰	50 871.9
4	罗马尼亚	15 786.8
5	挪威	108 729.2
6	葡萄牙	24 515.3
7	瑞士	93 259.9
8	塞尔维亚	9537.7
9	斯洛文尼亚	28 439.3
10	希腊	20 867.3
11	匈牙利	18 390.2
12	荷兰	57 025.0
13	德国	48 718.0

欧洲是近代工业发源地，德国、瑞士、奥地利是老牌的工业强国，本书将分别介绍在德国并购工程服务公司、在瑞士进行工业和服务领域的投资及在奥地利收购高科技汽车公司的案例；除了工业，欧洲国家的交通运输业、生物制药等行业在世界经济中占重要地位，本书后文分享了在希腊、荷兰开展物流领域的投资及收购法国制药公司的案例；随着全球环保意识的增强，欧洲国家在清洁能源领域的投资逐渐形成热潮，本书将以在罗马尼亚开展光伏项目建设、在葡萄牙风能领域开展投资的经验为例。此外，本书还将分享近期中国投资者在挪威、塞尔维亚、匈牙利、斯洛文尼亚进行投资的案例，希望能给读者启发。

---

[1] 数据来源：https://data.worldbank.org.cn/indicator/NY.GDP.PCAP.CD?locations=EU。

中国投资者赴欧投资的主要法律问题

除了在行业、商业方面的考虑外，赴欧投资还需要注意一些共性的法律问题，我们在此提炼了外商投资审查制度、经营者集中申报、特殊行业的监管审批和核心交易文件及条款四个方面。

1. 外商投资审查制度

中国投资者赴欧进行直接投资时，如东道国已建立了外商投资审查制度，则不可避免地会遇到东道国相关主管机构对境外投资者开展的外商投资审查。如不遵守相关审查制度，在极端情况下，可能会导致并购交易无效。应当注意到，目前欧洲国家对于外商投资审查政策呈逐渐收紧趋势，对并购交易而言，应及时仔细地评估拟进行的收购是否会触发东道国外商投资申报或批准要求、拟议交易是否需要事先取得主管当局的无异议函或者批准文件、针对外商投资审查程序将给拟议交易带来何种潜在风险，并对交易时间表的影响进行充分评估，以消除或者尽量降低对拟议交易的不利影响。2019 年 3 月 5 日，欧盟理事会通过了《建立对欧盟外商直接投资审查框架的第 2019/452 号欧盟条例》［Regulation（EU）2019/452 of the European Parliament and of the council establishing a framework for screening of foreign direct investments into the European Union，以下简称《欧盟外商投资审查条例》］，该条例于 2019 年 4 月生效，并已于 2020 年 10 月起正式实施。该条例赋予欧盟委员会（以下简称欧委会）参与成员国国家安全和公共秩序审查的权力，对可能影响某一个欧盟成员国或整个欧盟安全和公共秩序的外商直接投资建立了相关审查机制，该条例的实施及对外商直接投资审查机制的运行势必会对中国开展对欧投资产生影响。在该审查机制下，欧盟和成员国可基于安全或公共秩序的理由采取对外商直接投资的限制性措施，使成员国能够在一个成员国的外商直接投资可能影响其他成员国的安全或公共秩序时相互合作、互相协助，加强信息交流。成员国能够向计划实施或已完成投资的成员国提出评议，成员国的评议也应转交欧委会。欧委会还应酌情向计划实施或已完成投资的成员国发表意见。在以安全或公共秩序为由审查外商直接投资时，成员国和欧委会可考虑外商投资对以下方面的潜在影响：关键基础设施、关键技术、关键投入的安全性以及获取敏感信息或控制敏感信息的能力。

《里斯本条约》（Lisbon Treaty）将外国直接投资纳入欧盟的共同商业政策，欧盟对共同商业政策拥有专属权限。但是，公共安全与防御事务仍属于成员国的专属权限。因此，欧委会对外商投资审查的最终决定权仍由作为东道国的成员国享有，《欧盟外商投资审查条例》无法授予欧委会任何基于公共安全阻止或者否决外商投资的权力，亦无法强制要求成员国据此设立安全审查机制。

在我们选取的10个欧盟国家中，大多数国家在实践中已引入了合作机制，部分国家已经通过立法的方式将《欧盟外商投资审查条例》中的相关规定引入其国内法当中：如德国较早地建立了外商投资审查制度，早于《欧盟外商投资审查条例》通过的时间，近来也对《德国对外贸易法》进行了多处修改，建立了更加严格的外商投资审查机制；2020年奥地利通过了《奥地利外资审查规范》以引入《欧盟外商投资审查条例》的要求；芬兰通过修订《芬兰外国公司收购监督法》以补充规定《欧盟外商投资审查条例》中的相关内容；此外，法国、匈牙利、荷兰、葡萄牙、斯洛文尼亚也均设有外商投资国家安全审查机制，但是不同国家的审查机制在覆盖范围和制度设计上存在较大差异。

2. 经营者集中申报

相较于绿地投资，并购交易更加可能涉及经营者集中的审查。经营者集中，主要是指经营者之间实施合并，或者经营者取得其他经营者的控制权、影响力。在我国反垄断法的视域下，经营者集中是指以下三种情形：经营者合并、经营者通过取得股权或者资产的方式取得对其他经营者的控制权、经营者通过合同等方式取得对其他经营者的控制权或者能够对其他经营者施加决定性影响。本书提及的各国对于经营者集中的审查规则不尽相同，但经营者集中的核心内涵大体相当。

本书中的国家包括欧盟国家和非欧盟国家。宏观上，欧盟国家和非欧盟国家在经营者集中申报规定方面主要区别为：欧盟国家的经营者进行经营者集中申报时有两个对象，欧盟委员会和所在国反垄断主管机关。经营者要根据经营者集中的特定情形决定向何机关申报。非欧盟国家的经营者集中申报对象通常仅为所在国反垄断主管机关。

2.1 欧盟国家

欧盟成员国自愿将经营者集中审查权部分移交至欧盟。当特定集中行为触发了欧盟 2004 年 1 月 20 日第 139/2004 号条例 [EU Regulation No. 139/2004 dated January 20, 2004]（以下简称第 139/2004 号条例）中规定的申报标准时，参与集中的经营者应当向欧盟委员会进行申报。当特定集中行为不满足前述条例的申报标准但符合所在国的经营者集中申报标准时，经营者则应向所在国反垄断主管机关进行申报。

2.1.1 欧盟经营者集中申报

根据欧盟第 139/2004 号条例，任何出售公司控制权的行为在以下情况下应提交欧盟委员会事先批准：该交易涉及的所有公司（及其附属公司）的全球营业额超过 50 亿欧元；这些公司中至少有两家在欧盟内部开展业务，且各自的营业额超过 2.5 亿欧元。

若未达到上述标准，在满足以下所有四个条件时，仍应向欧盟委员会提交申请：所有有关公司在世界各地的总营业额超过 25 亿欧元；在至少三个欧盟成员国中，所有有关公司的总营业额均超过 1 亿欧元；在上述至少三个欧盟成员国中，至少两家有关公司各自的营业额总额超过 2500 万欧元；至少两家有关公司各自在欧盟内取得的营业额总额超过 1 亿欧元。

欧盟委员会对具有"欧洲"性质的经营者集中交易享有专属管辖权，欧盟成员国对此交易不具备管辖权。

2.1.2 所在国经营者集中申报

欧盟各国均规定了经营者集中申报相关的法律法规，当集中尚未达到第 139/2004 号条例中规定的标准但达到了各国国内反垄断法的标准，或者当合并主体的业务份额主要在某一欧盟成员国内时，经营者则可能需要向所在国的反垄断主管机关进行经营者集中申报。虽然欧盟各国均以欧盟的规定为参照制定国内的反垄断法，但是在经营者集中申报标准方面仍有较大差异。

例如，根据法国法律，当一家公司获得对另一家公司的直接或间接控制权时，该公司的收购行为被视为经营者集中。在此情形下，若同时满足以下两个条件，经营者则应向法国竞争管理局进行备案：第一，交易各方的全球营业额（不含税）超过 1.5 亿欧元；第二，交易各方中至少两方各自在法国的营业额（不含税）超过 5000 万欧元。

由此可以看出，欧盟各国可能规定了与第 139/2004 号条例中不同的经营者集中申报标准，经营者应当根据特定集中情况决定是否申报以及向何主体进行申报。

2.2 非欧盟国家

非欧盟国家由于通常不存在将国家权力转移至其他主体的情况，因而在进行经营者集中申报时可主要关注所在国的相关法律要求。如瑞士的相关法律规定：在有关企业共报告至少20亿瑞士法郎的营业额，或在瑞士达到至少5亿瑞士法郎的营业额，并且至少有两家企业分别报告在瑞士至少1亿瑞士法郎的营业额时，计划集中的企业必须在实施集中之前通知瑞士竞争委员会。

此外，还应当注意有些欧洲国家即使未加入欧盟，但由于其作为欧洲经济区（EEA）的成员国等原因，欧盟有关竞争的法律可能以转入国内法等方式影响国内的执法、司法。以挪威为例：挪威虽非欧盟的成员国，但其作为EEA的成员，其立法应符合欧盟单一市场立法。实践中，挪威虽无法在宪法上直接将欧盟法规和指令作为具有约束力的法律，但欧盟有关竞争的法律被不断地被转入挪威国内法。

3. 特殊行业的监管审批

如投资标的行业涉及东道国特殊监管领域的，在赴欧投资过程中需要提前了解东道国的行业监管框架、行业政策和是否涉及事前/事后的审批/备案程序。如涉及任何事前/事后的审批/备案程序，需要进一步了解审批/备案程序的办理方式、时间和进度，以调整拟议交易的时间表。通常在能源或者基础设施建设时需要审批文件，如在罗马尼亚，任何累计能够产生超过1兆瓦能量的发电活动均须罗马尼亚能源监管局签发设立批准程序。

4. 核心交易文件及条款

在不同的投资东道国，针对不同的投资项目，相关的交易习惯和监管要求会存在差异，因此中国投资者可以考虑在国内法律顾问的协助下，于交易的早期阶段即听取东道国当地的律师的意见，与当地的交易对手进行谈判、设计交易架构、开展尽职调查和准备交易文件。

在并购交易中，核心的交易文件包括股份购买协议（SPA）和股东协议（SHA）：SPA中的支付价格、股权分红锁定期、交割条件、责任限制、争议解决条款等是关键性条款；SHA中公司的治理结构、决议的通过、股东权利和僵局条款等则至关重要。如拟议并购为公开市场收购，则需要根据东道国及交易所关于证券上市交易的相关监管规则准备交易文件，如在斯洛文尼亚进行要约收购时，根据斯洛文尼亚法，收购要约和随附的招股说明书最为重要，收购要约针对要约发布时海信尚未持有的全部股份，且不以任何条件的成就为前提，在收购要约发布之前，招股说明书必须经斯洛文尼亚证券市场管理局批准。

在绿地投资或者新设公司的投资中，需要准备在当地设立公司的相关文件。例如在奥地利，需要公司设立时核心的文件，如申请公司登记时需要准备公司章程草案、任命董事总经理的股东决议文件、任命董事总经理的签字表格样本、经所有董事总经理签字的公司登记申请书等。

此外，根据投资的不同行业的监管要求，还会涉及一些特殊文件/协议。如投资标的行业涉及特许经营的，以投资者与东道国的主体双方签订特许经营协议的方式投资时，核心文件便是特许经营协议，此文件需要涵盖对于新设施的投资、担保条款、费用及支付方式、风险承担、协议的履行时间等条款。

股权并购在奥地利：在高科技汽车行业开展投资
Equity in Austria
Investing in the High-tech Automotive Industry

点 评

汽车行业是奥地利最重要的行业之一。总体而言，奥地利未对高科技汽车企业业务运营以及收购此类企业设置特别的限制。但在实施收购的过程中仍需结合其一般性规定进行综合考量，从而确定符合实际需要的交易方案。例如，规则要求股东会部分事项需要以绝对多数（股东会表决四分之三以上）投票通过，公司章程仅可设定更高的通过比例，因而若希望在交易完成后对公司各项事务均有绝对的控制权，则在确定收购比例时可能需要将该等规定纳入考量范畴。再如，规则赋予持有公司至少90%股份的股东以决议方式排除少数股东的权利，因而若希望取得标的公司100%的股份而交易过程中与小股东难以达成一致，则可考虑先行取得公司至少90%的股份并在交易完成后通过决议方式进一步取得剩余股份的方案。

此外，在公司治理层面，奥地利规则亦存在一些需注意的事项。例如，奥地利允许在有限责任公司中设置咨询委员会，但由于咨询委员会的设立和组织等方面没有具体的法律框架或规定，因此若对其职权和责任范围未做明确规定，则可能存在被认定为实质系监事会并需要遵守监事会相关规定的风险。因此，在收购完成后实施公司治理的过程中，需要关注当地的相关规定，确保公司的平稳有序运营。

在前往已建立外资审查制度的国家开展境外投资时，在交易的早期阶段，中国投资者应评估外商直接投资批准的相关要求。在严格监管外商投资的趋势下，2020年年中，奥地利通过新规强化了该国的外资审查制度，在很大程度上引入了《欧盟外商投资审查条例》（第2019/452号条例）的要求。

1. 奥地利的投资环境（Investment Environment in Austria）

1.1 概述（General Statement）

At the outset we want to establish that there are no legal requirements in Austria specifically with regards to the business operation of high–tech automotive businesses. Specific requirements may apply when acquiring land in connection therewith. Special requirements for foreign investors may depend on the specific situation and can only be evaluated on a case by case basis.

首先，我们想说明在奥地利国内没有关于高科技汽车企业业务运营的具体法律要求。但在取得与该行业有关的土地时，可能会适用一些相关的具体规定。对外国投资者的特殊要求可视具体情况而定，只能逐案进行评估。

In mid–2020, Austria has strengthened its foreign direct investment（FDI）control regime by enacting a new law, the Investment Control Act（Investitionskontrollgesetz in German, ICA）. The main change of the FDI control regime was to broaden the scope of its applicability, in particular by widening the relevant industry sectors and catching a wide range of deal structures such as indirect acquisitions and asset deals. Generally, the ICA is applicable to（i）direct and indirect acquisition of voting rights in（10, 25, and 50 percent thresholds apply）, controlling influence over, or substantial assets of an Austrian company,（ii）by one or more foreign persons（i.e., non–EU/EEA/Swiss citizens or entities）and（iii）if the Austrian target is active in certain relevant industry sectors. The relevant industry sectors are divided into two categories with different acquisition thresholds, namely（i）particularly sensitive sectors being subject to 10, 25 and 50 percent thresholds and（ii）other sensitive sectors being subject to 25 and 50 percent thresholds. Transactions requiring an FDI approval are deemed concluded under a statutory condition precedent until such approval—through the formal FDI proceeding or by way of a non-objection ruling—is being granted.

在2020年年中，奥地利通过制定一部新法律《投资监管法案》（德语为Investitionskontrollgesetz，简称ICA）增强了其对外商直接投资（FDI）的监管制度。外商直接投资监管制度的主要变化是扩大了其适用范围，特别是扩大相关行业部门并涵盖了广泛的交易结构，例如间接收购和资产交易。通常，ICA适用于：（i）直接和间接获得投票权（适用10%、25%和50%的门槛），对奥地利公司的控制权或实质性资产，（ⅱ）由一个或多个外国主体（非欧盟/欧洲经济区/瑞士公民或实体）和（ⅲ）奥地利目标公司是否活跃于某些相关行业。相关行业板块分为收购门槛不同的两类，即（ⅰ）特别敏感的行业受到10%、25%和50%的限制，以及（ⅱ）其他敏感行业受到25%和50%的限制。通过相关审查是需要经外商直接投资审查的交易成立的法定前提——通过正式的外商直接投资审查程序或无异议裁决——正式批准。

Given the severe sanctions in case of violation the Austrian FDI rules (including prison sentence of up to one year for implementing a transaction without necessary prior approval), foreign investors should evaluate the requirement of an FDI approval already at an early stage of any transaction.

鉴于违反奥地利外商直接投资监管规则的行为将受到严厉制裁（包括对未经必要事先批准的交易主体处以 年以下监禁），外国投资者应在任何交易的早期阶段评估外商直接投资批准的相关要求。

Austria has a very reliable and one of the most efficient legal systems in the European Union. Further, its geographic position in thecentre of Europe provides key strategic advantages for international investors, especially for investors in the automotive sector, with Austria being near the most relevant automotive clusters in Europe—Slovakia, Hungary and southern Germany.

奥地利的法律体系非常可靠，是欧盟最有效率的法律体系之一。此外，奥地利在欧洲中心的地理位置为国际投资者，特别是汽车行业的投资者提供了关键的战略优势，奥地利还靠近欧洲最相关的汽车产业集群——斯洛伐克、匈牙利和德国南部。

Further, Austria due to its position and its history traditionally serves as an East-West interface and hosts a large number of regional headquarters coordinating business operations in Central and Eastern Europe.

此外，奥地利由于区位和历史原因，传统上是联系东西方的纽带，在奥地利设有大量区域总部，以协调中欧和东欧的业务活动。

The key industrial sectors in Austria include the Food and Drink Industry, Mechanical and Steel Engineering, Chemical and Automotive Industry, Electrics and Electronics industry, Wood, Pulp and Paper industry.

奥地利的核心行业领域包括食品和饮料工业、机械和钢铁工程工业、化学和汽车工业、电子电气工业、木材、纸浆和造纸工业。

Further, it is interesting to point out that Austria has a very low strike rate. From 2005 to 2013, only two working days, on an annual average, were lost to strikes per 1000 employees.

此外值得注意的是，奥地利的罢工率非常低。从 2005 年到 2013 年，每 1000 名员工中每年平均只有两个工作日罢工。

1.2 研发和税收（R&D and Taxation）

Austria's R&D (Research and Development) expenditures grow above average and are already the second highest in the EU. Companies may benefit from an attractive funding system and a research premium of 14% for all R&D spending. Austria is therefore one of Europe's most dynamic R&D locations.

奥地利的研发支出高于平均水平，已经位居欧盟第二。奥地利的企业可以从优越的资助制度和高达 14% 的研发费用溢价中获益。因此，奥地利是欧洲最具活力的研发中心之一。

When it comes to taxation, Austria also offers attractive investment incentives. Businesses are subject to a uniform corporate income tax of 25% which may be reduced in the years to come. Tax burdens such as the trade or wealth tax, quite common in other countries, do not exist in Austria. The group taxation system makes it possible to offset the profits and losses of financially affiliated companies, including recognition of cross-border losses.

在税收方面，奥地利也提供了富有吸引力的投资激励措施。企业须缴纳统一的 25% 的企业所得税，该税率未来几年可能还会下调。在其他国家相当普遍的贸易或财富税等税收负担在奥地利并不存在。此外，集团税收制度可以抵消财务关联公司的损益，包括对跨境亏损的确认。

1.3 汽车行业（Automotive Industry）

The automotive industry ranks among the most important sectors in Austria. Specifically, the automobile manufacturing sector including the component supplier industry ranks among Austria's top three industrial sectors, and secures every ninth job in the country.

汽车行业是奥地利最重要的行业之一。具体来说，包括零部件供应商在内的汽车制造业位居奥地利国内行业前三名,奥地利国内每九个就业岗位中就有一个与汽车制造行业相关。

Europe's most diverse testing environment for autonomous driving, the world's lightest and most efficient high-performance batteries for electromobility and the promotion of the use of artificial intelligence are among the focal points in Austria in the field of mobility. More than 1600 patents were registered in the automotive sector in the period of 2011–2015.

欧洲最多样化的自动驾驶测试环境、世界上最轻和最高效的电动汽车高蓄能电池以及对人工智能应用的推动,都是奥地利汽车行业的研发重点。2011年至2015年,奥地利的汽车行业共注册专利1600多项。

Hardly any vehicles in the world today leave the assembly lines without components "Made in Austria". AVL List, Miba, Pankl Racing and TTTech are only a few examples of Austrian companies which have become indispensable in the automobile industry.

如今,世界上几乎没有一辆汽车在离开装配线时不包含"奥地利制造"的零部件。AVL李斯特、米巴(Miba)、Pankl Racing和TTTech只是奥地利汽车公司的几个例子,但这些公司已经成为奥地利汽车行业中不可或缺的一部分。

2. 案例分析:高科技汽车行业的投资(Case Study: Investment in a High-tech Automotive Business)

2.1 案件事实(Facts)

In 2013 a Chinese investor entered the Austrian market through the acquisition of shares in the wholly-owned subsidiary (Subsidiary) of an Austrian company (Parent Company). Both the Subsidiary and the Parent Company were limited liability companies. The Chinese investor acquired a 70 percent interest in the Subsidiary (Chinese Majority Shareholder). The transaction volume amounted to approx. EUR 7 Mio.

2013年,来自中国的投资者通过收购一家奥地利公司(以下简称母公司)的全资子公司(以下简称子公司)的股份进入奥地利市场。子公司和母公司均为有限责任公司。中国投资者(以下简称中国大股东)收购了该子公司70%的股权。交易额约为700万欧元。

The investment opportunity presented itself in the course of a restructuring process of the Parent Company, when, as part of the Parent Company's restructuring process, the Subsidiary was founded and the entire operative business of the Parent Company incorporated therein. The establishment of a subsidiary is quite common where the investor does not want to acquire the entire business of a company. In such a case, the part of the business which the investor wants to acquire is incorporated in the newly established subsidiary and in the following the shares of the subsidiary are acquired by the investor.

在母公司重组的过程中，子公司成立，母公司的全部经营业务被子公司所吸收，投资机会也随之出现。在投资者不想收购公司的整个业务的情况下，设立子公司是非常普遍的做法。在这种情况下，投资者想要收购的那部分业务被纳入新成立的子公司，随后投资者就会购买该子公司的股份。

The restructuring plan of the Parent Company provided for a 30 percent quota for the creditors of the insolvency proceedings. In order to meet this quota, the following measures were taken, namely:

母公司的重组计划为破产程序的债权人规定了30％的配额。为了达到这一配额，已经采取了下列措施：

• Foundation of a 100 percent subsidiary in the form of an Austrian limited liability company;

以奥地利有限责任公司的形式成立一个全资子公司；

• Contribution of the entire operative business into the Subsidiary;

整个公司的经营业务都收归于该全资子公司；

• Acquisition of 70 percent interest in the Subsidiary by the Chinese Majority Shareholder through a share purchase agreement.

中国大股东通过股权收购协议收购该子公司70％的股权。

图1　收购流程示意

The contribution of all assets into the Subsidiary included all assets and any rights and obligations pertaining thereto, except for any real estate owned by the Parent Company. The insolvency court subsequently approved the restructuring plan.

除母公司拥有的房地产外,所有资产以及与之相关的任何权利义务而产生的利益都应归属于该子公司。破产法院随后批准了重组计划。

2.2 交易完成后的法律问题(Legal Issues after the Conclusion of the Transaction)

2.2.1 设立咨询委员会(Setting up of an advisory board)

For corporate governance reasons, an advisory board was set up in the Subsidiary. The advisory board was given the competency to handle several agendas, which the general assembly is in principle responsible for.

出于公司治理的原因,在子公司设立了一个咨询委员会。该咨询委员会被赋予了处理原本由股东大会所负责的若干会议议程的职权。

In the following, disagreements arose between the shareholders regarding the prospective financing which lead to several practical issues:

之后,股东之间就预期的筹资问题产生了分歧,引发了一些实际问题:

The advisory board was practically used to handle all agendas, hence seizing competencies which were not explicitly allocated to the advisory board. As a consequence thereof, legal uncertainties arose, especially with regard to the resolutions which were passed by the advisory board because it defacto resembled a supervisory board.

实际上,咨询委员会负责处理所有的会议议程,因此掌握了并未被明确授予权限。由此产生了法律上的不确定性,特别是关于咨询委员会通过的决议,因为它实质上类似于公司的监事会(具体见下文第5条)。

The Chinese Majority Shareholder faced the issue that, initially, no Chinese managing director was appointed, which, even as majority shareholder, made it difficult to act quickly enough. The Chinese Majority Shareholder was therefore dependent on the only managing director of the Subsidiary at the time, who was also the minority shareholder of the Subsidiary (Austrian Managing Director).

中国大股东面临的问题是,因为最初没有任命任何中方董事总经理,使得其即使作为大股东,也难以迅速采取行动。因此,中国大股东只能依赖于当时子公司唯一的董事总经理,其也是子公司的一个少数股东(以下简称奥地利董事总经理)。

The Chinese Majority Shareholder wanted to limit the representation power of the Austrian Managing Director from sole power of representation to joint power of representation, with another managing director, to be appointed by the Chinese Majority Shareholder. The Austrian Managing Director resisted this strongly and managed to scare off several appointees of the Chinese Majority Shareholder (e. g. by threatening insolvency, personal liability, and through personal threats). This lead to the resignation of the appointees of the Chinese Majority Shareholder. As a result thereof, the company lacked any kind of representation. Therefore, a temporary managing director (Notgeschäftsführer in German) had to be appointed by the court.

中国大股东希望将奥地利董事总经理的代表权从唯一代表权限缩为与另一名中国大股东任命的董事总经理共享的联合代表权。奥地利董事总经理对此表示强烈反对，并设法吓跑了几位中国大股东任命的董事总经理（例如，威胁公司破产、承担个人责任以及人身威胁）。这导致中国大股东任命的几名董事总经理辞职。因此，该公司缺乏任何形式的有效代表，法院不得不为公司任命一名临时董事总经理（德语：Notgeschäftsführer）。

2.2.2 第三国董事总经理的具体要求（Specific requirements for third country national managing directors）

The Chinese Majority Shareholder wanted to appoint an individual who was not an EU national (Third-Country National) as managing director of the Subsidiary, which is not uncommon and only in certain cases bound to specific requirements. The appointment of a managing director is, in general, not conditional on any professional skills, personal capabilities, an Austrian citizenship (or citizenship of an EU country) or domestic residency of the managing director.

中国大股东希望任命一名非欧盟国家（第三国国民）的国民担任该子公司的董事总经理，这其实并不罕见，而且仅在某些情况下才受特定要求的约束。总体来说，董事总经理的任命不以任何专业技能、个人资质、奥地利公民身份（或欧盟国家公民身份）或国内居住权为条件。

In practice, Third-Country National managing directors may not always set up residency in Austria or any country within the EU but manage the company from a non-EU member state. As mentioned above, this is possible but may be problematic or even impermissible, if the managing director is involved in day to day business activities or none of the managing directors appointed by the company have domestic residency in Austria.

在实践中，第三国董事总经理可能并不总是在奥地利或欧盟内的任何国家拥有住所，而可能是在非欧盟成员国完成对公司的管理。如上所述，如果公司任命的董事总经理参与日常业务活动，或多位公司任命的董事总经理都没有在奥地利国内居住，这种跨国管理方式虽然也是有可能的，但还是会存在一些问题，甚至有时这种任命会被禁止。

As to the requirement of the managing director having domestic residency in Austria it may depend on where the company is located—competent courts in Vienna usually do not require the managing director to have domestic residency in Austria—and in case of multiple managing directors, whether at least one of the managing directors has domestic residency in Austria.

对于在奥地利拥有国内居留权的董事总经理的规定，可能取决于公司的所在地——例如维也纳有管辖权的法院通常不要求董事总经理在奥地利拥有住所——但如果公司有多位董事总经理，则至少要有一位董事总经理在奥地利拥有住所。

The reason for such a requirement is that the passive power of representation may be affected if none of the managing directors have residency in Austria or at least a local delivery address in order to receive any declarations on behalf of the company.

这一规定的原因是，如果所有的董事总经理都没有在奥地利国内的住所或者代表公司接收书面声明的地址，则该董事总经理对公司的消极代理权可能会受到影响。

As to the residence permit for Third-Country National managing directors, the following applies:

关于第三国董事总经理的居住许可，适用以下规定：

- Managing directors which have concluded a contract of employment with the Austrian company have to apply for a residence and work permit, whereas managing directors who have concluded a contract of employment with the foreign legal entity and shareholder of the Austrian company do not have to apply for a residence permit if dispatched by such shareholder to the Austrian company.

- 与奥地利公司签订雇佣合同的董事总经理必须申请居住和工作许可，而与外国法人及奥地利公司的股东签订雇用合同的董事总经理，如果被该股东派往奥地利公司，则无需申请居住和工作许可。

- Managing directors usually qualify as qualified workers as defined in the employment of foreign workers act (Ausländerbeschäftigungsgesetz in German) and can therefore apply for a so called *"Red-White-Red Card"*, which entitles its holder to residence and employment only with one specific employer-this is the first step to long-term residency in Austria. However, the qualification as such is not always definitive and should always be made on a case by case basis.

- 董事总经理通常有资格成为雇用外国工人法案（德语为 Ausländerbeschäftigungsgesetz）中所定义的合格工人，因此可以申请所谓的"红—白—红卡"，这使持有人能够在一个特定的雇主处居住和就业——这是在奥地利长期居住的第一步。但是，这样的资格并不总是确定的，需要逐案认定。

- Applications for a *"Red-White-Red Card"* have to be personally submitted by the applicant at the competent Austrian representation (consulate or embassy) in the applicant's home country or country of residence. Applicants who can either enter Austria without a visa (does not apply for Chinese citizens) or already have a valid residence title may submit their application directly to the competent residence authority in Austria.

- "红—白—红卡"必须由申请人本人在申请人所在国或居住国的奥地利代表处（领事馆或大使馆）提交。申请人如果免签入境奥地利（不适用于中国公民）或已经拥有有效居住权，可以直接向奥地利主管当局提交申请。

3. 法律框架（Legal Framework）

3.1 介绍（Introduction）

A limited liability company (LLC) or "GmbH" (Gesellschaft mit beschränkter Haftung) is the most common legal form of a corporation in Austria because it provides, among other things, for (a) an increased control of the management by the shareholders (b) low maintenance costs and a slender but highly efficient corporate governance framework that can be adapted to specific needs (c) a management that is subject to shareholders' instructions and most importantly (d) limited liability of the shareholders with regard to claims from third parties.

有限责任公司（LLC）或"GmbH"（德语：Gesellschaft mit beschr a nkter Haftung）是奥地利公司最常见的法律形式，因为它能够实现：（a）增加股东对管理层的控制权；（b）低维护成本、简洁且高效的公司治理结构，可根据具体需要进行调整；（c）受股东指示的管理层；（d）最重要的是股东对第三方索赔只承担有限责任。

As with all corporations, the LLC has legal capacity and is represented by its managing directors. In addition, statutory power of procuration (Prokura) may be granted to certain other persons. Compared to an AG (Aktiengesellshaft in German, means stock corporation), it is easier and more cost-effective to set up and maintain, as the minimum share capital is EUR 35 000 and the statutory formal requirements are less distinctive.

与所有其他类型的公司一样，有限责任公司具有法律行为能力，并由其董事总经理进行代表。此外，公司的法定代理权（Prokura）可以授予他人。与股份公司（AG，德语：Aktiengesellshaft）相比，由于有限公司的最低股本为35 000欧元，法定要求不是那么严格，因此建立和运营有限责任公司也相对更加容易，成本也更低。

The corporate organs of a LLC can be distinguished between those mandatory for every LLC, which include (a) the managing director and (b) the general assembly, those mandatory for some LLCs, which includes (c) the supervisory board and those optional, which includes (d) the advisory board.

在奥地利，一个有限责任公司的实际结构是可以不同于对每个有限责任公司结构的法律规定的，法律规定的公司结构包括（a）董事总经理，（b）股东大会，（c）监事会（其设立对于一些有限责任公司为法律强制性规定），以及（d）咨询委员会（其设立非法律强制性规定）。

Since not all statutory provisions regarding LLCs are mandatory, the legal provisions regarding the corporate governance of the company are supplemented and specified by its articles of association. The articles of association are therefore of particular importance as far as the competencies and the duties of the corporate bodies of the company are concerned.

由于并非所有涉及有限公司的法律条文都是强制性的，公司章程就成为公司治理法律条文重要的补充和细化。因此，对于公司法人的行为能力和职责来说，章程就显得尤为重要。

3.2 有限责任公司的成立及股本（Establishment and Share Capital of a LLC）

A LLC is established upon registration with the company register. Filing for registration requires the drafting of founding documents, such as the articles of association, the shareholder resolution appointing the managing directors, the specimen signature forms of the appointed managing directors and the company register application signed by all managing directors, notarized and apostilled, if signed outside of Germany or Austria, or super legalized if the managing director signs in a country which is not party to the Hague Convention (e.g. China).

有限责任公司经登记后成立。申请公司登记时需要准备公司成立文件草案，如公司章程、任命董事总经理的股东决议文件、任命董事总经理的签字表格样本、经所有董事总经理签字的公司登记申请书等公司设立文件，如果是在德国或奥地利以外的国家签字，则需要经过公证和认证，如果是在非《海牙公约》缔约国（如中国）进行签字，则还需经过特别认证。

Generally, the minimum share capital of a limited liability company is EUR 35 000, whereof only half of the amount (i.e. EUR 17 500) has to be paid in prior to the registration of the company.

一般来说，有限责任公司的最低股本为 35 000 欧元，其中只有一半（17 500 欧元）必须在公司注册前支付。

It is also possible to incorporate the company with a founding privileged share capital of (at least) EUR 10 000, whereof at least half of the amount (i.e. EUR 5000) must be paid in. However, the expires after 10 years, meaning that the share capital then has to be increased to EUR 35 000.

也可以用至少 10 000 欧元的创始特权股本成立公司，其中至少一半（5000 欧元）为必须缴纳。然而，创始特权会在 10 年后到期，这意味着股资届时必须增加到 35 000 欧元。

When choosing to incorporate a company with a founding privileged share capital of EUR 10 000, the share capital of the company still constitutes EUR 35 000.

当选择成立一家创始特权股本为 10 000 欧元的公司时，该公司的股本仍为 35 000 欧元。

3.3 股东大会 (The General Assembly)

The general assembly of a LLC is the supreme decision-making body of the company and is comprised of all shareholders. The general assembly is responsible for and decides on all matters, which are not explicitly excluded by law or the articles of association or assigned to other corporate bodies of the company.

有限责任公司的股东大会是公司的最高决策机构,由全体股东组成。法律和公司章程未明确排除或者未明确授权给公司其他机构的事项,由股东大会负责并作出决定。

3.3.1 股东决议 (Shareholder resolutions)

Resolutions are passed with a simple majority by votes cast. Resolutions such as aiming to amend the object of business or the articles of association or a resolution to implement restructuring activities (e.g. transformation or merger), however, may only be passed with a qualified majority (3/4). The articles of association may determine a higher quorum for both. Further, the general assembly is only quorate if shareholders representing at least 10% of the share capital are present. This requirement may also be amended through the articles of association (increased, reduced or even removed).

股东决议一般以简单多数的方式投票通过。但是,旨在更改公司经营目标、公司章程或实施重组活动(如改制或合并)的决议,只能以绝对多数(四分之三以上)的方式投票通过。公司章程可为这两种投票方式设定更高的法定人数。此外,只有代表公司至少 10% 股本的股东出席,才满足股东大会的法定人数。这一要求也可以通过公司章程进行修改(增加、减少甚至删除)。

3.3.2 少数股东权利 (Minority shareholder rights)

Minority shareholder rights are important in order to ensure that minority shareholders are not excluded from the decision making process completely and may exercise their rights as shareholders accordingly. Apart from any statutory provisions, minority shareholders' rights may also be supplemented and specified by explicitly listing such in the articles of association (e.g. determining that the amendment of the articles of association shall be subject to the consent of all shareholders).

少数股东权利是确保少数股东不被完全排除在决策过程之外,并能行使其股东权利的重要保障。除法定条款外,少数股东的权利还可以通过在公司章程中以明确列举的方式予以补充和规定(如确定修改公司章程须经全体股东同意)。

Statutory shareholder rights among other things include the following:
股东在其他事项中的法定权利包括以下内容：

● Dismissal of a supervisory board member

Shareholders holding a share in the amount of at least 10% of the share capital may file an application with the competent commercial court to have a supervisory board member removed. The court shall dismiss the supervisory board member only in case of an important reason. An important reason shall be affirmed by the competent court if the continuance of his/her role as supervisory board member is deemed inappropriate.

● 解雇监事

持股10%以上的股东，可以向有管辖权的商事法院申请解雇公司的监事。只有在有重大理由的情况下，法院才能支持股东解雇公司监事的请求。主管法院认为被申请解雇的监事不适宜继续担任监事职务的，应当认定为有重大理由。

● Convocation of a shareholders' meeting

If shareholders holding a share in the amount of at least 10% of the share capital (the articles of association may determine a lower percentage) demand the convocation of a shareholders' meeting, in writing and including the reason for the convocation, then such a meeting shall be convened by the managing directors without any delay.

● 召开股东大会

如果持股10%以上的股东（公司章程可以规定更低的持股比例要求）以书面形式写明召集事由要求召开股东大会的，董事总经理应该召开股东大会，不得有任何迟延。

● Inclusion of matters/issues in the agenda

Shareholders holding a share in the amount of at least 10% of the share capital may (the articles of association may determine a lower percentage) demand, in writing and including the reason, the inclusion of certain matters/issues into the agenda for the next general assembly, as long as such a demand is made within three days after the convocation of such general assembly.

● 将事项/问题列入大会议程

持股10%以上的股东（公司章程可以规定更低的持股比例要求）可以书面

要求将召集事由、具体事项列入下次股东大会议程，但必须在本次股东大会召开后三日内提出。

• Application to the court for a special audit

Shareholders holding a share in the amount of at least 10% of the share capital may file an application with the competent commercial court to substitute a shareholder resolution, which defeated a motion for the appointment of an expert auditor to audit the last annual financial statement.

• 向法院申请特别审计

如果股东大会作出了否认聘请专家审计人员审计上一年度财务报表的决议，持股10%以上的股东可以向主管商事法院提出申请，代替作出新的股东决议。

• Substitution of an auditor

An application may be filed with the competent commercial court, to substitute the appointed auditor if shareholders hold a share in the amount of at least 5% of the share capital or the nominal value of shares held amounts to at least EUR 350 000, provided that it appears appropriate due to any important reasons with regard to the person itself or on the grounds of bias.

• 更换审计师

如果股东持股5%以上或所持股份的票面价值达到35万欧元，则可向有管辖权的商事法院提出更换审计师的申请，但应有关于审计师本人或基于股东个人判断的正当的、重大的理由。

3.3.3 排除少数股东（Exclusion of minority shareholders）

An exclusion of minority shareholders may be effected, if one shareholder holds at least 90% of the share capital (shares held through affiliated companies are taken into account with regard to the 90% threshold).

如果一个股东持有公司至少90%的股份（通过关联公司持有的股份计算在内），则可以对少数股东进行排除。

In order to effect the exclusion, a squeeze out resolution has to be passed and the excluded shareholders have to receive appropriate and fair cash compensation. The minority shareholders have the right to demand judicial review of the awarded cash compensation, however they do not have the right to challenge the squeeze out as such.

必须通过决议的方式对少数股东进行排除，且被排除的股东必须获得合理、公平的现金补偿,排除行为才会有效。少数股东有权要求对所获现金补偿进行司法审查,但无权对此排除决议提出异议。

3.4 董事总经理(Managing Director)

A managing director is an individual (shareholder or third party) who is appointed by the shareholders of the LLC to manage the company's affairs and represent the company towards third parties independently. The managing director is either appointed by way of shareholder resolution at a shareholders' meeting or by written circular resolution (to be certified and if signed outside of Austria or Germany, also apostilled or super-legalized, if signed in a country which is not party to the Hague Convention, e. g. China.). A shareholder may also be appointed as managing director (the respective amount of salary must be determined at arm's length due to Austria's strict rules of capital maintenance) through the articles of association. The appointment of the managing director is effective as of the day specified in the appointment resolution—the registration of the managing director is not a precondition for the validity of the appointment.

董事总经理是由有限责任公司股东任命的个人(股东或第三方),负责管理公司事务,并独立对外代表公司。董事总经理可以通过股东大会的决议任命,也可以通过书面通知的方式任命(须经公证,若决议是在奥地利或德国以外的国家签署,则需经过认证,若在非《海牙公约》缔约国的国家签署,如中国,则还需经特别认证)。依据公司章程,还可以任命股东为公司的董事总经理(由于奥地利严格的资本维持规则,相关的工资数额必须按公平标准确定)。董事总经理的任命自任命决议规定的日期起生效,登记并非任命生效的前提条件。

3.4.1 代表权(Power of representation)

Only the managing directors can make binding declarations and sign contracts for the company, initiate proceedings before court, sign applications with the commercial register or undertake any other legal acts. Managing directors have to act in accordance with statutory provisions, the articles of association and any instructions given by the general assembly by way of shareholder resolution.

只有董事总经理才能代表公司做出有约束力的声明、签署合同、向法院提起诉讼、在商业登记处签署申请书或进行任何其他法律行为。董事总经理代表公司行事应当遵守法律条款、公司章程，与股东大会决议的指示保持一致。

With regard to the power of representation it is important to emphasize, that under Austrian law it is not permitted to restrict the power of representation of any managing director to specific types of business transactions or measures. However, there are certain limitations, such as the following:

关于代表权需要强调的是，根据奥地利法律，不允许将任何董事总经理的对公司的代表权限制在特定类型的商业交易或行为上。但是，也存在一些特定的限制，例如：

- General statutory limitations

The managing directors cannot enter into binding commitments for the company that would require either a change to the articles of association or the implementation of corporate re-organisations (such as mergers, spin-offs and such). Also, in case of transactions which constitute so called "self-dealings" (i.e., the company and a managing director personally enter into a contract) or double-representations (i.e., company A and company B enter into a contract but both are represented by the same managing director), prior approval of the shareholders is required.

- 一般法定限制

董事总经理不能对公司作出要求修改公司章程或实施公司重组的约束性承诺（如合并、分立等）。此外，如果交易构成"自我交易"（即公司和董事总经理个人签订合同）或双重代表（即 A 公司和 B 公司签订合同，但两者均由同一董事总经理代表），则需要事先获得股东的批准。

- Defining a list of reserved matters

The representation power of the managing directors can albeit only binding internally with no effect vis-à-vis third parties who are not aware of the restrictions—be limited by including a list of reserved matters (i.e. actions of the managing director that require prior consent of the shareholders) either in the articles of association or in the by-laws. Further matters may be added to or removed from the list at any time, either through an amendment to the articles of association or the by-laws, depending on where such reserved matters were included.

- 确定保留事项清单

公司章程或附则可以通过列举保留事项的方式对公司董事总经理的代表权

加以限制（即董事总经理的某些特定行为需要经过股东的事先同意才可实施），但这种限制仅对公司内部有效，对善意第三人不产生法律效力。通过修改公司章程或附则，可以随时在清单中进一步添加或删除事项，具体取决于该保留事项处在章程或细则中的位置。

- Instructions by shareholders

Even if not included on the list of reserved matters, shareholders may give binding instructions to the managing directors and insofar limit their power of representation.

- 股东指示

即使未被列入保留事项清单，股东也可以向董事总经理发出有约束力的指示，在一定程度上限制其代表权。

3.4.2 内部决议程序（Internal decision-making process）

To be distinguished from the power of representation as mentioned above is the internal decision-making process:

与前述代表权有所不同的是公司的内部决策程序：

All managing directors have to participate in the decision-making process or express their approval prior to the execution of the respective decision. Generally, all acts of the managing directors have to be unanimously approved by every managing director according to statutory law. Thus, none of the managing directors shall undertake any action alone except in a case of imminent danger. However, different rules regarding the internal decision-making process of the management board can be stipulated in the articles of association or bylaws for the management board: Responsibilities may be allocated among the managing directors, or entitle the managing directors to divide the areas of responsibility among themselves.

董事总经理在执行决策前，必须确保该所有的董事总经理都参与了该决策的决议程序并表示一致赞成。一般而言，根据法律规定，董事总经理的任何行为都必经过公司每一位董事总经理的一致同意。因此，除紧急情况外，董事总经理不得单独采取任何行动。然而，公司的章程或管理委员会附则可以规定不同的管理委员会内部决议程序：责任可以在董事总经理之间分配，也可以授权董事总经理自行划分其各自承担的职责范围。

The managing directors do not necessarily have to act simultaneously, however a managing director acting without the mandatory consent of all managing directors is in breach of his duty.

各位董事总经理不一定必须同时采取行动,但未经全体董事总经理的法定同意而采取行动是违反其职责的。

3.4.3 一般责任(General liability)

As mentioned above, the LLC is managed and represented solely by its managing directors who are responsible for the entire business of the company. Managing directors must exercise the duty of care and diligence of a prudent business person and face personal liability for all acts and omissions of the company specifically regarding the compliance with Austrian law. Consequently, a managing director may be liable under numerous provisions under Austrian administrative law, tax law and even criminal law (further below). However, generally speaking, managing directors are only liable towards the company and not towards third parties. Only in specific matters, managing directors are personally liable vis-à-vis the company's creditors.

如上所述,有限责任公司只由负责公司整个业务的董事总经理管理和代表。董事总经理应当履行商业人士的谨慎和勤勉义务,并根据奥地利的法律对公司的所有行为和疏忽承担个人责任。据此,根据奥地利行政法、税法甚至刑法的相关规定,董事总经理有承担责任的可能。然而,一般而言,董事总经理只对公司负责,而不对第三方负责。只有在特定事项上,董事总经理才对公司债权人负个人责任。

Provided, however, that the managing director acts according to administrative and tax obligations and duly pays the company's creditors, most risks and liabilities remain theoretical. Any material risks to managing directors (apart from possible administrative fines) usually only arise in the event of the company's insolvency, where the managing director is required to file for insolvency with the competent court without culpable hesitation.

然而,只要董事总经理依据其行政和税务义务行事,并按时偿付公司债权人,大多数风险和责任只是理论上的。董事总经理面临的任何重大风险(除了可能的行政罚款)通常只在公司破产的情况下才会出现,在这种情况下,董事总经理应当向主管法院申请破产,不得有任何迟延。

Also, the Business Judgment Rule provides for a safe harbour for managing directors. Managing directors have in any case acted with the duty of care and diligence of a prudent business person, if a business decision is made free of conflicts of interest, based on adequately available information and is justifiably assumed by the managing directors to be in the best interest of the company.

此外，商业判断规则为董事总经理提供了安全港。在任何情况下，董事总经理都有谨慎和勤勉的义务，应当根据充分可利用的信息做出没有利益冲突且符合公司最佳利益的商业决策。

3.4.4 撤销和辞职（Revocation and resignation）

The appointment of a managing director can be revoked by the shareholders at any time and for any reason. The resolution with which the managing director is appointed can also specify the date the revocation becomes effective.

股东可以随时以任何理由撤销对董事总经理的任命。股东大会任命董事总经理的决议也可以指定撤销任命的生效日期。

Even though the appointment can be revoked at any time, the employment relationship of such managing director does not necessarily automatically end as a result thereof. Thus, there may be a continuing financial obligation of the company vis-à-vis such managing director. Following the effective revocation the managing director has to be deleted from the company register.

即使股东可以随时撤销对董事总经理的任命，但与该董事总经理的雇用关系不一定自动终止。因此，公司可能仍然负有对该董事总经理的财务支付义务。在撤销任命的决定生效后，应当从公司注册簿中删除该董事总经理。

The resignation from the position of managing director is effective only after the expiration of two weeks as of declaration of the intended resignation towards the general assembly, provided that the resignation of the managing director was included in the agenda. Otherwise, two weeks as of declaration towards every individual shareholder.

在董事总经理的辞职事宜已经列入股东大会的议程的前提下，董事总经理向股东大会作出辞职声明两周后，该辞职行为才能生效。否则，辞职行为只能在辞职的董事总经理向每一名股东分别作出辞职声明满两周后生效。

3.5 监事会（Supervisory Board）

The supervisory board shall oversee management and monitor its actions. Only an individual (and not a legal entity) may be a member of the supervisory board. Further, a supervisory board has to comprise of at least three members. However, more members may be appointed as there is no statutory maximum number for a supervisory board.

监事会对公司管理层负有监督义务，监督管理层的各项行为。只有个人（而非法人实体）可以是监事会成员。此外，监事会必须至少由三名成员组成。但由于监事会没有法定的最高人数限制，公司可以任命更多的监事成员。

Members of the supervisory board are appointed by the shareholders (not applicable to such which are appointed by the works council, as further described below). Shareholders may revoke such an appointment at any time and without giving any explanation, as long as at least three members remain (minimum legal requirement) and the resolution is passed with the required majority (75 percent of the votes cast at the meetings where more than half of the share capital is represented).

监事会成员由股东任命（不适用于下文提及的由公司工会任命的监事）。股东可以随时无理由地撤销对监事的任命，但剩余监事至少还应有 3 人（满足最低法定要求）。撤销监事任命的决议应当以法定多数的形式投票通过（出席会议的股东持有公司一半以上的股份，且须经出席会议的股东所持表决权 75% 以上通过）。

3.5.1 法定监事会和任意监事会（Mandatory supervisory boards and voluntary supervisory boards）

Whereas a supervisory board is only mandatory in cases as statutorily set forth, a supervisory board may also be established voluntarily, although this is rarely the case in practice. However, the competencies and areas of responsibility as defined in the statutes may not be limited or restricted, for both the mandatory supervisory board and voluntary supervisory board.

尽管监事会只能根据法律的强制性规定成立，但公司也可以根据实际情况自愿设立监事会，不过这种情况较为罕见。但是，无论是法定监事会还是任意监事会，都不得限制或缩减法律规定的监事会的职权和责任范围。

3.5.2 任职资格（Required attributes of the members of the supervisory board）
Specifically with regard to personal capability, nationality and residency.
具体包括个人能力、国籍和居住权。

A member of the supervisory board must be aged 18 or above and mentally healthy in order to duly act on behalf of and represent the company. Aside therefrom there are no further statutory requirements, specifically none regarding the personal capabilities or professional qualifications or any certain level of experience in a certain field of business.

监事会成员必须年满18岁，精神健康，方可代表公司行事。除此之外，法律没有作其他要求，特别是没有对个人能力、专业资格或在某一业务领域任何特定的经验水平作出要求。

Notwithstanding the aforementioned, however, certain criteria have been developed through case law, namely that a member of the supervisory board has to be capable of fulfilling his/her statutory duties, i. e. the supervision of the managing directors and the conduct of their business. Consequently, the requirements and professional qualifications for members of the supervisory board depend on the nature and size of the business of the respective company.

尽管有上述规定，判例法中还是制定了某些标准，比如监事会成员必须有能力履行其法定职责，即对董事总经理及其行为进行监督。因此，对监事会成员的要求和专业资格就取决于公司业务的性质和规模。

This means that a member of the supervisory board should be able to recognize difficult legal and economic relationships, assess their impacts on the respective company, as well as recognize (contingent) risks for the company and may not rely on his/her missing intellectual capacities or on his/her missing experience or knowledge.

这就意味着，监事会成员应当有能力能够识别复杂的法律、经济关系，评估其会对公司产生的影响，识别其可能会给公司带来的潜在风险，智力、相关知识或工作经验不足无法完成前述职责。

If members of the supervisory board do not fulfill their duties with the due diligence of a prudent member of a supervisory board, they are liable vis-à-vis the company and the creditors of the company who suffered a damage due to the undue performance of these members of the supervisory board.

如果监事会成员未能履行审慎、勤勉的职责，则该监事会成员应当对因其失职而给公司和公司债权人带来的损失承担责任。

3.6 咨询委员会（Advisory Board）

The advisory board, as mentioned above, is an optional corporate body of the LLC, which may be set up and organised in a number of different ways, especially with regards to its competencies, areas of responsibilities, and (number of) members.

如上所述，咨询委员会是有限责任公司中的一种可选择是否设立的法人团体，其设立和组织方式多种多样，特别是在其职权、职责范围和成员人数等方面可以有很多选择。

In order to legally analyse the advisory board, it has to be differentiated between an advisory board functioning as a corporate body of the LLC (regulated in the articles of association) and an advisory board set up on a contractual basis. The latter usually only serves as an advisory panel to the shareholders of the LLC, meaning that even if the managing directors were instructed by the shareholders (either by way of shareholder resolution or in the articles of association) to include members of the advisory board in the decision making process, such non-compliance would neither lead to any company law related sanctions nor affect the decision as such.

对咨询委员会进行法律分析，应当将其区分为由公司章程规定的以有限责任公司法人团体形式运作的咨询委员会，和依据合同设立的咨询委员会。后者通常为有限责任公司股东的一个顾问团队，这就意味着即使董事总经理根据股东决议或公司章程将咨询委员会成员纳入公司的决策过程中，此类不合规行为不会受到公司法上的任何处罚，也不会影响该决策的效力。

3.6.1 咨询委员会的设立（Setting up of an advisory board）

Advisory boards in LLCs, although permissible, often create several legal uncertainties, depending on the specific structure and organization of the advisory board. This is partly because there is no specific legal framework or any particular statutory provisions regarding the setting up and organization of advisory boards.

虽然法律允许在有限责任公司中设置咨询委员会，但由于咨询委员会的结构和组织特性，往往会造成一些法律上的不确定性。部分原因是在咨询委员会的设立和组织等方面没有具体的法律框架，也没有任何具体的法律规定。

In practice, an advisory board may be either set up in addition to or instead of a supervisory board. Depending thereupon, the function of the advisory board and the obligations of the members of such corporate body may vary.

在实践中，可以在监事会之外设立咨询委员会，也可以不设立监事会，由咨询委员会代替。因此，不同公司咨询委员会的职责及其成员的义务也可能不同。

3.6.2 作为监事会的咨询委员会（Advisory board acting as a supervisory board）

According to the Austrian Supreme Court, an advisory board being allocated competencies, which in principle lie in the core competency of the supervisory board, shall be treated as such. Core competencies include, among other things, the right to inspect the books, to convoke the general assembly and to supervise and monitor the management and its activities.

根据奥地利最高法院的规定，如果咨询委员会被赋予监事会的核心职权，则该咨询委员会应当被视为监事会。核心职权主要包括检查公司账簿、召集股东大会以及监督管理层及其活动等。

The assessment of whether an advisory board defacto acts as a supervisory board has to be made on a case by case basis, taking into account the case specific organization with regard to its competencies and areas of responsibilities. The legal consequences of such qualification would result in the advisory board being obligated to comply with all statutory rules applicable to the supervisory board.

咨询委员会是否在实质上成为监事会，应当逐案进行评估，同时要考虑到该咨询委员会具体的职权和责任范围。若咨询委员会被认定为事实上成为监事会，那么法律后果为该咨询委员会应当遵守适用于监事会的所有法律规定。

4. 交易完成后的经验与教训（Lessons Learned After the Conclusion of the Transaction）

4.1 公司治理（Corporate Governance）

Setting up an advisory board may lead to a number of unintended legal implications; therefore a profound knowledge of Austrian law is imperative in order to not overstep any provisions regarding competencies (statutory or as defined in the articles of association). The Chinese investor has to be cautious in defining and determining the scope of the competencies and areas of responsibility. Otherwise, among other things, the advisory board may overstep its competenciesand be qualified as a supervisory board and hence the statutory rules regarding supervisory boards would apply.

设立咨询委员会可能会带来一些无法预测的法律后果；因此，必须深入了解奥地利法律，以免违反任何有关其职权的法律规定或公司章程规定。中国投资者必须谨慎确认和决定咨询委员会的职权和责任范围。否则，如果咨询委员会超越其职权而被认定为监事会，那么所有关于监事会的法律规定都将适用于该咨询委员会。

4.2 对其他股东的依赖（Dependency on Other Shareholders）

The Chinese investor should always have the ability to convoke a shareholders' meeting. A shareholders' meeting may be effected either by a managing director appointed by the investor himself/herself or in accordance with any convocation competencies as defined either in the statutes (e. g. minority shareholder rights) or the articles of association. In any case, the investor should not be solely dependent on the participation of other shareholders. The investor should also implement a control mechanism in order to be able to closely monitor and supervise the actions of the other shareholders.

中国投资者应始终保证自己有能力召开股东大会。股东大会可以由投资者本人任命的董事总经理召开，也可以由法律规定的（如少数股东权利）或公司章程中规定的具有召开股东大会权限的任何人召开。在任何情况下，投资者都不应仅依赖于其他股东。投资者应设立一种控制机制，以使其能够密切监测、监督其他股东的各项行为。

4.3 居住和工作许可（Residency and/or Work Permit）

The Chinese investor should make sure that all residency and/or work permit requirements (e. g. eligibility to apply for a red-white-red card or any alternatives thereto) have been fulfilled, prior to the appointment and/or dispatch of a Third-Country National as managing director (or any other executive position).

中国投资者在任命、派遣第三国国民担任公司董事总经理或其他任何高管职务之前，应当确保其满足所有的居住、工作许可要求，例如申请"红—白—红卡"或其他有同等效力的资格证。

作者简介

Christian Mikosch specialises in corporate law, international commercial law and mergers and acquisitions with particular expertise in the CEE/SEE (Central and Eastern Europe/Southern and Eastern Europe) region. Besides being the head of Wolf Theiss' China Desk, Christian is lecturing at the University of Vienna and the Donauuniversität Krems. Christian is also responsible for the firm's work in Kosovo. Prior to joining the firm, Christian gained valuable experience while working in New York. Christian holds LL. M. degrees from both the University of Manchester and the University of Rotterdam and regularly lectures on legal topics at various universities. He is admitted to the bar in Austria and in the Czech Republic.

Christian Mikosch 专攻公司法、国际商法和并购业务，尤其擅长中东欧和东南欧地区的业务。除了担任 Wolf Theiss 中国业务的负责人之外，Christian 还在维也纳大学和克罗姆斯多瑙大学任教。除此之外，克里斯蒂安还负责律所在科索沃地区的业务。在加入该所之前，Christian 在纽约工作，积累了宝贵的经验。Christian 拥有曼彻斯特大学和鹿特丹大学的法学硕士学位，并定期在多所大学开设法律讲座。他在奥地利和捷克共和国均获得了律师资格。

Martin Laschan is a member of the Corporate and M&A team in the Vienna office and has been involved in several matters involving clients from different business sectors. As a native Chinese speaker, he is an active member of the firm's China Desk and is involved in most China related projects. He is currently studying law at the University of Vienna. He has also gained international experience participating in an exchange program at the Taiwan University and working for one of the leading law firms in Taipei. In addition, his experience includes working for the German Trade Office in Taipei.

Martin Laschan 是维也纳办公室公司与并购团队的成员，曾参与多项来自不同业务领域的客户的业务。他以中文为母语，作为律所中国办公室的主要成员，参与了大部分与中国相关的项目。他目前在维也纳大学进修法律。曾参加台湾大学的交换项目，并曾在台北一家知名律师事务所工作，积累了国际业务方面的工作经验。此外，他还曾供职于台北的德国贸易办事处。

股权并购在法国：在制药行业开展投资
Equity in France
Investing in the Pharmaceutical Industry

点 评

　　通过本文作者的介绍可以了解到，法国的制药行业处于世界领先地位，具有广阔的市场。但是制药行业在法国属于强监管的领域，主要反映在卫生、经济和社会等诸多方面。法国政府制定了强有力的监管框架，以确保在法国生产或分销的药品的质量和安全。本文介绍的案例为2017年中国投资者收购一家法国制药集团。本案中，中国投资者拟收购的法国制药集团的股权由创始家族和某些关键员工持有，股权比较分散，但这种分散的股权结构在法国公司中比较常见。与多方当事人进行谈判是此类交易的难点之一，当事人可能存在不同的利益诉求，甚至对公司最佳利益的认知也存在分歧。该难点的解决方案之一是确定一个牵头方，让其代表其他卖方处理谈判的所有环节。

　　另外，需要关注的是，除了常规的反垄断申报，从外商投资监管的角度来看，虽然外商投资在法国是自由的，但如外商投资涉及有关国家利益的"敏感"领域，则需要提交相关政府部门进行外国投资筛查。此外，出于数据统计的需要，非法国居民获得法国公司10%及以上的股本或投票权的交易应向法兰西银行进行申报。

　　最后，如果中国投资者拟收购的法国公司属于法国法律中规定的"中小企业"，则在签署任何出售超过公司50%股本的交易之前，应将该等交易通知公司员工，以使公司员工能够提出购买公司拟出售的全部股本的反要约，虽然实践中这种情况非常罕见。在本案中，主要法律问题之一是要按照卖方的法律义务来设计交易，而卖方的义务包括将交易信息通知到每名员工，并咨询员工代表意见。在履行通知行为后，2个月的期限已届满，或者获得所有员工的弃权书之前，投资者不得签署任何具有约束力的协议。同时，在没有获得对买方具有约束力的协议的情况下，卖方也不希望将此类战略性交易通知其员工。该问题的解决方案是让中国买方签署一份有利于卖方的出售期权，该期权可在上述信息通知和咨询行为完成后行使。为了保护买方，最终的股权收购协议会作为出售期权协议的附件。这种解决方案在法国交易中很常见，但需要向外国投资者进行解释与说明，避免产生不必要的误解，从而影响正常的交易。

1. 法国的制药行业（Pharmaceutics in France）

The pharmaceutical industry in France is a vibrant and expanding sector, bringing together those companies which develop, manufacture, and market medication; including traditional, well-established pharmaceutical laboratories, as well as biotechnology start-ups. Pharmaceutical companies may deal with regulated drugs, medical devices, but also operate on non-regulated markets (such as certain homeopathic drugs, healthcare cosmetics, etc.).

法国的制药行业是一个充满活力和不断扩大的行业，汇集了开发、制造和销售药物的公司，包括传统的、成熟的制药实验室以及生物技术初创企业。制药公司可以经营受管制药品、医疗器械，但也可以在不受管制的市场（如某些顺势疗法药品、保健化妆品等）中开展业务。

This sector is propelled by world leading players as well as a strong network of mid-size and small companies, backed with highly recognized research and development (R&D) teams and infrastructures. Moreover, in the coming years the French government is willing to implement various measures that would aim to enhance the attractiveness of the industry for French and international investors (through the reduction of authorization delays for instance).

该行业的发展由世界领先的企业以及强大的中小型企业网络推动，并拥有具有高认可度的研发团队和基础设施支持。此外，在未来几年，法国政府愿意采取各种措施以提高该行业对法国和国际投资者的吸引力（例如，通过减少在政府授权方面的迟延）。

1.1 法国在全球制药行业中发挥关键作用的三个重要因素（Three Important Factors as to Why France Plays a Key Role in the Global Pharmaceutical Industry）

1.1.1 一流的研发能力（First-class R & D activities）

R&D spending in France is among the highest in the world. Such investments are encouraged by various tax incentives. The pharmaceutical industry, in particular, has made significant investments in R&D.

法国的研发支出是世界上最高的。这些投资受到各种税收优惠的鼓励。特别是在制药行业，研发投入是非常巨大的。

The quality of the French academics and, consequently, the possibility to hire high-level profiles, combined with a strong network of R&D centers and public laboratories, has made the French pharmaceutical companies amongst the most innovative and secured ones in the world market. What is more, the country is top of the list for international companies when it comes to choosing the location of their R&D centers.

法国学术人员的素质较高，因而更可能聘请到高层次人才，再加上研发中心和公共实验室强大的联结网络，使法国制药公司成为世界市场中最具创新性和安全性的公司群体之一。此外，当跨国公司在选择研发中心的位置时，法国是最优先的选择。

1.1.2 巨大的国内市场（A significant domestic market）

France is one of the biggest worldwide consumers of medication. Despite the complexity of pharmaceutics distribution in France, which is constrained by various regulations, and the fact that some percentage is reimbursed to end-users by the French social security scheme, this market represents a significant volume, which makes the domestic market interesting to French pharmaceutical companies.

法国是全球最大的药物消费国之一。尽管法国的药品分销很复杂，受到各种法规的限制，而且法国社会保障制度对终端消费者给予了一定比例的补偿，但巨大的市场规模使得法国制药公司对法国国内市场仍抱有兴趣。

1.1.3 一流的市场参与者（Leading players）

The top French pharmaceutical players are among the leading exporters of pharmaceutics in the world. For instance, the export of drugs amounted to 30 billion euros in 2019[1], mainly in the European Union (59.4%), but also worldwide, in constant increasing.

法国顶级制药公司是世界上主要的制药出口商之一。例如，2019 年药品出

---

[1] French Pharmaceutical Industry-Key data 2020, See https://www.leem.org/publication/french-pharmaceutical-industry-key-data-2020.

口额为 300 亿欧元，[1]主要面向欧盟出口（59.4%），同时也广泛地向全球市场出口，并不断增加出口金额。

The industry is led by several big players with worldwide presence and reputation, but many smaller players also exist beside them—from the very small enterprises to mid-size companies with a strong culture for innovation and, often, internationally oriented.

法国制药行业由几家拥有全球知名度和声誉的大型企业领导，但除此之外还有许多小型企业——从非常小的企业到具有强大创新文化的中型企业，这些企业通常都是国际化的。

1.2 制药行业的监管规定（Regulatory Requirements Regarding the Pharmaceutical sector）

The pharmaceutical industry is characterised by significant risks, namely sanitary, economic, and social. Therefore, a strong regulatory framework has been put in place by the French government in order to ensure the quality and security of pharmaceutical products which are produced and/or distributed in France.

制药行业存在重大风险，主要是在卫生、经济和社会等方面。因此，法国政府制定了强有力的监管框架，以确保在法国生产或分销的药品的质量和安全。

As a consequence, where regulated drugs and medical devices are involved in the target company's business, a specific due diligence review shall be performed by a specialized regulatory advisor, who will be able to assess the compliance of the products and, as the case may be, the plants or the distribution scheme of the target company, please see below for further developments on the due diligence review.

因此，如果目标公司的业务涉及受管制药品和医疗器械，则应由专门的监管顾问进行具体的尽职调查，该顾问将会评估公司产品的合规性，在某些情况下还要评估目标公司工厂和分销计划的合规性，更具体的信息请参阅下文有关尽职调查的内容。

---

〔1〕 法国制药行业 2020 年度关键数据，参见 https://www.leem.org/publication/french-pharmaceutical-industry-key-data-2020。

2. 交易结构（Transaction Structure）

2.1 投资项目介绍（Introduction of the Investment Project）

In 2017, our Chinese client acquired a French group of companies running a pharmaceutical activity. The target group included a parent company, whose capital was shared between various individual holders and subsidiaries dedicated to R&D, manufacturing and distribution of drugs, medical devices, and natural healthcare products. Most of the companies were incorporated as simple joint-stock companies under French law, some were incorporated in foreign jurisdictions.

2017年，我们的中国客户收购了一家经营制药业务的法国集团。目标集团包括一家母公司，其股份由多位个人股东持有，这些子公司致力于药物、医疗器械和天然保健产品的研发、制造和分销。大部分公司是根据法国法律成立的简单股份制公司，还有一些公司是在法国以外的司法辖区成立的。

The group's parent company was still held by the founding family and certain key employees. Such a breakdown of the ownership is common in French mid-size companies in which the founders have allowed their heirs or trusted employees to enter the share capital, for various reasons (such as for wealth planning or management incentive planning purposes).

该集团的母公司仍由创始家族和某些关键员工持有。这种所有权的细分在法国中型公司中很常见，因为各种原因（如财富规划或管理激励计划目的），创始人允许其继承人或受信任的员工持有公司股份。

As a result, one of the difficulties in such transactions is to negotiate with multiple contacts who may not all have the same interests nor even the same views on the company's best interests. One way to manage this difficulty is to have one or two of the sellers take the leadership and handle the negotiation for the others. However, in such a case, it is necessary to ensure that they get the approval of their partners in order to avoid delays and inefficient discussions; in any case, any transaction document—including letters of intent, term sheets, and NDA (non-disclosure agreement, NDA)—must be executed by all parties to the contemplated transaction.

因此，与多个不同的当事人进行谈判是此类交易的困难之一，这些当事人可能并不都有相同的利益追求，甚至对公司的最佳利益有不相同的看法。解决这个问题的办法之一是让一到二个卖方牵头,来为其他卖方处理谈判。但是在这种情况下,必须确保牵头人得到其他人的授权,以避免时间的拖延和无效的讨论;在任何情况下,包括意向书、投资条款清单和保密协议(NDA)在内的任何交易文件,都必须经过拟进行交易的各方当事人签署。

2.2 交易程序和交易文件(Transaction Process and Documents)

It is common for transactions in France that the first document to be executed would be the confidentiality agreement (NDA). This agreement aims to frame the exchanges of information between parties during the negotiation period, which may end either with the execution of transaction agreements or with the surrender of the project.

在法国,交易中签订的第一份文件通常是保密协议(NDA)。保密协议的目的在于为交易各方在协商阶段提供一个信息交流的框架,该协议可能随着交易合同的执行或项目的移交而终止。

The NDA can be either mutual (both parties may exchange/receive information from the other) or unilateral (one party may provide the other one with information about its business). In the case of the acquisition of a company's whole share capital, the NDA is commonly unilateral, since the buyer will request information from the seller about the target company. Also, it is to be noted that French legal advisors (*avocats* in French) do not usually execute any NDA since their professional rules include appropriate confidentiality obligations.

保密协议可以是相互的(双方可以交换、接收对方的信息),也可以是单方的(一方可以向另一方提供有关其业务的信息)。在收购公司全部股本的情况下,NDA 通常是单方的,这是因为买方会要求卖方提供目标公司的相关信息。此外需要注意的是,法国的法律顾问(法语为 avocats)通常不执行任何保密协议,因为他们的专业规则中就包括合理的保密义务。

The NDA shall be carefully negotiated in order to avoid obligations on the receiving party that would be impossible to apply in practice (while they are commonly included in NDAs). Such provisions may put the receiving party at risk of being recognized as liable in case of any claim from the disclosing party, since it will not be able to prove the fulfillment of its obligations.

保密协议应谨慎协商,以避免信息接收方实际上无法履行某些义务(然而 NDA 中通常会规定这些义务)。这些规定可能会使信息接收方面临承担责任的风险，因为一旦信息披露方提出任何索赔，信息接收方无法证明其履行了协议规定的义务。

Together with the execution of the NDA, our client had to countersign a process letter issued by the sellers. Such letters are issued in cases where a bid process takes place and aim to set out the conditions and timelines of such a process, including the conditions in which potential bidders may run their due diligence reviews, release a letter of intent, and be selected for either a second, in-depth due diligence review or directly to negotiate the final documents. Additionally, data room regulations are sometimes set out and shall be executed by the bidders.

在执行保密协议的同时，我们的客户必须在卖方签发的过程信函上签字。此类信函是在投标过程中签发的，目的是说明投标过程中的条款以及时间线，潜在的投标者可能会对信函中包含的条款进行尽职调查、发出意向书，还可能会被选中进行第二次深入尽职调查或者直接进入最终交易文件的协商环节。此外，信函中有时也会设置对数据存储空间的规定，这些规定都是投标者应该要执行的。

At the end of the bid process, our client, having considered the findings of his due diligence review, decided to move forward with the transaction and issued a binding offer to the sellers. After comparison with those issued by other bidders, our client has been retained for the transaction documents final negotiation phase, which will lead to the finalization of the share purchase agreement (SPA), as well as the representation and warranties agreement through which our client would acquire all shares and securities issued by the target company.

在投标程序结束时，我方客户在考虑了尽职调查审查的成果后，决定继续推进交易，并向卖方发出具有约束力的要约。在与其他投标人提供的报价进行比较后，卖方选择了我方客户进入交易文件的最终协商阶段，在这个阶段，交易双方会签订最终的股份购买协议（SPA）以及陈述和保证协议，通过这些协议我方客户将会获得目标公司所有的股份和证券。

The SPA is commonly executed under conditions precedent, which must be fulfilled before the closing date stipulated in the agreement. On closing, the transaction was completed, and our client became the owner of the shares on that date.

一般情况下，在所有的先决条件均于协议中约定的交易完成日之前已满足时，交易各方才会执行 SPA。投标结束时，交易完成，我方客户成为目标公司股份的所有者。

It is to be noted that we were able to assist our client from the start of the process, which allowed us to assist him in the drafting and negotiation of all documents from the very beginning, and to help reduce the cultural gap in the negotiations.

值得注意的是，我们从交易程序开始就能够为客户提供帮助，这使我们能够第一时间帮助客户起草、协商所有的交易文件，并帮助客户减少谈判中的文化差异。

2.3 尽职调查（Due Diligence）

As part of the transaction process, the due diligence review of the target group's business and organization is a major step. It consists in investigating the entirety of the target's business and organization in order to identify and limit certain acquisition risks. Its main goal is to identify deal-breaking issues; to validate the target's valuation; and, eventually, to properly cover identified risks in the representations and warranties. Since our client was an industrial company and not a financial investor, the goal of its due diligence review (especially the business and financial ones) was also to identify synergy opportunities that could arise following the transaction.

作为交易过程的一部分，对目标集团的业务和组织进行尽职调查是一个重要环节。它包括调查目标的整个业务和组织以识别和限制某些收购风险。它的主要目标是发现破坏交易的问题、验证目标公司的估值、最终在陈述和保证条款中适当地涵盖已经识别的风险。由于我们的客户是一家工业企业而非金融投资者，尽职调查的目的（尤其是业务尽职调查和财务尽职调查方面的）也是为了发现交易后可能出现的协同机会。

In the case of our transaction, since the target group was acting in a strongly regulated sector, a key concern was about the compliance of the companies' manufacture plants, products, and distribution scheme with the applicable healthcare regulation. Since the group was also running an IP-sensitive activity, it was essential to make an in-depth intellectual property due diligence in order to assess the validity of all the patents, trademarks, and other IP rights ownership.

在我们的交易中，由于目标集团处于受严格监管的行业中，因此，公司的制造厂、产品和分销计划是否符合适用的医疗法规就是一个关键问题。由于该集团还正在开展一项与知识产权相关的敏感业务,因此必须进行深入的知识产权尽职调查,以评估所有专利、商标和其他知识产权所有权的有效性。

From a practical point of view, most of the due diligence reviews in France are based on virtual data rooms in which potential purchasers and their advisors can review the documents uploaded by the target company and the sellers. However, especially when sensitive business or IP information on the target company is to be communicated, as is often the case for pharmaceutical companies, a physical data room may be set up. Moreover, a "clean team agreement" may be executed between parties who are also competitors in order to reduce antitrust liability risk linked to the exchange of sensitive and confidential information between competitors.

从实用的角度来看,法国的尽职调查大多是基于虚拟的数据储存空间(虚拟数据库),潜在买家及其顾问可以在虚拟数据库中审查目标公司和卖家上传的文件。但是,特别是当涉及目标公司的敏感业务或知识产权信息时,制药公司就经常会遇到这种情况,此时就可以建立一个实体的数据储存室。此外,有竞争关系的企业之间也可以签订"清洁团队协议",以减少竞争对手之间敏感和机密信息的交换所带来的反垄断法律责任风险。

2.4 竞争法申报(Competition Law Filings)

M&A transactions between industrial parties may involve a high concentration of companies running the same type of activities. Those transactions involving French parties are subject to one of two levels of control: either at the French level, made by the French *Autorité de la concurrence*, or at the EU level, made by the European Commission.

同行业与企业间的并购交易可能会涉及经营同类业务的经营者高度集中的问题。涉及法国主体的交易会受到两种控制制度之一的制约:一种是来自法国竞争管理局的法国方面的控制,另一种是来自欧盟委员会的欧盟方面的控制。

2.4.1 法国竞争法(French Competition Law)

According to French law, the acquisition of a company is deemed to be a concentration of companies when a company acquires the direct or indirect control of another company (art. L. 430-1, French Commercial Code).

根据法国法律,当一家公司获得对另一家公司的直接或间接控制权时,该公司的收购行为被视为经营者集中(《法国商法典》第 L. 430-1 条)。

In such a case, a filing shall be made to the French Competition Authority if both the following requirements are met (art. L. 430-2, French Commercial Code):

在这种情况下，如果同时满足以下两个条件，则应向法国竞争管理局进行备案（《法国商法典》第 L. 430-2 条）：

- The worldwide turnover (without taxes) of the parties to the transaction is in excess of 150 million euros;
- 交易各方的全球营业额（不含税）超过 1.5 亿欧元；
- The turnover (without taxes) made in France, by at least two of the parties to the transaction individually, is in excess of 50 million euros.
- 交易各方中至少两方各自在法国的营业额（不含税）超过 5000 万欧元。

It should be noted that these amounts may differ in transactions involving retail companies for instance (but that was not the case for our client).

需要注意的是，以上数额可能在涉及零售类企业交易时会有所不同（我方客户不属于这种情况）。

The filing will be made by means of a notification to the French Competition Authority by the purchaser as soon as the transaction project is sufficiently clear and certain (regarding the conditions, the identity of the parties, and the timeline of the transaction). In practice, the SPA will include the obtention of the Authority clearance as a condition precedent to the completion of the sale. The notification can be informally submitted before the execution of the SPA in order to let the Authority begin its review as early as possible and to minimize the delay between the signing of the SPA and the closing of the transaction, (which could last up to 25 days following the reception of the complete notification subsequent to the signing of the SPA). Also, the employees' representatives shall be informed within three days following the filing of the formal notification.

一旦交易项目足够清晰和确定（关于交易条件、双方身份和交易时间表），买方将以通知的方式向法国竞争管理机构提交备案。在实践中，股份购买协议（SPA）将获得授权许可作为完成交易的先决条件。该通知可在 SPA 执行前非正式提交，以便当局尽早开始审查，并尽量减少签署 SPA 和交易完成日间的时间间隔（签署 SPA 并向竞争管理局提交交易通知后，竞争管理局的审查时间最多会持续 25 天）。同时，应在提交正式通知后的三天内通知员工代表。

The control run by the Authority consists of an initial short process (about one month), or a longer process (about four months) if, after the first step, there remains a serious doubt regarding the risk of a restriction to the effective competition within the considered market.

竞争管理局所进行的管制包括初步的较短程序（约 1 个月），和后续的较长程序（约 4 个月）。如果经过初步的较短程序之后，竞争管理局仍然严重怀疑相关市场内的有效竞争会被该交易项目限制，其将会启动后续较长时间的管制程序。

After conducting a competitive assessment of the transaction and ascertaining whether or not it contributes to economic progress, the French Competition Authority may (Art. L 430-7, French Commercial Code):

在对该交易进行竞争性评估并确定其是否有助于经济发展后，法国竞争管理局可以采取以下措施（《法国商法典》第 L 430-7 条）：

- prohibit the transaction and, where appropriate, order the parties to take measures to restore sufficient competition; or
- 禁止该交易，并酌情要求交易各方采取措施来恢复市场的充分竞争；或
- authorize the transaction by requiring the parties to take any measure to ensure sufficient competition or by requesting for them to respect certain requirements to make the new group contribute sufficiently to "economic progress" in order to offset the harm done to competition, (in such a case, the process timeline could be extended).
- 批准该交易，但同时要求交易各方采取任何措施以确保充分竞争，或者要求交易各方遵循某些要求以使合并后的企业能够为经济发展做出充分贡献，以抵消合并对竞争带来的损害（这种情况下的时间线可以被延长）。

Failure to notify a concentration or to comply with the Authority's orders will usually lead to a fine upon discovery by the French Competition Authority. Both companies and directors involved can be fined in this regard. Fines for companies should be calculated as a percentage of their worldwide turnover.

未履行经营者集中的通知义务或未能遵循竞争管理局指令的，经竞争管理

局查明后，通常会被处以罚款。有关公司和管理人员都会被处以罚款，对公司罚款的数额根据其全球营业额的1%计算。

2.4.2 欧盟竞争法（EU competition law）

According to EU Regulation No. 139/2004 dated January 20, 2004, any sale of the control of a company should be submitted to the prior approval of the European Commission when:

根据欧盟2004年1月20日第139/2004号条例，出现以下情况，任何出售公司控制权的行为应提交欧盟委员会事先批准：

- The worldwide turnover of all companies concerned by the transaction (and their affiliates) is above 5 billion euros;
- 该交易涉及的所有公司（及其附属公司）的全球营业额超过50亿欧元；
- At least two of these companies have activities within the EU with an individual turnover above 250 million euros for each.
- 这些公司中至少有两家在欧盟内部开展业务，且各自的营业额超过2.5亿欧元。

If these thresholds are not met, a filing shall nonetheless be made with the European Commission when all four of the following conditions are met:

如果未达到上述标准，但满足以下四个条件时，仍应向欧盟委员会提交申请：

- The total turnover achieved worldwide by all the companies concerned represents an amount of more than 2.5 billion euros;
- 所有有关公司在世界各地的总营业额超过25亿欧元；
- In each of at least three EU Member States, the total turnover of all the companies concerned is greater than 100 million euros;
- 在至少三个欧盟成员国中，所有有关公司的总营业额均超过1亿欧元；
- In each of at least three of the EU Member States referred to above, the total turnover achieved individually by at least two of the companies concerned is greater than 25 million euros;
- 在上述至少三个欧盟成员国中，至少两家有关公司各自的营业额总额超过 2500 万欧元；
- the total turnover achieved individually in the EU by at least two of the companies concerned represents an amount greater than 100 million euros.
- 至少两家有关公司各自在欧盟内取得的营业额总额超过 1 亿欧元。

When these requirements are met, the transaction is considered as "European", and the European Commission shall therefore have exclusive jurisdiction, which means that Member States' authorities are not competent (unless the European Commission partially or totally transfers the case to them).

当满足这些要求时，该交易就被视为具有"欧洲"性质，欧盟委员会对该交易就具有专属管辖权，这意味着欧盟成员国政府对此交易不具备管辖权（除非欧盟委员会将案件管辖权部分或全部地移交给他们）。

A filing scheme similar to the one described above for filings with the French Competition Authority shall apply to filings with the European Commission (employees' representatives shall be informed as well).

向欧盟委员会进行交易备案应当同样适用上述提到的备案规则（同样应该通知员工代表）。

2.4.3 外商投资监管（Foreign investments regulation）

According to French law, foreign investments in France shall be free (Art. L. 151-1, French Monetary and Financial Code). Regardless of the political majorities running the government, the French State traditionally endeavors to attract foreign investments to support the country's economic growth and employment.

根据法国法律，在法国进行外商投资应是自由的（《法国货币和金融法典》第 L. 151-1 条）。不管多数党如何管理政府，法国历来都会努力吸引外国投资，以支持国家的经济增长和就业。

However, the French State considers that certain business or industrial sectors are "sensitive" for its national interest. Consequently, when a foreign investor is contemplating an investment in a company involved in such a sensitive sector (representing the acquisition of the control of such company or a branch of activity, or leading to the holding of more than 25% of its voting rights), the contemplated transaction shall be submitted to the prior approval from the French Minister of the Economy (Art. L. 151-

3, French Monetary and Financial Code). The French government recently updated the list of the business sectors deemed to be sensitive. Among them are investments in sectors relating to materials, products or services essential to the interests of the country, especially regarding the protection of public health (Art. R. 151-3, II, 8°, French Monetary and Financial Code).

然而，法国认为某些商业或工业行业是关乎国家利益的"敏感"领域。因此，当外国投资者考虑投资涉及"敏感"行业的公司时（具体表现为获得该公司或分支机构的控制权，或导致其持有超过25%的表决权），该等拟议交易应事先获得法国经济部长的批准（《法国货币和金融法典》第L.151-3条）。法国政府最近更新了被认为是敏感行业的行业名单。其中包括对与国家利益至关重要，特别是在保护公共健康方面的材料、产品和服务相关行业的投资（《法国货币和金融法典》第R.151-3条，第II款，第8项）。

When a contemplated transaction involves a target running an activity likely to fall under one of these sensitive sectors, the prior approval of the government shall be requested. The government will assess—on a case-by-case basis—the sensitivity of any contemplated transaction, with regard to the specificities of the target company's activities, their importance, etc.

当拟议交易涉及的目标公司所经营的业务可能属于这些敏感行业之一时，应事先取得政府批准。政府将根据目标公司活动的特殊性以及重要性等具体情况评估拟议交易的敏感性。

Following such assessment, the government will either (i) fully approve the contemplated transaction, (ii) approve the transaction provided that certain measures and conditions are implemented, or (iii) refuse the approval.

进行上述评估后，政府将（i）完全批准拟议交易，(ii) 在实施某些特定措施和完成某些条件的情况下批准该交易，或 (ii) 拒绝批准。

It shall be noted that if there is any doubt as to the necessity of submitting a contemplated transaction to such foreign investment screening scheme, the parties may file a "prior request for examination of an activity", for the purpose of determining whether all or part of the contemplated investment falls within the scope of the screening scheme.

应当注意，如果对将拟议交易提交外国投资筛查的必要性存在任何疑问，各方可以提出"事先审查某项活动的请求",以确定拟议投资的全部或部分是否属于筛查的范围。

Compliance with this foreign investments screening scheme is key and in case of non-compliance, the Government may issue injunctions to the parties, along with significant financial penalties, and ultimately, the transaction may be considered as null and void.

遵守外国投资筛查非常重要。如果不遵守外国投资筛查,政府可能会向当事方发出禁令,并处以巨额罚款,最终,拟议交易可能会被视为无效。

Therefore, in the case of an investment made by a Chinese entity in a French pharmaceutical company, the necessity to obtain such prior approval must be cautiously considered and the filing of a prior request for examination can be considered in case of doubts, in order to avoid any sanctions. In the case described herewith, we recommended to our client to establish contact with the administration.

因此,如果中国投资者对法国制药公司进行投资,必须谨慎考虑获得此类事先批准的必要性,如有疑问,可以考虑提出事先审查的请求,以避免受到任何制裁。在上述情况下,我们建议客户与主管部门进行沟通。

In addition to the foreign investments screening scheme described above, transactions further to which a non-French resident acquires at least 10% of the share capital or voting rights of a French company, involving an amount of more than 15 million euros, are considered as foreign investments and shall be declared to the *Banque de France* for statistical purposes only (Art. R. 152-3, French Monetary and Financial Code).

除上述外国投资筛选外,非法国居民若进一步收购法国公司10%及以上的股权或表决权,涉及金额超过1500万欧元的交易,将被视为外国投资,应向法兰西银行进行申报,该项申报仅出于统计目的(《法国货币和金融法典》第R. 152-3条)。

2.4.4 员工知情权(Employees' information)

Employees of a target company which falls under the category of "small or medium enterprises" (PME), as defined by French law, shall be informed of any contemplated sale of more than 50% of the share capital before its signing, in order to allow them to submit a counter-offer to purchase all the shares that are supposed to be sold (Art.

L. 23-10-1 *et seq.*, French Commercial Code)。

如果目标公司属于法国法律中规定的"中小企业"（PME），则在签署任何出售超过公司50%股本的交易之前，应将该交易通知公司员工，以使公司员工能够提出购买公司拟出售的全部股本的反要约（《法国商法》第 L. 23-10-1 条起）。

As a consequence, this must be taken into account in the step plan of the contemplated transaction, as well as in its structuration: no binding agreement shall be executed before such information is delivered and before:

因此，在拟议交易计划的步骤和结构中应当考虑到这个问题，在上述信息通知到员工以及下列时间节点之前，不得签署任何具有约束力的协议：

- the end of the information-consultation with the works council; or
- 与工会进行信息咨询之后；或者
- the expiry of a two-month submission period if the company does not have a works council.
- 如果公司没有工会，则在2个月的提交期限截止后。

In practice, however, it is often possible to obtain a waiver from all the employees in order to speed up the process, as was the case in the considered transaction with our Chinese client.

然而在实践中，就像我方中国客户进行的交易情况一样，为加快交易进程，公司通常可以寻求从所有员工那里获得弃权书。

On a practical note, counteroffers from employees are very rare and the sellers have no legal obligation to consider them.

实际上，员工提出反要约的情况非常罕见，卖方也没有法律义务去考虑这些反要约。

As stated above, in companies having a works council ("comité d'entreprise" or "CSE"), such representative body shall be informed and consulted on the contemplated transaction, prior to signing any binding agreement (but once the discussions on the transactional documents are nearly ended). This information shall comprise the context of the transaction, its rationale, details on the potential purchaser as well as a description of the potential impact of the transaction on the company's business and employees' working conditions. A transaction timetable shall also be included. The works council is bound to render its opinion within one month following the notification of the transaction (extended to two months if the works council appoints an expert to run further investigations).

如上所述，在有工会（法语为 comité d'entreprise 或简称为 CSE）的公司中，在签署任何有约束力的协议之前（但在有关交易文件的讨论即将结束时），应就拟进行的交易通知该代表机构并征询其意见。该信息应包括交易的背景、交易的理由、潜在买家的详细信息以及交易对公司业务和员工工作条件的潜在影响的描述。交易时间表也应包括在内。工会须在接到交易相关的通知后一个月内提出意见（如工会委任专家进行进一步调查，则可延长至两个月）。

2.5 项目融资方式（Project Financing Method）

In our specific case detailed herein, the financing method used by the Chinese investor to pay the purchase price on closing date was a combination of self-financing through intra-group sources and bank financing through the conclusion of the bank loan documentation between the investor and a banking company internationally recognized.

在本文详述的具体案例中，中国投资者在交易完成日支付购买价款所采用的融资方式包括来自集团内部的自筹资金，以及投资者与国际认可的银行签订银行贷款文件的银行融资。

2.6 交易文件中的关键条款（Key Terms in Transaction Documents）

2.6.1 股份购买协议（SPA）

As regards the SPA, a specific attention should be granted to the following types of provisions (of course, this list is not exhaustive and should be adapted with regard to the contemplated transaction specificities).

关于 SPA，应特别注意以下类型的条款（当然，该清单并非详尽无遗，应根据预期的具体交易情况进行调整）。

Purchase price: This clause will usually be drafted in common by the parties and their legal and financial advisors. Under French law, a price is necessary for the sale to be valid. The price may be clearly stipulated in the SPA or only determinable (according to a formula provided in the agreement, and usually based on financial elements that were not known on the date of execution of the SPA, but which will be determined for the closing date). In practice, there are many options for the structuration of the price and its payment (locked box, etc.).

收购价格：本条款通常由各方及其法律和财务顾问共同起草。根据法国法律，报价是有效销售的必要条件。给出收购价格可在 SPA 中明确规定或仅规定定价方式（根据协议中规定的计算公式，结合在 SPA 实施日未知但在交易完成日能够确定的财务因素来定价）。在实践中，收购价格的构成和支付有很多选择（如锁箱机制等）。

In certain cases, a price adjustment mechanism based on the closing accounts will be included in the SPA, and/or an earn-out provision, (according to which the purchase price will be modified after the closing date, depending on future financial results of the company when the control is sold). The earn-out clause is often used when a seller remains in the target company for a certain period of time after the transaction, as an inducement mechanism.

在某些情况下，SPA 中会包含基于成交账户的价格调整机制，同时还可能会有收购价款的支付按照被收购主体的业绩情况进行分期支付的安排（根据此条款，在交易完成日之后，收购价格还会被调整，价格会根据控制权售出之后公司未来的财务状况来确定）。当卖方在交易后的一段时间内仍然留在目标公司时，收购价款的支付按照被收购主体的业绩情况进行分期支付的安排往往是一种激励机制。

Conditions precedent: As was the case for our client's transaction, most significant, industrial M&A transactions are structured with the signing of the SPA followed by a closing of the transaction. The completion of the sale will usually be made a condition of the obtention of certain authorizations (including change of control approval by certain important counterparties such as clients, providers, or lenders, when requested by the agreements in place), or of the performance of certain actions by the target company or the sellers (carve-out, etc.). These conditions precedent shall be met on closing date. They are of high importance since they will allow the purchaser to withdraw from the transaction when such conditions precedent, which are considered deal-breakers, are not met. As previously explained, among the conditions precedent are usually the authorizations needed to be obtained in order to complete the contemplated transaction (foreign investment authorizations, competition authorities' authorizations, etc.).

先决条件：与我们客户的交易一样，行业并购最重要的交易结构是在交易完成后签署 SPA。完成股份的出售是获得某些授权（包括在协议要求的情况下获得某些重要交易对象如客户、供应商或贷款人等的控制权变更批准）或是目标公司或卖方进行某些行为（如股权剥离等）的条件。这些先决条件应于交易完成日前满足。它们非常重要，因为这些先决条件将允许买方在无法满足一些被认为是破坏交易的先决条件时退出交易。如前所述，获得授权通常被认为是一项完成预期交易的先决条件（如外商投资授权、竞争管理局授权等）。

Closing deliveries: In relation to the conditions precedent or other subjects, the SPA will provide a list of documents to be provided by each party to the other, and such provision will constitute a condition precedent to the closing of the transaction. Usually, closing deliveries will include the documents linked to the authorizations to be obtained, but also waivers, corporate registers, as well as documents which have been identified as necessary during the due diligence review (such as waivers from the banks or the security holders, missing corporate documents that were not provided in the data room, or corporate authorizations).

交割交付：SPA 将列明应由交易各方向其他各方提供的关于先决条件及其他事项的文件清单，同时提供该文件清单也将成为完成交易的先决条件。一般来说，交割交付包括取得各类授权文件、弃权书、公司登记册以及尽职调查中必要的各类文件（如银行或证券持有人的弃权书，数据库中未包含的公司文件，或公司授权书）。

Management in the interim period: The SPA will commonly include a provision according to which the sellers will bind themselves not to take certain strategic or financial decisions during the period between the signing and the closing date. According to such a provision, they may commit themselves to running the day-to-day business, but they must refrain from taking those decisions, listed in the SPA, which could impact the future of the company, at least without the purchaser agreement. Such prohibited decisions usually include the distribution of dividends; the sale of company assets; significant changes to the company's business; and the hiring/firing of key employees.

过渡期管理：SPA 通常会包含约束卖方在 SPA 签署日和交易完成日之间不得做出某些战略决定或财务决策的条款。根据该条款，卖方会承诺其继续经营日常业务，但未经买方同意，卖方不得作出 SPA 中列出的可能影响公司未来的决策。该等被禁止的决策行为通常包括分配股息、出售公司资产、对公司业务作出重大变更以及雇用或解雇关键员工。

On the closing date, the sale will be fully completed, without the need of a notarial deed or other equivalent agreement, as soon as all the conditions precedent are satisfied, the share transfer order is executed, and the price is paid (it is common in France to get the sellers' bank confirmations that the price has been fully received on their accounts in order to declare the transaction closed). It is to be noted that State registration fees, as of 0.01% of the sale price (when the target company is a joint-stock company), must be paid within one month following the closing date and are usually borne by the purchaser.

于交易完成日，无需获得公证书或其他同类协议，只要先决条件得到满足、股份转让已实施并支付价款（在法国常见做法是，获得卖方银行确认价款已经完全到账的函件即可认为交易完成），股份出售就能完全完成。需要注意的是，国家登记费用应在交易完成日后的一个月内由买方支付，（目标公司为股份公司的情况下）数额为交易价格的 0.01%。

In our case, taking the numerous sellers into consideration, a single bank account called "pivot account" has been set up in order to receive the payment of the price from the Chinese purchaser in a single wire transfer, such sum being subsequently allocated between the sellers.

在我们的案例中，考虑到卖家数量众多，我们设立了一个名为"pivot account"的专用银行账户，以便在一次电汇中收到中国买家的支付价款，随后再在众多卖方中进行分配。

2.6.2 陈述和保证 (Representations and warranties)

Representations and warranties are the assertions made by the seller, regarding the target company, to the purchaser. These assertions may cover a wide range of matters such as tax, corporate regulation, labor law, product compliances, financial figures, real estate, etc. In case of breach of a representation (such as the existence of undisclosed litigation, or mistakes, or omissions in the financial statements), the seller shall guarantee its financial consequences. Also, specific warranties may be provided to cover the issues raised by the purchaser's advisors while they ran their due diligence reviews. The conditions of the warranty/ies shall be drafted carefully and may include sellers' liability limitations, as well as threshold amounts below which the warranty cannot be called, or above which the purchaser will not be indemnified.

陈述和保证是卖方就目标公司的情况向买方做出的声明。这些声明可能涵盖税务、公司法规、劳动法、产品合规性、财务数字、房地产等广泛的事项。为防止违反陈述（如存在未披露的诉讼，或财务报表中存在错误和遗漏），卖方应对其财务结果进行保证。此外，针对买方顾问在进行尽职调查时提出的问题可能也要提供特定的保证。保证条款应仔细起草，其中可能包括对卖方责任的限制，还可以设定一项保证责任的数额标准，规定低于该标准则保证不会生效，或者规定高于该标准则买方不会得到赔偿。

Representations and warranties are usually included within the SPA, but they may sometimes, for various reasons, be included in a separate agreement. Common practice in France tends to include them as part of the SPA. A separate agreement may be of interest when the parties are not exactly the same as in the SPA. In our case, minority shareholders did not want to be bound by such representations and warranties. Therefore, we included the representations and warranties in a separate agreement for more convenience and confidentiality.

陈述和保证条款通常规定在 SPA 中，但有时出于其他原因也可能规定在一个独立的协议中。在法国，该条款通常是 SPA 的一部分。当 SPA 中各方的意见不完全一致时，通常会有意签订一份独立的协议。在我们的案例中，目标公司少数股东不愿意被陈述与保证条款所约束，出于便利和保密的考虑，我们就把陈述与保证条款单独规定在一份独立的协议中。

In addition, the purchaser may ask the seller(s) to subscribe a specific on-demand guaranty within a bank in order to cover certain indemnities that may be due by the seller under the representations and warranties provisions (other guaranty schemes to secure sellers undertakings may also be contemplated).

此外，买方可要求卖方在银行认购一份特定的见索即付保函，以支付卖方根据陈述与保证条款需要应付的某些赔偿（也可考虑其他保证卖方承诺的担保方案）。

2.7 主要法律问题（Main Legal Issues）

In our case, one of the main legal issues was to structure the transaction in compliance with the legal obligation of the sellers to inform each employee individually, as well as to consult employee representatives. The difficulty is that sellers could not sign any binding agreement before this was done and the two-month delay had expired, or all waivers were obtained. In the meantime, the sellers did not want to inform their employees of such a strategic transaction without a binding agreement from the purchaser.

在我们的案例中，主要法律问题之一是要按照卖方的法律义务来设计交易框架，而卖方的义务包括将交易信息通知到每名员工，并咨询员工代表意见。问题在于，在履行通知行为后 2 个月的期限已届满或者获得所有员工的弃权书之前，卖方不得签署任何具有约束力的协议。同时，在获得没有买方具有约束力的协议的情况下，卖方也不希望将此类战略性交易通知其员工。

The solution was to make the Chinese purchaser sign a put option to the benefit of the sellers, that may be exercised upon completion of the information and consultation processes mentioned above. In order to secure the purchaser, the final SPA was attached to the put option agreement. This solution is common in French transactions but needs to be explained in detail to foreign investors.

该问题的解决方案是让中国买方签署一份有利于卖方的出售期权，该期权可在上述的信息通知和咨询行为完成后行使。为了保护买方，最终的 SPA 会附在出售期权协议之后。这种解决方案在法国交易中很常见，但需要向外国投资者详细解释。

Put option agreements need to be drafted carefully in order to protect the purchaser's interests, and schedules are also of importance since they shall include all the agreements (in final version) that will be executed for the purpose of the transaction.

出售期权协议需要仔细起草以保护买方的利益，而且时间表应包括为交易目的而签署的所有协议最终版本，因而也很重要。

2.8 非法律问题及相关解决方案（Non-legal Issues and Relevant Solutions）

Strong administrative and governance obligations to which our Chinese client was subject in China were among the issues we met, since it sometimes implied a lack of responsiveness which could be detrimental in the context of a bid process, as was the case in the considered transaction.

我们遇到的问题之一是，中国客户在中国负有很强的行政和管理义务，因此有时会导致其缺乏灵活性，这可能对竞标过程造成不利影响，在我们的交易中所发生的情况也的确如此。

Having a local counsel in France to assist in the negotiations and to liaise with the French counterparties since the beginning (and not only for running the due diligence review and drafting final transactional documentation) was also of importance to our client in order to soften and streamline the exchanges despite cultural differences which may arise in the course of the negotiation. Indeed, the quality of the communication is definitely key to closing a transaction in France.

在法国聘请当地律师协助谈判，并从一开始就与法国交易方保持联系对我们的客户来说是非常重要的，不仅是为了进行尽职调查审查和起草最终交易文件，前期沟通也利于在交流协商过程中缓解可能会出现的文化差异，提高沟通效率。实际上在法国，沟通的质量绝对是完成交易的关键因素。

— 作者简介 —

Nathalie Younan is Partner of FTPA Avocats and Head of Corporate/M&A practice. Nathalie Younan represents several French groups of companies in implementing their legal strategies, for their external growth and restructuring. Drawing from years of international experience, she often acts for foreign companies established, inter alia, in the United States, in Europe or in the Middle East, in their projects in France (incorporation, acquisitions, commercial contracts, closing down of subsidiaries, etc.). Nathalie Younan holds a Master's degree in Torts and Contracts Law from Paris I Panthéon-Sorbonne University, a Master's degree in Litigation and Arbitration from Paris II Panthéon-Assas University, and an LL. M degree from Harvard Law School. Nathalie Younan has been registered within Paris Bar and the New York Bar and is a member of the NYSBA and IBA.

Nathalie Younan 是 FTPA 律师事务所合伙人，兼企业与并购业务部门的负责人。她代表法国领先的公司集团实施法律策略，以促进外部增长和重组。她凭借多年的国际经验，为在美国、欧洲、东亚或中东建立的知名外国公司在法国开展业务提供法律服务（公司设立、并购、设立合资企业、少数并购项目、商业合同、关闭子公司等）。Nathalie Younan 拥有巴黎第一大学（先贤祠·索邦大学）的侵权法和合同法硕士学位，巴黎第二大学（先贤祠·阿萨斯大学）的诉讼和仲裁硕士学位，以及哈佛大学法学院的法律硕士学位。Nathalie Younan 具有巴黎和纽约州的律师执业资格，是纽约州法律协会（NYSBA）和国际律师协会（IBA）会员。

Mathieu de Korvin is on associate of FTPA Avocats, mainly advising on corporate law and mergers and acquisitions. Mathieu de Korvin received a Master in Financial Law from University of Paris-Dauphine, and a Master in Business Administration from University of Paris I Pantheon-Sorbonne. He is admitted to the Paris Bar in January 2016, and is a member of the French-Chinese Economic Law Association.

Mathieu de Korvin 是 FTPA 律师事务所的律师，主要为客户提供公司法及投资与并购方面的法律服务。Mathieu de Korvin 拥有巴黎多芬纳大学的金融法硕士学位，以及巴黎第一大学（先贤祠·索邦大学）的工商管理硕士学位。他于 2016 年 1 月获得巴黎律师执业资格，是法中经济法律协会会员。

以芬兰为主导的项目投资：在房地产开发行业开展投资
Finnish-led Project Investment Investing in the Real Estate Development Industry

点 评

  本文分析的案例极具国际性，该投资项目涉及多个国家和司法辖区，包括芬兰、荷兰、中国、俄罗斯四个国家。一家芬兰建筑公司（该公司是芬兰最大的建筑公司之一）与中国公司在荷兰设立的一家公司共同组建了合资企业，该合资企业通过持有俄罗斯项目公司的股份，拟在俄罗斯建立一个集商务、娱乐、酒店和办公等多功能为一体的商业中心。该项目的目标是开发和建造房地产，并在完工后向国际房地产投资者或房地产基金出售和/或租赁已开发的房产。本文作者担任芬兰建筑公司的法律顾问，并在管理该投资项目中发挥了主导作用。

  由于项目的参与各方有不同的背景和工作方法，整合不同的观点和方法是一项非常具有挑战性的工作。本文作者详细介绍了该投资项目以芬兰为"出发点"，最终延伸到俄罗斯境内的特殊交易结构。在该项目中，中国的投资者作为其中的重要投资方，不仅需要了解芬兰的商业文化，还需要对俄罗斯乃至荷兰的商业环境都有所了解。这是非常有趣的商业体验与挑战，也是中国企业对外投资一次有益的尝试，即不仅可以只面向一个国家为投资目的地，还可以尝试更加国际化的交易模式与结构。当然，这种交易的风险也是比较大的，一旦失败，付出的成本也较大。所以，如果未来拟采用此种模式进行境外投资，则需要尽可能早地聘请法律顾问并介入交易前期的可行性论证，这样可以更大程度保护投资者的合法权益，减少后期大幅调整交易方案的风险，以期减少交易成本，让投资者在商业模式上投入更多的精力，从而更加快速地推进项目进程。

1. 芬兰的商业（Business in Finland）

For decades Finland has been growing its foothold in international trade. With a major airport in the metropolitan Helsinki area (Helsinki-Vantaa Airport) and significant ports in the South of Finland (Port of Hanko, Port of Helsinki and Port of Hamina-Kotka), Finland has become a central logistics hub for through-transportation of goods to Russia, the Nordic countries as well as Central European countries, making it an attractive location for foreign investors.

几十年来，芬兰在国际贸易中积极扩大其优势。借助于赫尔辛基大都会区的主要机场（赫尔辛基-万塔机场）和芬兰南部的重要港口（汉科港、赫尔辛基港和哈米纳-科特卡港），芬兰已成为向俄罗斯、北欧国家以及中欧国家中转和运输货物的中央物流枢纽，这使其成为一个对于外国投资者而言极具吸引力的国家。

From pure nature to technological innovations, Finland is a pioneering hub for continuous development of new ideas with worldwide reach. Finland is one of the safest countries in the world and this in turn is reflected in Finland's business life. Finland is one of the least corrupt countries in the world. The low level of corruption creates a business platform in which doing business is straight-forward and simple. The judicial system is independent and impartial and is generally respected. One can expect a case to be processed fairly with no prejudice and in accordance with the legislation.

从自然到技术创新，芬兰都是具有开拓性的中心，持续产出具有全球影响力的新思想。芬兰是世界上最安全的国家之一，而这也反映在芬兰的商业方面。芬兰是世界上腐败程度最低的国家之一，这为其创造了一个直接、便于交易的商业平台。因司法系统独立、公正，公信力高，人们可以预见案件将依法得到公平处理。

1.1 港口和赫尔辛基-万塔机场（The Ports and Helsinki-Vantaa Airport）

Key factors to the efficient logistics services and inbound and outbound cargo traffic are the Ports of Hanko, Helsinki and Hamina-Kotak as well as Helsinki-Vantaa Airport, a major Nordic airfreight and passenger hub. As the fastest route between the Nordics and Asia, Helsinki-Vantaa Airport is an increasingly popular connection to the Far-East Asia. Excellent logistics service providers and an extensive network of roads, railways, inland waterways and pipelines support the domestic logistics network inside Finland. This powerful combination has made Finland the "Gateway to Europe" accounting for significant quantities of European road-and water-transport.

汉科港、赫尔辛基港和哈米纳-科特卡港以及赫尔辛基-万塔机场（北欧的主要空运和客运枢纽）均是高效的物流服务和出入境货物运输的关键因素。作为北欧和亚洲之间速度最快的航线，赫尔辛基-万塔机场与远东地区的连通越来越受欢迎。优秀的物流服务提供商和广泛的公路、铁路、内陆水道和管道网络为芬兰境内的国内物流网络提供支持。这种强大的组合使芬兰成为"通往欧洲的门户"，成为大量欧洲公路和水路运输的枢纽。

1.2 排名前列的基础设施（Highly Ranked Infrastructure）

According to the World Economic Forum, the quality of the Finland's infrastructure is among the best in the world, reflecting excellent facilities for maritime, air, road and railroad transport, ranked 23rd, respectively, in 2018. New rail freight route between Kouvola, Finland and Xi'an, Zhengzhou, China was opened in 2018. Trains on the new northern route take 10—12 days to complete a one-way journey, whereas a cargo ship takes an average of eight weeks. New route takes four days less than the current connection between Zhengzhou and Hamburg, Germany. This rail route is already in use by various companies from all around the Nordics and Central Europe.

根据世界经济论坛的数据，芬兰是世界上基础设施质量最优的国家之一，芬兰的基础设施在2018年排名世界第23位，包括出色的海运、空运、公路和铁路运输。芬兰科沃拉和中国郑州、西安之间的新铁路货运线于2018年开通。新北部货运线上的火车仅需要10—12天即可完成单程运输，而一艘货船则平均需耗用8个星期。新北部货运线相较于当前连通中国郑州和德国汉堡的线路可节省4天时间。来自北欧和中欧各地的诸多公司均已使用该货运线。

1.3 广泛应用的信息技术（Extensive use of Information Technology）

Finland also makes extensive use of Information Technology to deliver optimized supply chain solutions. Recently, a fast and cyber secure submarine cable connection between Helsinki and Rostock in Germany was completed, and this established a new digital link between the two countries. Finland has also attracted major data center investments from companies such as Google, Telecity Group and Yandex. This can be attributed to the cool climate of the North as well as highly skilled professionals and excellent infrastructure.

芬兰还广泛利用信息技术来提供优化的供应链方案。最近，赫尔辛基与德国罗斯托克之间已经建成了快速、安全的海底电缆网络连接，这在两国之间建立了新的数字化联系。芬兰还吸引了重要数据中心如 Google（谷歌）、Telecity Group 和 Yandex 等公司的投资。这可以归功于北方凉爽的气候，还有高水平的专业技术人员和优良的基础设施。

2. 交易结构（Transaction Structure）

2.1 简介（Introduction）

A few years ago HPP Attorneys Ltd (HPP) worked as the Finnish counsel in a large tripartite project involving parties from three countries and cultures. A Finnish construction company, one of the largest in Finland, and a Chinese company formed a joint venture in order to build a multifunctional commercial, entertainment, hotel and office center in Russia. The target of the project was to develop, construct, sell and/or lease developed property to international real estate investors or real estate fund after completion.

几年前，HPP 律师事务所（HPP）在一个大型三方项目（项目涉及三个不同文化的国家）中担任芬兰法律顾问。一家芬兰建筑公司（该公司是芬兰最大的建筑公司之一）与一家中国公司组建了一家合资企业，以便在俄罗斯建立一个集商务、娱乐、酒店和办公为一体的多功能商业中心。该项目的目标是开发和建造房地产，并在完工后向国际房地产投资者或房地产基金出售和/或租赁已开发的房产。

During the project HPP acted as the legal advisor to the Finnish construction company. HPP also took a leading role in the legal project management and at the end of the day acted as the legal advisor for the entire project coordinating the legal work amongst all parties.

在项目中，HPP 作为芬兰建筑公司的法律顾问行动，在法律项目管理中发挥了主导作用，并在项目尾声作为整个项目的法律顾问，协调各方的法律工作。

The project had a clear international emphasis as the parties involved in the project had diverse backgrounds and methods of working. Consolidation of different ideas and methods was an interesting challenge for HPP and eventually being able to act as trusted advisor in many aspects of the project proved to be very fruitful not only to HPP, but to all parties involved.

由于参与各方有不同的背景和工作方法,该项目具有明显的国际性。对于 HPP 来说,整合不同的观点和方法是一个有趣的挑战,最终,HPP 在项目的许多方面充当可信赖的顾问,这次合作对 HPP 和所有相关方而言都非常有收获。

The international aspects and emphasis were not only limited to the partnership between the Chinese and Finnish entities in the development and construction of the commercial center. At least third of the tenants of the commercial center were of international background. This meant that the project had to meet high standards of not only the Chinese, Russians and Finns, but also parties from many countries and persons with many nationalities as well.

该项目的国际化方面和国际重要性不仅体现于中国和芬兰法人实体在商业中心开发和建设方面的合作关系,且体现于至少有三分之一的商业中心租户具有国际背景。这意味着该项目不仅要满足中方、俄罗斯方和芬兰方的高标准,还要符合其他各国的群体或个人的高标准。

2.2 项目的法律结构（Legal Structure of the Project）

The structuring of the project included multiple countries and multiple jurisdictions. The Finnish construction company established a company under the Dutch law. The Chinese entity established two companies under Dutch law, one for financing of the project and one for cooperating in the project with the Dutch B.V. owned by Finns. Together, the Dutch B.V. owned by the Finns and the Dutch B.V. owned by the Chinese formed a joint venture with 50/50 ownership. The joint venture, again a Dutch B.V., owned all shares in a special purpose vehicle (SPV), which was established and operated under Russian law. The SPV LLC, a Russian subsidiary of the SPV, was established to develop and construct the project in Russia. A Russian subsidiary of the Finnish construction company, again a Russian LLC, was appointed as the contractor.

该项目的结构涉及多个国家和司法管辖区。这家芬兰建筑公司根据荷兰法律成立了一家公司。中国法人实体根据荷兰法律成立了两家公司,其中一家为项目提供资金,另一家在项目中与芬兰法人实体持股的荷兰私人有限责任公司合作。芬兰方持股的荷兰私人有限责任公司和中方持股的荷兰私人有限责任公司成立了一个合资企业，两家公司分别持有合资企业 50% 的所有权。该合资企业（亦为荷兰私人有限责任公司）持有特殊目的公司（SPV）的所有股份，该特殊目的公司根据俄罗斯法律而设立和运营。SPV 的俄罗斯子公司是有限责任公司（LLC）形式，该子公司成立的目的是在俄罗斯开发和建设该项目。芬兰建筑公司的俄罗斯子公司担任承包商，该公司亦为俄罗斯有限责任公司（LLC）形式。

The project was originally introduced two years before the investment decision when the Finnish and Chinese parties first met. About a year from the first meeting, the Finnish and Chinese parties entered into a joint investment agreement and during the same year the SPV and the SPV LLC were established. Two years from the first meeting the SPV LLC made the first phase investment decision in the project and the Russian subsidiary of the Finnish construction company signed a project management contract for the first phase of the project. During the same year the SPV acquired the ownership of another entity OOO SPV. At the same time the building permit for the site was received. Mere two years later the commercial center was ready for grand opening.

当芬兰方与中国各方初次会面时，该项目的合作动议第一次被提出，两年后双方作出投资决定。大约在第一次会议召开的一年后，芬兰方和中国各方签订了联合投资协议，同年，SPV 和 LLC 特殊目的公司成立。在第一次会议召开的两年后，LLC 特殊目的公司做出了项目第一阶段的投资决策，芬兰建筑公司的俄罗斯子公司就项目的第一阶段签署了项目管理合同。同年，SPV 获得了另一家实体——OOO 特殊目的公司的所有权。同时，项目参与方收到了该地的建筑许可证。仅经过两年，商业中心即将盛大开业。

OOO SPV and the Russian subsidiary of the Finnish construction company worked closely under the supervision of the Board of Directors of OOO SPV and it included both Chinese and Finnish board members. OOO SPV managed the Tender Commission, which approved all sub-contractors and suppliers. The duties of OOO SPV also included acceptance of working documentation, acceptance of work, taking care of lease contracts as well as invoicing and monitoring of payments. The Russian subsidiary of the Finnish construction company, in addition to acting as the general contractor, was also responsible for the design of the project and had the main responsibility for project management. The Russian subsidiary of the Finnish construction company was also in charge of sub-contractoragreements after OOO SPV had given its approval. There were project management agreements between OOO SPV and the Russian subsidiary of the Finnish construction company. One project management agreement consisted of design and construction work and the other work regarding the lease agreements i. e. marketing services and negotiations with tenants to enter into lease agreements.

在OOO特殊目的公司董事会的监督下，OOO特殊目的公司和芬兰建筑公司的俄罗斯子公司开展密切合作，董事会包括来自中国和芬兰主体的成员。OOO特殊目的公司管理招标委员会，所有分包商和供应商须经招标委员会批准。OOO特殊目的公司的职责还包括接收工作文件、接受工作分派、处理租赁合同以及开具发票和监督付款。芬兰建筑公司的俄罗斯子公司除担任总承包商外，还负责项目的设计，并主要负责项目管理。在OOO特殊目的公司作出批准以后，芬兰建筑公司的俄罗斯子公司也负责处理分包商协议。OOO特殊目的公司与芬兰建筑公司的俄罗斯子公司签订了项目管理协议。项目管理协议包括设计和建造工作以及关于租赁协议约定的其他工作，即营销服务和与租户协商签订租赁协议的工作。

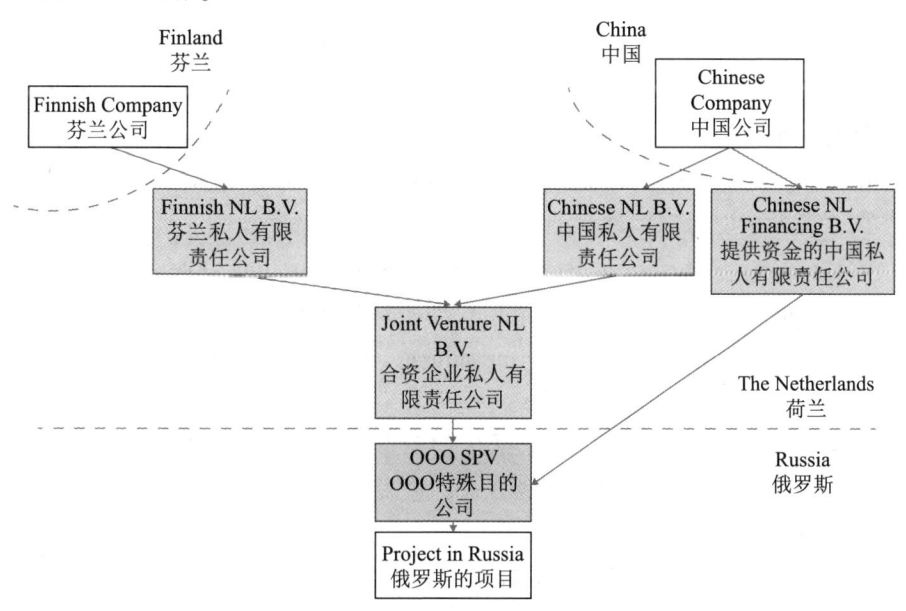

Chart 1　Legal Structure cf the Project
图1　项目的法律结构

2.3 芬兰竞争法申报（Finland's Competition Law Filings）

Under Finnish law, certain mergers, acquisitions, public bids and other transactions that may bring about a so-called concentration have to be notified to a governmental authority. The Finnish Competition Act provides a system of merger control for operations that affect the Finnish economy. It largely copies and partially incorporates the system of European Union's merger control and prohibits concentrations that create or strengthen a dominant position resulting in a significant restriction of effective competition on the Finnish market or a part thereof. The provisions regarding merger control set forth in the Finnish Competition Act apply to mergers, acquisitions, public bids and all other transactions that may bring about a concentration. In accordance with this act, concentrations shall be deemed to arise where:

根据芬兰的法律，一些可能引起集中的合并、收购、公开招标和其他交易须向政府主管机关通报。《芬兰竞争法》针对影响芬兰经济的业务规定了兼并控制制度。它主要效法并部分吸收欧盟的合并控制制度，禁止产生或加强支配地位、从而严重限制芬兰市场或芬兰部分市场有效竞争的集中。《芬兰竞争法》中关于合并控制的规定适用于合并、收购、公开招标以及可能导致集中的所有其他交易。根据该法，在以下情况下，应认为出现集中：

i. two or more previously independent undertakings merge;

两个或两个以上之前独立的企业合并；

ii. one or more persons or legal entities already controlling at least one undertaking, or one or more undertakings acquire, whether by purchase of securities or assets, by contract or by other means, direct or indirect control of the whole or parts of one or more other undertakings; or

一个或多个个人或法人实体已经控制至少一个企业，或者一个或多个企业通过购买股权或资产、合同或其他方式，直接或间接控制一个或多个其他企业的全部或部分；或

iii. a full-function joint venture is established.

建立一个全功能的合资企业。

A concentration that meets certain thresholds as regards the turnover of the undertakings concerned will have to be notified to the Finnish Financial Supervisory Authority (FSA). A concentration remaining below the threshold turnover levels may be effectuated without a notification to the FSA.

如企业营业额达到某些规模的集中度，必须向芬兰金融监督局（FSA）进行报告。对于没有达到营业额规模的集中，则无须向 FSA 报告。

Section 22 of the Finnish Competition Act provides that a concentration must be notified to the FSA if the combined turnover of all undertakings concerned exceeds €350 million in the calendar year preceding the concentration; and at least two undertakings concerned each achieved a turnover of at least €20 million in the Finland in that year.

《芬兰竞争法》第 22 条规定，如果在集中之前的一年，所有相关企业合并的年度营业额超过了 3.5 亿欧元，并且至少有两家相关企业该年度在芬兰国内分别实现了至少 2000 万欧元的营业额，则必须向 FSA 报告此次集中。

A concentration that has been effectuated without having been duly notified or without the parties observing the appropriate waiting period will be regarded as being null and void under the laws of Finland.

根据芬兰法律的规定，未经按时报告或当事方未经适当等待期限而实施的集中将被视为无效。

In addition, the FSA has wide powers to impose fines and orders in the context of concentration control. Failure to notify a concentration will usually lead to a fine upon discovery by the FSA. Both companies and directors involved can be fined in this regard.

此外，FSA 拥有广泛的权力，可以在控制集中的背景下进行罚款和下达指令。如未能报告集中，一经发现，FSA 通常会进行罚款。涉及的公司和董事都可能因此而被罚款。

In this project, there was no obligation to notify FSA, or similar authorities in Russia, because the client of HPP did not acquire control of the target company and it did not concern a full-function joint venture.

该项目无须向 FSA 或俄罗斯的类似机构作出通知，因为 HPP 的客户没有获得对目标公司的控制权，而且目标公司也不是一个全功能的合资企业。

2.4 外商投资审查（Foreign Investment Screening）

The transactions discussed in this project did not trigger foreign screening system in Finland. However, due to the revision of Finland's foreign investment screening system in 2020, we will have a brief introduction here.

本项目交易不触发芬兰的外商审查制度。然而，由于2020年芬兰对外商投资审查制度做出了修订，本文在此处予以简要介绍。

Finland's act on foreign investment screening [Act on the Monitoring of Foreign Corporate Acquisitions (172/2012, as amended), Act] entered into force in 2012. The Act was amended as of 11 October 2020.

芬兰的外商投资审查法案（《外国公司收购监督法》172/2012修订本，以下简称法案）于2012年生效。该法案于2020年10月11日被修订。

The Ministry of Economic Affairs and Employment is responsible for handling matters concerning the monitoring and confirmation of corporate acquisitions. The Ministry also serves as the national contact point in the cooperation between Member States and the EU.

经济事务和就业部负责审查并批准有关公司收购事项。该部还作为欧盟成员国与欧盟之间合作的国家联络主体。

The review process starts when an investor submits an application to the Ministry. There are no formal requirements for the contents of the application, but the Ministry has published instructions for drafting an application. The application must be made by the potential foreign investor and not a Finnish holding or special purpose vehicle established by the foreign investor. After receiving such application, the other authorities can be invited to give advice by the Ministry.

当投资者向经济事务和就业部提交申请时，审查程序便开始。对于申请书的内容没有正式规范，但是该部已经发布了申请书起草的指导意见。申请必须由潜在的外国投资者提出，而不是由外国投资者设立的芬兰控股公司或特殊目的公司提出。收到申请后，该部可以邀请其他主管机关提供意见。

In the event, if the Ministry finds that the acquisition may endanger a very important national interest, it transfers the matter to the Government's plenary session for resolution. The Government's plenary session then makes the decision about whether to restrict or approve the transaction. The vast majority of transactions submitted to date have been approved by virtue of this rule.

如果该部认为特定收购可能危及非常重要的国家利益，该部会将其移交给政府全体会议解决。政府全体会议将作出限制或批准该交易的决定。迄今为止，已提交的绝大多数交易已根据该法案获得批准。

3. 项目融资方式（Project Financing Method）

Both the Chinese and Finnish shareholder invested altogether approximately EUR 40 million in the project. As mentioned above, the Chinese entity established a Dutch B. V. to finance the project, which offered a bank loan to the SPV LLC. Most of the financing in the first phase came through China. Provisions regarding financing were included in the shareholders' agreement.

在本项目中，中国和芬兰股东共投资约 4000 万欧元。如上所述，中国实体成立了荷兰私人有限责任公司，并为该项目提供资金，该公司向 LLC 特殊目的公司提供银行贷款。第一阶段的大部分融资来自中国。有关融资的规定已包含在股东协议中。

4. 交易文件中的关键条款（Key Terms in Transaction Documents）

4.1 芬兰买卖协议（SPA）符合北欧传统（The Finnish SPA Falls Under the Nordic Tradition）

Unlike in Common Law countries such as the UK and the United States, Finnish agreements can be fairly simple and short. The fundamental legislation that governs the transfer of shares of companies and transfer of assets is Finnish Corporations Act（2006/624, as amended）. The Finnish Corporations Act is comprehensive and enables short agreements. Many key terms can be traced from the legislation and only special terms are usually listed. That being said, Finnish SPAs have been influenced by their Common Law counterparts and therefore are more detailed than before.

与普通法国家（如英国和美国）不同，芬兰的协议可以相当的简单和短小。适用于公司股份转让和资产转让的基本立法是《芬兰公司法》（2006/624 修订本）。《芬兰公司法》内容全面，并允许当事方达成简短的协议。在立法中可以找到许多关键条款，协议通常只列出特殊条款。不过，芬兰的 SPA 受到了普通法方面的影响，因此比以前更为详细。

With respect to the SPA, the following terms are of great importance（please note that this is not an exhaustive list, but just some examples）:

关于 SPA，下述条款十分重要（请注意，此处并非穷尽性的列举，而是仅举几例）：

Payment of the purchase price: it goes without saying that the manner in which the purchaser will pay the purchase price for the shares should be written down very precisely. Earn-out arrangements are also quite common in Finland; these are payment arrangements, which are linked to the post-closing performance of sellers (in many cases the sellers/managing directors of target companies stay also after closing).

支付购买价款：不言而喻，购买者支付股份购买价格的方式应该被非常准确地记录下来。在芬兰，收购价款的支付按照被收购主体的业绩情况进行分期支付的安排也很常见；这些付款安排与卖方交割后的业绩挂钩（在许多情况下，目标公司的卖方/董事总经理在交割后也会留任）。

In addition, a clause regarding so-called leakage can be needed, i. e. prohibiting the target company to make any distributions during the locked box period between signing of the transaction documents and executing the deed of transfer/closing. Leakage can mean, for example, any dividend or other distribution of assets declared, paid or made by the target company to a seller or an affiliate, or any transfer of title and ownership of any of the company's assets to a seller or seller's affiliate for a value which is less than the fair market value of such assets.

此外，可能需要一个关于所谓防"泄漏"的条款，即该条款禁止目标公司在签署交易文件和执行转让/交割协议之间的"锁箱"期间内进行任何股息分配。"泄漏"行为，例如目标公司向卖方或关联公司宣布、支付或作出的任何股息或其他资产分配，或任何以低于市场公允价值的价格将公司资产的所有权转让给卖方或卖方的关联公司的行为。

Completion actions: It is common practice in Finland to include a clause in the SPA, stipulating what party needs to complete which actions at or prior to the day the deed of transfer is executed closing of the transaction. For example, the delivery of waiver letters of banks regarding their rights pursuant to the release of a right of pledge on the relevant shares, etc.

交割行为：在芬兰，通常会在SPA中加入一项条款，规定某方当事人需要在转让协议执行当日（或之前）完成某些行为（进行交易交割）。例如，提交由银行出具的解除相关股份质押的豁免函等。

Limitation of liability: in the event that one of the parties to the SPA is in breach of its contractual obligations contained therein, the other party may hold the defaulting party liable.

责任限制：如果 SPA 的一方违反其中包含的合同义务，另一方可要求违约方承担责任。

In this respect, it is common practice to include wording pertaining to the limitation of liability, as well as certain thresholds in SPA; usually certain thresholds are included in the share purchase agreement. These limitations usually only apply to breaches of the warranties; typically, in case of damages under the indemnifications, the liability of the seller is unlimited (obviously, this also depends on the negotiations). The seller usually warrants to the buyer that each statement listed under the section on Warranties are true and correct as of the signing date and shall be deemed to have been repeated on the closing date. The purchaser usually warrants that the Warranties shall be true and correct in all material respects at and as of the closing, except to the extent Warranties relate to an earlier date (in which case such Warranties shall be true and correct on and as of such earlier date).

在这方面，通常的做法是在 SPA 中列入与责任限制有关的措辞，以及特定的标准。这些限制通常仅适用于违反保证的行为；通常，在赔偿损失的情况下，卖方的责任是无限的（当然也取决于谈判结果）。卖方通常向买方保证，截至签署日，保证条款下列出的每一声明均为真实、准确的，且在交割日，应视卖方同样作出上述声明。买方通常承诺保证条款的所有重要方面在交割时和交割前均是真实和准确的，除非保证条款涉及较早的日期（在此情况下，此类保证条款应当在该较早日期当日和之前均为真实、准确的）。

Upon signing of the SPA, the shares are not transferred yet. In order to transfer title to shares in a private limited liability company under Finnish law there needs to be a corporate resolution by the seller and the buyer to approve and enter into the relevant share transfer and the related agreements, an agreement between the seller and the buyer regarding the transfer of the shares in the target, and, if share certificates have been issued regarding the shares of the target, the share certificates must be physically transferred (duly endorsed) into the possession of the buyer to perfect the relevant share transfer. The target's shareholder register needs to be updated.

签署 SPA 后，股份尚未转让。根据芬兰法律，为了将股份所有权转让给私人有限责任公司，卖方和买方需要通过公司决议批准并签订股权转让协议和相关的协议，卖方与买方须就目标公司的股份转让达成协议，并且，在已针对目标公司的股份签发股权证书的情况下，经正式批准的股权证书必须被现场递交给买方所有，以完成相关股份的转让。目标公司的股东名册需要更新。

Applicable law is almost always agreed upon in the SPA. Often the agreement is construed in accordance with and is governed by the laws of Finland. Laws of Finland usually refers to the Finnish laws, regulations, judgments or other legally binding requirements or rules of any governmental authority in Finland, including, for the avoidance of doubt, the regulations of the European Union. Finnish law is a safe choice to use in agreements between Finnish entities but also between a Finnish entity and a foreign entity.

SPA通常会就适用的法律达成一致。协议通常根据芬兰法律进行解释并受其管辖。芬兰法律通常是指芬兰的法律、法规、判决或其他由政府主管机关作出且具有法律约束力的要求或规则，为避免疑义，该类法律还包括欧盟的法规。对于芬兰实体之间以及芬兰实体与外国实体之间达成的协议，适用芬兰法律是一个安全的选择。

Arbitration: Agreeing on arbitration is rather common in Finnish agreements. Though the Finnish justice system is highly respected, the judicial process can take long and is, first and foremost, public. Usually it is agreed upon that disputes relating to the agreement shall be finally settled by arbitration in accordance with the Arbitration Rules of the Finland Chamber of Commerce. The number of arbitrators tends to vary between one and three. Sometimes parties agree that each party can appoint one arbitrator and the third arbitrator is appointed by the Arbitration Institute of the Finland Chamber of Commerce.

仲裁：在芬兰协议中，仲裁协议相当普遍。虽然芬兰司法系统受到高度尊重，是首要的、最重要的并且公众化的争议解决方式，但司法程序可能需要耗费很长时间。通常，协议中会约定有关协议的争议最终应根据《芬兰商会仲裁规则》通过仲裁来加以解决。仲裁员的数量往往在1人到3人之间。有时，在各方同意的情况下，各方可以各指定一名仲裁员，芬兰商会仲裁院可任命第三位仲裁员。

4.2 股东协议关键条款（The Important Terms of SHA）

● Important resolutions: certain resolutions should be adopted by the shareholders with a special majority of the votes. In Finland most resolutions of the general meeting are adopted by a normal majority. In case a client only holds a minority stake in a company it is therefore of great importance that certain, essential resolutions can only be adopted if the minority shareholders consent as well. Essential resolutions are (amongst others): the winding up or liquidation of the company, amendment of the articles of association, any sale of all or a substantial part of the business of the company and making participations in the capital of other companies.

● 重要决议：股东应以特别多数票通过某些决议。在芬兰，股东会的大多数决议都以一般多数同意通过。如果客户只持有公司的少数股权，那么应加入只有少数股东同意才能通过特别决议的条款，这一点非常重要。特别决议指（以及其他）：公司的解散或清算、公司章程的修订、公司全部或大部分业务的出售以及参与对其他公司的投资。

● Information rights: in principle, each shareholder should be informed by the board of managing directors regarding the business of the company. In the SHA this right of information can be made more concrete and broadened (e. g. the obligation of the company to submit to the shareholders a quarterly report which shall inter alia consist of a balance sheet, profit and loss account and cash flow statements).

● 知情权：原则上，董事总经理委员会应通知每位股东公司业务的经营情况。在 SHA 中，这种知情权利可以更加具体、更加广泛（例如，公司有义务向股东提交季度报告，其中应包括资产负债表、损益表和现金流量表）。

● Transfer of shares: It is common practice in Finland to incorporate share-transferring restrictions (e. g. in the form of an offering requirement whereby the offering shareholders should offer the shares first to the other shareholder). The pricing mechanism is always one of the topics regarding which parties need to negotiate. These kinds of restrictions are sometimes written into Articles of Association.

● 股份转让：在芬兰，通常采用股份转让限制机制（例如以要求出售股份的股东应首先向另一股东发出要约的形式来进行限制）。定价机制始终是交易相关方需要协商的主题之一。此类限制有时会被载入公司章程。

● Tag/drag along: Tag/drag along clauses are used in the event that a shareholder envisages to sell all its shares in the target company to an interested buyer. In such an event, the minority shareholder has the right to sell and transfer all the shares it holds in the target company to the interested buyer as well under the same conditions (i.e. the tag along). The drag along is also usually included; this means that if a (majority) shareholder wants to sell its shares in a target company that then the other (minority) shareholders are forced to sell their shares as well against the same conditions.

●随售/拖售权：如股东欲将目标公司的所有股份出售给感兴趣的买方，则会使用随售/拖售条款。在这种情况下，小股东有权按照相同条件将其持有的目标公司的股份转让给感兴趣的买方（即随售权）。拖售权也是经常被设置的条款，这就意味着如果股东（大股东）希望转让其持有的目标公司的股份，其他股东（小股东）也将被迫按照相同条件转让其持有的目标公司的股份。

● Good/Bad leaver provisions: in many cases if the managing directors of the target company hold shares as well, provisions are included to cover the situation that the employment or management agreement with such managing director is terminated. It is common practice that in such a case the managing director/shareholder is forced to sell its shares in the company against a certain price. The price depends on the question what the reason for termination of the employment/management agreement was.

●正常离职/不良离职条款：在许多情况下，如果目标公司的董事总经理也持有股份，则条款会涵盖与该董事总经理的雇用或管理协议终止的情况。在这种情况下，通常的做法是该董事总经理/股东被迫以一定的价格出售其在公司的股份。价格取决于终止雇用/管理协议的具体原因。

5. 主要法律问题（Main Legal Issues）

As mentioned above, HPP had a leading role in assisting and supporting the entire project. This meant coordinating the Finnish and Chinese project related actions in a Russian context. Both the Finnish party and the Chinese party aimed to develop a commercial center, which met the highest western standards. Operating with both Finnish and Chinese parties in a complex project environment involving many jurisdictions can be difficult as the laws and regulations differ greatly between Finland, China and Russian, not to mention the cultural differences between the three countries. At the end of the day all legal issues were clarified in a timely manner despite of the challenging work environment. The key to this was hard-working and great collaboration between all parties with a clear business goal in mind, which resulted in successful completion of the project.

如上所述,HPP 在协助和支持整个项目方面发挥着主导作用,这种主导作用意味着在俄罗斯的背景下协调与芬兰和中国项目相关的行动。芬兰交易方和中国交易方均希望建立一个符合西方最高标准的商业中心。由于芬兰、中国和俄罗斯的法律法规和文化存在较大差异,因此,在项目涉及多个司法管辖区的复杂背景下,与芬兰和中国交易方合作可能会很困难。尽管工作环境充满挑战,但最终,所有法律问题都得到了及时解决。成功完成项目的关键在于各方之间的努力和良好的合作,以及明确的业务目标。

6. 其他问题与解决方案（Other Issues and Relevant Solutions）

Other issues which we came across when working with Chinese clients in this project are:

在与中国客户就本项目进行合作时,我们遇到的其他问题有:

- The fact that in many projects time is of the essence, a swift follow-up/turnaround of the different versions of the documentation is a key factor. In case of Chinese buyers, specific approvals are required, which may put the Chinese buyers in a worse position compared to some other buyers, especially in case of auction processes. Slow and formal decision making may prejudice the possibility to buy the target project, and for example, the local purchasers may have less mandatory internal approvals and they may, therefore, be much faster and be in a better position to compete for the target project.

- 在许多交易中,时间至关重要,快速跟进或者流转不同版本的交易文件是关键。如果买方来自中国,则需要经过特别批准,这可能使中国买方相较于其他买方处于不利地位（特别是在拍卖过程中）。缓慢、过于正式的决定程序可能会降低中国买方买到目标公司的可能性,例如,本地购买者须经过的强制性内部批准较少,因此,在竞争目标项目时,本地购买者所需时间更少、处于更加有利的位置。

- It is very important to be open and transparent from the very beginning of a collaboration to avoid frustration/loss of trust. This applies also for instance to the timing of specific approvals from Chinese authorities or the parent company.

● 为了避免焦虑或者对彼此失去信任，在合作的早期阶段保持公开、透明十分重要。这也适用于须经中国主管机关或母公司特别批准的情况。

Based on HPP's experience, it is also essential to have someone in the project who can speak Mandarin and understands the cultural differences; in almost all transactions and projects involving Chinese parties, HPP is not only giving legal advise, but advising also on and bridging cultural gaps.

根据 HPP 的经验，有一位能用中文交流并了解文化差异的人是交易顺利进行必不可少的要件；在几乎所有涉及中国参与方的交易和项目中，HPP 不仅提供法律服务，还在弥合文化差异的方面提供建议。

— 作者简介 —

Mäkinen Markku, managing partner of HPP Attorneys, specializes in mergers and acquisitions, investment and capital markets transactions. Markku also advises clients in complex infrastructure projects. Prior to joining HPP Markku worked as an in-house counsel at Nokia Corporation. He has extensive experience in demanding technology projects in an international environment. At Nokia he led several legal teams including Nokia China and Nokia North America legal teams. Markku has acted as the Managing Partner of HPP since 2015. His working languages are Finnish and English. He is member of the Finnish Bar.

Mäkinen Markku 是 HPP 律师事务所的管理合伙人，专攻并购、投资和资本市场领域，还为客户提供复杂基础设施项目的法律咨询服务。加入 HPP 之前，Markku 在诺基亚公司担任公司的法律顾问。对在国际环境下有高度技术要求的项目，他具有丰富的经验。在诺基亚工作时，他领导多个法律团队，包括诺基亚中国和诺基亚北美法律团队。自 2015 年以来，Markku 一直担任 HPP 的管理合伙人。他的工作语言是芬兰语和英语，是芬兰律师协会会员。

Zhou Yanhuan specialises in M&A. She assists clients in legal questions related to M&A, corporate and contract law and advises both Finnish and international clients. Her working languages are Finnish and English. She is member of the Finnish Bar.

Zhou Yanhuan 专攻并购业务。她协助客户处理有关并购、公司法和合同法相关法律问题，并为芬兰和国际客户提供咨询建议。工作语言是芬兰语和英语，是芬兰律师协会会员。

HPP ATTORNEYS(**HPP**) is a full-service business law firm advising domestic and international clients on all aspects of their business operations. HPP has significant cross-border experience and regularly works with multinational clients and leading law firms around the world, particularly on transactions, investments and disputes, and can advise its clients in a variety of languages including Swedish, English, French, German, Russian and Mandarin.

HPP 是一家提供全方位服务的商业律师事务所, 为国内外客户就其业务运作的各个方面提供咨询服务。HPP 具有丰富的跨境业务经验, 并经常与跨国客户和全球领先的律师事务所合作, 尤其是在交易、投资和纠纷解决方面, 并且可以为客户提供多种语言的咨询建议, 包括瑞典语、英语、法语、德语、俄语和普通话。

HPP lawyers are recognised as leading practitioners in Finland in their chosen fields of M&A, dispute resolution, competition, public procurement, transport, technology media and telecoms and insurance.

HPP 的律师在并购、争议解决、竞争法、政府采购、运输、科技媒体与电信和保险等领域被认为是芬兰领先的从业者。

HPP's lawyers have broad experience of advising on projects in various sectors ranging from real estate development projects to renewable energy projects to technology projects. In doing so, HPP puts together multidisciplinary teams of lawyers from different legal or sector specialisms to ensure the project developer has access to comprehensive and tailored advice to assist them in executing their project in the most efficient and risk-adjusted manner.

从房地产开发项目到可再生能源项目, 再到技术项目, HPP 的律师在各个领域的项目咨询方面拥有丰富的经验。为此, HPP 将来自不同法律专业或不同行业的跨学科律师团队组合在一起, 以确保项目开发商能够获得全面和量身定制的法律建议, 帮助他们以最有效且经过风险调整的方式来执行项目。

投资在罗马尼亚：光伏项目建设
Investments in Romania
the Construction of Photovoltaic Projects

点 评

本文作者来自沃尔夫·泰斯律师事务所，曾为中国客户就开发光伏项目提供法律服务，结合项目经验，本文作者从公司形式的选择、土地收购、规划建设、设立批准与电网连接、生产许可、电力销售等方面全流程地介绍了在罗马尼亚进行的光伏项目建设。

投资光伏行业，根据罗马尼亚能源法规，建设光伏项目可能涉及一系列审批程序。例如，可能涉及罗马尼亚能源监管局签发设立批准程序，任何累计能够产生超过1兆瓦能量的生产活动均须设立批准，设立批准使投资者有权开发或翻新能源生产设施，但未赋予投资者以任何方式出售和/或运输所产生的能源，或从事需要不同批准和许可的活动的权利。再如，获得设立批准后，为合法、合规地进行电能生产，还需取得由罗马尼亚能源监管局签发的相应生产许可证，从而获得根据适用的法律规定生产电能并进行商业化的权利。因而在投资罗马尼亚光伏行业时，需关注可能涉及的审批程序以确保各项程序的及时履行和项目的平稳运作。

同时，在罗马尼亚开展投资，对于财产所有权及转让开展尽职调查工作至关重要。罗马尼亚历史上曾进行过较为广泛的财产国有化，后续罗马尼亚政府颁布多项法案对相关财产进行返还或予以补偿。如果权利人向主管机关提出归还其原财产的请求，在最终决定作出前，相关的处置行为则受到限制。因而若在罗马尼亚投资的资产涉及前述情形，则在投资前开展较为深入的尽职调查工作可能对降低后续标的资产出现争议、纠纷等风险具有重要意义。

一段时间以来，审查外商直接投资（DFI）已成为中东欧各国的热门话题。一些国家对外商直接投资采取了更严格的审查措施，允许对可能带来安全风险的交易进行审查。根据《欧盟外商投资安全审查条例》（Regulation（EU）2019/452）要求，罗马尼亚政府2022年4月18日以政府紧急法令形式通过《竞争法》修正案，即紧急法令（GEO 46/2022），对外国直接投资建立了较为严格的安全审查制度。

We are hereby summarising a case where a Chinese company instructed Wolf Theiss Rechtsänwalte GmbH & Co KG（the Firm）to provide full legal advice with respect to the development of a photovoltaic project, starting from the acquisition of land rights until the Project became fully operational.

我们在此总结一家中国公司委托沃尔夫·泰斯律师事务所就光伏项目的开发提供全方位法律咨询服务的案例，从土地权收购开始，到本项目全面投入运营，本所全程提供法律服务。

We have included a description of the legal steps and procedures, which have been observed and followed by the Company in order to ensure the full legal and regulatory compliance of the Project. Each step contains a brief explanation of relevant legal requirements as well as noteworthy issues encountered in the Firm's practice related thereto, along with recommendations and/or possible solutions, if applicable.

本文介绍了相关法律步骤和程序，公司应当遵守并遵循这些步骤和程序，以确保本项目完全符合法律法规。每个步骤均包含对相关法律要求的简要说明，以及本所在相关实践中遇到的值得注意的问题，并提出相应的建议和/或可能适用的解决方案。

1. 公司结构、投资政策与融资（Corporate Structure, Investment Policies and Financing）

1.1 罗马尼亚公司法（Company Law in Romania）

The first step investors must take is to decide on the type of company best suited for their envisaged objective. In Romania the two most commonly encountered types of company are the joint stock company and the limited liability company（in Romanian, "societate pe actiuni", respectively "societate cu raspundere limitata"）.

第一步，投资者需要确定最适合其预设目标的公司类型。在罗马尼亚，股份公司和有限责任公司是最常见的两种公司类型（罗马尼亚语中分别为"societate pe actiuni"和"societate cu raspundere limitata"）。

In our specific case, the client opted for an SPV, a limited liability company with a sole shareholder corporate structure. Under Romanian company law, any person and/or legal entity may become the sole shareholder in a single, individual limited liability company; as such, the same person and/or legal entity may not act as sole shareholder in multiple companies, under the penalty of winding up and liquidation of the more recently established company.

在这一具体案例中，客户选择了特殊目的公司，即一家具有单一股东公司结构的有限责任公司。根据罗马尼亚公司法，任何自然人和/或法人实体可成为一人有限责任公司的单一股东；鉴于此，同一自然人和/或法人实体不得在多家公司中担任单一股东，否则较后成立的公司将面临停业清算的处罚。

A limited liability company with a sole shareholder corporate structure has certain advantages over a joint stock company when both are established for the same purposes, such as:

相较于因相同目的而成立的股份公司而言，具有单一股东公司结构的有限责任公司具有一定的优势，例如：

- The minimum share capital is only 200 RON, the equivalent of 50 EUR as opposed to 90 000 RON or 20 000 EUR required for a joint stock company;

- 最低股本仅为200列伊，相当于50欧元，而股份公司则要求90 000列伊或20 000欧元；

- Does not necessarily require a board of directors or a censor committee and is generally more manageable than a joint stock company;

- 不要求必须设置董事会或审查委员会，并且通常相较于股份公司更加易于管理；

- A sole shareholder type of limited liability company does not require holding a general shareholder assembly and it is sufficient to keep a register of the sole shareholders decisions.

- 单一股东类型的有限责任公司无须召开股东会议，只需保留单一股东所作决议的记录即可。

On the other hand, a limited liability company presents certain key differences from a joint stock company, such as:

另一方面，有限责任公司与股份公司具有一些关键差异，例如：

- More restrictive voting conditions—requires the majority of both share numbers and shareholder numbers;
- 在投票条件上存在更多限制——要求股份数量和股东人数均占大多数；
- Shares may not be sold to a third party without the unanimous consent of the remaining shareholders;
- 在未经其余股东一致同意的情况下，股份不能出售给第三方；
- The share capital must be registered and paid in full before the limited liability company is legally registered.
- 在有限责任公司依法登记前，股本须完成登记并足额支付。

All operations, queries and amendments related to companies, their articles of incorporation and corporate structure are conducted through and registered with the National Trade Registry Office of Romania (hereinafter the Trade Registry) for third party publicity purposes.

为向第三方公示之目的，所有与公司、公司章程和公司结构相关的活动、查询和修改均应通过罗马尼亚国家交易登记处（以下简称交易登记处）进行并在此登记。

1.2 公司税务与财务规定（Company Tax and Fiscal Provisions）

In Romania, as of 2019 the company income tax is (i) 16% applied to the profit margin if the annual turnover rate is over EUR 1 000 000 or (ii) 1% of the annual turnover rate if the company is classified as a micro-enterprise with at least 1 employee. This tax is due by the client's SPV and not by the sole shareholder, which will be subject to the tax law from his state of origin unless the client opts for distribution of dividends, which is subject to Romanian law.

2019年罗马尼亚公司所得税为：（i）若年营业额超过1 000 000欧元则为利润的16%；（ii）如公司被分类为微型公司并具有至少1名雇员则为年营业额的1%。该税务由客户的特殊目的公司而非公司的单一股东支付，股东税务事宜受其所属地税法管辖，除非客户选择分配股息，此情形下股息分配所涉税务事宜受罗马尼亚法律管辖。

It is also important to note that in Romania fiscal amendments are usually frequent and take place particularly fast. For example, in 2018 companies from the IT sector as well as IT employees were declared exempt from the corporate income tax/income tax, in order to stimulate development of the IT sector. The same measures were taken in 2019 for employees in the construction sector, based on their employer's turnover from construction projects. As such, it can be expected that such fiscal amenities will also be provided in the future, based on the economical and financial policies the instated government.

同样值得注意的是，在罗马尼亚，财政修正案通常频繁、迅速地发布。例如，在2018年，罗马尼亚宣布免征IT公司以及员工企业所得税和个人所得税，以刺激IT行业的发展。2019年，基于雇主从建筑项目获得的营业额，对建筑行业的雇员亦采取了同样的措施。因此，基于政府的经济和财政政策，可以预期政府未来还将提供此类财政便利。

As for the renewable energy project developed by the client, special taxes and regulations, as well as further details related to the green certificates support scheme will be detailed below, with respect to the setting-up authorization and licensing process.

至于中方客户开发的可再生能源项目，就其设立批准和许可过程方面，将在下文详细说明相关的特殊税收和法规，以及与绿色证书支持计划相关的进一步细节。

2. 土地收购 (Acquisition of Land)

2.1 确定适于本项目的土地 (Identification of Suitable Land for the Project)

After setting up the SPV as a limited liability company, the next step of the project concerns the acquisition of real estate on which the project will be developed.

在设立特殊目的公司作为有限责任公司后，本项目下一个步骤是收购可用于项目开发的不动产。

In principle, in Romania identifying real properties suitable to the client needs is made through a real estate broker, who is knowledgeable about the area and may provide additional information regarding the real properties. This was also the situation in the case at hand, where the client used the services of an international broker to identify and initiate preliminary discussions regarding the land pertaining to the future Project.

原则上,在罗马尼亚,会通过不动产经纪人确定适合客户需求的不动产,不动产经纪人对地区十分了解并可提供有关不动产的其他信息。本项目中也是如此,客户通过国际经纪人的服务以确定关于未来项目用地的事项,并就此启动初步讨论。

In Romania all real estate, such as plots of land or buildings and constructions, must be registered with the National Office for Cadastre and Real Estate Publicity (the Land Book Office) for publicity against third parties; each individual piece of land, with or without buildings built thereon, has a unique Land Book number and a unique cadaster number by which it can be identified. The Land Book contains information about the characteristics of the property including surface area, the owners, as well as encumbrances affecting such property (mortgages, liens, etc.). However, as of the moment of this case study, the national Land Book and cadastral registration of all real estate assets in Romania is not yet complete, and as such, some lands may be entirely absent from the aforementioned records.

在罗马尼亚,所有的不动产(例如土地或楼房建筑)须在国家地籍和不动产公示办公室(以下简称地籍办公室)登记,以便对第三方进行公示;每块单独的土地,无论其上是否建有建筑物,均有一个独特的土地簿编号和地籍编号,以用于识别该块土地。土地簿包含有关该不动产特征的信息(例如,面积、所有权人,以及影响该财产的权利负担(如抵押、留置权等)。但是,截至撰写本案例研究之时,罗马尼亚全部不动产的国家土地簿制作和地籍登记尚未完成,因此,上述记录中可能对一些土地完全没有记载。

If the address of the property and cadastral number is known, a Land Book excerpt issued by the Land Book office at the request of the interested parties is sufficient to provide the prima facie information about the property.

如果已知不动产的地址及其地籍编号,则由地籍办公室应有意各方的要求出具的土地簿摘录须提供与该不动产相关的初步信息。

It is also worth mentioning that according to the Romanian regulations, land is divided into 2 categories: inside the built-up area, or outside of the built-up area of municipalities. The general rule is that no building permit may be issued for any zones outside of the built-up area; however, there are a few exceptions, some of which may be considered to also include any energy production and transportation projects and infrastructure. In any case, no building permit will be issued for those plots of land that are still in agricultural use, these plots of land must be first deregistered from the competent agricultural authority.

值得一提的是，根据罗马尼亚的规定，土地分为两类：一是在城市建成区内的土地，二是在城市建成区外的土地。一般规则是，对于在城市建成区以外的任何区域，均不会签发建筑许可证；但是，此处有一些例外，例如，其中一些可能被认为是任何能源生产和运输项目的区域，以及基础设施的区域。无论如何，对于那些仍用于农业的土地，不会向其签发建筑许可证，这类土地必须首先在主管农业部门注销。

In addition, depending on the classification mentioned above, the investor may be required to prepare different zoning plans in accordance with the Planning Certificate (certificat de urbanism in Romanian) issued by the local authorities, depending on the scope, dimension and impact of the project.

此外，根据上述分类，投资者可能被要求根据地方当局颁发的规划证书（罗马尼亚语为 certificat de urbanism）准备不同的分区计划，这具体取决于项目的范围、规模和影响。

2.2 尽职调查（Due Diligence）

During the period of 1945—1989, all private property was abolished and/or severely limited during the time period in Romania. All privately-held companies were nationalized, taken over by the State and became public companies and all living spaces were no longer privately owned, but rather leased to individual persons and families. All agricultural work was done by specially constituted legal entities called cooperative agricole, and individual persons were not allowed to have lands over a certain surface area.

在 1945—1989 年，所有私有财产均被废止或严重受限。所有私营公司均被国有化，由国家接管并成为公共公司，所有居住空间不再由私人所有，而是租赁给个人和家庭。所有农业工作均由特别组成的法律实体完成，其名称为农业合作社，个人不得在特定区域内拥有土地。

After the above mentioned time period, starting with 1990, the Romanian government issued several reparation laws. These enactments gave the former owners and/or their heirs or legal successors the right to have their former properties returned in kind or receive compensatory damages when normal restitution was no longer possible.

在上述期间后，从1990年开始，罗马尼亚政府颁布了多项赔偿法。这些法令赋予前业主和/或其继承人或法定承继人收回此前被没收的同类财产，或在财产不能正常恢复原状的情况下获得补偿性赔偿的权利。

Without going into detail concerning the procedures set forth by the above mentioned restitution laws, if the entitled person issues a request to the competent public authority for the restitution of the former property, all future sales and/or transmission of ownership are blocked, until the final and irrevocable solving of the request has been made.

在此不详述上述归还法律规定，如果权利人向主管公共机关提出归还其原财产的请求，则在对请求作出最终的、不可撤销的决定前，针对该财产未来的所有出售和/或所有权的转移都将被阻止。

Moreover, in Romania, it is necessary to perform a review of all past transfers of title to the maximum extent possible, in order to ensure that there is an unbroken and valid chain of titles from the original owner to the current owner.

此外，在罗马尼亚，有必要尽最大努力对此前全部的所有权转让行为进行审查，以确保从最初财产所有人到当前财产所有人的所有权链条有效且不间断。

As such, conducting a due diligence investigation on the property titles and transmissions is of key importance as it can avoid possible litigations with the former owners and even the full loss of ownership rights.

因此，对财产所有权及其转让进行尽职调查至关重要，因为它可以避免与前财产所有人发生可能的诉讼甚至所有权的完全丧失。

The due diligence report can also actively determine if there are any other key issues or significant risk factors involved in the acquisition transaction and may determine possible solutions and/or remedies thereof.

尽职调查报告还能主动确定收购交易中是否存在其他关键问题或重大风险因素，并可针对问题或风险决定可能的解决方案或补救措施。

In the case at hand, the legal due diligence revealed certain defects, but these were addressed as appropriate solutions were identified.

在本案例中，法律尽职调查发现了一些问题，但在确定适当的解决方案后，这些问题得到了解决。

The due diligence was performed not only with respect to legal aspects, but also cadastral (measurements of the properties), technical (proximity of utilities) and environmental aspects.

尽职调查不仅针对法律方面的问题,还针对地籍(不动产的测量)、技术(邻近设施)和环境方面的问题。

2.3 获取土地权利 (Obtaining Rights over the Land)

Once the due diligence confirmed the ownership title and the suitability of the land for the Project, relevant rights in land were obtained by notarized agreement.

一旦尽职调查确认了用于本项目的土地的所有权和适用性,土地的相关权利将通过公证后的协议获得。

As the Romanian Civil Code, all sale and purchase agreements concerning ownership rights and/or any other real estate rights must be notarized in order to be valid. The public notary will also ensure that the transfer of ownership/other real estate rights is registered with the Land Book Office for third party publicity.

根据《罗马尼亚民法典》,所有关于所有权和/或任何其他房地产权利的买卖协议必须经过公证才能生效。公证人还将确保所有权和/或其他房地产权利的转让登记于地籍办公室,以向第三方公示。

For the notarization of the sale and purchase, the seller must provide the notary with ownership documents (and a fiscal certificate in case of buildings), as well as other additional documents that may prove ownership of the land. In addition, both parties must present the notary valid IDs/trade registry excerpts for companies, and the power-of-attorney (POA) in notarized form.

对于买卖的公证,卖方须向公证人提供所有权文件(若是建筑物,还需财务证书)以及可能证明土地所有权的其他文件。此外,双方还须向公证人出示有效的身份证/公司交易登记摘录,以及公证形式的授权书(POA)。

In case the interested party opts for financing the land acquisition through a bank, additional agreements are entered into, such as the loan agreement between the financing bank and the company. In most cases, the bank will secure the loan agreement by setting up a mortgage on the purchased land, in which case a mortgage agreement may also be concluded between the parties in notarized form and registered with the Land Book Office.

如果意向方选择通过银行为土地收购提供融资，则融资银行与公司之间会签订其他协议，如贷款协议。在大多数情况下，银行将对购买的土地设立担保来担保贷款协议，双方可以公证的形式签订担保协议并在地簿办公室登记。

In the case at hand, the Company decided to acquire full ownership over the envisaged land for the Project. However, in other cases investors sought to acquire only building rights over the land (in Romanian, superficies agreement).

在本案例中，公司决定收购本项目所需土地的全部所有权。然而，在其他情况下，投资者只希望收购土地上的建筑权利（罗马尼亚语为 superficies agreement）。

3. 规划与建设（Planning and Construction）

3.1 规划证（Planning Certificate）

According to the Romanian regulations, the first step of the permitting procedure is the issuance by the competent local authority of a planning certificate. The planning certificate informs the applicant on the legal, economic and technical regimes of the land on which the construction is intended to be developed (or, as the case may be, of the construction which is intended to be refurbished) as well as on the legal requirements that must be observed within the development process (such as rezoning of the land, and/or endorsements from public institutions that are prerequisites for the issuance of a building permit). Typically, this planning certificate is valid for a time period no longer than 24 months from its issuing date.

根据罗马尼亚的规定，许可程序的第一步是由地方主管部门颁发规划证。规划证会告知申请人关于其拟开发建筑物（或视情况而定，可能为拟翻新建筑物）所在土地需遵守的法律、经济和技术制度，以及在开发过程中必须遵守的法律要求，例如重新划分土地和/或获得公共机构的认可是签发建筑许可证的先决条件。通常，此规划证的有效期为自签发日起不超过24个月。

3.2 对地区分区要求的修改（Amendment of Local Zoning Requirements）

For each urban area, the local authorities adopt a General Zoning Plan (in Romanian, Plan Urbanistic General, PUG) which contains general urbanism and construction requirements in the municipality.

对每个城区，地方当局采用总体分区规划（罗马尼亚语为 Plan Urbanistic

General，以下简称 PUG），该计划包含辖区的总体城市规划和建设要求。

Considering that, in the case at hand, the project was different from the local regulations originally envisaged by the local authorities for that particular zone through the PUG, the Company was required to prepare and have approved by the local municipal council, documentation amending the PUG, namely a Zonal Urbanism Plan (in Romanian, Plan Urbanistic Zonal, PUZ). For the purposes of the PUZ, some endorsements had to be obtained from the competent authorities, in particular from the utility providers, environmental authorities, as well as the county council.

在本案例中，本项目用地不同于地方当局最初在 PUG 中对该特定区域的设想，因此公司被要求准备用于修改 PUG 的文件，并使其经当地市政委员会的批准，该文件即为区域城市规划（罗马尼亚语为 Plan Urbanistic Zonal，以下简称 PUZ）。为满足 PUZ 的目的，其须获得主管机关——特别是公共设施提供方、环保机关和县级政府部门的认可。

It should be noted that, considering the zoning documents are approved through a local council decision, any third party that justifies an interest and considers itself damaged by this administrative decision can challenge the validity of said decision and thus, the new zoning regulations in a court of law; we have observed that there is an ongoing trend in Romania that some non-governmental associations which claim to defend the architectural heritage of the major cities challenge any and all decisions related to zoning plans and/or any other aspect related to building permits.

应注意的是，鉴于分区文件由地方政府部门决定批准，任何证明其具有相关利益并认为其因此行政决定而受到损害的第三方可以在法庭上质疑上述决定的有效性，并进而质疑新分区规则的有效性；我们注意到，在罗马尼亚一直存在一种趋势，即一些声称捍卫主要城市建筑遗产的非政府组织会质疑任何与分区计划和/或与建筑许可其他方面有关的决定。

3.3 建筑许可证（Building Permit）

After meeting each of the requirements established by the planning certificate mentioned above, as well as making any necessary amendments to the zoning plans and regulations, the investor was able to finally request the competent authority (i.e., in most cases, the mayor) to issue the relevant building permit.

在满足上述规划证书确定的每项要求，以及对分区计划和规定进行必要的修改后，投资者最终得以要求主管机关（在大多数情况下，为市长）签发相关的建筑许可证。

The building permit is the final administrative act by which the competent local authorities approve any works related to building, demolishing, refurbishing or modifying constructions, it is legally binding for the investor concerning the rights and obligations regulated thereunder.

建筑许可是地方主管机关批准任何与建筑、建筑的拆除、翻新或改造相关事宜的最终行政行为，其规定的权利和义务对投资者具有法律约束力。

The planning certificate must expressly state the purpose for which the building permit is required, as well as all the prior endorsements and/or authorizations listed which must be obtained from the relevant authorities. These include: (i) water management and waste water collection; (ii) access to public roads and/or transportation facilities; (iii) fire security permit; (iv) environmental agency point of view or endorsement; (v) other endorsements required depending on the location of the land.

规划书须明确载明建筑许可证的目的，以及载明必须从有关机关获得的全部事先同意和/或授权。其中包括：(i) 水管理和废水收集；(ii) 使用公共道路和/或交通设施；(iii) 消防安全许可；(iv) 环保机构的同意或看法；(v) 取决于土地具体位置须取得的其他同意事项。

The request for the issuance of the building permit was accompanied by the following documents: (i) the planning certificate issued specifically for the building permit; (ii) proof of ownership for the land with updated Land Book and cadastral excerpt; (iii) technical documentation for the effective construction works; (iv) all of the endorsements and authorizations mentioned in the above paragraph.

在请求签发建筑许可证时，应附有下列文件：(i) 专为建筑许可证签发的规划证书；(ii) 附有最新土地簿和地籍摘录的土地所有权证明；(iii) 有效建筑工程的技术文件；(iv) 以上所述文件的全部同意和授权书。

In addition, for the building permit the investor was required to pay a fee of 1% from the total estimated value of the works in the municipality's account. Under normal circumstances, the estimated value of the works is the one stated in the technical documentation for the construction works; however, in our experience, local authorities have established minimum thresholds under which such a tax cannot go below. Also, some local authorities have developed a practice of adding a multiplier to the 1% based on the category/location of the land—i. e. , the more central the zone, the higher the multiplier—which can cause instability when determining a budget for the desired project.

此外，为取得建筑许可证，投资者需向市政当局的账户支付工程估价1%的费用。在正常情况下，工程估价是建筑工程技术文件中所载的价格；但是，根据我们的经验，地方主管机关已制定了最低门槛的情况下，税收不能低于此水平。此外，一些地方机关已经发展出一种做法，即根据土地的类别和位置，以1%为基准向其增加倍数的做法，即越接近区域中心的位置，倍数越高，这导致了确定项目预算时的不稳定性。

In the case at hand, the building permit was valid for a period of 12 months (out of a maximum period of 24 months from the issuing date), while the works had to commence no later than 12 months from the issuing date under penalty of the building permit becoming void. An additional extension may be requested only once, for a period of 12 months, for which another fee in equal amount of 30% of the initial building permit fee must be paid.

在本案例中，建筑许可证的有效期为12个月（处于最长期限内，在签发日期起的24个月的最长期限内）[1]，但工程必须自签发之日起12个月内启动，否则将面临建筑许可证无效的处罚。额外延期只能申请一次，可延期的期限为12个月，为此，必须另外支付相当于初始建筑许可费30%的费用。

At the end of the completion of the works, a handover protocol was signed between the Company and the contractor, which was endorsed by the representatives of the local municipality.

在工程竣工时，公司与承包商签订了移交协议，该协议得到了当地市政当局代表的认可。

Under Romanian regulations, ownership over the construction is acquired gradually as the construction works are finalized, with full ownership existing as of the handover protocol. Failure to comply with the obligations established under the building permit, as well as absence of the handover protocol will lead to the construction being consid-

---

[1] 建筑许可证有一个从签发之日起算为期24个月的最长有效期限，但除非另行支付费用申请延期12个月的，自签发之日起12个月未能施工将导致建筑许可证无效。——译者注

ered as not completed, with all legal consequences thereof which may include court litigation between the company and the contractor, expiration/voiding of the building permit.

根据罗马尼亚法律,在建筑工程逐渐完工的过程中,相关主体将陆续获得建筑物的所有权,并于订立移交协议时获得全部的所有权。若未能遵守建筑许可证规定的义务,以及没有移交协议,将致使工程被视为未完成,其所有的法律后果可能包括:公司与承包商之间的诉讼,以及建筑许可证过期与失效。

Upon finalizing the construction works, the buildings were registered with the Land Book.

在完工后,相关建筑物在土地簿上进行登记。

4. 设立批准与电网连接（Setting up Authorization and Connection to the Grid）

4.1 设立批准（Setting-up Authorization）

The first step under the Romanian energy regulations for the establishment of a photovoltaic project was the issuance of a setting-up authorization by the Romanian Energy Regulatory Authority (ANRE).

根据罗马尼亚能源法规建设光伏项目的第一步是由罗马尼亚能源监管局（ANRE）签发设立批准书。

We note that the setting-up authorization entitles the investor to develop or refurbish energy production facilities, but not to sell and/or transport by any means the resulted energy, activities that entail different authorizations and permits for which the obtaining procedures will be detailed below.

我们注意到,设立批准书使投资者有权开发或翻新能源生产设施,但无权以任何方式出售和/或运输所产生的能源,或从事需要不同批准和许可的活动,本文将在后文详细说明这类批准和许可的获取程序。

A setting-up authorization is required for any production aggregate capable of producing more than 1 million watt (MW) of energy, which was also the case at hand. The minimum validity period for the setting-up authorization is one year, and a maximum of either (i) 25 years for production, transportation, distribution or energy market administration or (ii) 10 years for energy sales and/or energy trading on the appropriate regulated market. In the case at hand, the setting-up authorization was granted for a period of three years.

任何累计能够产生超过 1 兆瓦能量的生产活动都须设立批准书，本案例亦是如此。设立批准的最短有效期为 1 年，最长有效期则为：（i）对生产、运输、分销或能源市场管理而言，为 25 年；或（ii）对在受适当监管的市场上进行的能源销售和/或能源交易而言，为 10 年。在本案例中，设立批准的有效期限为 3 年。

For the purposes of having the setting-up authorization issued, the following documents were submitted: (i) trade registry excerpt regarding the investing company; (ii) copies of the last financial statement registered by the investor with the fiscal authorities and a full accounting balance sheet; (iii) shareholders/associates affidavit; (iv) proof of ownership/ownership title for the land on which the project will be developed or refurbished; (v) excerpts that prove registration of ownership rights with the Land Book Office; (vi) table of contents containing all plots of land involved in the project development; (vii) proof of intent regarding the development/refurbishment of energy production aggregates and proof of publishing in local media; (viii) technical memorandum detailing conditions and works to be executed, also containing economical forecasts and indexes; (ix) proof of financing for the project development issued by the designated banking institution; (x) authorization issued by the competent environmental agency; (xi) layout and placement plan of the energy production aggregates; (xi) total estimated duration of the project and (xii) affidavit concerning the exclusive use of ANRE-confirmed contractors and suppliers.

为使有关机关签发设立批准之目的，在本案例中须提交以下文件：（i）关于投资公司的交易登记摘录；（ii）投资者在财政部门登记的最后一份财务报表副本和完整的会计资产负债表；（iii）股东、关联人的宣誓书；（iv）用于项目开发或翻新的土地的所有权证明；（v）证明在地籍办公室进行所有权登记的摘录；（vi）载有项目开发所涉所有土地的目录；（vii）关于能源生产总量的开发、整修的意向证明和在当地媒体公示的证明；（viii）详细说明将要进行的工作及其条件，并包含经济预测与指标的技术备忘录；（ix）指定银行机构签发的项目开发融资证明；（x）由环保主管机构签发的批准；（xi）能源生产总量的安排和规划；（xi）项目预计持续的总时间和（xii）排他性使用 ANRE 确认的承包商和供应商的宣誓书。

4.2 电网连接（Connection to the Grid）

In order to obtain the connection to the grid, the following steps were taken: (i) the issuance of an emplacement endorsement; (ii) the issuance of the interconnection technical approval (ATR) providing for the grid connection alternative to be used by the applicant, as identified in the solution study, endorsed by the grid operators; (iii) the conclusion of the interconnection agreement; (iv) the performance of the actual connection works; (v) the testing of the connection installation; (vi) the putting into function of the connection installation; and (vii) the putting under voltage of the connection installation.

为接入电网，本案例中采取了以下步骤：（i）签发放置批准；（ii）按照解决方案研究中所确定的事项，经由电网运营商认可，签发为申请人提供可采用的电网连接替代方案的互连技术批准（ATR）；（iii）订立互连协议；（iv）履行实际连接的工作；（v）测试连接装置；（vi）将连接装置投入使用，以及（vii）放低连接装置的电压。

5. 生产许可（Production License）

After the company has obtained the setting-up authorization, an additional step is required for the legal and compliant production of electrical energy, which is the issuance of the corresponding production license by ANRE.

在公司获得设立批准后，为了合法、合规地进行电能生产，仍需要采取额外的步骤，即由 ANRE 签发相应的生产许可证。

In addition to the regular documents concerning trade registry excerpts of the investment company, financial statements and powers of attorney, the investor will submit the following documents: (i) addresses of all electrical energy production facilities for which the Setting-up Authorization was issued; (ii) technical characteristics of the energy production facilities and electrical networks of the investor; (iii) organizational chart of the investing company; (iv) list of personnel and their qualifications employed by the investor, or, in absence of any employees, any electrical services agreement concluded with an ANRE-authorized electrician or specialist; (v) estimated turnover of the production facilities; (vi) Handover Protocol as proof for putting into function the energy production facilities; (vii) ownership documents and/or property titles over the production facilities and the corresponding land; (viii) the ATR mentioned in the previous chapter and (ix) proof of initiating the procedure for obtaining the environmental authorization.

除了投资公司的交易登记摘录、财务报表和授权书等常规文件，投资者还将提交以下文件：(i) 已签发的设立批准所针对的电能生产设施的地址；(ii) 投资者的能源生产设施和电网的技术特征；(iii) 投资公司的组织结构图；(iv) 关于投资者雇用的人员及其资格的清单，或在没有任何雇员的情况下，与ANRE授权的电工或专家签订的任何电力服务协议；(v) 生产设施的估计营业额；(vi) 证明能源生产设施投入使用的移交协议；(vii) 生产设施和相应土地的所有权文件和/或财产权利；(viii) 前一章提到的ATR和(ix) 启动获得环保批准程序的证明。

ANRE will analyze the request and issue a response no later than 60 calendar days from the registration date, while also making additional requests for amendments to the request if necessary. If amendments are required, they will be addressed by the investor no later than 90 days from the ANRE request date.

ANRE将在登记日后的60个自然日内分析请求并作出回复，同时，还会在必要时提出更改请求的要求。如果要求进行更改，投资人须自ANRE作出要求之日起90日内对此进行处理。

If all the required documentation is complete, ANRE will within 60 days of receiving the request/the amendments to the request ifapplicable, issue the appropriate license (i. e. the energy production license) which entitle the investor to produce and commercialize electrical energy in accordance with applicable legal provisions.

如果必备的文件都已齐全，ANRE将自收到请求或收到对请求的更改（如果适用）后60日内签发相应的许可证（如能源生产许可证），使投资者有权根据适用的法律规定，生产电能并使其商业化。

6. 支持计划认证、国家援助与融资解决方案（Accreditation for the Support Scheme, State Aid and Financing Solutions）

In order to promote the production of renewable energy, the Romanian Parliament enacted Law no. 220/2008, which provided for a support scheme based on green certificates granted to producers of energy and the obligation of specific legal entities to acquire and hold a certain amount of green certificates. The support scheme was enforced and applied to projects completed until 31 December 2016. As such, all of the following details and procedures described below are made in consideration of the support scheme which the client benefitted from, but is not available for future investments.

为了促进可再生能源的生产，罗马尼亚议会颁布了第 220/2008 号法律，该法基于授予能源生产者的绿色证书以及特定法律实体获取和持有一定数量绿色证书的义务，规定了一项支持计划。该支持计划曾实施并适用于 2016 年 12 月 31 日前完工的项目。因此，下述所有细节和程序均考虑到客户可从中受益的支持计划，但其不适用于未来的投资。

With the exception of the green certificates support scheme, which was a direct implementation of EU directives and regulations for stimulating renewable energy production and consumption, Romanian legal provisions did not provide any other incentives for the development of the client's project.

绿色证书支持计划是对欧盟刺激可再生能源生产和消费指令及法规的具体实施。除绿色证书支持计划外，罗马尼亚的法规没有为客户项目的开展提供任何其他激励措施。

At the current moment, there is no legal provision and/or international accord with respect to stimulating investments made by Chinese entities. As such, there is no preferential tax for foreign investments—such a measure is prohibited by EU competition regulations to discourage masked or indirect forms of state aid.

目前，在促进中国实体的投资方面，并无法律规定和/或国际协议。因此，对外国投资并无税收优惠——欧盟竞争法规禁止采取这种措施以阻止隐蔽的或间接的国家援助。

Furthermore, at the time the green certificates support scheme was implemented, this was more efficient than any other fiscal or other type of incentives, as a single green certificate was worth between EUR 30 and EUR 50 for produced Megawatt.

此外，在绿色证书支持计划实施时，该计划比任何其他财政或其他类型的激励措施更加有效，因为为用于生产所需的兆瓦电量而申请的绿色证书，其单个价值在 30 欧元到 50 欧元之间。

As for the financing necessary to complete the client's project, we have not conducted any negotiations and/or legal services on behalf of the client in this regard. As such, it is reasonable to assume that the financing was individually acquired by the client, possibly from a Chinese investment bank.

至于完成客户的项目所必须的融资，我们在此方面并未代表客户进行任何谈判和/或法律服务。因此，可以合理地假设，客户独立地获得了融资，且融资可能来自一家中国投资银行。

Depending on the type of renewable energy, each legal entity involved in the energy production sector would receive a certain number of green certificates for each MW of energy produced. For solar energy, a number of (6) green certificates were initially granted. The client obtained the maximum number of green certificates.

根据可再生能源的类型，涉足能源生产行业的各法律实体将获得一定数量的绿色证书用于每兆瓦能源的生产。针对太阳能，最初授予绿色证书的数量为6份。客户获得了数量最多的绿色证书。

The participation into the support scheme was confirmed by ANRE through the accreditation process, which could be obtained in one or two stages. In case of the 2-stage accreditation for green certificates, a preliminary accreditation period was requested, during the testing period.

参与支持计划的事宜由 ANRE 以认证程序确认，该认证程序可以在一或两个阶段内完成。在通过两个阶段的认证获得绿色证书的情况下，在测试期内须进行初始认证。

Starting with July 2013, the Romanian authorities suspended from trading a certain number of green certificates. The sale of these certificates was re-scheduled to take place until 2030.

从2013年7月开始，罗马尼亚当局暂停了对一定数量的绿色证书的交易。预计到2030年绿色证书交易才会被重新提上日程。

7. 电力销售与绿色证书 (Sale of Electricity and Green Certificates)

In accordance with the Romanian regulations, the sale of electricity and green certificates can be made only in a transparent and anonymous manner, on the centralized energy and green certificate market operated by the Romanian company OPCOM.

根据罗马尼亚的法规，只能在罗马尼亚公司 OPCOM 运营的能源和绿色证书集中市场内，以透明和匿名的方式出售电力和绿色证书。

Green certificates (GC) can be traded on 2 different platforms, which are: (i) the centralized green certificates market (GC Centralized Market), and (ii) the green certificates market for bilateral contracts (GC Bilateral Contracts Market). Both trading markets operate parallel with the electricity market and both are under the supervision of the Romanian Energy Market Operator Company (in Romanian abbreviated as OPCOM).

绿色证书可以在两个不同的平台上交易，这些平台是：(i) 集中式绿色证书市场（以下简称绿色证书集中市场），以及 (ii) 双边合同的绿色证书市场（以下简称绿色证书双边合同市场）。两个交易市场都与电力市场并行运营，且二者均受罗马尼亚能源市场运营公司（罗马尼亚语缩写为 OPCOM）的监督。

As of 2013 and considering the regulation of the two above-mentioned markets, trading Green Certificates outside of those markets based on sale-purchase agreements concluded under normal circumstances is no longer permitted and any such arrangements are automatically considered null and void. The OPCOM rules are meant to create a centralized and standardized market/trading platform for the competitiveness, transparency and non-discrimination of the trading environment.

截至2013年，考虑到对上述两个市场的监管，基于在一般情况下达成的买卖协议而在这些市场之外进行的绿色证书交易将不再被允许，任何此类交易将自动被视为无效。OPCOM 的规则旨在为维护交易环境的竞争力、透明度和无歧视性而创建一个集中的、标准化的市场/交易平台。

OPCOM has the following attributes related to the administration of the GC market, based on the GC market regulation: (i) establishes and maintains the Green Certificates registry and the registry of all market participants; (ii) records the participants' codes in market that are issued by the national electrical network distributor; (iii) manages in a transparent and non-discriminatory manner all trading performed on the GC market; (iv) establishes the guidelines for market participation and submits it to ANRE for approval; (v) receives, validates and processes the sale/purchase offers on the market; (vi) makes public the closing price of each trading session on the GC Centralized Market (vii) ensures the publicity of trading sessions and organizes each session (viii) sends monthly status reports and updates to ANRE.

基于绿色证书市场的规定，OPCOM 在绿色证书市场管理这一方面具有以下特点：(i) 确立和维护绿色证书登记和所有市场参与者的登记；(ii) 记录由国家电网分销商发布的市场参与者代码；(iii) 以透明和非歧视的方式管理在绿色证书市场上进行的所有交易；(iv) 制定市场参与指南并提交给 ANRE 批准；(v) 接收、确认和处理市场上的销售、购买报价；(vi) 公布绿色证书集中市场上每个交易时段的收盘价；(vii) 确保交易时段的公开性，并对各交易时段进行组织；(viii) 每月向 ANRE 发送情况报告及其更新状况。

As opposed to the GC Bilateral Contracts Market, where the price of a green certificate is freely negotiated by the parties (within the mandatory trading value range), on the GC Centralized Market the certificates are traded at the closing price of the GC Centralized Market determined on the basis of the respective offers to buy and to sell submitted on the GC Centralized Market in that respective month.

与在绿色证书双边合同市场内绿色证书的价格由各方自由协商（在法定的强制交易价范围内）相反，在绿色证书集中市场上，证书以基于各月提交的买卖报价确定的收盘价进行交易。

In accordance with the GC Market Regulation, a green certificate can be subject to successive trading and shall be registered in the account of the economic agent to which the GC is transferred and, finally, to the account of the economic agent, which will use the GC in order to prove the fulfilment of the GCs mandatory purchase quota. Transfer of GCs from the account of the seller to the account of the buyer will be performed by OPCOM, only after payment confirmation, and will be effective after the registration in the green certificates register.

根据绿色证书市场规则，绿色证书可以连续交易，且应登记于受让证书的经济代理人的账户，并最终移转至经济代理人的账户，经济代理人将使用该绿色证书以证明其满足了法定的购买额度。OPCOM 在确认付款后将绿色证书从卖方账户转移到买方账户，且该转移将在于绿色证书登记处进行登记后生效。

On a more general level, the entire electricity market is divided in several sub-markets, which consist of: (i) the bilateral contracts market; (ii) the double-negotiated bilateral contracts market; (iii) the day-ahead market; (iv) the intraday market and (v) the balancing market.

在更普遍的层面上，整个电力市场分为几个子市场，包括：(i) 双边合同市场；(ii) 双重谈判双边合同市场；(iii) 日前市场；(iv) 日内市场及 (v) 平衡市场。

For the bilateral contracts market, parties can opt for 2 types of contracts: classic bilateral contracts and continually-negotiated bilateral contracts. The former type is a non-amendable type of contract in which the partiescan not modify the mandatory clauses and the latter are more permissive with respect to negotiation of essential clauses.

对于双边合同市场，缔约方可以选择两种合同：传统双边合同和持续谈判双边合同。前者是一种不可修改的合同，各方不能修改合同的强制性条款；后者则在基本条款的谈判方面更加宽松。

The double-negotiated bilateral contracts market is optional and investors can participate by submitting a simple request, as well as withdraw in the same manner, aspects which are meant to contrast the mandatory nature of the previously detailed bilateral market.

与前述双边市场的强制性不同的是，双重谈判双边合同市场具有可选择性，投资人可以提交一份简要请求的方式参与其中，也可以同样的方式撤回请求。

In addition, investors can also choose to participate in the day-ahead market, which is organized with one day prior to the conclusion of the contracts and where offers are considered valid based on market clearing price. Each market participant may submit only one buy and only one sell offer for each day of trading. OPCOM is obligated to notify each participant regarding acceptance or withdrawal of their offers.

此外，投资者还可以选择参与于合同签订前一天组织且根据市场清算价格确定报价有效的日前市场。每个市场参与者在每个交易日仅可提交一个买入或卖出报价。OPCOM 有义务通知每位参与者报价是接受还是撤回。

On the intra-day market, which is also an optional and free for participation market, electricity is traded on an hourly basis of the delivery day, based on a participation agreement form concluded with OPCOM.

日内市场也是可选择且可免费参与的市场，在该市场内的交易日，基于与 OPCOM 达成的参与协议，电力以小时为单位进行交易。

Finally, on the balancing market, the transmission system operator buys and sells electricity from the participants under regulations proposed by the operator and endorsed by ANRE. This market was set up in order to ensure some degree of stability within the

National Energy System. Participants are directly registered by the operator, which then proceeds to check the offers and calculate necessary quantities for transaction on the market. Participation on this market is mandatory for all eligible energy license holders.

最后,在平衡市场上,根据由运营商提出并由 ANRE 认可的规则,传输系统运营商从参与者处购买和销售电力。建立这个市场是为了确保国家能源系统具有一定程度的稳定性。参与者直接由运营商进行注册,随后,运营商会查看报价并计算市场交易的必要数额。所有符合条件的能源许可证持有者都必须参与此市场。

The Client successfully registered on the relevant markets and is trading both energy and green certificates.

我们的客户在相关市场成功注册可进行能源和绿色证书的交易。

— 作者简介 —

Andrei Sălăgeanu is an Associate with the Wolf Theiss Bucharest office and member of the Real Estate team. He specializes in real estate law, as well as in litigation and dispute resolution matters. Andrei has acted on behalf of numerous real estate developers in all legal matters related to their day-to-day activities, providing representation in all sales-related activities and negotiations, as well as SPA drafting and review. He has also provided legal representation in civil & commercial litigation files with a strong emphasis on banking consumer disputes and enforcement proceedings. He is a graduate of the University of Bucharest Law School and is a member of the Bucharest bar.

Andrei Sălăgeanu 是 Wolf Theiss 布加勒斯特办公室的合伙人,也是房地产团队的成员。他专攻房地产法、诉讼和争议解决业务。Andrei 曾代表众多房地产开发商处理与他们日常活动相关的所有法律事务,在所有与销售相关的活动和谈判中提供代理服务,包括 SPA 协议的起草和审核。他还在民商事诉讼中担任诉讼代理人,重点关注银行消费者纠纷解决和执行程序。他毕业于布加勒斯特大学法学院,并且是布加勒斯特律师协会的成员。

投资在挪威：在多种行业开展投资
Investments in Norway
Investing in Multiple Industries

点 评

中国是挪威在亚洲的最大贸易伙伴。据中国外交部统计，2023年，两国的双边贸易总额达143.46亿美元，[1]由此可见，两国之间的投资往来密切。根据本文作者的统计，在过去几年中，中国投资者在挪威境内的几次较大的交易均成为挪威的头条新闻。

在公开公布的交易当中，以下交易被认为是非常经典的，如国内上市公司曲美家居收购了挪威上市公司 Ekornes ASA（Ekornes 是欧洲最大的家具制造商之一，总部位于挪威，该公司主要以其"Stressless"系列的躺椅而闻名，它在独有的细分领域中开展经营，可增补曲美家居的现有产品）；奇虎360科技有限公司牵头收购了 Opera Software AS（Opera 网络浏览器的开发者）；华彬集团收购了 Voss of Norway ASA（高端饮用水品牌 VOSS）等交易。其中特别值得关注的交易是 2018 年曲美家居对家具制造商 Ekornes ASA 的收购。在收购时，Ekornes ASA 是一家挪威上市公司。经历与公司管理层和董事会进行磋商的漫长过程后，自愿要约于 2018 年 6 月发出，在收到超过 98% 的股东对要约作出的承诺后，2018 年 9 月曲美家居完成全部股权的收购。我们作为中国律师也有幸参与了该项目的后期募集资金部分的法律服务。

本文作者没有拘泥于一个案例展开介绍，而是基于其丰富的项目经验，总结提炼了相关案例中共通的一些问题展开分析，我们选取了两个重要问题列示如下，希望对读者有所帮助：

一是关于交易对价支付的问题。几乎无一例外，多数卖方在交割时更乐于

---

[1] 数据来源：驻挪威王国大使馆经济商务处。

接受现金对价,这也是支付对价的一种主要方式,现金对价的资金来源通常为债或股权。在本文作者为中方投资者就其在挪威境内的并购提供咨询的所有交易中,挪威参与方往往首先会倾向于以现金结算。本文作者确曾数次见到已上市的买方试图推迟支付现金对价或通过发行买方(或其已上市的母公司)股票收购公司的方式来支付对价。但卖家通常对此不愿接受,交易陷入困境往往是这个原因。虽然也可以考虑其他形式的对价,但这在实践中并不常见。

二是关于设立咨询委员会的问题。在本文作者参与交易过程且涉及中国投资者的几个案例里,为适用法律的强制性规定,各方同意设立目标公司的咨询委员会,并以此作为管理层与员工讨论的平台。但是,根据挪威法律,选举成立董事会更加有利。因为在挪威,咨询委员会不是正式的法人机关,而是根据公司法特别安排的,因此,关于设立咨询委员会相关条款的约定很少。

1. 挪威和北极地区:关于投资的潜力(Norway and the Arctic Region: On the Potential for Investments)

1.1 概述(Introduction)

Norway, the northernmost outpost of Europe, has for several decades been one of the world's largest exporting countries of oil and gas. Following the breakthrough during the 1960's with the discovery of petroleum in the floor of the North Sea, Norwegian economy has boomed and is, per capita, one of only four countries with a gross domestic product of more than USD 75 000 (excluding islands and micro states such as Monaco and Lichtenstein).[1] Much of the critical infrastructure along the Norwegian coastline is connected to the petroleum industry, with large operational centres at several points along the coast. With respect to the export of natural gas, there are also pipelines on the ocean floor to Scotland, England, Germany, the Netherlands and France.

挪威是欧洲最北端的前哨,几十年来,该国一直是世界上最大的石油和天然气出口国之一。随着20世纪60年代在北海海床发现石油的突破,挪威经济蓬勃发展,该国是人均国民生产总值超过75 000美元的仅有的四个国家之一

---

[1] The other three being Luxembourg, Ireland and Switzerland. Sourced from the World Bank. 2019 GDP per Capita Statistics.

(不包括岛屿和摩纳哥、列支敦士登等小型国家)。[1]挪威海岸线上的许多关键基础设施均与石油工业有关,在沿海的几个地点设有大型运营中心。在天然气出口方面,挪威有连通苏格兰、英格兰、德国、荷兰和法国的海底管道。

The People's Republic of China is the largest trading partner of Norway in Asia. According to the Foreign Ministry of China, the bilateral trade between the two countries amounted to an aggregate amount of USD 14.346 billion in 2023. Negotiations are underway with the hopes of reaching a free-trade agreement between the two nations, with Norway eager to obtain duty-free trade of industrial products, including its second largest export, seafood, and China hoping to gain improved access to various Norwegian markets.

中国是挪威在亚洲最大的贸易伙伴。据中国外交部统计,2023年两国的双边贸易总额达143.46亿美元。促成两国之间达成自由贸易协定的谈判正在进行当中,挪威希望实现对工业产品及其第二大出口产品——海产品的自由贸易,而中国希望能够进一步改善进入挪威各类市场的机会。

While Norway cannot reasonably be described as a major force itself in world trade, with the tonnage of cargo passing through even the largest port only constituting a fraction of the cargo tonnage of the largest ports on the European continent, Norway sits at a strategically important location for the transportation of goods in our time, being the link between the European continent and the Arctic. As the polar ice cap has been drastically reduced, new trade routes of great international significance may open up in the Arctic seas, potentially reducing the lead time to delivery of goods from the far east to Europe by several weeks. Furthermore, this has opened up for the potential to make good use of the vast resources offered by the Arctic oceans—both in respect of oil, natural gases and seafood.

将挪威称为世界贸易的主要力量似乎有些夸大(即使航经挪威最大港口的货物吨位也只占欧洲大陆最大港口货物吨位的一小部分),但不可否认的是在当今时代,挪威确实位于货物运输的重要战略位置,是欧洲大陆和北极之间的纽带。随着极地冰盖大幅减少,可能将在北极海域开辟具有重大国际意义的新贸易航线,这可能会使从远东到欧洲交付货物的前置时间缩短数周。此外,新航线

---

[1] 另外三个是卢森堡、爱尔兰和瑞士。数据来自世界银行2019年人均GDP统计。

的开辟也是为了充分利用北冰洋蕴藏的大量资源（包括石油、天然气和海产品）。

With the advent of more energy-efficient and environmentally friendly means of maritime transportation, Norway may evolve into an important gateway to Europe and to the Arctic in the near future. Indeed, the People's Republic of China has recognized the significance of the Arctic heralding a new era in global logistics by expressing a desire to "*advance Arctic-related cooperation under the Belt and Road Initiative, so as to build a community with a shared future for mankind and contribute to peace, stability and sustainable development in the Arctic*".[1] In respect of what is being coined as the Polar Silk Road, it has further been acknowledged by the People's Republic of China that: "*The utilization of sea routes and exploration and development of the resources in the Arctic may have a huge impact on the energy strategy and economic development of China.*"[2]

随着更节能、更环保的海上交通方式的出现，在不久的将来，挪威可能会发展为通往欧洲和北极的重要门户。中国曾表示，希望"在'一带一路'的倡议下，推动关于北极地区的合作，为人类构建未来共享的北极社区，推动北极地区的和平、稳定与可持续发展"。[3]这说明中国已经认识到北极在新时代全球物流中的重要性，进一步认可了所呈现出的"极地丝绸之路"："对海上航线的利用以及北极资源的勘探和开发可能对中国的能源战略和经济发展产生巨大影响。"[4]

Norway welcomes Chinese investments both with respect to business and infrastructure, and neither Norway nor its neighbours in the Arctic region (in particular Russia and Canada) will on its own be in a position to sustainably develop industrial and logistics infrastructure on the northernmost part of the globe without the participation of other important trade and development partners. From the perspective of Chinese interested parties, both capital investments (share transactions) and infrastructure projects may be of particular interest in light of the ambitious outline for the *Polar Silk Road*.

---

〔1〕 White paper: The State Council Information Office of the People's Republic of China (2018): *China's Arctic Policy*, 1st edition.

〔2〕 White paper: The State Council Information Office of the People's Republic of China (2018): *China's Arctic Policy*, 1st edition.

〔3〕 白皮书：《中国的北极政策》，中华人民共和国国务院新闻办公室2018年第1版。

〔4〕 白皮书：《中国的北极政策》，中华人民共和国国务院新闻办公室2018年第1版。

投资在挪威：在多种行业开展投资

挪威欢迎中国在商业和基础设施方面进行投资，若无他国的重要贸易和开发合作伙伴参与其中，挪威及其在北极地区（特别是俄罗斯和加拿大）的邻国均无法凭借自身在全球最北端可持续地开发工业和物流基础设施。从中国有意参与方的角度来看，鉴于其建设"极地丝绸之路"这一构想，资本投资（股权交易）和基础设施项目可能均会对其产生特别意义。

In 2019, the most active sectors in private M&A (Merger and Acquisition) in Norway was (according to Merger Market data) technology, media and telecommunications (22.2% of all reported deals), business services (17.7% of all reported deals) and industrials and chemicals (12.6% of all reported deals). However, in terms of deal value, the category of energy, mining and utilities was by far largest with a total deal value of all reported deals of USD 10.9 billion. This includes, for example, the acquisition of Cape Omega AS, a company providing infrastructure for transporting natural gas produced on the Norwegian continental shelf and exploration and development of oil and gas assets, for an undisclosed consideration by the Switzerland-based alternative asset management Partners Group Holding AG. The transaction was subject to approval by the Norwegian Ministry of Petroleum and Energy and was completed in June 2019.

2019年，挪威私人并购最活跃的领域是（根据Merger Market数据）技术，媒体和电信（占所有报告交易的22.2%），商业服务（占所有报告交易的17.7%）以及工业和化工（所有报告交易的12.6%）。其中，能源、采矿和公用事业类别迄今为止交易金额最大，所有已报告交易的交易总额为109亿美元。例如，收购Cape Omega AS，这是一家提供基础设施的公司，该基础设施可用于运输在挪威大陆架上生产的天然气以及勘探和开发油气资产，总部位于瑞士的可替代资产管理合作伙伴集团未公开收购价格。该交易经挪威石油和能源部批准，并于2019年6月完成。

With this as a starting point, we will in this chapter explore the particulars of Chinese inbound investments in Norway. We will both draw upon our particular experiences as a law firm and offer insight into aggregated data on Chinese inbound investments to Norway over the last couple of years. In any case, we will not focus on any sectors in particular, instead taking a broad perspective, as the Polar Silk Road vision is in itself having a broad scope and further aims to enable investments across a wide variety of sectors.

以此为出发点，本章将探讨中国投资者在挪威境内投资的具体情况。作为一家律师事务所，我们将利用我们的特殊经验，深入研究过去几年中国对挪威境内投资的汇总数据。总之，我们不会仅关注具体某个行业，而是会采取一种广泛的视角，正如"极地丝绸之路"具有广阔的前景，使跨越多个领域的投资成为可能。

1.2 挪威企业能吸引投资的重要因素（The Important Factors for Norwegian Ventures to Get Investments）

1.2.1 挪威可提供大量自然资源供养持续增长的全球人口（Norway can offer vast natural resources critical to sustaining an ever-growing global population）

Norway can play a key role in the future globalised economy by fulfilling a growing demand for protein sources and/or livestock consumption for human. According to an estimate by the United Nations, it is anticipated that there will be nearly 10 billion people on Earth by 2050. At the same time, it is urgent that the emissions of greenhouse gas are reduced. While the global supply of protein sources is steadily increasing, it is unequally available, and the demand is not met, in particular in third world countries. The lack of protein nutrients has been deemed a major global challenge. Sustainably managed, the oceans provide vast resources, and the Arctic region provides a great untapped potential in this respect. Being at the forefront of both fisheries and aquaculture industries and the sustainable management of fish stocks, Norway may be a key player in "feeding the world" in years to come.

挪威可通过满足人类对蛋白质和/或畜牧类产品不断增长的消耗需求，在未来的全球化经济中发挥关键作用。根据联合国的估计，预计到2050年，地球上将有近100亿人。与此同时，减少温室气体的排放量迫在眉睫。虽然全球蛋白质的供应量正在稳步增加，但其分布不均衡也无法满足需求，在第三世界国家尤为如此。蛋白质营养成分的缺乏被视为一项主要的全球性难题。通过可持续管理，海洋可提供大量资源，而北极地区在这方面提供了巨大的潜力。挪威处于渔业和水产养殖业以及鱼类资源的可持续管理的最前沿，可能成为未来几年"为世界提供食物"的关键角色。

1.2.2 挪威为中国投资者的经营而开放（Norway is open for business for Chinese investors）

While the revised National Security Act (2019) empowers Norwegian authorities to screen foreign direct investments in Norway on grounds of national security matters, the scope of the act is limited to businesses handling classified information (state secrets) or vital national interests. While the latter exception includes critical infrastructure in the definition of national interests, it remains a fact that there is no formal obstacles or thresholds to foreign direct investments in Norwegian companies or infrastructure originating in the People's Republic of China.[1] Several large corporations in Norway are owned, wholly or in part, by Chinese entities, and the Norwegian government is eager to attract more business with China following the normalisation of the diplomatic and political relations between the two countries in 2016.

虽然经2019年修订的《挪威国家安全法》授权挪威主管机关根据国家安全事项筛查外国对挪威进行的直接投资，但该法案的范围仅限于涉及机密信息（国家机密）或重要国家利益的企业。虽然后一种例外包括属于"国家利益"定义中的关键基础设施，但事实上，对外方给挪威公司或中方在挪威的基础设施建设直接投资并无正式的障碍或限制。[2]挪威的几家大公司全部或部分由中国实体拥有，自2016年中国和挪威两国的外交和政治关系正常化后，挪威政府希望吸引更多与中国一同开展的业务。

1.2.3 信息技术的广泛使用（Extensive use of information technology）

In an effort to diversify the economy and move into the "post-petroleum age", the burgeoning technology industry is central to the Norwegian Government's strategy of "green growth". Indeed, one of the major transactions involving Chinese buyer's in Norway in recent years was the acquisition of Opera Software AS, the creator of the Opera web browser, by Qihoo 360 Technology Co., Ltd. and others in 2016. Most aspects of daily life in Norway is in part subject to digital innovations, including in the

---

[1] It should be noted that there is a requirement that the CEO and at least half of the elected members to the Board of Directors are residents of Norway or the European Economic Area. This requirement may be waived by the Ministry of Trade and Fisheries upon application.

[2] 应当指出的是，此处具有一项要求，即首席执行官和至少一半的董事会当选成员应是挪威或欧洲经济区的居民。经向贸易和渔业部申请，此项要求可被豁免。

sphere of citizen's interaction with the government, payment services, etc.

为了实现经济多元化和步入"后石油时代",新兴技术产业是挪威政府"绿色增长"战略的核心。2016年,奇虎360科技有限公司及其他公司收购了Opera Software AS (Opera 网络浏览器的创建者)。事实上,这是近年来中国买家在挪威开展的主要交易之一。挪威的日常生活部分受到数字创新的影响,包括公民与政府的互动、支付服务等领域。

1.3 某些行业的监管要求(Regulatory requirements regarding certain sectors)

As mentioned above, some foreign direct investments may be subject to screening under the National Security Act. While its scope is broad, it would be an overstatement to claim that it is a barrier to Chinese (mainland) inbound investments on a general level. Furthermore, there is generally no requirement of any licenses to invest in or operate a business in Norway, unless sector-specific restrictions apply.[1] For sake of giving a correct picture of the regulatory landscape that a potential investor would have to navigate, we will give two brief examples of relevant regulatory requirements to be aware of in industries closely related but with very different approaches to regulating foreign ownership: Fisheries and aquaculture (fish farming).

如前文所述,某些外国直接投资可能需要根据《挪威国家安全法》进行筛查。虽然其范围很广,但通常来说,如称其为中国入境投资的一个障碍则未免夸大其词。此外,除适用某些限制的特殊行业外,通常在挪威投资或营业不需要获得任何许可。[2]为了准确描述潜在投资者必须确定的监管情况,我们将在渔业和水产养殖业(鱼类养殖)提供两个需注意的监管要求的简要示例,渔业和水产养殖业虽密切相关,但二者对外国所有权的监管体制差异很大。

1.3.1 渔业(Fisheries)

The fisheries and aquaculture sectors provide the third largest chunk of the total value of exports from Norway at approximately 12.5 billion US dollars in 2020. While both fisheries and aquaculture exports fish and fish-based products, there is significant

---

[1] For example, investment in power generating infrastructure, such as wind farms, are subject to a comprehensive regulatory regime. In many cases, however, the threshold to operate may only be a basic duty to self-certify compliance, e.g. with respect certain environmental requirements.

[2] 例如,对风电厂等发电基础设施的投资受到全面监管制度的约束。然而,在许多情况下,经营标准仅为自身确认是否合规的基本义务,例如,遵守某些环保方面的要求。

differences between the regulatory regimes applicable. As such, these are usually considered to be different industrial sectors altogether.

2020 年，挪威渔业和水产养殖业的产值约为 125 亿美元，是挪威出口总值中的第三大部分。虽然渔业和水产养殖业均出口鱼类和鱼类产品，但二者适用的监管制度存在显著差异。因此，二者通常被视为完全不同的产业。

With respect to inbound investments to Norway in the fisheries industry, a restrictive approach has been taken to ensure that a high degree of Norwegian ultimate ownership and title to fishing rights (quotas). This is one of the very few sectors where a requirement of obtaining permits to acquisition of rights/quotas apply. Fishing rights/quota primarily attach to fishing vessels. As a main rule, due to the acquisition permit system and the so-called "active duty requirement", only fishermen in active duty onboard may own more than 50% of quotas/fishing rights. Non-active rights holders are restricted to owning *less than* 50%. This threshold applies both to shares and voting rights, and the authorities take a strict approach with respect to any attempt to circumvent this rule via voting arrangements, etc.

关于对挪威境内的渔业投资，挪威已采取限制性措施，确保挪威拥有高度的最终所有权和捕捞权（配额）。这是极少数须获得权利/配额许可证的行业之一。捕捞权/配额主要与渔船相关。作为一项主要规则，由于许可证取得制度和所谓的"现时义务要求"，只有现时从事捕捞活动的渔民可以持有超过 50% 的配额/捕鱼权。非现时从事捕捞活动的渔民持有的配额/捕鱼权不可超过 50%。该限制适用于股票和投票权，对于通过投票安排等方式规避规则的任何企图，主管机关会采取严格的处理方法。

Furthermore, a specific restriction on foreign ownership applies. Irrespective of whether foreign shareholders are in active fishing duty or not, foreign persons or entities cannot own more than 40% of a set of quotas/permits. Again, the authorities take a strict approach to this threshold. While there has been significant interest from certain Chinese parties in investing in fishing vessels with quotas, for example to ensure supply of raw materials for use in food production, this threshold has in practice barred several interested parties from moving ahead with investment plans as it restricts the ability to take control in such ventures.

此外，对外国所有权适用具体的限制。无论外国股东是否现时从事捕捞活动,外国自然人或实体都不能持有超过40%的配额/许可证。同样,主管机关对该限制采取严格的处理方法。虽然中国的某些投资方十分有意向对具有配额的渔船进行投资(例如,投资该类渔船以确保用于食品生产的原材料供应),但由于该限制束缚了控制此类项目的能力,实际上阻碍了数个有意的投资方推进投资计划。

1.3.2 水产养殖业(Aquaculture)

With respect to aquaculture (fish farming) there is in principle no restriction on foreign ownership. The vast majority of fishfarming facilities is currently based on in-water fish pens, and the market is dominated by large Norway-based actors like MOWI (formerly Marine Harvest), Lerøy Seafood Group, Cermaq[1] and SalMar. These are indeed also the fourth largest fish farmers globally. Foreign investors are continually looking to get into the Norwegian market by acquiring licenses, but sale of licenses are very rare. New licenses are rarely issued, partly as a means to control the spread of fish health problems (salmon lice, pancreatic disease, etc.), and this currently represents a major obstacle to foreign investment.

对于水产养殖(鱼类养殖),原则上对外国所有权没有任何限制。当前绝大多数的养鱼设施以水中的鱼栏为基础,该市场主要由挪威的大型从业者支配,如MOWI(前身为Marine Harvest)、Lerøy Seafood Group、Cermaq[2]和SalMar。事实上,这些企业也是全球第四大鱼类养殖商。外国投资者不断寻求通过获得许可证进入挪威市场的机会,但许可证的销售非常罕见。挪威很少签发新的许可证,一定程度上是一种控制鱼类疾病(鲑鱼虱、胰腺疾病等)传播的手段,这也是目前外国投资的主要障碍。

However, plans and investments are being made to establish facilities for onshore farming for the entire lifespan of the fish. Technology based on recirculation and recycling of water in large on-shore tanks are currently being tried out, but there are inherent issues with on-shore farming that still needs sorting out before mass commercialisation of on-shore fish farming can happen. In particular, outages relating to supply of oxygen or fresh water could in theory kill off entire stocks of fish in a matter of minutes. Should the technology be able to deal with this hazard, there is great potential in

---

[1] A majority of shares in Cermaq is owned by the Japanese Mitsubishi corporation.
[2] Cermaq的大部分股份由日本三菱公司持有。

both onshore farming projects and investments in the companies developing the technological solutions.

但是，正在进行中的规划和投资是为了建立用于鱼类整个生长周期的陆上养殖设施。目前，对大型陆上水箱内的水循环和水回收利用技术正在测试，但是，在陆上养殖大规模商业化之前，仍有一些固有问题需要解决。尤其是氧气或淡水的供应中断理论上可以在几分钟内致使整个鱼群死亡。一旦该技术能够应对这种风险，那么对于陆上养殖和开发该技术的公司的投资将均具有很大的潜力。

2. 交易结构（Transaction Structure）

2.1 投资项目简介（Introduction of the Investment Projects）

Over the last few years, several inbound transactions to Norway by Chinese investors have made headlines in Norway. Of the ones announced publicly, the following are considered the most significant:[1]

在过去几年中，中国投资者在挪威境内的几次交易均成为挪威的头条新闻。在公开公布的交易当中，以下交易被视为最重要的交易（如表1所示）:[2]

表1 重要交易信息

Buyer/买方	Target/目标公司	Sector/行业	Value/价格（USD）	Announced/公告日
QuMei Investment AS 曲美投资股份公司	Ekornes ASA	Furniture/家具	$696 000 000	May 2018/2018年5月
Qihoo 360 Technology Co., Ltd. 奇虎360科技有限公司；Beijing Kunlun Tech Co., Ltd. 北京昆仑万维科技股份有限公司；Golden Brick Capital Management Ltd. 金砖资本管理有限公司；	Opera Software AS	Technology (developer of the Opera web browser) 技术（Opera网络浏览器的开发者）	$575 000 000	July 2016 2016年7月

---

[1] Source: Mergermarket.
[2] 数据来源于 Mergermarket。

续表

Buyer/买方	Target/目标公司	Sector/行业	Value/价格（USD）	Announced/公告日
Reignwood Group 华彬集团	Voss of Norway ASA	High-end consumer water brand VOSS 高端饮用水品牌VOSS	$ 84 000 000	Jan 2016 2016年1月
Bluestar Elkem Investment Co., Ltd. 蓝星埃肯投资股份有限公司	REC Solar Holdings AS	Solar panels 太阳能电池板	$ 566 000 000	Nov 2014/ 2014年11月
China National Bluestar (Group) Co., Ltd. 中国蓝星集团股份有限公司	Elkem ASA	Silicone products and alloys 硅产品及合金	$ 2 349 000 000	Jan 2011/ 2011年1月

The latest major transaction was the 2018 acquisition by the well-respected QuMei Furniture Group Co., Ltd. of the Norway-based furniture manufacturer Ekornes ASA. Ekornes is one of the largest manufacturers of furniture in Europe. Being primarily known for its "Stressless" range of recliners, it operates in an exclusive segment that complements the existing offering of QuMei Furniture. Ekornes was at the time of acquisition a listed company. After a lengthy process with the management and Board of Directors of the Company, the voluntary offer was issued in May 2019. After receiving acceptances for the offer from well in excess of 98% of the shareholders, the remaining shares were redeemed.

最近的主要交易是2018年著名的曲美家居集团股份有限公司对总部位于挪威的家具制造商Ekornes ASA的收购。Ekornes是欧洲最大的家具制造商之一，该公司主要以其"Stressless"系列的躺椅而闻名，它在独有的细分领域中开展经营，可增补曲美家居的现有产品。在收购时，Ekornes是一家上市公司。经过与公司管理层和董事会进行磋商的漫长过程后，自愿要约于2019年5月发出。在收到超过98%的股东对要约作出的承诺后，剩余的股份被回购。

However, the table above clearly shows us that the various transactions span across a range of industries and, as such, the industry specific examples provided in this chapter should not in any way be seen as limiting the generality of the issues raised in this article.

但是，上表清楚地说明，各交易跨越多种行业，因此，在任何方面，本章中提供的行业特别示例均不应被视为限制了本文中提出的问题的一般性。

In this part of the article, we will draw upon the experiences relating to several of such major Chinese acquisitions in Norway. In addition, where relevant, we will draw upon recent cases in which we have had the pleasure to advise on aspects of the acquisition of Norwegian companies by Chinese entities, drawing upon our collective experiences as a full-service law firm. Due to Norwegian client-privilege rules being very strict, we offer specifics to the extent we are legally allowed to.

在本文的这一部分，我们将介绍中国收购方在挪威进行的几项重大收购的相关经验。此外，在近期收购类的案例中，我们有幸为中国实体收购挪威公司提供方方面面的建议，我们将借鉴其中的相关经验，同时，我们也将总结作为一家提供全方位服务的律师事务所的全部经验。由于挪威的"客户特权"规则非常严格，我们将在法律允许的范围内提供具体信息。

2.2 交易文件（Transaction Documents）

In connection with a share purchase transaction, the seller and the buyer will enter into a share purchase agreement (SPA), which will govern the rights and obligations of the parties with respect to the sale and transfer of the shares in the capital of the target company.

就股份购买交易而言，卖方和买方将签订股份购买协议（SPA），买卖双方出售和转让目标公司股份的权利和义务将适用该协议。

Under Norwegian law, it is common practice that the parties enter into a non-disclosure agreement prior to exchange of information with respect to the target company. Such NDA is often entered into in combination with a letter of intent, memorandum of understanding or term sheet setting out the main terms of the transaction, such as price, right to perform due diligence investigation on the target company, indicative time line, exclusivity, appurtenant agreements as a condition for the contemplated transaction, such as shareholder agreements, choice of law and venue. Even though a letter of intent or similar is of a non-binding character the main terms of the transaction is negotiated at such stage of the process and any deviation from such terms must in practise and in order to gain commercial acceptance be explained through specific findings during the due diligence investigation, other information received from the target company or the seller or supported by deviation from assumptions set out in the term sheet. It is therefore recommended that legal advisors are engaged at an early stage of the process.

根据挪威法律，通常的做法是，双方在就目标公司的信息进行交换之前，先行签订保密协议（NDA）。此类 NDA 通常与列明价格、对目标公司进行尽职调查的权利、指示性时间安排、排他性、作为拟议交易条件的附属协议（例如股东协议、法律和地点的选择等）等交易主要条款的意向书、合作备忘录或投资条款清单相结合而订立。虽然意向书或类似文件不具有约束性，但在交易过程的这一阶段会对交易的主要条款进行磋商。在实践中，为了获得商业认可，任何偏离这些条款的行为均须通过尽职调查期间的具体调查结果、自目标公司或卖方获得的其他信息加以解释，或通过条款中假设的偏离行为加以支持。因此，建议法律顾问在交易过程的早期阶段就参与其中。

Several of the transactions listed above, most recently the Ekornes ASA acquisition, did not entail any SPA. Prior to the Board issuing its recommendation, however, listed companies and an offeror is expected to enter into a co-operation or transaction agreement, provided that the offer will be recommended by the Board of Directors to the shareholders. Such agreements will often set out details concerning the procedure concerning the offer and the recommendation thereof. However, prior to announcing a recommended offer, the Board may have a lengthy process with the interested party subject to an NDA.

上述几项交易（最近的一项交易是对 Ekornes ASA 的收购）并未涉及任何股份购买协议。然而，在董事会提议之前，如果上市公司和要约人预计会签订合作或交易协议，将由董事会向股东提出要约。此类协议通常会载明有关要约程序及其提议的细节。但是，在公布提出的报价之前，董事会可能需要就 NDA 与利益相关方进行漫长的协商流程。

2.3 尽职调查（Due Diligence）

It is common practice in merger and acquisitions conducted in Norway to perform a due diligence review, in particular with the purchase of at least 90% of the shareholding. In acquiring a public listed company, the due diligence is more limited. In cases related to acquiring a portion of the shareholding, the performance of a due diligence may require a consent of the other shareholder(s) either due to a shareholder's agreement or as a requirement from the board of directors of the target company wanting to ensure equal treatment of the shareholders. The due diligence is in most cases carried out prior to negotiating the share purchase agreement or merger agreement. The purpose of such an investigation is identifying key issues relating to the transaction and resolve such issues in the transaction documents either through representation and warranties, indemnification or as issues to be resolved as a condition and prior to closing or directly lowering the purchase price.

在挪威进行的合并和收购中,进行尽职调查是惯例,特别是在购买目标公司 90% 以上股份的情况下。在收购一家上市公司时,尽职调查受到更多的限制。在收购部分股权的情况下,开展尽职调查可能需要得到其他股东的同意,这可能是基于股东协议,也可能是基于目标公司董事会确保平等对待股东的要求。在大多数情况下,尽职调查开展于就股份购买协议或合并协议进行谈判之前。此类调查的目的是确定与交易相关的关键问题,并通过陈述、保证、赔偿、以问题的解决作为交割前的条件并直接降低购买价格。

2.4 竞争法备案(Competition Law Filings)

2.4.1 挪威与欧盟竞争法(Norwegian and EU competition law)

Under Norwegian law, all corporate transactions, mergers and amalgamations (concentrations) that *"will create or strengthen a significant restriction of competition"* are prohibited to the extent that no particular exception applies. All concentrations above a certain revenue-based threshold [1] shall be notified to the Norwegian Competition Authority for assessment. The Norwegian Competition Act 2004 (Competition Act) provides a system of merger control for all businesses and operations relevant to the Norwegian economy.

---

[1] Subject to section 18 of the Norwegian Competition Act, the obligation to provide notification of a concentration does not apply *"if the undertakings concerned have a combined annual turnover in Norway below 1 billion kroner (ca. USD 114 million), or only one of the undertakings concerned have an annual turnover in Norway that exceeds 100 million kroner (ca. USD 11.4 million)"*. Note, however, that a transaction involving entities that fall well below the threshold could still be considered as prohibited on the grounds that the concentration will restrict competition in a market.

根据挪威法律，所有"将造成或加强对竞争的显著限制"的公司交易、兼并和合并（集中）均被禁止，无一例外。所有超过某一限制（该限制基于收入而定）[1]的集中均应向挪威竞争主管机关进行报告以备评估。2004年《挪威竞争法》（以下简称《竞争法》）规定了适用于与挪威经济相关的所有企业和业务的兼并控制制度。

Norway is not a European Union (EU) member state. However, as a member of the European Economic Area (EEA), Norway is nevertheless subject to EU competition law rules in the sense that the legislation of Norway and other EEA, EFTA states shall be in line with EU Single Market legislation. While Norway is constitutionally unable to take EU regulations and directives as binding law directly, EU acts relating to competition is continuously transposed into domestic Norwegian law. As such, concentrations that create or strengthen a dominant position resulting in a significant restriction of effective competition is prohibited. The questions of whether effective competition is prohibited is assessed on the basis of relevant markets for the products and/or services involved, both in a broad and narrow sense.

挪威并非欧盟（EU）的成员国。但是，作为欧洲经济区（EEA）的成员，挪威和其他欧洲经济区（EEA）、欧洲自由贸易联盟（EFTA）的国家的立法应符合欧盟单一市场立法，从这种意义上说，挪威仍然遵守《欧盟竞争法》的规则。虽然挪威在宪法上无法直接将欧盟法规和指令作为具有约束力的法律，但欧盟有关竞争的法律不断地被转入挪威国内法。因此，造成或加强支配地位从而严重限制有效竞争的集中将受到禁止。有效竞争是否受到阻止的问题，须根据所涉产品和/或服务的相关市场（在广义和狭义上）进行评估。

Under the Competition Act, concentrations shall be deemed to arise where:

根据《竞争法》，出现下列情形时，应认为集中出现：

(a) two or more previously independent undertakings or parts of undertakings merge; or

(a) 两个或两个以上之前独立的企业或企业的一部分合并；或者

(b) one or more persons already controlling at least one undertaking or one or

---

[1] 根据《挪威竞争法》第18条规定，"如果相关企业在挪威的年营业总额低于10亿克朗（约合1.14亿美元），或仅有一个相关企业在挪威的年营业额超过1亿克朗（约合1140万美元），则不适用报告集中的义务。"但请注意，相关实体低于限制的交易仍可能因市场竞争被集中所限制而被禁止。

more undertakings acquire direct or indirect control on a lasting basis of the whole or parts of one or more other undertakings.

(b) 已经控制至少一个或多个企业的一个或多个自然人,直接或间接获得对一个或多个其他企业的全部或部分进行持久控制的权利。

The creation of a joint venture performing on a lasting basis all the functions of an autonomous economic entity, shall constitute a concentration within the meaning of the first paragraph (b).

设立一个持久地履行自治经济实体的所有职能的合资企业,应构成(b)款所述的集中。

It is irrelevant whether the acquisition occurs by purchase of securities or assets, by contract or by other means. It is further not relevant to assess whether the acquisition is made by obtaining direct or indirect control of the whole or parts of one or more other undertakings.

收购系通过购买证券或资产、合同或其他方式进行与集中的认定无关。收购系通过直接或间接控制一个或多个企业的全部或部分亦与此无关。

While concentrations exceeding the above-mentioned threshold values (as regards the turnover of the undertakings concerned) will have to be notified to the Competition Authority of Norway, a concentration remaining below the threshold turnover levels may be effectuated without a notification to the Competition Authority. Subject to section 18 of the Competition Act, the Competition Authority may direct to involved parties to give notification where the threshold has not been exceeded. The applicable deadline for the Competition Authority to give such order of forced notification is the earlier of three months from the date of the agreement concerning the concentration and three months from the date when control is obtained. Concentrations may under any circumstance be notified to the Competition Authority on a voluntary basis.

虽然超出上述限额(与相关企业的营业额有关)的集中必须向挪威竞争管理局报告,但对于低于营业额标准限制的集中,则可以不经向竞争管理局报告而实行。根据《竞争法》第18条的规定,竞争管理局可以指示参与方在未超过限制的情况下作出报告。竞争管理局发出强制报告命令的截止日期是自集中协议签订之日起三个月内和获得控制权之日起的三个月内。在任何情况下,均可以自愿地向竞争管理局报告集中。

A concentration that has been effectuated without having been duly notified or without the parties observing the appropriate waiting period will be regarded as being null and void under the laws of the Norway.

根据挪威法律，未经及时通知或当事方未遵守适当等待期限而实施的集中被视为无效。

The Competition Authority has wide powers to impose fines and orders in the context of concentration control. Failure to notify a concentration will usually lead to a fine upon discovery by the Competition Authority. Both companies and directors involved can be fined in this regard. Fines for companies may run up to 1 percent of the total turnover in the year preceding the year of the fine in the event of failure to give mandatory notification and up to 10 percent of the total turnover in the event of a breach of the general prohibition relating to acts restricting competition.

竞争管理局拥有广泛的权力，可以在集中控制的范围内进行罚款和下达指令。如未能报告集中，一经发现，竞争管理局通常会进行罚款。涉事公司和董事都可能因此而被罚款。如未能履行强制性报告义务，则公司应缴的罚款最多可达罚款前一年总营业额的1%，如违反了与限制竞争相关的法案的一般性义务，则罚款最多可达总营业额的10%。

With respect to the transactions listed in the section 2.1 above, several of the transactions will have been above the threshold for notification either nationally or at the EU level (see below), but in several instances it would be sufficient to give simplified notice as there was no overlap in terms of the markets in which the buyer and the target operated (vertically or horizontally).

就上文第2.1节中列出的交易而言，一些超出国家或欧盟层面报告限制（见下文）的交易需要向监管部门报告，但在某些情况下，由于买方与目标公司在并不重合的市场范围内开展经营（在纵向或横向的意义上），因此，仅向监管部门进行简化性的报告即可。

2.4.2 欧盟竞争法（EU competition law）

Under the Economic Concentration Regulation 139/2004, any concentration with an EU dimensions will be subject to the examination and clearance by the EU commission. The concept of a "concentration" includes both merger of independent entities, acquisition of direct or indirect control and the establishment of joint ventures entailing joint control of a full-function joint venture.

根据第 139/2004 号经济集中条例，任何具有欧盟规模的集中都将受到欧盟委员会的审查和批准。"经营者集中"的概念包括独立实体的合并和直接或间接地控制以及建立合资企业（包括共同控制一个职能完备的合资企业）。

Whether or not there is an EU dimension depends on whether the companies involved in the concentration reach the turnover thresholds. There are to alternative turnover thresholds, of which at least one must be met for the transaction to be considered having an EU dimension:

经营者集中是否达到欧盟规模视参与集中的公司是否达到营业额限制而定。除营业额限制外，还另有其他限制，即若交易满足以下至少一个条件，则应视其具有欧盟规模：

(i) a combined worldwide turnover of all the merging firms over €5000 million, and an EU-wide turnover for each of at least two of the firms over €250 million.

(i) 所有合并公司的全球总营业额超过 50 亿欧元，并且至少两家公司在欧盟范围内的营业额超过 2.5 亿欧元。

(ii) a worldwide turnover of all the merging firms over €2500 million, and a combined turnover of all the merging firms over €100 million in each of at least three Member States, a turnover of over €25 million for each of at least two of the firms in each of the three Member States included under ii, and EU-wide turnover of each of at least two firms of more than €100 million.

(ii) 所有合并公司的全球营业额超过 25 亿欧元，并且所有合并公司的总营业额在至少三个成员国内超过 1 亿欧元，至少两个公司的营业额在 (ii) 中所述的三个成员国内超过 2500 万欧元，以及欧盟范围内至少两家公司的营业额超过 1 亿欧元。

If any alternative threshold is exceeded, the concentration must be notified to the EU Commission. Similar to the national notification regime, a simplified procedure will apply if the involved firms are not operating in the same or related markets, or if they have only very small market shares not reaching specified market share thresholds.

如经营者集中超出了任何一项其他限制，则必须上报至欧盟委员会。与国家报告制度类似，如果涉及的公司不在相同或相关市场中营业，或者它们的市场份额极小，未达到规定的市场份额限制，则将适用简化程序。

A particularly relevant example would be the 2011 acquisition of the Norwegian silicone and alloy products manufacturer Elkem ASA by China National Bluestar (Group) Co., Ltd. (Bluestar). The involved parties exceeded the notification thresholds as each party had an EU-wide turnover in excess of the threshold (EUR 250 million). As Bluestar's parent company China National Chemical Corporation was wholly owned by the People's Republic of China, the Commission considered the hypothetical case of how it would affect competition if "*assuming all Chinese State-owned firms in the sector acted as one*". While, the pertinent entities did in fact not act in concert, this serves to underline the broad assessment undertaken by the Commission. At the end of the investigations, the European Competition Commissioner, Mr Joaquín Almunia, said: "*The Commission examined this merger carefully for possible coordination by the Chinese State of market behaviour of Chinese State-owned companies in the same sector as we also do for mergers involving European State-owned undertakings,*" adding that "*this case is a further illustration of our continuous effort to preserve effective competition in the market while being fair and transparent*".

一个与此十分相关的案例是2011年中国蓝星（集团）股份有限公司（以下简称蓝星）对挪威硅及合金产品制造商Elkem ASA的收购。由于参与方在欧盟范围内的营业额超过了限制（2.5亿欧元），因此超出了须进行报告的标准。由于蓝星的母公司中国化工集团公司是中国国有全资子公司，因此，竞争委员会考虑到，如果"假设此行业的所有中国国有企业如同一个整体行动一致"，则竞争会受到何种影响。虽然有关实体事实上并非行动一致，但这使得委员会强调进行全面的评估。在调查结束时，欧洲竞争委员Joaquín Almunia先生谈道："委员会仔细调查了此次合并，以确定在同一行业中中国国有企业可能进行合作的市场行为可能造成的影响，这正如我们对欧洲国有企业合并进行的审查一样"，他还补充说："这个案例进一步说明了我们在保持市场有效竞争的同时，为维护市场公平透明作出持续性努力。"

3. 项目融资方式（Project financing method/methods）

3.1 挪威境内并购交易的对价（Introduction on Consideration in M&A Transactions in Norway）

Almost without exception, most sellers prefer cash consideration upon closing, and this is also the main form of consideration, funded by debt or equity or typically, a combination. In all transactions where we have advised a party concerning M&A transactions in Norway originating in China, the starting point from the Norwegian party or parties have been a preference for settlement in cash. Time and again we do see attempts by listed interested parties to defer the consideration (e.g. by vendor notes) and/or to settle the consideration upon acquisition of private companies by issuing shares in the buyer (or its listed parent company). While sellers generally do not prefer this, it is perhaps particularly relevant in the context of distressed transactions. Other means of consideration may be considered,[1] but this is not at all very common in practice.

几乎无一例外，多数卖方在交割时更乐于接受现金对价，这也是支付对价的一种主要方式，现金对价的资金来源通常为债或股权或者债股结合的方式。在我们为中方就挪威境内的并购提供咨询的所有交易中，挪威参与方往往首先会倾向于以现金结算。我们确曾数次见到已上市意向方试图推迟支付现金对价（例如，通过卖方票据）和/或通过发行买方（或其已上市的母公司）股票收购私人公司的方式来支付对价。但卖家通常对此不愿接受，在陷入困境的交易中可能尤为如此。其他形式的对价也可以考虑，[2]但这在实践中并不常见。

In some cases, the buyer and the seller are not able to easily come to an agreement as to the enterprise value of the target. In these instances, both industrial investors and private equity investors may offer to bridge the gap in respect of the differing viewpoints on valuation by means of an earn-out component. This is also commonplace to try to incentivise management or founder to stay on board for a certain period. A usual

---

[1] For example, payment-in-kind, warrants or options, etc.
[2] 例如，实物、认股权证或期权等。

pitfall from the seller's perspective is that a demanding transaction process "drains" the company of a certain amount of energy and leaving a perceived vacuum in the period immediately following closing. In these instances, getting a head start on fulfilling the financial targets usually associated with the earn-out turns out to be very hard.

在某些情况下，买方和卖方无法轻易就目标企业的价值达成协议。在这些情况下，产业投资者和私募股权投资者可以通过收购价款分期支付的方式来弥合不同估值之间的差距。激励管理层或创始人在一定时期内留在董事会也是普遍的做法。从卖方的角度来看，一个常见的隐患是，苛刻的交易过程会"耗费"公司的许多精力，使得公司立刻在交割后的一段时间内处于明显的真空状态。在这种情况下，结合收购价款分期支付安排，开始实现财务目标往往十分困难。

3.2 通常的融资方式（Usual means of financing）

As mentioned above, the most common form of consideration is by cash payment as a lump sum. According to the offer documents publicly available, this was for example also the case with respect to the recent acquisition of Ekornes ASA by QuMei Furniture. With respect to the financing of the consideration, a certain amount of equity will be required as banks and financial institutions will in most cases be hesitant to offer loan financing arrangement for the entire consideration to be paid at closing. The reason for this is that the value of the assets available as security will in most cases not be considered sufficient to make a fully leveraged transaction prudent and the lender wants the borrower to have "skin in the game".

如上所述，最常见的对价形式是一次性的现金支付。例如，根据公开的发行文件，曲美家居对 Ekornes ASA 的收购即是如此。至于对价的融资，则需要一定的股权，这是因为在多数情况下，银行和金融机构不愿提供用于在交割时支付全部对价的贷款融资安排。因为在大多数情况下，可用作担保的资产不足以使杠杆交易的进行完全审慎可靠，并且贷方希望借方可以"亲临游戏"以在交易中承担一定的风险。

The terms of the financing offered will depend on the individual circumstances pertaining to each transaction, but in general higher credit risk (and other risks) will imply higher interest rate and stricter financial and other covenants. The arrangement of security satisfactory to the lender (s) will also be part of the negotiations.

具体的融资条件由交易的具体情况决定。但总体而言，信用风险（以及其他风险)越高,意味着利率越高,融资条款和其他的约定条款越严格。贷方满意的担保安排也将成为谈判的一部分。

We have seen in the last few years that credit worthy buyers with highly levered loans, have been able to rearrange financing on more borrower friendly terms shortly after closing, either in the loan or bond market. This requires of course that the borrowing terms permits early prepayment of the original loan and a favorable loan/bond market. One example is the aforementioned recent acquisition of Ekornes ASA by QuMei Furniture: approximately 12 months after it was closed, Ekornes QM Holding AS (QuMei Furniture's acquisition vehicle) issued a NOK 2 billion bond loan maturing in October 2023 and which was listed on Oslo Stock Exchange. According to the publicly available prospectus, the purpose of said issue was, in part, to apply the net proceeds of the issue amount towards repayment in full of existing shareholder loans.

在过去的几年,我们注意到高借贷但信用评级优秀的买家,能够在贷款市场或债券市场交易结束不久,以更有利于借款人的条件实行再融资。当然,这不仅需要一个更有利的贷款市场或债券市场,也需要借款条款允许提前偿还原始贷款。例如,在前述曲美家居收购Ekornes ASA的案例中,曲美家居在收购完成约12个月后,Ekornes QM Holdings AS(曲美家居的收购实体)发行了一笔2023年10月到期、价值20亿挪威克朗的债券贷款,并于奥斯陆证券交易所上市。根据公开的招股说明书可知,该发行的部分目的是将发行净额用于全额偿还现有的股东贷款。

With respect to vendor notes (short-term loan from seller to purchaser), the entire consideration may be deferred, although this is not very common in practice. It is usually a written precondition stated in the vendor note that the purchaser shall use such loan solely for paying the purchase price for the shares. Subject to the terms of the vendor notes, for which the parties are free to agree whatever they find acceptable, the purchaser has to repay the vendor loan including interest within a certain term.

供应商票据(卖方发放给买方的短期贷款)可以推迟所有对价的支付,但这在实践中并不常见。通常,在供应商票据中会写明一个前提条件,即购买者仅能使用此类贷款来支付股票的购买价格。根据供应商票据的条款(当事人可以自由地对他们认为可以接受的任何条款达成协定),买方须在一定期限内偿还供应商贷款及利息。

3.3 以目标公司的资产作为并购融资的担保（Taking the Target Company's Assets as Security for Acquisition Financing）

Note that prior to 2020, upstream financing from the target company (in other words financing the transaction by means of a loan or other means of financial assistance, including the furnishing of security, from the target company itself) was limited to the amount (s) which the company could legally distribute to shareholders as dividends. This applied both with respect to private and public limited liability companies.

请注意，在2020年之前，目标公司的上游融资（换句话说，是通过目标公司本身的贷款或其他金融援助手段，包括提供担保）为交易融资的金额不得超过公司可以合法地作为股息分配给股东的金额。这适用于私营和公共有限责任公司。

However, with effect from 1 January 2020, the aforementioned rules [1] have been changed with respect to private companies and are now more flexible with respect to the possibility of using the target company's assets as security for acquisition financing. The cap equal to the distributable dividend amount do not apply if the following two conditions are fulfilled：

但是，自2020年1月1日起，上述规则[2]已针对私人公司进行了更改，现在将目标公司的资产用作收购融资担保的可能性更加灵活。如果满足以下两个条件，则交易融资的金额等于可分配股息金额上限的限制则不适用：

Firstly, the company to which the upstream financing is granted must be domiciled in the EU/EEA. This applies only directly to the recipient of the financing, and parent companies of the recipient may therefore be domiciled outside of the EU/EEA.

首先，必须在欧盟/欧洲经济区注册其上游融资的公司。这仅直接适用于融资的接受者，因此，接受者的母公司则可能位于欧盟/欧洲经济区之外。

Secondly, the acquisition of shares in the company granting the upstream financing must result in the creation of a group of companies in which the buyer will become the parent company with determinative influence over the target company.

其次，获得上游融资的股份收购必须导致创建多家公司，其中买方将成为

---

〔1〕 See section 8-10 of the Norwegian Private Limited Liability Companies Act as amended.
〔2〕 参见经修订的《挪威私人有限责任公司法》第8—10条。

对目标公司具有决定性影响的母公司。

If the above conditions are fulfilled, the target company may grant credit, pledge its assets or provide other forms of financial assistance [1] subject to compliance with certain formal procedures and up to an amount as determined by the board of directors, provided that this does not interfere with the statutory requirement of having "*adequate equity and liquidity*".[2] These formal procedures include a credit evaluation of the borrower, a board resolution, a shareholder resolution approving the board's resolution by a two thirds majority and a duty to publicly register a statement from the board of directors of the target company stating, inter alia, that "*it is in the interest of the company to provide the assistance*". If the formal procedures are not followed, the upstream financial assistance may be at risk of being invalid.[3]

如果满足上述条件，则目标公司可以授予信贷，抵押其资产或提供其他形式的融资援助，[4]但要遵守某些正式程序，但最高限额不超过董事会确定的数额，也不得干扰法定要求，即"拥有足够的股本和流动性"。这些正式程序包括对借款人的信用评估、董事会决议、以三分之二多数同意批准董事会决议的股东决议以及目标公司董事会经注册的公开声明，声明中需要包括："提供符合公司利益的援助"。如果不遵循正式程序，上游融资援助可能会面临无效的风险。[5]

4. 交易文件中的关键条款 (Key Terms in Transaction Documents)

4.1 股份购买协议（SPA）

With respect to the SPA, the following terms are of great importance (please note that this is not an exhaustive list, but just some examples):

关于股份购买协议（SPA），下述条款十分重要（请注意，此处并非穷尽性的列举，而是仅举几例）：

● Payment of the purchase price is commonly governed by share purchase agreements in Norway as a payment in cash at closing. In many cases it is stipulated as a

---

[1] This exception does not apply to public companies.
[2] See section 3-4 of the Norwegian Private Limited Liability Companies Act.
[3] Pursuant to section § 8-11 of the Norwegian Private Limited Liability Companies Act.
[4] 此项例外不适用于公众公司。
[5] 根据《挪威私人有限责任公司法》第8-11条。

condition that key shareholders re-invest a portion of the purchase price in a joint holding company together with the purchaser in order to ensure a carried interest. Earn-out arrangements are also quite common in Norway. By earn-out clauses we mean payment arrangements linked to the post-closing performance of sellers (in many cases the sellers/managing directors of target companies' stay also after closing). However, be aware that in Norway if earn-out payments or similar is linked to a duty and obligation to stay-on for a certain period as an employee, the payment of the earn-out will likely be considered as salary and taxed as salary by the Norwegian tax authorities.

● 挪威通常规定在交割时以现金支付购买价格。在许多情况下，这会被规定为主要股东与买方一同向联合控股公司再次投入购买价格的条件，以确保附股权益。在挪威，收购价款分期支付安排也很常见；这些付款安排与卖方交割后的业绩挂钩（在许多情况下，目标公司的卖方/董事总经理在交割后也会留任）。但是，请注意，在挪威，如果收购价款分期支付或类似的安排与雇员在一定期限内保持留任的责任和义务挂钩，则相关款项将被挪威税务主管机关视为工资薪金，并按工资薪金的税率计税。

● Adjustment of the purchase price: Increasingly, the traditional Closing Accounts mechanism by which the final purchase price is settled on the basis of balance sheet adjustments after the actual closing date, is being replaced by the "Locked Box" mechanism. A particularly important part of the Locked Box is the Leakage clause, under which the seller and target company is prohibited from declaring any dividend, making any distributions, or incurring new debt, settling debt or other payments outside ordinary course of business in the period between the Locked Box accounts date (which may be prior to signing of the transaction documents) and the execution of the deed of transfer/closing.

● 购买价格的调整：传统的交割账户机制，即在实际交割日后根据资产负债表的调整结算最终购买价格的机制，正在逐渐被"锁箱"机制取代。"防泄漏"条款是"锁箱"的一个十分重要的部分，根据该条款，在"锁箱日"（可能在交易文件签署之前）和转让/交割契约签署之间，卖方和目标公司不得在正常营业过程之外宣布任何股息、进行任何分配、产生新的债务以及对债务或其他付款进行结算。

● Limitation of liability: In the event that one of the parties to the SPA is in breach of its contractual obligations contained therein, the other party may hold the defaulting party liable. In this respect, it is common practice to include wording pertaining to the limitation of liability. Usually, certain thresholds are included in the share purchase agreement. These limitations usually only apply to breaches of the warranties; typically, in case of damages under the indemnifications, the liability of the seller is unlimited (obviously, this also depends on the negotiations). It should be considered whether and to what extent liability for Seller's Knowledge should be excluded.

• 责任限制：如果 SPA 的任何一方违反了合同中包含的义务，另一方可要求其承担违约责任。在这方面，通常的做法是在合同中加入与责任限制有关的措辞。通常，某些限制包含在股票购买协议中。这些限制通常仅适用于违反保证的行为；一般而言，在赔偿损失的情况下，卖方的责任是无限的（显然，这也取决于谈判）。应当考虑在何种程度上或者是否应免除卖家的知情责任。

Also to be considered are escrow arrangements with respect to parts of the purchase price, whether to include a MAC clause (materially adverse conditions) as a closing condition, the amount and level of disclosure relating to representations and warranties, etc.

还应当考虑的是，与部分购买价格相关的第三方托管是否应包括作为一项交割条件的 MAC 条款（重大不利条件）以及包括与陈述和保证相关的披露信息量和程度等。

Upon signing of the SPA, the shares are not transferred immediately. Under the laws of Norway, the legal title to the transferred shares is completed by means of notification from the shareholder to the target company represented by its board of directors, documentation that such notification has been recorded in the shareholders registry and documentation of approval of the new shareholder by the board of directors of the target company. In general, no corporate actions or entering into of any contracts in Norway requires the presence or assistance of a notary.

签署 SPA 之后，股份不会立即转让。根据挪威法律，转让股份的法定所有权须通过股东向目标公司（由董事会代表）发出通知的方式完成，且该通知应以文件的形式记录于股东登记处，目标公司董事会的新股东作出的批准亦应以文件的方式记录。一般而言，在挪威，任何公司行为或订立任何合同均不需要公证人在场或协助。

4.2 股东协议 (Shareholders' agreement, SHA)

With respect to the SHA, the following terms was of vital importance in the case presented herein:

关于 SHA,以下条款对于本文中的案例至关重要:

• Important resolutions: Certain resolutions should be adopted by the shareholders with a special majority of the votes and in order for such provisions to be valid pursuant to Norwegian company law also recorded in the articles of association of the target company. In Norway most resolutions of the general meeting are adopted by a normal majority such as appointing board of directors, declaring dividends and approving the annual accounts. Resolutions such as share capital increase and other changes to the articles of association is resolved by a super majority (2/3 of the voting rights). In case a client only holds a minority stake in a company it is therefore of great importance that certain, essential resolutions only can be adopted if the minority shareholders consent as well. This is usually governed as an agreed voting restriction under the SHA. Essential resolutions are (amongst others), amendment of the articles of association, including changes to the share capital by way of rights issues, direct issues, any sale of all or a substantial part of the business of the company and making participations in the capital of other companies.

• 重要决议:股东应以特别多数票的方式通过某些决议,以使这些条款符合挪威公司法和目标公司的章程。在挪威,股东大会的大多数决议以普通多数票的方式通过,例如任命董事会成员、宣布股息和批准年度结算。增加股本和以其他方式变更公司章程等决议应以特别多数票(投票权的 2/3)通过。在客户只持有公司少数股权的情况下,应加入只有少数股东同意才能通过基本决议的条款,这一点非常重要。这通常被视为 SHA 约定的投票限制。基本决议包括:修改公司章程、以发行附加股或直接发行等方式变更股本、出售公司全部或大部分业务以及参股其他公司,等等。

• Information rights: In principle, each shareholder should be informed by the board of managing directors regarding the business of the company. In the SHA this right of information can be made more concrete and broadened (e.g. the obligation of the company to submit to the shareholders a quarterly report which shall inter alia consist of a balance sheet, profit and loss account and cash flow statements) depending on the size of the target company and its administration.

• 知情权：原则上，董事总经理委员会应告知每位股东公司业务的经营情况。在 SHA 中，视目标公司的规模及其管理而定，该知情权可以更加具体、更加广泛（例如，公司有义务向股东提交季度报告，其中应包括资产负债表、损益表和现金流量表）。

• Transfer of shares: In Norway, if not stated otherwise in the company's articles of association, the other shareholders have a pre-emptive right to share that are being transferred in a private limited company. It is recommended to include further details on the restriction of transferring shares in the target company. It is common practice in Norway to incorporate further details on the share-transferring restrictions such as pre-emptive rights, pricing, settlement and procedure (e.g. in the form of an offering requirement whereby the offering shareholders should offer the shares first to the other shareholder). The pricing mechanism is always one of the topics regarding which parties need to negotiate. It is also common practice to deviate from pre-emptive rights in applying a tag or drag along in connection with the transfer of shares.

• 股份转让：在挪威，除非公司章程另有规定，股东有权优先购买在私人有限公司内部转让的股份。建议在协议中包含有关限制目标公司转让股份的进一步细节。在挪威，通常的做法是进一步纳入股权转让限制的具体条款，例如优先购买权、定价、结算和程序（例如以出售要求的形式，按照该要求，出售股份的股东应首先向其他股东出售股份）。定价机制始终是各方需要协商的主题之一。在股份转让时，除优先购买权之外，适用随售和拖售条款也是常见的做法。

• Tag/drag along: We recommend the inclusion of wording pertaining to the event that a shareholder envisages to sell all its shares in the target company to an interested buyer. In such an event, the minority shareholder has the right to sell and transfer all the shares it holds in the target company to the interested buyer as well under the same conditions (i.e. the tag along). The drag along is also always included; this means that if a (majority) shareholder wants to sell its shares in a target company that then the other (minority) shareholders are forced to sell their shares as well against the same conditions. The threshold for exercising drag-along rights is usually agreed at a threshold of 50% ownership or more but is of course negotiable at lower levels.

• 随售/拖售权：我们建议，在股东试图将其持有的目标公司全部股份出售给有意向的买方的情况下，加入与此相关的条款。在这种情况下，小股东有权按照相同条件将其持有的目标公司的股份转让给有意向的买方（即随售权）。拖售权也是经常设置的条款，这意味着如果股东（大股东）希望出售其持有的目标公司的股份，其他股东（小股东）也将被迫按照相同条件出售其持有的目标公司的股份。通常会将行使拖售权的限制约定为所有权的50%或以上，当然，也可以协商至更低。

- Good/Bad leaver provisions: In many cases if the managing directors of the target company hold shares as well, provisions are included to cover the situation that the employment or management agreement with such managing director is terminated. It is common practice that in such a case the managing director/shareholder is forced to sell its shares in the company against a certain price. The price depends on the question what the reason for termination of the employment/management agreement was. Such provisions are likely to have a tax implication for the managing director in terms as sale of shares in these events being classified as salary tax and not capital gains under Norwegian law.

- 正常离职/不良离职条款：在许多情况下，如果目标公司的董事总经理也持有股份，则条款会涵盖与该董事总经理的雇用或管理协议终止的情况。在这种情况下，通常的做法是董事总经理/股东被迫以一定的价格出售其在公司的股份。价格取决于终止雇用/管理协议的具体原因。此类条款可能会对董事总经理产生税务方面的影响，因为在这种情况中，股份出售被归类为工资薪金税种，而非挪威法律规定的资本收益。

In several cases involving Chinese investors where we have been privy to the transaction process, parties agree to the establishment of an advisory board of the target company, in particular as a measure to make the strict rules applicable with respect to employee participation in corporate bodies more practicable. [1] However, the election

---

[1] Both in private and public companies, employees have a general right to representation on the company board of directors if the total number of employees exceed 30. With higher numbers of employees, further requirements come into play, such as the obligation to establish a corporate assembly with powers to elect the board. In practice, many companies avoid the duty to establish a corporate assembly in addition to the board of directors by entering into an agreement between the company and the unions representing the employees. One measure that may be relevant in this respect that we have seen in practice has been the creating of an advisory board to function as a platform for discussion between management and employee reps.

into the board of directors is more favourable under Norwegian law. This because in Norway, an advisory board is no formal corporate body. Since the advisory board is particularly arranged for under the various companies acts [1], the only relevant provisions are included in the SHA and/or an agreement entered into between the company and the relevant employee unions.

在我们参与了交易过程且涉及中国投资者的几个案例里，各方同意设立目标公司的咨询委员会，并以此作为一项特别措施，使员工参与公司法人团体的严格规则更加切实可行。[2]但是，根据挪威法律，选举成立董事会更加有利。这是因为在挪威，咨询委员会不是正式的法人主体。由于咨询委员会是根据各种公司法[3]而特别安排的，因此，唯一的相关条款包含在SHA和/或公司与相关的员工工会达成的协议中。

4.3 上市公司交易简述（Brief on Transactions in Listed Companies）

A brief mention should be given to the particulars of purchasing a listed company. Even though no agreement will generally be entered into with each individual shareholder in the event of an acquisition of a listed company, it is nevertheless common for the interested party to enter into a co-operation or transaction agreement (the difference being in name only) with the target company. In addition to setting out the terms on which the Board will recommend the offer, the agreement may give the offeror rights to carry out a limited due diligence review, etc. Furthermore, pre-approval of the voluntary offer to be made will be obtained in writing prior to the public announcement of the offer. Due care should under any circumstance be taken to ensure that any such dealings are in the strictest compliance with, inter alia, the Securities Act.

---

[1] Norway has two statutory acts of company regulations: The Private Limited Liability Companies Act (Private LLCA) and the Public Limited Liability Companies Act (Public LLCA). While the two instruments closely mirror each other in many respects, the Public LLCA is adapted to the requirements of public (in particular listed) companies, with less lenient share transfer restrictions, etc.

[2] 在私营和上市公司之中，如果员工的总数超过30人，则员工有权在董事会中进行陈述。随着员工人数的增加，将具有更多的要求，如设立有权选举董事会的公司大会的义务。在实践中，除了董事会外，许多公司通过由工会代表员工与公司签订协议的方式设立公司大会，避免相关的责任。在这一方面，我们在实践中遇到一项措施是建立一个咨询委员会，作为管理层和员工代表之间进行讨论的平台。

[3] 挪威有两个公司法：《私人有限责任公司法》（Private LLCA）和《公共有限责任公司法》（Public LLCA）。虽然二者在许多方面密切相关，但Public LLCA适用于公共（特别是上市）公司的要求，股权转让限制更为严格。

简要陈述上市公司购买流程。一般来说,即使在收购上市公司时不会与每个股东签订协议,但有意方与目标公司签订仅有名称差异的合作或交易协议是常见的做法。除了载明董事会提出要约的条款之外,协议还可赋予要约人进行有限尽职调查的权利。此外,在要约公开之前,须以书面形式获得自愿要约的预先批准。在任何情况下均应当审慎,以确保此类交易严格遵守证券法。

5. 主要法律问题(Main Legal Issues)

One of the main legal issues during the negotiations with respect to most transactions is the non-compete clause in the SPA (in the event of an outright sale with no continued co-ownership) and/or in the SHA (in the event where the previous owners continue to own a minority share). It is indeed common practice in the Norway to include either unilateral or mutual non-compete and non-solicitation clauses in the SPA and/or SHA, prohibiting one or either party from engaging in competing business. In one case we experienced clients wanting to have the possibility to engage in competing business with a specific competitor or investing in a specific competitor. This is, with the sole exception of minority investments (generally less than 5% of outstanding shares) in the shares of publicly traded companies, not common practise and should be dealt with an early stage of the process. We have experience in finding agreements where very limited ownership in a third party has been accepted, but such arrangements are not commonplace and will, as mentioned above, not generally be accepted by the buyer. In the event of a breach of a non-compete clause often it is agreed between parties that the breaching party is liable to cover the other party's loss in such event and also pay a defined liquidated damage. Note, however, that irrespective of whether the pertinent agreement (SHA or SPA) is made subject to Norwegian law, Chinese law or the laws of a third country, the non-competition restrictions cannot go so far as to be deemed onerous and unreasonable under Norwegian law. Provisions of Norwegian and EU competition law will also come into play in the assessment of the validity of non-compete clauses.

对大多数交易而言,谈判期间的主要法律问题之一是 SPA(完全出售股份,前股东不再继续持有共同所有权的情况下)和/或 SHA 中(前所有者继续拥有少数股份)中的不竞争条款。在挪威,通常的做法是在 SPA 和/或 SHA 中加入单方或双方的不竞争和不招揽条款，以禁止任何一方从事竞争性的业务。在一个案例中，我们曾遇到客户希望与特定竞争对手从事竞争性业务或向其投资的情况。这种做法并不常见，唯一的例外是对于上市公司的少量投资（该少量投资一般为已发行股份的 5%），应在交易过程的早期阶段及时处理。我们曾发现接受持有第三方极少数所有权的协议，但这种安排并不常见，如上所述，买方通常对此不会接受。在违反不竞争条款的情况下，交易方通常会一致同意：违约方有责任支付另一方因此而遭受的损失，并支付约定的违约赔偿金。但是，请注意，无论相关协议（SHA 或 SPA）受挪威法律、中国法律抑或第三国法律的管辖，不竞争限制都不能被挪威法律视为繁重的、不合理的条款。挪威和欧盟竞争法的规定也将在评估不竞争条款的有效性时发挥作用。

6. 其他问题和相关解决方法（Other Issues and Relevant Solutions）

Other issues which we come across when assisting our Chinese clients are:
在向中国客户提供协助时，我们遇到的其他问题包括：

(i) The fact that in many transactions time is of the essence; a swift follow-up/turnaround of the different versions of the transaction documentation is key. In case of Chinese buyers, we have experienced that specific approvals from Chinese authorities may be required, in particular where the ultimate Chinese owner is wholly or partly owned by the state. On the basis of this, we have often found it necessary to sit down with the Norwegian party or parties to create an understanding of the fact the regulatory framework in China will require all boxes to be ticked and that a certain amount of patience is required. It is advisable for Chinese interested parties to be up-front with any such requirements with the Norwegian party, as this fosters trust between the parties. Especially in case of auction processes, however, time-consuming procedures and requirements for clearances or permits in China may prejudice the possibility to buy the target company (since for example local purchasers have less mandatory internal approvals). Accordingly, the common approach by Chinese buyers is in our experience to approach potential targets outside of structured sales processes initiated by the sellers themselves.

(i) 在许多交易中，时间至关重要；不同版本交易文件的快速跟进或者流转是关键。如果买方来自中国，我们遇到过需要经过中国主管机关特别批准的情形，特别是在中国的最终买方由国家全资或部分所有的情况下。在此基础之上，我们经常发现有必要与挪威交易方共同了解中国的监管框架，以使交易满足所有的标准，这需要一定的耐心。对于中国的有意方，明智的做法是及时向挪威方表明任何此类要求，以增进双方之间的信任。不过，在中国进行清关或获得许可证等耗费时间的程序和要求（特别是在拍卖过程中）可能会降低购买目标公司的可能性（例如，由于本地购买者须经的内部强制性批准较少）。因此，根据我们的经验，中国买方通常的方法是在卖方自身发起的出售程序之外与潜在的目标公司接洽。

(ii) To avoid frustration/loss of trust it is key to be transparent at an early stage regarding the expectations of each party, the expected timeline and specific approvals required from for example Chinese authorities or the parent company.

(ii) 为了避免焦虑或者彼此失去信任，在合作的早期阶段就各方的期许保持信息沟通透明十分重要，例如，中国主管机关或母公司预期的时间安排和要求的特别批准。

(iii) If a legal opinion on the transaction documents is required, it is prudent to agree on the scope at an early stage as this is not a usual requirement in Norway. Legal opinions are usually only issued in connection with lending documentation and liens and mortgages attached to it.

(iii) 如果须就交易文件提出法律意见，则应尽早就其范围达成一致意见，因为这并非挪威常见的要求。法律意见通常仅与贷款文件以及附加的留置权和抵押相关。

In our experience it is essential to have someone who has experience with Chinese investors, can speak or liaise with Chinese speaking advisors, and understands the cultural differences in order to bridge and manoeuvre through different market practise.

根据我们的经验，有一位具有与中国投资者打交道的经验、能够与说中文的顾问沟通并能理解文化差异的人是不可或缺的，以便通过不同的市场实践弥合差异、把控交易。

Some Chinese businesspeople may consider the Norwegian style of commercial dealing as brash and too forthright or outspoken. Norwegian corporations are, however, getting ever more experience in dealing with Chinese businesses. When the cultural differences are bridged and each party is transparent with respect to its expectations of the other party, the cooperation between Norwegian and Chinese businesspeople usually work very well.

中国商人可能认为挪威的商业交易风格是傲慢、过于直率或直言不讳的。然而，挪威公司在处理中国企业的事务方面获得了越来越多的经验。当义化差异得到弥合，且任何一方对他方的期许得到坦诚透明的回应时，双方的合作通常进展十分顺利。

— 作者简介 —

Lars Berge Andersen is a partner and Head of SANDS Energy, Shipping & Offshore Department. He has previously lived and worked as a lawyer in Shanghai. For more than 15 years he has advised Norwegian investments in China and Chinese investments in Norway and other countries. He is also the Chairman of the Norwegian-Chinese Chamber of Commerce and was previously a board member of the Norwegian Business Association in China.

Lars Berge Andersen 是 SANDS 能源、航运和海洋部门的合伙人兼负责人。他曾在上海生活和工作过。为挪威在中国的投资以及中国在挪威和其他国家的投资提供建议方面，拥有超过 15 年的工作经验。他还是挪威中国商会的主席，并曾经任职中国挪威商业协会的董事会成员。

SANDS is a full-service business law firm based in Norway with approximately 160 lawyers and associates across offices in Oslo and several other cities. Established in 1989, the firm has for the last few years been the fastest growing outfit on the Norwegian business law arena. SANDS have significant strengths both as a transactional adviser as well as in litigation.

SANDS 是一家提供全方位服务的商业律师事务所，总部位于挪威，在奥斯陆和其他几个城市的办事处设有约 160 名律师和合伙人。该事务所成立于 1989 年，过去几年一直是挪威商法领域发展最快的公司。SANDS 在交易项目法律顾问和诉讼方面均具有明显优势。

投资在葡萄牙：在风能领域开展投资
Investments in Portugal
Investing in the Wind Energy Industry

点 评

葡萄牙位于欧洲伊比利亚半岛的西南部，毗临大西洋，海岸线长达832千米，有着独特的地理优势。它的地理位置、气候和地质特点赋予它得天独厚的清洁能源资源。北部和中部地区常年不断的西风和绵延不尽的山峦为建设风力发电站创造了理想的条件。同时葡萄牙原本是一个能源系统高度依赖石油和天然气进口的国家，发展风力发电站是葡萄牙利用其自然资源、降低严重依赖石油能源的有效方法之一。因此，风力发电获得了来自葡萄牙政府的政策支持。

行业监管政策上，葡萄牙的电力行业基本实现了完全的自由化和私有化，发电、配电和供电等业务分拆，发电厂的运营等需要取得主管机关颁发的运营许可证书。同时，本文作者结合在葡萄牙风力发电领域的项目经验，对葡萄牙风力发电领域的股权投资项目的操作流程、反垄断申报、项目融资方式、交易协议重点关注事项（如付款、交割、特殊权利条款等）进行了详细的介绍。本文为拟投资葡萄牙风力发电市场的中国投资者介绍该领域的基本监管面貌并提供操作指引。

1. 葡萄牙的风能生产 (Wind Energy Production in Portugal)

Energy decisions play a major role in the achievement of sustainable development and consequently on the economic, environmental and social welfare of future generations. Combining energy efficiency with renewable energy resources constitutes a key strategy for a sustainable future, emphasised in the European and Portuguese policy guidelines. The wind power sector stands out as a fundamental element for the achievement of the European renewable objectives. Currently, most of the energy planning models focus predominantly on the economic and environmental dimensions of the problem.

能源决策在实现可持续发展以及最终对人类后代的经济、环境和社会福利方面发挥着重要作用。欧洲和葡萄牙的政策指导方针强调,将能源效率与可再生能源相结合是可持续未来的关键战略。风电部门是实现欧洲可再生能源目标的基本要素,目前大多数能源规划模型主要关注经济和环境维度的问题。

Portugal is a country with an energy system highly dependent on oil and gas imports. Meanwhile, the share of renewable energy sources (RES) in the total primary energy consumption has been increasing.

葡萄牙是一个能源系统高度依赖石油和天然气进口的国家,但同时可再生能源在一次能源消费总量中所占的份额也在不断增加。

According to the official reports, the increasing demand for electricity in Portugal over the next ten years will be mainly supported by new investments in renewable projects with a focus on solar, and wind power technologies and the new national strategy for hydrogen. The rising trend of the wind power demonstrates that wind power will influence significantly the power generation in Portugal with a fundamental role in future electricity plans, particularly in regard to meeting the renewable and Kyoto protocol commitments.

根据官方报告,专注于太阳能、风能技术的可再生能源项目的新投资,以及国家氢能战略推动着未来十年葡萄牙电力需求的增长。风力发电的增长趋势表明,风力发电将对葡萄牙的发电产生重大影响,在未来的电力计划中,尤其是在履行可再生能源和京都议定书承诺方面发挥着根本作用。

1.1 葡萄牙在风能生产中发挥关键作用 (Portugal Plays a Key Role in the Wind Energy Production)

Data from the Portuguese power utility Redes Energeticas Nacionais (REN), the national TSO, shows that renewable sources accounted for 61.7% of Portugal's electricity in 2020.

国家电力系统运营商(TSO)葡萄牙电力公司 Redes Energetica Nacionais

(REN)的数据显示，2020年，可再生能源占葡萄牙发电量的61.7%。

Hydro sources had the largest contribution (28%), followed by wind (24%), biomass (6.7%) and photovoltaic (PV) sources (2.6%). Wind power production is massively obtained in the Center and North regions of Portugal, together representing 87% of the overall production.

在葡萄牙的可再生能源发电量中，水电占比最大（占28%），其次是风能（占24%），生物发电（占6.7%）和光伏发电（PV）（占2.6%）。葡萄牙的中部和北部地区获得了大量的风力发电，占总发电量的87%。

The first floating wind farm in Portugal was built in 2019, 20 km off the Portuguese coast, near Viana do Castelo. The project is called WindFloat Atlantic and is one of the largest floating wind farms in the world with an installed capacity of 25MW.

葡萄牙的第一个浮动风力发电场建于2019年，离葡萄牙海岸20公里，靠近维亚纳堡（Viana do Castelo）。该项目被称为WindFloat Atlantic，是世界上最大的浮动风电场之一，装机容量为25兆瓦（MW）。

In the 2005–2015 decade, the wind energy installed capacity increased almost 400% and was by far the type of RES with the highest absolute variation (i.e., 3971 MW). Portugal's wind power is expected to grow to around 9 GW by 2030, which is enough to cover more than 40% of the country's electricity consumption. Portugal's ambitious national energy and climate plan foresees raising renewables contribution to primary energy consumption from 31% in 2020 to 47% in 2030. For that effect, Portugal is pioneering several developments in environmentally sustainable energy production operations.

在2005—2015年的十年间，葡萄牙的风能装机容量增加了近400%，风能是迄今为止绝对变化最大的可再生能源类型（3971兆瓦）。预计到2030年，葡萄牙的风力发电量将增长到9千兆瓦左右，这足以满足该国超过40%的电力消费。葡萄牙雄心勃勃的国家能源和气候计划预计可再生能源对一次能源消耗的贡献将从2020年的31%提高到2030年的47%。为此，葡萄牙正在开发多项环境可持续能源生产业务。

Moreover, in February 2019, the Government passed legislation that allows project operators in Portugal to add turbines to up to 20% of the grid connection capacity at existing wind farms without regulatory permission. The measure seeks to boost wind capacity while protecting electricity consumers by setting a fixed 15-year tariff of € 45/MWh for the additional electricity generated.

此外，2019年2月葡萄牙政府通过了一项法案，该法案预计将允许葡萄牙的项目运营商在未经监管许可的情况下，在现有风力发电场的电网连接容量中增加多达20%的涡轮机。该措施旨在提高风力发电能力，同时为新增发电量设定45欧元/MWh的15年固定电价，以保护电力消费者。

Overall, wind power generation, together with solar energy, is becoming the new paradigm in energy production in Portugal.

总体来说，风力发电和太阳能正在成为葡萄牙能源生产的新模式。

1.2 葡萄牙能源生产部门的监管要求（Portuguese Regulatory Requirements Regarding the Energy Production Sector）

The Portuguese electricity sector is currently almost fully liberalised and privatized. This is because of the implementation of EU directives, such as Directive 2009/72/EC on the common rules for the internal market in electricity and the privatisations after the measures imposed under the financial assistance plan (2011 to 2014) as part of the conditions imposed by the Troika (representing the EU in its foreign relations, in particular concerning its common foreign and security policy). Generation, distribution and supply activities are unbundled (which refers to legal and accountability separation), although the transmission activity underwent a process of ownership unbundling. The transmission activity is unbundled at the legal and ownership level, and from the remaining activities of the sector. This is even though only legal and ownership unbundling were necessary in relation to the generation and supply activities. Unbundling requirements also apply to the distribution activity from the remaining activities in the electricity sector (with the DSO being autonomous) from a legal, organisational and decision-making perspective.

目前，葡萄牙的电力行业基本实现了完全的自由化和私有化，这是因欧盟指令的执行，例如关于电力内部市场统一规则的2009/72/EC号电力指令，以及根据2011—2014年的财政援助计划采取措施后，作为欧盟"三驾马车"（代表欧盟处理外交关系，尤其是关于共同外交和安全政策方面）施加条件的一部分而进行的私有化。葡萄牙的发电、配电和供电等业务是分拆的（主要体现在法律和承担责任方面的分拆),且输电业务还经历过所有权的分拆。尽管输电业务仅在法律和承担责任方面与发电和供电进行了必要的分拆,其与电力行业内的其他业务也实现了分拆。此外,电力行业内其他分配业务(在输电系统运营商自主运营的情况下)也同样可以在法律、组织和决策等方面实现分拆。

The Portuguese Electrical System essentially consists of four different activities (which are mostly unbundled) that are carried out through the: generation of electricity; transmission of electricity through very high and high voltage grids; distribution of electricity through high, medium and low voltage grids; supply of electricity to consumers.

葡萄牙电气系统主要由四种不同的业务组成(大多都是分拆运行的),这些业务通过以下方式进行:发电;通过超高压和高压电网输电;通过高、中、低压电网分配电力;向消费者供电。

Generation and supply activities are not strictly regulated. They are liberalised and can be developed by any company that goes through the licensing, registration or prior communication procedure (as applicable). Generation of electricity is divided into an ordinary and special regime. The ordinary regime includes thermoelectric plants, whereas the special regime comprises generation from renewable sources, cogeneration, small production and production regulated by any other special regimes, such as the generation of electricity for self-consumption.

葡萄牙的发电和供电业务不受严格监管,是自由化的,可以由任何经过许可、注册或通过事先沟通程序(如适用)的公司开发。发电分为普通制度和特殊制度。普通制度适用于热电厂,而特殊制度适用于可再生能源的发电、热电联产、小规模发电和由任何其他特殊制度管制的发电业务,如自用发电。

The operation of electricity generation plants requires an operation licence from the General Director for Energy and Geology (issued after the commissioning of the power plant) or an operation certificate (if the installation of the same was only subject to prior communication). The operators of power plants must comply with the law and Entidade Reguladora dos Serviços Energéticos (ERSE) 's regulations, particularly in relation to technical operation of the plant and payment of regulated tariffs of access to the grid; and compliance with the clauses of the power purchase agreement with the last resort supplier (this applies to generators in the special regime with guaranteed remuneration)。

发电厂的运营需要能源和地质局长颁发的运营许可证（在发电厂授权后授予）或运营证书（若同一电量的装配仅需事前沟通）。发电厂的运营商必须遵守法律和葡萄牙能源服务管理局（ERSE）的规定，特别是与发电厂的技术操作和上网电价支付有关的规定；以及遵守与最终供应商签订的购电协议的条款（适用于在特殊发电制度下报酬有保障的运营商）。

Portugal and Spain have been integrating their electricity markets into a single Iberian Electricity Market (MIBEL). They share a common spot market operator (OMIE) which has been operating in both countries since July 2007 and a forward market operator (OMIP) since July 2006.

葡萄牙和西班牙已将它们的电力市场整合成一个统一的伊比利亚电力市场（MIBEL）。它们共同拥有一个自2007年7月开始运营的现货市场运营商（OMIE）和一个自2006年7月开始运营的远期市场运营商（OMIP）。

2. 交易结构（Transaction Structure）

2.1 投资项目介绍（Introduction of the Investment Project）

One of our non-EU clients negotiated an investment in a Portuguese group active in the renewables generation industry, for the acquisition by our Client of shares representing 100% of its capital.

我们的一位非欧盟客户与一家活跃于可再生能源发电行业的葡萄牙集团进行了投资谈判，拟收购其100%的股份。

2.2 交易文件（Transaction Documents）

In connection with the Transaction, the seller and our client entered into a share purchase agreement (SPA). Said SPA governed the rights and obligations of the seller and our client with respect to the sale and transfer of the shares in the capital of the target company.

在交易中，卖方和我方客户签订了股份购买协议（SPA）。上述SPA规定了卖方和我方客户在出售和转让目标公司股份方面的权利和义务。

Under Portuguese law, it is common practice that parties enter into a non-disclosure agreement (NDA) with respect to their intentions regarding the envisaged transaction. A non-disclosure agreement creates a legal obligation between the parties securing that certain information (e.g. the envisaged transaction) remains protected/confidential. Such NDA is usually the first transaction document to be entered between parties.

根据葡萄牙法律，各方就拟进行交易的意图达成保密协议（NDA）是一种商业惯例。保密协议规定了交易各方的法律义务，以确保某些信息（如双方设想的交易）仍然受到保护和保密。这样的保密协议通常是交易各方签订的第一份文件。

Following the signing of an NDA, the parties often enter a term sheet. The term sheet governs the initial intentions of parties with respect to the transaction (e.g. the purchase price for the shares). It is therefore essential that professional legal advisors are engaged in the transaction at an early stage.

签署保密协议后，双方通常会签署投资条款清单。投资条款清单规定了交易方的初始意图（如股份购买价格）。因此专业法律顾问在早期阶段参与交易是很必要的。

2.3 尽职调查（Due Diligence）

Simultaneously with the drafting of the transaction documents, it occurred a due diligence regarding the target company and the business carried out by it. The purpose of such an investigation is to identify key issues relating to the transaction and the target company, which is of paramount importance to the buyer for the calculation of the price that it will offer for the shares.

在起草上述交易文件的同时，需对目标公司及其开展的业务进行尽职调查。进行调查的目的是确定本次交易以及目标公司中存在的关键问题，这对买方计算其对股份的报价至关重要。

Following identification of certain issues, we have sought protection against those issues in the transaction documents. In general, potential risks can be limited/covered by means of lowering the purchase price; including specific conditions precedent or conditions subsequent; including representations and warranties and including specific indemnifications.

在确定交易中存在的问题之后，我们在交易文件中对这些问题进行了处理。一般而言，可以通过以下方式规避潜在风险：降低购买价格；加入特定的先决或后续条件条款；加入陈述和保证条款，以及加入具体赔偿条款。

2.4 竞争法申报（Competition Law Filings）

Under Portuguese law, certain mergers and acquisitions that may bring about a so-called concentration have to be notified to governmental entities. The Portuguese competition legislation provides a system of merger control for operations that affect the Portuguese economy. It largely copies and partially incorporates the system of European merger control and prohibits concentrations that create or strengthen a dominant position resulting in a significant restriction of effective competition in the Portuguese market or a part thereof. The provisions regarding merger control set forth in Portuguese competition legislation apply to mergers, acquisitions, public bids and all other transactions that may bring about a concentration. In accordance with this legislation, concentrations shall be deemed to arise when a change of control in the whole or parts of one or more undertakings occurs on a lasting basis as a result of:

根据葡萄牙法律，某些可能导致集中的兼并和收购必须向政府申报。葡萄牙竞争法设定了一种合并控制体系，以对影响葡萄牙经济正常运行的经营活动加以控制。它在很大程度上复制并部分吸收了欧洲并购控制体系，禁止在葡萄牙的市场或部分市场中形成或强化支配地位而严重限制有效竞争的经营者集中行为。葡萄牙竞争法中关于合并控制的规定适用于合并、收购、公开招标和所有其他可能导致集中的交易。根据该法，当一个或多个企业的全部或部分控制权基于以下原因而持久地发生变化时，应视为集中：

● a merger between two or more previously independent undertakings or parts of undertakings; or

● 两个或两个以上之前独立的企业或企业的一部分之间的合并；或

● the acquisition, directly or indirectly, of control of all or parts of the share capital or parts of the assets of one or various undertakings (to which a market turnover can be attributed), by one or more persons or undertakings already controlling at least one undertakings, or;

● 一家或多家公司的控制人，直接或间接地取得其他公司的全部或部分股份或部分资产（包括市场营业额在内）的控制权，或

● the creation of a joint venture performing on a lasting basis all the functions of an autonomous economic entity (a full-function joint venture).

● 建立了一个能够持续进行所有自主经营活动的的合营企业（全功能合营

企业)。

A merger that meets certain thresholds as regards the turnover of the undertakings concerned will have to be notified to the Autoridade da Concorrência (AdC). A concentration remaining below the threshold turnover levels may be completed without a notification to the AdC.

参与集中的企业营业额达到某些规模的集中度时,应向葡萄牙竞争管理局(AdC)提交通知。参与合并的企业营业额未达规定数额的,无需向AdC提交通知即可完成交易。

Concentrations must be notified to the AdC if they meet one of the three alternative jurisdictional thresholds set out in the Portuguese competition legislation:

满足以下葡萄牙竞争法规定的三种情形中任意一种的合并交易行为,应向AdC提交通知:

• the parties' aggregate Portuguese turnover exceeds EUR100 million and the individual Portuguese turnover of each of at least two parties exceeds EUR5 million;

• 合并各方在葡萄牙的营业额合计超过1亿欧元,且至少有两方在葡萄牙的营业额都超过500万欧元;

• the acquisition, creation or reinforcement of a share exceeding 50% in the national market (or in a substantial part of it) for a particular good or service;

• 该交易使某一特定商品或服务在葡萄牙国内市场(或相当大一部分市场)获得、创造或巩固超过50%的市场份额;

• the acquisition, creation or reinforcement of a national market share exceeding 30% but lower than 50% in the Portuguese market or in a substantial part of it and the Portuguese individual turnover of at least two undertakings exceeds EUR5 million.

• 该交易使某一特定商品或服务在葡萄牙国内市场(或相当大一部分市场)获得、创造或巩固超过30%但低于50%的市场份额,且至少有两方在葡萄牙的营业额都超过500万欧元。

A merger that has been completed without having been duly notified or without the parties observing the appropriate waiting period will be regarded as being null and void under the laws of Portugal.

根据葡萄牙法律,未经正式通知AdC或当事各方未遵守合理的等待期即完成的集中将被视为无效。

In addition, the AdC has wide powers to impose fines and orders in the context of concentration control. Failure to notify a concentration will usually lead to a fine upon discovery by the AdC. Both companies and directors involved can be fined in this regard.

此外，AdC 在控制经营者集中方面拥有广泛的罚款和命令权力。经 AdC 查明合并交易方应向其通知集中情况而未通知的，相关公司和管理人员都会被处以罚款。

In the case of our client, the acquisition of 100% of capital in the Portuguese wind power production triggered an obligation to notify the AdC.

就我方客户来说，收购葡萄牙风力发电公司 100% 的资本就会使其负有向 AdC 通知交易行为的义务。

3. 项目融资方式 (Project Financing Method)

The project financing methodology is also key when structuring a Portuguese M&A transaction as Portuguese law provides for the prohibition of financial assistance. As such, a Portuguese company cannot provide funds or security for a party to acquire its shares as that is deemed to be financial assistance. A transaction involving financial assistance is deemed to be null and void by Portuguese law.

在设计葡萄牙并购交易方案时，项目融资方式也是关键，因为葡萄牙法律禁止经济援助行为。据此，葡萄牙公司无法为另一方获得其股份提供资金或担保，因为该行为将被视为经济援助。葡萄牙法律认为包含经济援助行为的交易是无效的。

Please note that intra-group financing is a commonly used finance arrangement in Portugal. In addition, many transactions involving Chinese buyers are financed via bank credit facilities. We do see that it is quite difficult for Chinese buyers to have a transaction funded through China. To avoid this, transactions can also be financed via bank credit facilities or through intra-group finance arrangements.

需要注意的是，集团内部融资在葡萄牙是一种常用的融资安排。许多涉及中国买方的交易都是通过银行信贷融资进行的。因为我们发现中国的买方在中国很难获得支持交易的资金。为了解决该问题，交易还可以通过银行信贷或通过集团内部融资安排来获得资金支持。

4. 交易文件中的关键条款（Key Terms in Transaction Documents）

4.1 股份购买协议（SPA）

With respect to the SPA, the following terms are of great importance (please note that this is not an exhaustive list, but just some examples):

关于SPA，以下为十分重要的条款（请注意此处并非详尽列举，仅列举部分）：

Payment of the purchase price: the manner in which the purchaser will pay the purchase price for the shares should be written down very precisely. Earn-out arrangements are also quite common in Portugal; these are payment arrangements, which are linked to the post-closing performance of the target.

付款方式：应当详尽约定买方股份购买价格的付款方式。收购价款的支付按照被收购主体的业绩情况进行分期支付的安排在葡萄牙也很常见，这是一种与以后公司盈利能力挂钩的付款安排。

Completion actions: It is common practice in Portugal to include a clause in the SPA stipulating the actions that must be completed by each party at (or prior to) the day in which the transfer of the shares occurs (closing of the transaction). For example, the delivery of corporate resolutions from the seller and the buyer approving the transaction, or the delivery of waiver letters from banks regarding their rights pursuant to the release of a right of pledge on the relevant shares etc.

交割条件：在SPA中加入一项规定各方在股份交易完成之日当天或之前必须履行特定行为的条款，在葡萄牙是很常见的一种做法。例如，买卖各方应提交公司批准该项交易的决议，或提交由银行出具的解除相关股份质押的豁免函等。

Representations and Warranties (R&W): one of the most difficult parts of negotiation in a SPA is the R&W section. Obtaining from the Seller comprehensive R&W is fundamental to grant protection to the buyer. Also the seller is expected to represent that all information made available in the due diligence phase is complete, accurate and not mis-leading.

陈述和保证（R&W）：SPA中协商过程中最困难的部分之一就是陈述和保证部分。从卖方获得全面的陈述和保证是买方获得保护的基础。此外，卖方应表示在尽职调查阶段提供的所有信息都是完整、准确且无误导性的。

Limitation of liability: in the event that one of the parties to the SPA is in breach of its contractual obligations contained therein, the other party may hold the defaulting party liable. In this respect, it is common practice to include wording pertaining to the limitation of liability; usually certain thresholds are included in the SPA. These limitations usually only apply to breaches of the R&W; typically, in case of damages under the indemnifications, the liability of the seller is unlimited (obviously, this also depends on the negotiations).

责任限制条款：如果一方违反了 SPA 中规定的合同义务，另一方可要求违约方承担责任。对此，SPA 中通常也会包含与责任限制有关的措辞以及一些责任限制的条件。这些责任限制通常只在违反 R&W 义务的情形下适用；一般情况下，如果承担责任的方式为赔偿损失，那么卖方的责任就是无限的（但这也取决于各方的协商情况）。

Interim period: it is common practice in Portuguese transactions that the shares are not transferred upon signing of the SPA; such transfer only occurs after successful accomplishment of certain conditions precedent (e.g. regulatory approvals, merger control approvals, financing parties approval). Given this, it is fundamental that the SPA contains appropriate provisions governing the management of the target company in the period between signature of the SPA and transfer of the shares (closing of the transaction). In addition, a clause regarding the so-called leakage can be needed (i.e. prohibiting the target company to make any dividend distributions in the period between signing of the SPA and transfer of the shares/closing).

过渡期条款：在葡萄牙较为常见的做法是，在签署 SPA 时先不转让股份；相关股份仅在成功完成某些先决条件后（例如监管部门批准、并购控制部门批准、融资方审批等）才发生转让。据此，在 SPA 中加入一条在 SPA 签署日到股份转让日期间对目标公司管理层进行约束的合理条款是至关重要的。此外，还需要一条有关"防泄漏"的条款（即禁止目标公司在签署 SPA 和转让、交割股份之间进行任何股息分配）。

Non-compete/no-solicitation: one of the main legal issues during the negotiations with respect to the transaction documents is the non-compete/no-solicitation clause. It is common practice in Portugal to include such provisions in the transaction documents prohibiting the seller to engage in competing business and employ/solicit key employees from the target company.

竞业禁止/招揽禁止：竞业禁止/招揽禁止条款是交易文件谈判中的主要法律问题之一。在葡萄牙，通常做法是在交易文件中加入该条款，禁止卖方从事竞争性业务或从目标公司招揽雇用关键员工。

4.2 股东协议（Shareholders Agreement，SHA）

In the event that the seller remains with a participation in the target company, it is common practice that the parties enter into SHA governing their relationship as shareholders of the target company. With respect to the SHA, the following terms are (amongst others) of vital importance：

如果卖方仍然保留目标公司股东地位，则通常的做法是交易各方作为目标公司的股东订立一份股东协议来约定他们之间的关系。关于SHA，以下为非常重要的条款：

Material resolutions：certain resolutions should be adopted by the shareholders with a special majority of the votes. In Portugal most resolutions of the general meeting are adopted by a simple majority (50%). In case a client only holds a minority stake in a company it is therefore of great importance that certain, essential, resolutions can only be adopted if the minority shareholders consent as well. Essential resolutions are (amongst others)：the increase/decrease of share capital (anti-dilution provisions), winding up or liquidation of the company, amendment of the articles of association, any sale of all or a substantial part of the business of the company, acquisition of participations in the capital of other companies, approval of budget/business plan, etc.

重大决议：某些决议应由股东以特别多数票通过。在葡萄牙，大多数股东大会的决议是以简单多数（50%）通过的。如果客户只持有公司的少数股权，那么应加入只有少数股东同意才能通过重要决议的条款，这一点非常重要。重要的决议包括：增加/减少股本（反稀释条款）、公司解散或清算、修改公司章程、出售公司全部或大部分业务、收购其他公司的资本、预算/商业计划的批准等。

Information rights：in principle each shareholder should be informed by the board of managing directors regarding the business of the company. In the SHA this right of information can be made more concrete and broadened (e. g. the obligation of the company to submit to the shareholders a quarterly report which shall inter alia consist of a balance sheet, profit and loss account and cash flow statements).

知情权：原则上，董事会成员应当通知每一位股东关于公司业务的运营情况。在 SHA 中，这种信息权利还可以更具体和广泛（例如，公司有义务向股东提交季度报告，其中应包括资产负债表，损益表和现金流量表）。

Transfer of shares: it is common practice in Portuguese transactions to include in a SHA share-transfer restrictions (e. g. in the form of a right of first refusal granted to the non-selling shareholder whereby the selling shareholders should offer the shares first to the other shareholder). The pricing mechanism is always one of the topics regarding which parties need to negotiate.

股份转让：葡萄牙的交易惯例是在 SHA 中设置股份转让限制条款（例如授予未出售股份的股东优先购买权，出售股份的股东应首先向其他股东出售股份）。定价机制始终是各方需要协商的议题之一。

Tag/drag along: it is common practice in Portuguese transactions to include provisions so that in the event that a shareholder envisages to sell all its shares in the target company to an interested buyer, the minority shareholder has the right to sell and transfer all the shares it holds in the target company to the interested buyer as well under the same conditions (i. e. the tag along). The drag along is also always included; this means that if a (majority) shareholder wants to sell its shares in a target company, then the other (minority) shareholders may be forced by the selling shareholder to sell their shares as well for the same conditions.

随售权/拖售权条款：在实践中一种常见的做法是规定随售权条款，规定当一个股东欲出售自己所持有的目标公司所有股份给有意的买方时，少数股东有权在相同条件下出售自己所持目标公司所有股份给前述有意的买方（即随售权）。设定拖售权条款也很常见，该条款意味着当多数股东欲出售自己所持目标公司全部股份时，少数股东所持目标公司股份也将被迫由多数股东以相同的条件强制出售。

Good/Bad leaver provisions: in many cases, if the managing directors of the target company hold shares, provisions are included to cover the situation where the employment or management agreement with such managing director is terminated. It is common practice that in such a case the managing director/shareholder is forced to sell its shares in the company against a certain price. The price depends on the reason for termination of the employment/management agreement.

正常离职和不良离职条款：很多情况中，如果目标公司的总经理持有其公司股份，且该总经理的雇用或管理协议终止，此时就需要正常离职和不良离职条款。在这种情况下，总经理会被要求以特定价格强制卖出其持有的目标公司股份。出售价格取决于终止雇佣或管理协议的具体原因。

Deadlock provisions：It is common practice in Portuguese transactions to insert provisions in a SHA dealing with situations in which the shareholders are not in agreement as regards the future of the target company. Accordingly, if a shareholder is not able to approve certain resolutions (due to the fact that it does not hold the required majority), such shareholder is granted a put option/call option to be exercised at a certain price so that he can leave the company or acquire the entire capital.

僵局条款：在葡萄牙的交易中通常会在股东协议中设置僵局条款来处理股东就目标公司的未来发展无法达成一致意见的情况。据此，如果一个股东由于未能持有公司的足够股份而导致无法通过某些决议，则股东有权以特定的价格行使看跌期权或看涨期权，以使其能够出售其股份离开公司或购买全部公司的股份。

5. 其他问题及解决方案 (Other Issues and Relevant Solutions)

Other issues which we come across when assisting our Chinese clients are：
我们在协助中国客户时还遇到过以下其他问题：

The fact that in many transactions time is of the essence; a swift follow-up/turnaround of the different versions of the transaction documentation is key. In case of non-EU buyers, such as Chinese buyers, specific approvals are required. Especially in case of auction processes, this may prejudice the possibility to buy the target company (since for example local purchasers have less mandatory internal approvals).

在许多交易中，时间是一个关键因素。在不同版本的交易文件中进行快速跟进和转换是关键。如果是非欧盟买方，例如中国买方，则还需要获得特定的许可。特别是在拍卖过程中，这可能会影响购买目标公司的可能性（因为葡萄牙当地的买方内部审批限制更少）。

To avoid frustration/lost of trust it is key to be transparent at an early stage already regarding specific approvals from, for example, Portuguese regulators/authorities.

为了避免焦虑或者彼此失去信任，买方在授予具体许可时，比如在葡萄牙监管部门授予许可的早期阶段，对具体进展保持充分披露是很关键的。

In our experience it is also important to have somcone who can speak Chinese and understands the cultural differences; in almost all transactions we are not only advising on civil law and tax law, but we are also bridging cultural gaps.

根据我们的经验，能有一个会说中文且能够理解文化差异的人很重要，因此几乎在所有交易中，我们除了要提供民法和税法方面的建议，还要做弥合文化差异的工作。

— 作者简介 —

Gonçalo Anastácio is a partner at SRS Advogados and heads both the Competition & EU Department and the Energy Department. He is a highly recognized lawyer in his field, both nationally and internationally, including being ranked Band 1 by Chambers & Partners and being inducted into the Hall of Fame by Legal 500.

Gonçalo Anastácio 是 SRS Advogados 的合伙人，同时也是竞争法和欧盟法部门以及能源部门的负责人。他在国内外都是该领域公认的杰出律师，包括被领先的法律目录评为第一名（Band 1 by Chambers & Partners）并被法律 500 强举荐进入名人堂（Hall of Fame by Legal 500）

With over 25 years of experience, Gonçalo has been involved in many of the most high-profile competition and regulatory cases in Portugal. He is fluent in Portuguese, English, French, Spanish, and Italian. He graduated in Law from the University of Coimbra (1995), holds a post-graduate degree in European Studies from the Collège des Hautes Études Européennes of Sorbonne, and a master's degree in European Law from the Lisbon University, where he was a teacher (assistant) for a decade at the undergraduate level and subsequently for the postgraduate course on Competition and Regulatory Law, among others, mainly on topics of European Law, Competition Law, Law of the Economy, and Regulatory Law.

Gonçalo Anastácio 拥有超过 25 年的执业经验，参与了许多葡萄牙最引人注目的竞争和监管案件。他精通葡萄牙语、英语、法语、西班牙语和意大利语。他于 1995 年在科英布拉大学获得了法律学位，后在巴黎索邦大学获得了欧洲研究的研究生位,并在里斯本大学获得了欧洲法硕士学位,在那里他曾担任助教十年,随后在竞争法和监管法研究生课程中担任讲师,主要讲授欧洲法、竞争法、经济法和监管法等方向。

Gonçalo Anastácio is also a member (and former president) of the International Chamber of Commerce (ICC) Competition Commission for Portugal and has been a member of working groups on draft proposals for the transposition of European Directives and the preparation of competition-specific statutes. He is a member of several scientific bodies and reviews, including the Circle of Portuguese Competition Lawyers, of which he was one of the founders, its first secretary general, and is currently a member of the Advisory Board. Gonçalo was also part of the first group of practitioners to receive the title of Specialist Lawyer in European and Competition Law from the Portuguese Law Society (2004).

Gonçalo Anastácio 还是国际商会(ICC)葡萄牙竞争委员会的成员(以及前主席),并且曾是起草欧洲指令和准备特定竞争法规的工作组成员。他是葡萄牙竞争法协会的成员,也是该协会的创始成员之一,曾担任第一任秘书长,目前是咨询委员会的成员。他还是葡萄牙律师协会(2004年)首批获得欧洲法和竞争法专家律师称号的从业者之一。

SRS Advogados is a leading multi-practice Portuguese law firm with over 140 lawyers in domestic Portuguese offices in Lisbon, Funchal and Oporto. Its international footprint comprises offices in Angola, Brazil, Macau, Malta, Mozambique and Singapore.

SRS Advogados 是一家领先的综合性葡萄牙律师事务所,在葡萄牙里斯本、丰沙尔和波尔图办公室拥有140多名律师。其国际办公室分布于安哥拉、巴西、澳门、马耳他、莫桑比克和新加坡。

股权并购在瑞士：在工业和服务领域开展投资

点 评

　　瑞士一直以来从其经济富足屹立于欧洲。瑞士已经与欧盟实现了经济一体化，并且拥有领先的高新技术产业，相较于其他欧洲国家，瑞士的税率更具有优势，因而吸引了很多投资者来投资。本文作者为来自瑞士菲谢尔律师事务所（Vischer）的 Lukas Zuest 和 Peter Kuehn，就中国投资者投资瑞士的优势、中国投资者在瑞士的并购交易、交易文件中的重点条款以及在瑞士投资时需要考虑的一些其他重要方面进行深入探讨。由于比较熟悉中国投资者的交易习惯与投资兴趣，本文作者对交易中一些需要特别考虑的问题予以提示，供读者进行参考。具体如下：

　　瑞士对境外投资的限制非常少。因此，瑞士卖方并不会首先考虑中国海外直接投资法律法规规定的境外批准或备案要求。根据本文作者的实践经验，如果中国买家尽早以透明的方式处理中方内部交易所需程序和具体要求，瑞士卖方将会觉得合作更顺畅，随后的出境审批或备案程序也能够更及时地融入交易流程。

　　近期，瑞士公司卖家经常要求买家购买并购保证保险（W&I 保险），以弥补违反陈述和保证条款带来的损失或索赔请求。W&I 保险是一种专业保险产品，旨在弥补违反陈述和保证条款所带来的损失或并购交易中的赔偿索赔。保障因未知或未披露事项而产生的损失或责任，并为经济损失提供补偿。实践中，绝大多数的保单是买方保单。必须强调的是，保险从不对一个谨慎的被保险人能够并且应当识别的风险负责。因此，缔结一份买方 W&I 保险并不能免除买方对目标公司进行尽职调查的工作。相反，保险仅对买方在尽职调查中已经核实的事项的陈述与保证条款进行承保。如果保险公司认为被保险人对特定事项的尽职调查报告不够全面和具体，那么其承保范围将会被限制甚至是被排除。此外，想要购买 W&I 保险的买方需要雇佣保险经纪人协助进行保险的购买。

与其他司法管辖区不同，瑞士法律没有一般的外国投资控制法规。然而，关于收购位于瑞士的不动产（包括对持有此类不动产的公司的大量持股），如果收购的不动产不打算用作永久性商业机构（例如工厂建筑、仓库、办公室、购物中心、商店、宾馆、餐馆，等等），包括适当的土地储备，则中国投资者需要根据莱克斯—科勒法案（Lex Koller 法）[1]获得特别许可。如果交易受 Lex Koller 法约束，则最迟须在交割前获得所需的许可。

1. 瑞士作为中国投资地的优势

1.1 瑞士与欧盟已实现经济一体化

瑞士位于欧洲中心。尽管瑞士不是欧盟成员国，但在经济层面上，它与欧盟已实现一体化，瑞士与欧盟间的贸易未受影响。自 1973 年以来，瑞士与欧盟签订了多项自由贸易协定。

多年来，瑞士与欧盟签署了多项双边条约，使其进一步融入欧盟内部市场。除此之外，由于拆除贸易技术壁垒协议，作为一般规则，任何通过瑞士合格测试的相关产品都可以被贴上 EC 标签并出口到欧盟，无需通过双重测试或根据相关欧盟安全标准做进一步检查。该协议惠及了不同产地的商品。因此，对于意在向欧洲推出工业产品的中国制造商，瑞士是一个有吸引力的欧洲测试市场，因为瑞士准入的工业产品一般也意味着欧盟准入。

瑞士和欧盟之间的人员自由流动协议于 2002 年生效，为瑞士国民与欧盟 27 国[2]及欧洲自由贸易联盟（EFTA）[3]国家的国民自由流动提供保障。只要他们具备医疗保险，合适的住宿条件和足够的资金（储蓄或收入）来养活他们自己和他们的家庭，该协议即授予那些国民居留和工作许可。欧盟 27 国和欧洲自由贸易联盟国家的公民移居到瑞士或者在瑞士找到工作的，他们需要做的仅仅是在入境 14 天内到有关部门登记注册，在就职 8 天前提供有效的劳动协议、房

---

[1] 译者注：Lex Koller 译为"莱克斯—科勒法案"，是瑞士对外国人在瑞士购买房地产进行限制的一部法律。

[2] 奥地利、比利时、保加利亚、塞浦路斯、捷克共和国、丹麦、爱沙尼亚、德国、芬兰、法国、希腊、匈牙利、爱尔兰、意大利、拉脱维亚、立陶宛、卢森堡、马耳他、荷兰、波兰、葡萄牙、罗马尼亚、斯洛伐克、斯洛文尼亚、瑞典、西班牙。

[3] 冰岛、挪威、列支敦士登。

屋租赁或购买协议以及填写完整的申请表，便可取得外国居民身份证。

1.2 瑞士与中国的自由贸易协定

2013年7月6日，中国和瑞士签订了自由贸易协定（以下简称中瑞自贸协定），此协定已于2014年7月1日生效。中瑞自贸协定是中国与世界20强经济体的第一个自贸协定，也是第一个与欧陆国家签订的自贸协定。

自从中瑞自贸协定生效后，瑞士对来自中国的、列入瑞士特殊偏好表的货物（对于来自中国香港特区的进口货物，适用欧洲自贸联盟与中国香港特区的自贸协定）取消了所有适用于工业品和其他非农业/养殖/渔业产品，包括纺织品和鞋类的关税，以及减少或取消了众多适用于农业/养殖/渔业产品的关税。

瑞士鼓励中国制造商考虑结合中瑞自贸协定、瑞士与欧盟、欧洲自贸联盟以及与其他40个国家的30个自贸协定的优势，将瑞士作为通向所有这些国家的"门户"。

"门户"并不意味着中国公司可以轻而易举地将瑞士当作货物出口欧盟或其他与瑞士签订贸易协定的国家的中转站，甚至作为通道而享受零关税。自由贸易的难易程度取决于瑞士与目的国贸易协定中的原产地规则，这需要由国际贸易法律专家进行具体分析。

一般来说，原产地规则对在贸易协定成员方境内创造的附加值有最低规定。中国公司可以以低关税或零关税向瑞士出口零部件和半成品，以满足中瑞自由贸易协定中的原产地规则，并在瑞士境内处理或加工这些零部件和半成品，或者将其与瑞士生产的零部件进行组装，以符合瑞士与最终出口目的国在贸易协定中对"原产于瑞士"的要求。这些产品将被视为瑞士制造，拥有积极的形象含义和效应，并在出口最终目的国时享受有关贸易协定的优惠税率。

1.3 瑞士拥有领先的高新科技技术

瑞士位于欧洲的心脏地带，分别与德国、法国、意大利以及奥地利接壤，自然资源贫乏，但却是高科技工业的重镇，如制药、化学制品、信息与通信技术、金融科技、生物技术、生命科学、医疗技术，以及机械、电力和金属工业。

众多国际知名生产商和跨国生物制药公司[1]不仅将其总部设在瑞士，而

---

[1] 例如：ABB, Geberit, Georg Fischer, Givaudan, Glencore, Holcim, Logitech, Lonza, Micronas, Nestlé, Nobel Bio-care, Novartis, Oerlikon, Rieter, Roche, Schindler, Schweiter, Syngenta, Straumann, Sulzer, Swatch, Tyco, 等等。

且在此建有重要的生产和研发场所。因为瑞士能够提供世界上最高品质的生活，这里拥有无与伦比的安全环境、高质量的学校，多语种的文化环境中英语被广泛使用，种种条件使这个国家对人才产生了强烈的吸引力。

瑞士拥有多所欧洲领先的理工科院校，例如苏黎世联邦理工学院（ETH）和洛桑联邦高等工业学院（EPFL）。长期以来，这些院校已经形成了与高科技企业携手合作、共同开展应用类研发项目的优良传统。

中国投资者应当知悉的一项重要因素是：瑞士对于对外技术转让不设任何限制，但是受技术出口法规限制的军用物资以及军民两用产品除外。

1.4 中国企业在瑞士设立欧洲总部的优势

中国企业设立欧洲总部或者分销中心，瑞士是首选地。

瑞士拥有优质的中小学校、知名的高等院校、特有的双轨教育体系以及世界最高品质的生活环境，对于国外人才具有强烈的吸引力。瑞士通过其卓越的产品和服务在国际人才市场上胜出，将大量尖端人才引入高素质高技能的劳动力大军。

在欧洲范围内，瑞士的职场最富有多元文化背景并且工作者可使用的语种最多。在苏黎世、巴塞尔和日内瓦的大都会区域均为多元文化和多语言社区，在那里英语几乎随处可闻，英语已经成为几乎所有国际性的瑞士公司，通用的工作语言。

瑞士是拥有最开明的劳动法的欧洲国家之一，其工会化程度低，工会行事温和，社会环境、经济、政策等所有因素都鼓励用工，并从根本上促成了瑞士的低失业率，截至2021年1月，瑞士失业率为3.7%。与欧盟27国同期平均7.3%的失业率相比，瑞士的失业率非常低，比奥地利的5.7%、德国的4.6%还要低。

只要遵守劳动法规定的通知期，劳动合同可以随时终止，不需要理由，也不需要支付遣散费。但是滥用性解雇和法定解雇保护的情形除外。

瑞士交通发达。苏黎世国际机场是瑞士与德国南部地区的国内与国际交通枢纽，该机场的航线通达世界所有主要城市，其中包括中国的北京、上海和香港。其他规模稍小的国际机场位于巴塞尔和日内瓦。从苏黎世国际机场起飞，欧洲所有国家的首都均可以在1—2小时之内抵达。国内/国际公路与铁路运输极为便利，因为已建立了覆盖面广泛的公路与公共交通网络，城际铁路至少每小时发一班车，而地区性的火车发车则更为频繁。瑞士耗费巨资建设铁路和公路，建成了创纪录的最长公路隧道——圣哥达隧道使其穿越阿尔卑斯山脉，并将欧洲北部与南部联结在一起。

虽然瑞士没有滨海区域，但是在巴塞尔—莱茵港口设有三处集装箱装卸设施，可满足进出瑞士的海运运输需求。莱茵河自巴塞尔至鹿特丹全程通航，航程约830公里，耗时3—4天，反向则耗时一周。中古时期，巴塞尔就因莱茵河港口成为北海与地中海之间的重要枢纽。

1.5 瑞士的自由法律框架

关于直接投资，瑞士的法律框架清晰明了，对投资者而言非常具有吸引力。对于来自国外的直接投资，瑞士法律没有特殊规定。通常情况下，瑞士对于外商投资无特殊审批要求，对于由内资或者外资所控制的瑞士公司也不会施行不同的法律法规。

仅有个别例外：

● 外国企业或者外国控股企业如果要投资或买卖住宅房地产（其中包括购买民用住宅房地产公司的控股权）通常仍属于禁止之列（另请参阅第4.3节）。

● 在某些监管领域，例如金融服务、公共交通、能源、广播电视、电信，外国投资者必须通过一家获得此类业务牌照的瑞士公司或者分支机构加以运作，其前提条件是，该牌照或许可的颁发对象是外国公司或者外国控股的公司。

1.6 瑞士公司的注册手续简洁明了

股份有限公司是瑞士公司的经典形式：责任有限，股份便于交易，股份转让仅受公司章程的限制，股东不会被商业登记处披露，并且通常情况下股东不可能被排除在公司外，但在上市公司以及公司合并时，极少数股东可以被排除。股份有限公司由股东大会和董事会管理，受外部审计的约束，在满足特定条件下，审计可能被限制或豁免。

有限责任公司，同样施行责任有限但更关注公司成员组成。公司成员由商业登记处向公众披露，股份转让须经股东会议同意。原则上，公司由全体股东管理而非董事会管理。有正当理由时，可以排除股东。与股份有限公司不同，在有限责任公司的章程中可以引入竞业禁止条款、额外的货币出资以及实物出资。

有限责任公司的最低注册股本为20 000瑞士法郎，股份有限公司为100 000瑞士法郎。公司成立时，有限责任公司的注册股本应当全额支付。而对于股份有限公司，在成立时则应当支付至少20%且不少于50 000瑞士法郎的注册股本。

注册股本应当在公司创立之前存入以公司名义持有的银行账户中。该账户直到公司在商业登记处完成注册之前，都将被冻结。

如果注册股本以实物而非现金支付，则需要在实物出资协议中充分详细地描述相关实物出资。发起人应当以书面形式报告该实物出资的性质和状态以及其估值的合理性。最终，由一名持证审计师审查发起人的报告，并确认其完整性和正确性。

1.7 瑞士对于跨境资本流动不设限制

瑞士拥有欧洲第二大金融中心，诸多世界最大的金融服务提供商如瑞士瑞信银行、瑞士联合银行（UBS）、瑞士再保险公司、苏黎世金融服务集团等选择在这里建立其欧洲总部。另外，中国建设银行和中国工商银行在苏黎世也设有分行。

瑞士对于跨境（汇出和汇入）支付转账或者资本流动没有设置任何限制。

1.8 瑞士提供比其他欧洲国家更具优势的税率

在欧洲范围内，瑞士是一个低税率国家。较之大多数欧洲国家，瑞士普通企业所得税税率很低。

公司所得税为三级税制，即联邦、州和乡镇。在多数州/直辖市，瑞士联邦政府征收的7.8%的企业所得税税负占全部企业所得税比例不到50%。

由于瑞士26个州和各个城市市政府均有权自主决定其所征收的所得税税率，因此，26个州都竞相压低其税率（且各州内的每个市政府之间也如此）。因此，瑞士各州之间总体企业所得税税负介于11.9%到21.6%之间，例如2021年：楚格市的企业所得税率为11.9%，卢塞恩市的企业所得税率为12.3%，巴塞尔市的企业所得税率为13.0%，沙夫豪森市的企业所得税率为14.2%，苏黎世市企业的税率为19.7%[1]。随着瑞士公司税法的改革已于2020年1月1日生效，许多州已经降低了其普通企业所得税率。为确保一个有竞争力、吸引力和可靠的税收框架，对研发费用的额外减税或税收抵免，经合组织的"专利盒子"税收模式，向瑞士转移业务时对任何隐藏的准备金或商誉进行免税，以及各州降低与参股、专利或公司间贷款相关的资本税的权利都已引入瑞士税法。

对持股超过股本10%或价值超过1 000 000瑞士法郎部分股权且出售前至少

---

[1] 根据规划，截至2023年将降至18.2%。

应持有一年取得的红利,以及对持股超过10%而取得的资本收益[1],联邦政府免收企业所得税。

瑞士达成有约束力的税务裁定的做法很可能是独一无二的。瑞士税务裁定的实践做法不是受到经合组织和欧盟调查的一类特殊税收安排,而是主管税务机关与纳税人就特定事项的税务影响而达成的有约束力的共识,如合并计划、公司重组或其他活动。税务的裁定可以在几周内获得(加急案件可以更快),它给纳税人提供了更好的确定性。

1.9 中瑞避免双重征税协定为来自中国的投资者在瑞士的投资提供优惠条件

瑞士与中国签订了避免双重征税协定即中瑞DTA,为投资瑞士提供了更好的条件。

例如,根据相关协定,支付给在另一方缔约国持有派息人至少10%股权资本的关联公司(合伙企业或个人除外)的股息免征任何预扣税。根据瑞中DTA,如果股息受益人是公司(出于财政透明考虑,合伙企业和个人除外)、居住于缔约国另一方并且直接持有派息公司至少25%的资本,那么股息的最高预扣税将是5%。

2. 案例分析

中国最大的手工工具(manual tool)[2]和叉车生产供应商,其公司上市于中国证券交易所,作为我们的中国客户,已经通过一家总部位于瑞士的私募股权公司收购了欧洲领先的工业和服务领域中的高品质办公设备和存储系统制造商和分销商(约有500名员工)。购买价格近2亿瑞士法郎。

此次交易架构为股权转让,我们的中国客户收购了瑞士目标集团100%的控股股份。以下各节是对中瑞并购交易以及此次交易的概述。

2.1 概述

瑞士并购交易除股权转让的其他类型还包括资产转让、法定兼并以及上市公司的公开收购。瑞士并购市场十分精密成熟,不仅是大型并购项目,对中小

---

[1] 出售前至少应持股一年。
[2] 手工工具是指用于握持、以人力或以人控制的其他动力作用于物体的小型工具,一般有手柄,便于携带。

型目标公司的收购通常也遵循标准化程序。

如今许多交易的构建方式是让不同的潜在买家参与竞标程序，在竞标的每个阶段（包括指示性报价、确定的有约束力的报价或最终报价），最优秀的报价将成功进入下一轮竞标，直至最终出现最具吸引力的买家候选人，获得完成交易的机会。

通常，瑞士并购交易的初始步骤之一是签订非披露协议（NDA）或保密协议（CA），以保护可能流向意向买家的敏感信息。

此后，双方通常会签订意向书（letter of intent）、条款清单（term sheet）或条款纲要（heads of terms）、谅解备忘录（memorandum of understanding）或类似文件，以阐明双方的大致意图以及预想交易的基本条款。

之后，买家将对目标群体进行尽职调查，这不仅涉及潜在的法律问题，还涉及财务、税务和任何其他相关方面（如知识产权、信息技术、环境等）。业务和技术尽职调查通常由买方完成。

最终在拍卖中竞拍成功的买方将被邀请参与交易文件的谈判，例如此次交易中的股份购买协议（SPA）。

签署股份购买协议后，双方必须在交割前执行某些操作，并努力实现交割条件。特别是，他们将处理必需的监管文件（例如，相关司法管辖区的合并控制许可，我们的中国客户在此次交易中亦是如此），获得重要第三方的控制批准的某些变更（包括在我们中国客户的情况中，相关中国证券交易所对此次交易的批准），安排收购融资，将并购保证（W&I）保险落实到位，根据具体情况，执行某些剥离交易并准备辅助协议（如过渡服务、租赁、咨询或新的关键管理人员雇佣协议）。

一旦实现交割条件（或在允许的情况下放弃交割条件），双方将完成交易。在双方法律顾问最大程度共同核实、完成、初始化交割文件的情况下进行交割前准备，以此控制双方在实际交割时所需的投入。交割时，股份以合法效力转让给买方，并将（第一批）购买对价支付给卖家。在后续阶段，根据目标公司的表现，可能需要根据具体情况支付进一步的购买对价或盈利能力支付（earn-out）。

最后，买方可能要进行某些事后管理操作，例如，选举新的董事会成员，重新命名目标公司，在目标集团实施新的规章，等等。

2.2 瑞士的合并控制法规

在计划进行经营者集中行为当年的财政年度内，相关企业（或译为合并企业）必须在实施集中行为之前向瑞士竞争委员会（COMCO）发出通知：

- 相关企业共报告至少 20 亿瑞士法郎的营业额，或在瑞士达到至少 5 亿瑞士法郎的营业额，并且，
- 至少有两家企业分别报告在瑞士至少 1 亿瑞士法郎的营业额。

对于保险公司、银行和其他金融中介机构，适用特殊周转计算方法。

如果其中一家企业在终局不可上诉的裁决中被认定在瑞士市场占据主导地位，并且如果经营者集中涉及市场或相邻市场或其上游或下游市场，则必须进行通告。

如果初步评估显示规划中的经营者集中将产生或加强支配地位，瑞士竞争委员会将展开调查。除非瑞士竞争委员会在收到通告一个月内通知涉事企业其将开展调查，否则企业可以完成集中。若开展调查，除非有关各方延迟否则调查将在四个月内完成。

如果调查指出经营者集中会出现以下情形，瑞士竞争委员会可以禁止集中或允许附条件和义务的集中：

- 集中将产生或加强支配地位，并可能消除有效竞争；并且
- 集中不会改善在另一市场的竞争条件，从而超过支配地位带来的负面影响。

对瑞士竞争委员会的决定不满可以在瑞士联邦行政法院提出质疑，其裁决可诉至瑞士最高法院。

3. 交易文件中的主要术语

3.1 购买协议（SPA）

最为重要的是，购买协议包含双方各自在特定交易中的义务，即卖方向买方交割股份时出售和转让的义务，以及买方在交割股份时支付购买对价完成购买获得股份的义务。

购买对价可以分期支付。如果在交割时未支付全款，则通常需要支付大部分款项，支付款项也可能包含基于未来盈利能力的部分。双方可以协商采用"锁箱机制"（Locked Box Purchase Price），以最近适当的资产负债表日期为准，

确定股权收益，卖方必须保证在交割前不会泄露任何信息。另外购买价格可能受到交割后价格调整机制的影响。卖方会设立一个结算账户，并设定与初步购买价格相关的参数（如净价、净债务和净营运资金等），这些参数将在交割后由买方进行审核，并根据商定的调整金额进行相应的付款。

其实，购买协议一旦签署，其将从签约到交割引导缔约双方，甚至可能包含交割后的某些操作（见上文第2.2节）。

购买协议还将就双方的相关特定领域提供各种陈述和保证。例如，卖方将声明并保证其拥有股份所有权，其有资格达成购买协议，并且目标集团不存在不同领域的主要未披露事项，如财务报表、重大合同（客户、供应商、融资协议、证券等）、合规、知识产权/信息技术、就业、社会保障、养老金、不动产、环境、保险、税务等。

买方在尽职调查中识别的风险可能会被"独立担保"（independent guarantees）承担或被"补偿"（indemnities）。为承担某些风险，双方可能会同意托管一定的购买对价。

卖方还将寻求通过某些责任限制来控制其风险，包括对"损害"的具体定义，在买方提出索赔要求之前"损害"必须超出适当的披露概念、某些门槛或免赔额，通常还会规定责任上限、关于适用的诉讼时效，甚至包括当买方未遵守某些索赔通知程序时而导致权利的消灭。

当自然人作为卖方时，买方可以通过寻求竞业禁止担保来保护其收购的业务的顺利进行。

最后，双方将通过协议规定解决争议时所适用的瑞士实体法并确定仲裁条款。

3.2 股东协议（SHA）

由于我们的中国客户收购了100%目标股份，因此不必签订股东协议（SHA）。然而，在非收购全部股份的交易中，买方通常会与少数股东签订股东协议。

股东协议的条款通常包含有关目标公司（及其子公司）的公司治理、董事会组成、信息权利、重要董事会和股东决策目录、转让限制、随售和领售条款、购买权、退出条款、正常和不良离职者情形、竞业禁止承诺，可能还有处罚、沟通规则、保密条款，等等。

有时，双方同意将其股份委托第三方代理以确保股东协议，特别是转让规则的执行。

3.3 法人组织文件

除了主要交易文件、购买协议和股东协议，瑞士并购交易通常还需要某些附属协议（见上文第2.2节）和其他法人组织文件：

首先，可能要求缔约双方获得其法人权力机关对交易的批准。

卖方还需根据需要取得目标公司的公司决议。例如，在记名股票的情况下，公司章程可能普遍规定股份转让需要经董事会批准。买方期待看到此类董事会决议，并且在交割时登记在公司股东名册上。

此外，买方通常需要向目标公司提交权益所有人通知，以说明自然人所最终代表的受益所有人。基于此，目标公司应当发布一份接到该通知的受益所有人名单。但依据瑞士公司法规定，如果没有被通知受益所有人的话，则不需公示通知名单。例如，在我们的中国客户的案例中，上市（控股）公司在这个意义上没有受益所有人。

买方也许想要修改董事会组成并包括自己的代表以取得完全控制。有时，作为董事会成员的卖家可能立即在交割后辞职，或者在适当的交易过渡期后辞职。为此，买方必须提交一份商业登记申请，视情况包括选举新董事会成员的临时股东大会会议记录、前董事会成员的辞职信、经公证的签字样本和新董事会成员的护照复印件等附件。

4. 需要考虑的其他重要方面

4.1 融资及购买对价支付——一些实际问题

瑞士目标公司的中国买家通常会以自己的（集团内）资金或向某家中国银行借贷来为收购提供经费。如果买方希望在瑞士的银行贷款来为收购提供经费，瑞士本土银行和非瑞士银行（中国工商银行和中国建设银行在瑞士设有分支机构）都可以提供银行贷款。

瑞士对境外投资没有任何限制。因此，瑞士卖方并不会首先考虑到中国海外直接投资法律法规规定的境外批准或备案要求。根据我们的实践经验，如果中国买家尽早以透明的方式处理这些程序和具体要求，瑞士买家将会觉得合作更为顺畅，随后的处境审批或备案程序也能够充分地融入交易流程。

在一些交易中，中国买家开了一家瑞士特殊目的公司（SPV），实际收购了瑞士目标公司。如果在交割时购买价款已经在该 SPV 的瑞士银行账户里，因为资金仅在瑞士境内进行转移，会特别有利于交易的交割。

然而，如果购买价款必须在交割日从中国转到瑞士，那么在指示买方银行在交割日将资金汇给卖方时，双方必须考虑到瑞士和中国之间的时差。在这种情况下，中国买家甚至可能在瑞士时间的实际交割日之前向银行提出汇款要求。

4.2 并购保证（W&I 保险）

近期，瑞士公司卖家经常要求买家购买并购保证保险（W&I 保险），以弥补违反陈述和保证条款带来的损失，或弥补索赔请求。W&I 保险是一种专业保险产品，旨在弥补违反陈述和保证条款所带来的损失，或并购交易中的赔偿索赔。保险保障因未知或未披露事项而产生的损失或责任，并为经济损失提供补偿。

原则上，有两种主要的 W&I 保险保单：卖方保单和买方保单。卖方保单是约定买方向卖方提出索赔，然后卖方向保险公司索赔。从根本上说，这是第三方责任险。在买方保单情形下，买方直接向保险公司提出索赔。从根本上说，这是赔偿保险。卖方通常不参与索赔处理，并且排除了保险人对卖方的追索权，除非损害是因卖方的故意不当行为或欺诈造成的。实践中，绝大多数的保单是买方保单。

必须强调的是，保险从不对一个谨慎的被保险人能够并且应当识别的风险负责。因此，缔结一份买方 W&I 保险并不能豁免买方对目标进行尽职调查工作。相反，保险仅对买方在尽职调查中已经核实的事项的陈述与保证条款进行承保。如果保险公司认为被保险人对特定事项的尽职调查报告不够全面和具体，那么承保范围将会被限制甚至是被排除。

想要购买 W&I 保险的买方需雇用保险经纪人，保险经纪人通常会获得 3—5 家保险公司的非约束性报价（NBI），其中列出了承保范围和保险费的基本概要。基于 NBI，买方选择一家保险公司开始承保流程。在承保流程进行中，保险公司主要根据买方顾问的尽职调查报告和虚拟数据室里提供的关于目标公司的文档进行风险评估。在承保流程顺利完成后，保险公司向买方发出 W&I 保险的初步保单，并通常可以在一定程度上再进行协商。

4.3 不动产相关问题——Lex Koller 法

与其他司法管辖区不同，瑞士法律没有一般的外国投资控制法规（见本文

第1.5节)。然而，关于收购位于瑞士的不动产（包括对持有此类不动产的公司的大量持股），如果收购的不动产不打算用作永久性商业机构（例如工厂建筑、仓库、办公室、购物中心、商店、宾馆、餐馆等)，包括适当的土地储备，则外国买家需要根据 Lex Koller 法获得特别许可。如果交易受 Lex Koller 法约束，则最迟须在交割前获得所需的许可。

5. 总结

瑞士已经成为中国企业寻求在欧洲直接投资、建立欧洲总部或销售和营销中心、配送中心、研发中心，并对具有欧洲分销网络的欧洲高端技术的制造商以及生产商进行收购的主要国家。过去十几年里，在瑞士，由中国控制且极具规模的公司或分公司的数量已增长了十倍。

思想敏捷、开放的中国投资者不仅能够将业务导向且务实的理念带入与瑞士方的新业务合作，也能够适应当地的现状和习俗，因而有很大机会在瑞士投资合作成功。

— **作者简介** —

Lukas Zuest 主要的执业领域为中瑞双向直接投资，交易（兼并和收购）和中瑞双边贸易。自2007年以来他一直在上述领域执业，并熟悉相关的注意事项。在完成其瑞士法律教育后，他顺利地取得了新加坡国立大学和华东政法大学联合培养的法学硕士学位。他曾在上海的一家国际律师事务所有四年半的工作经验。他的工作语言是德语、英语和汉语。他是 Vischer 中国业务主管和瑞中经济协会（SCCC）的董事会成员。

Peter Kuehn 专注于并购、银行、金融和私募股权。此外，他还就公司、合同和航空等领域的法律方面向瑞士和国际客户提供咨询服务，并且在房地产和跨境法律问题方面经验丰富。Peter 求学于德国康斯坦茨大学（获法学博士学位）和伦敦国王学院（获国际金融法律硕士学位），于2005年获得德国律师资格，于2008年获得瑞士律师资格。Peter 获得瑞士证券交易所的认可，可作为股票发行人的代表。他曾任职多家律师事务所和一家国际航空公司的法律部门。他也是多家瑞士公司的董事会成员。

Vischer an influential and innovative Swiss law firm, dedicated to providing effective legal solutions for Swiss and international clients, covering business, tax and regulatory matters. Working from modern offices in Zurich, Basel and Geneva, our more than 115 attorneys, tax advisers and public notaries are organized under the direction of experienced partners in practice teams, covering all areas of commercial law. With significant trade between China and Switzerland, many Chinese clients need expert advice to navigate the challenges of Swiss legal frameworks, whilst working with a different culture and language. Vischer's China Desk team, consisting of Chinese speaking Swiss and Chinese lawyers, provides you with the legal bridge you need to effectively complete investment and trade deals, mitigate risks and manage disputes. Vischer works for Chinese listed companies, state-owned enterprises and private entrepreneurs. Vischer has extensive experience in Sino-Swiss M&A, foreign direct investments, and commercial projects, bringing pragmatic, timely and expert advice to support your objectives. As a Chinese client looking to do business in Switzerland, Vischer can help with due diligence, negotiations and legal services, with prompt and practical solutions that focus on major risks. Vischer is used to helping Chinese clients to make fast, informed decisions, providing concise advice to support negotiations, contracts, arbitration and dispute management.

Vischer 是一家颇具影响力和创新精神的瑞士律师事务所，致力于为瑞士和国际客户提供有效的法律解决方案，内容涵盖商业、税务和监管事宜。Vischer 在苏黎世、巴塞尔和日内瓦拥有现代化办公场所。在执业经验丰富的合伙人的领导下，115 多名律师、税务顾问和公证人组成不同的专业团队，涵盖整个商经法律领域。随着中瑞之间的重要贸易往来，许多中国客户需要专家建议来应对来自瑞士法律框架的挑战，并同时使用不同的文化和语言。Vischer 的中国业务团队由会中文的瑞士和中国律师组成，为客户搭建法律桥梁，有效完成投资和贸易交易，降低风险以及管理纠纷。Vischer 为中国上市公司、国有企业和私有企业服务。Vischer 在中瑞并购、外商直接投资和商业项目领域拥有丰富的经验，为客户目标提供务实、及时和专业的法律意见。对于希望在瑞士发展业务的中国客户，Vischer 提供尽职调查、谈判和法律服务，以及着眼于主要风险的及时且实用的解决方案。Vischer 致力于协助中国客户作出快速且明智的决策，为其提供简明的建议，以支持谈判、合同、仲裁和争议管理。

投资在塞尔维亚：绿地投资
Investments in Serbia
Green Field Investments

点 评

　　塞尔维亚和中国签署了一项自1996年9月起生效的双边投资条约，该等条约约定，签署国有义务鼓励来自另一个签署国的个人或法人实体的相互投资，有义务公平和平等地对付所有此类投资并使投资人在该另一签署国的领土上获得全面的保护和保障，应提供协助并确保向另一签署国国民签发签证和工作许可证方面更加便捷等事宜，为两国间的投资活动提供了规则层面的保障。

　　根据本文作者的介绍，在塞尔维亚国内法层面，塞尔维亚政府向外国投资者提供各种福利政策以促进外国投资，其形式包括国家援助、税收优惠和税收减免、海关激励和/或强制性社会保障激励等方式。其中最为常见的是根据政府通过的《投资法令》授予奖励，该法令规定了对于特定行业的投资项目，如制造业、服务中心服务相关的项目（即主要向塞尔维亚以外的用户提供信息、通信和技术ICT服务）等，根据投资者付出的合理投资费用（指自提交申请之日起至投资项目实现期届满之日为止的重要和非重要资产的投资成本，和/或在实现充分雇用后的两年内向与投资项目相关的新雇员支付的薪金总额）按特定比例授予奖励，可授予的激励总额取决于投资项目以及项目执行的具体流程。在投资过程中，投资者可对塞尔维亚政府提供的激励政策予以适当关注，或在一定程度上减轻资金压力。

1. 简介（Introduction）

Chinese investments in Serbia come in various forms and shapes. Some of them are purely commercial projects, while others have great infrastructural significance and are considered not only important for Serbia, but for the entire Balkan and Southeast Europe region.

中国在塞尔维亚的投资形式多样。其中一些是纯粹的商业项目，而另一些则在基础设施方面具有重大意义，这些项目不仅对塞尔维亚十分重要，而且对整个巴尔干和东南欧地区都很重要。

One of the best examples of the significance of Chinese investments into Serbia in recent years has been the takeover of the Smederevo Steel Plant, by global steel giant, Hesteel Group Co. Ltd (the Hesteel Group).

全球钢铁巨头中国某钢铁集团对斯梅代雷沃钢铁厂的收购，是体现近年来中国对塞尔维亚进行投资至关重要的最好例证之一。

Smederevo Steel Plant, formerly one of ex-Yugoslavia's leading companies, known for high steel outputs and lucrative engagements on the market, faced significant problems at the end of the previous century, which led to bankruptcy of this once mighty state-owned company. After an unsuccessful attempt at privatization performed by the American corporation U.S. Steel in 2003, the company once again came into state ownership in 2012, being sold to the Republic of Serbia for a symbolic price of USD 1. Faced by uncertain times, burdened by debts, and employing somewhere close to 5000 workers, future for the Smederevo Steel Plant seemed bleak.

斯梅代雷沃钢铁厂曾是前南斯拉夫一流的公司之一，以高水平的钢产量和高利润的业务而闻名，该公司在20世纪末曾面临重大问题，这导致了这家一度强大的国有公司破产。2003年，一家名为"美国钢铁"的美国公司对其进行私有化尝试失败，此后，该公司于2012年再度成为国有企业，被以1美元的象征性价格出售给塞尔维亚共和国。斯梅代雷沃钢铁厂面临着复杂的环境、负担着沉重的债务、同时还雇用着近5000名工人，这使该公司的前景看似十分惨淡。

In April 2016, Smederevo Steel Plant, supported and supervised by the Government of the Republic of Serbia, as its majority shareholder, and Hesteel Group, signed the Agreement on Sale and Purchase of Assets, by which the majority of the Steel Plant's key assets (i.e., 98 separate proprietary packages) were sold to Hesteel for EUR 46 000 000.

2016年4月，斯梅代雷沃钢铁厂在其大股东塞尔维亚共和国政府的支持和监督下，与中国某钢铁集团签署了《资产买卖协议》，通过该协议，以 46 000 000 欧元的价格向中国某钢铁集团出售钢铁厂的大部分主要资产（即 98 个独立的资产包）。

The transaction itself was structured as an assets acquisition carve-out, whereby Hesteel Group chose to set-up a new limited liability company in Serbia to which the Smederevo Steel Plant's key assets were to be transferred, together with its employees, while Smederevo Steel Plant remained to exist as a separate shell company still liable and responsible for debts accrued in previous years, ultimately to be borne by the Republic of Serbia and its tax payers.

该交易本身的结构是资产收购剥离，在本次交易中，中国某钢铁集团选择在塞尔维亚设立一家新的有限责任公司，斯梅代雷沃钢铁厂的主要资产与其雇员将被一同转移至该公司。而斯梅代雷沃钢铁厂将作为一个独立的空壳公司继续存在，并仍对此前的累计债务承担责任，该债务并最终由塞尔维亚共和国及其纳税人承担。

Besides from paying EUR 46 000 000 for the Steel Plant assets, Hesteel Group also promised to inject further EUR 300 000 000 of its own funds into equity of HBIS Group Serbia Iron & Steel (the Hesteel Serbia), which is the official name of Hesteel Group's newly established subsidiary in Serbia. With Hesteel Serbia's registered and paid-in monetary capital currently amounting to approx. EUR 308 000 000, the promises of Hesteel Group regarding the long-term nature of their investment into Serbia seem to be well performed.

除为钢铁厂的资产支付 46 000 000 欧元以外，中国某钢铁集团还承诺进一步将其自有资金 300 000 000 欧元注入某钢铁集团塞尔维亚钢铁公司（中国某钢铁集团在塞尔维亚新成立的子公司的正式名称，以下简称某钢铁集团塞尔维亚公司）的股本。随着某钢铁集团塞尔维亚公司完成登记注册，并获得近 308 000 000 欧元的实收货币资本，中国某钢铁集团对塞尔维亚进行长期投资的承诺似乎得到了较好履行。

The investment of Hesteel Group attracted significant attention from European media, whereby the attempts of the largest Chinese steel-producer to gain a fixed manufacturing foothold in Europe did not go unnoticed. Reports of European Commission investigations into potential state-aid issues were published, which, however, ultimately resulted in the EU's antitrust body finding no issues with the Steel Plant takeover and its previous business operations.

中国某钢铁集团的投资引起了欧洲媒体的极大关注，中国最大的钢铁制造商尝试在欧洲获得固定生产点的尝试引起欧洲媒体关注。欧盟委员会公布了关于潜在的国家援助问题的调查报告，但最终欧盟反垄断机构认为钢铁厂的收购及其先前的业务经营不存在任何问题。

All the attention given to this transactions has, since the takeover, been proven to be quite deserved, since Hesteel Serbia became the second-largest exporter in Serbia, with its reported revenue in 2017 amounting to USD 750 000 000 and expected to be somewhere close to USD 1 000 000 000 in 2018.

自收购以来，所有对此交易的关注都被证实是值得的，这是因为某钢铁集团塞尔维亚公司成为塞尔维亚的第二大出口商，据报告，该公司2017年的收入达到750 000 000美元，在2018年，收入预计将接近1 000 000 000美元。

Hesteel Group's example since served to attract further investments by Chinese companies in Serbia, some of which will be mentioned in the following paragraphs, with all such investments being an important contribution to Serbia's overall efforts on economic and financial stability in recent years.

中国某钢铁集团的案例吸引了中国企业在塞尔维亚的进一步投资，其中企业一些将在下文中提及。近年来，塞尔维亚致力维护经济和金融稳定，这些投资在这些方面作出了重要贡献。

We so far had the opportunity to advise several Chinese investors on proposed greenfield investments in Serbia. As each of these transactions is a specific case requiring unique approach and legal assistance, our Chinese clients in most of the cases found the below information very helpful and necessary in order to assess the liability of the investments and the business climate in Serbia in general.

迄今，我们有机会向几位中国投资者就向塞尔维亚拟议的绿地投资提供建议。由于这些交易均具有特殊性，需要独特的方法和法律协助，在多数情况下，我们的中国客户发现以下信息对于评估塞尔维亚的投资责任和商业环境而言十分有用和必要。

2. 国家概况（Country Overview）

Serbia is a landlocked country in Central Southeast Europe. It is bordered by Hungary to the north; Romania and Bulgaria to the east; the Republic of Macedonia to the south; and Croatia, Bosnia and Herzegovina, and Montenegro to the west. With population of approx. 8 million, its capital and largest city is Belgrade, with approx. 1.6 million inhabitants. The official language of Serbia is Serbian, and the official currency is the Serbian dinar (RSD).

塞尔维亚是东南欧中部的内陆国家。它在北方与匈牙利接壤,在东部与罗马尼亚和保加利亚接壤,在南部与马其顿共和国接壤,在西部与克罗地亚、波斯尼亚和黑塞哥维那以及黑山接壤。其人口约为800万人。它的首都、也是最大的城市贝尔格莱德拥有约160万居民。塞尔维亚的官方语言是塞尔维亚语,官方货币是塞尔维亚第纳尔(RSD)。

Thanks to its highways (Corridors 10 and 11) and extensive river network (the total length of navigable rivers and channels is 1395 km), especially Danube river which passes through the country and its capital city Belgrade, Serbia is connected with other important countries such as Austria, Germany, Slovakia, Italy, Turkey, Greece, and many more. Furthermore, Serbia has a very favorable geographical position and a mild climate.

塞尔维亚发达的高速公路(走廊10号公路和走廊11号公路)和广阔的河流网络(通航河流和河道的总长度为1395公里),特别是通过国家境内及其首都贝尔格莱德的多瑙河,使其与其他重要的国家例如奥地利、德国、斯洛伐克、意大利、土耳其、希腊等连通。此外,塞尔维亚拥有非常有利的地理位置和温和的气候。

After renewing its membership in the International Monetary Fund (IMF) in December 2000, Serbia reintegrated into the international community by rejoining the World Bank's International Bank for Reconstruction and Development (IBRD) and the European Bank for Reconstruction and Development (EBRD). Significant progress has been made in trade liberalization and enterprise restructuring, as well as privatization of previously state-owned companies, including telecommunications and small and medium-sized firms.

2000年12月以来,塞尔维亚在国际货币基金组织(IMF)的成员资格续期,塞尔维亚重新加入了世界银行的国际复兴开发银行(IBRD)和欧洲复兴开发银行(EBRD),并借此重返国际社会。在贸易自由化、企业重建以及前国有企业（包括电信和中小企业）的私有化方面，塞尔维亚取得了重大进展。

Serbia is also a candidate for the European Union (EU) membership as of 2012, with accession negotiations ongoing. Serbia signed a Stabilization and Association Agreement with Brussels in May 2008. Further, the Interim Trade Agreement with the European Union was fully implemented in February 2010, allowing significant freedom for establishment of trade on the European Union single market. Serbia is also pursuing membership in the World Trade Organization (WTO).

截至2012年，塞尔维亚也是欧盟成员国的候选国，塞尔维亚加入欧盟的谈判持续开展。塞尔维亚于2008年5月与布鲁塞尔签署了《稳定与结盟协定》。此外，与欧盟签订的《临时贸易协定》在2010年2月全面实施，该协定使塞尔维亚获得在欧盟单一市场上开展贸易的重大自由。塞尔维亚也积极寻求加入世界贸易组织（WTO）的机会。

3. 塞尔维亚绿地投资法律概述 (Legal Overview of Greenfiled Investments in Serbia)

The purpose of the following paragraphs is to provide you with a general outline of basic legal rules and principles typically relevant for a foreign investor considering a greenfield investment in Serbia.

下文将对塞尔维亚的基本法律规则和原则进行总体概述，特别是那些与外国投资者考虑在塞尔维亚进行绿地投资相关的规则和原则。

In order to present a clear picture of the investment climate, as well as the legal aspects concerning foreign greenfield investments in Serbia, the following sections hereof will present a general outline significant for receiving a precise and useful information on typical questions and dilemmas faced in the course of execution of an investment in Serbia.

为了清楚地展现塞尔维亚关于外国投资者在塞尔维亚进行绿地投资的投资环境以及法律问题，以下各节将提供一个总体的概要，这一概要十分重要，可以帮助您准确了解在塞尔维亚进行投资的过程中面临的典型问题和困境。

3.1 外国投资 (Foreign Investments)

Foreign investments in Serbia generally include but are not limited to (i) rights acquired by an investor on the basis of shares or stocks in Serbian companies or a branch established in Serbia, (ii) rights of ownership and other property rights on mobile property or real estate in Serbia, (iii) PPP agreement or rights arising from a license or permit issued by public authorities for performing licensed business activities; etc.

对塞尔维亚的外国投资总体上包括但不限于：(i) 投资者因在塞尔维亚的公司或在塞尔维亚境内建立的分支机构持有股份或股票而获得的权利；(ii) 对塞尔维亚境内的动产或不动产持有的所有权和其他财产权；(iii) 公私合作协议或为开展特许经营活动而由公共机关签发的执照或许可证所产生的权利等。

As of 2000, Serbia has attracted more than EUR 27 billion of foreign direct investments and grown into one of the premier investment locations in Central and Eastern Europe.

截至 2000 年，塞尔维亚吸引了超过 270 亿欧元的外国直接投资，并成为中欧和东欧的主要投资地点之一。

Besides investments from the European Union, the Serbian infrastructure, electric power, food, telecom and automotive sectors are attracting attention from Chinese investors as well. In 2014, the Serbian government had announced that China National Electric Engineering Co. (CNEEC) publicized plans to invest in Serbia. During 2016, a consortium consisting of CNEEC and Scarborough group signed a contract worth EUR 230 million on building a power plant in Serbia. In 2017, Mei Ta Group, Chinese producer of automotive parts, finished the construction of the production plant as a part of their 60 million EUR investment in Serbia. In addition to that, several Chinese construction companies are currently executing infrastructure projects in Serbia as part of the Chinese Government's Belt and Road Initiative (BRI), including a EUR 302 million section of the Corridor 11 Highway constructed by Shandong High-Speed Group, a EUR 208 million section of the Corridor 11 Highway constructed by China Communications Construction Company Ltd. (CCCC), and a 350 million USD section of Belgrade-Budapest Railway built by China Railway International and CCCC, on which works started in November 2017. Chinese construction companies are also seen as probable contractors for several other infrastructure projects, thereby suggesting a very suitable investment climate for Chinese investors.

除来自欧盟的投资以外，塞尔维亚的基础设施、电力、食品、电信和汽车行业也吸引了中国投资者的关注。2014年，塞尔维亚政府宣布，中国电力工程有限公司（CNEEC）公布了在塞尔维亚投资的计划。2016年，由中国电力工程有限公司和斯卡伯勒集团组成的财团签署了一项价值2.3亿欧元的合同，以在塞尔维亚建设一座发电厂。2017年，中国汽车零部件生产商美塔集团完成了生产工厂的建设，这是其在塞尔维亚所进行的6000万欧元投资的一部分。除此之外，一些中国建筑公司目前正在塞尔维亚开展基础设施项目，这些是中国政府"一带一路"倡议的一部分，其中包括由山东高速集团以3.02亿欧元的总价建设的"11号走廊"公路段，由中国交通建设有限公司（CCCC）以2.08亿欧元的总价建设的"11号走廊"公路段，由中铁国际和中国交通建设公司以3.5亿美元的总价建设的贝尔格莱德—布达佩斯铁路段（该工程于2017年11月开工）。中国建筑公司也被视为其他几个基础设施项目的可能承包商，这意味着对于中国投资者而言，塞尔维亚具有非常合适的投资环境。

Foreign investors in Serbia have various investment protection rights and typically enjoy national treatment. Article 17 of the Constitution of the Republic of Serbia broadly states that foreigners, in accordance with international treaties, have all the rights guaranteed under the Constitution and applicable laws in the Republic of Serbia, except for those rights which are reserved solely for domestic nationals.

在塞尔维亚的外国投资者拥有各种投资保护权，通常享受国民待遇。《塞尔维亚共和国宪法》第17条对此作出了规定：根据国际条约，外国人享有所有《塞尔维亚共和国宪法》和在塞尔维亚境内所适用的各种法律所保障的权利，但仅适用于国内公民的权利除外。

Bilateral treaties and international conventions additionally provide for a more favorable treatment of foreign investors originating from countries that are signatories to such treaties or conventions. Investors may also enjoy benefits arising from preferential trade agreements to which Serbia is a party, including but not limited to free trade agreements concluded with Russia, Belarus, Kazakhstan, Turkey, CEFTA and EFTA, as well the Stabilization and Association Agreement with the EU.

双边条约和国际公约还为来自签署国的外国投资者提供了更有利的待遇。投资者还可享受来自塞尔维亚加入的优惠贸易协定的优惠，包括但不限于与俄罗斯、白俄罗斯、哈萨克斯坦、土耳其、中东欧自由贸易区和欧洲自由贸易联盟达成的自由贸易协定，以及与欧盟达成的稳定与结盟协议。

The Republic of Serbia and the People's Republic of China signed a Bilateral Investment Treaty which is in effect since September 1996 (Investment Treaty). Pursuant to Art. 2 of the Investment Treaty, the signatories are obligated to encourage mutual investments coming from individuals and/or legal entities based in the country of the other signatory. Further, the signatories are obligated to treat all such investments fairly and equally, with full protection and safety on the territory of the other signatory.

塞尔维亚共和国和中华人民共和国签署了一项自1996年9月起生效的《双边投资条约》(以下简称《投资条约》)。根据《投资条约》第2条，签署国有义务鼓励来自另一个签署国的个人或法人实体的相互投资。此外，签署国有义务公平和平等地对待所有此类投资，并使投资人在该另一签署国的领土上获得全面的保护和保障。

The Investment Treaty also stipulates that each signatory shall provide assistance and ensure easier terms for issuance of visas and work permits to the nationals of the other signatories, as it may be necessary for performance of any investment related activities by such persons. Provisions such as these may prove to be very useful in practice, especially if implementation of foreign investment in Serbia entails establishment of a local legal entity, which is to be represented and managed by a foreign national.

《投资条约》还规定，签署国应提供协助并确保向另一签署国国民签发签证和工作许可证方面的条款更加便捷，因为这对于该等主体进行任何与投资相关的活动而言可能是十分必须的。在实践中，当在塞尔维亚进行外国投资需要设立一个由外国国民代表并管理的地方法律实体的情况下，这些规定被证明是非常有用的。

3.2 投资融资与激励 (Investment Financing and Incentives)

One of the most important question that foreign investors come across while evaluating their potential investment into Serbia is the issue of securing of appropriate financing for their investment. There are several options in this regard that are usually utilized by the investors, such as self-funding, securing loans from banks and financial institutions, obtaining government incentives, etc.

外国投资者在评估其对塞尔维亚的潜在投资时遇到的最重要问题之一，是保证为其投资获得适当的融资。在这一方面，投资者通常会作出几种选择，例如自筹资金、从银行和金融机构获得贷款、获得政府激励等。

In our experience, it is common for foreign investors in Serbia to pre-dominantly finance the investments by themselves, through the use of their own funds and assets. Foreign investors usually choose this type of investment financing to show that their investment is serious and long-term, thereby implying that they are committed to their investment in Serbia. Besides from sending a strong message on the market, such scenario also leads to a more favorable position with the government, and may be of significant influence on the process of award of subsidies to the investor.

根据我们的实践经验，塞尔维亚的外国投资者在多数情况下通过自有的资金和资产为投资提供资金。外国投资者通常选择此类融资方式，来表明他们的投资是严肃的、长期的，从而体现他们致力于在塞尔维亚进行投资。除了在市场上发出强有力的信息，这种方案还会使得投资者在与政府交涉时处于更有利的地位，并可能对投资者获得补贴的过程产生重大影响。

On the other hand, debt-financing is becoming more significant in Serbia in recent years, with banks being prepared to offer suitable commercial terms through loans. Some of the largest investments in recent years involved the use of syndicated loans, while crediting by international banking institutions (European Bank for Research and Development, International Monetary Fund, etc.) for major infrastructural projects also became more important.

另一方面，近年来，在塞尔维亚债务融资变得越来越重要，银行正准备通过贷款提供合适的商业条款。近年来，一些规模最大的投资利用了银行贷款，而国际银行机构（欧洲研究与发展银行、国际货币基金组织等）对主要基础设施项目的贷款也变得更加重要。

It should also be noted that alternative ways of funding of certain parts of the investment project may be available, such as the use of financial leasing agreements, franchising, securing of corporate or intracompany loans, etc.

还应该指出的是，对于投资项目的某些部分而言，另有一些可供选择的融资方式，例如利用融资租赁协议、特许经营、公司担保或公司内部贷款等。

An interesting note in terms of investment financing for any prospective Chinese investor is the fact that the Bank of China has its own local subsidiary in Serbia, serving the role of financial support for all potential investors, with its financial operations being conducted in Serbian dinars, Chinese yuan, Euro and other currencies, depending on the necessities of each specific case.

对于任何潜在的中国投资者来说,在投融资方面一个值得注意的事项是,中国银行在塞尔维亚当地拥有分支机构,可为所有的潜在投资者提供财务支持,根据个案的需要提供以塞尔维亚货币第纳尔、中国货币人民币、欧元和其他货币为流通币种的财务业务。

In order to promote a positive investment climate, the Republic of Serbia offers various benefits to foreign investors that decide to invest their funds into Serbia. As a general comment, the investment incentives may encompass various forms, depending on the type of investment and related project, and are usually given in the form of a state aid, tax incentives and tax relief, customs incentives and/or compulsory social security incentives.

为了构建积极的投资环境,塞尔维亚向决定对塞尔维亚投资的外国投资者提供各种福利。一般来说,投资激励措施可能包括各种形式,具体取决于投资的类型和相关项目,并通常会以国家援助、税收优惠和税收减免、海关激励和/或强制性社会保障激励的形式提供。

The most common incentive scheme applied to new investments in Serbia is the awarding of incentives under the Government-adopted Investment Decree, which defines the amount of incentives that may be awarded depending on the justifiable costs of an investment made by the investor. These justifiable costs (as per Article 3 of the Investment Decree) are:

适用于塞尔维业新投资的最常见的激励方案是根据政府通过的投资法令予以奖励,该法令规定了根据投资者付出的合理投资费用予以奖励的金额。这些合理投资费用(根据《投资法令》第3条)是指:

- costs of investment into material and non-material assets, during the period starting from the date of submission of the application for incentives until the date of expiry of the investment project realization period; and/or
- 自提交激励申请之日起至投资项目实现期届满之日止的重要和非重要资产的投资成本;和/或
- costs of gross salaries paid to new employees related to the investment project during a two-year period, after reaching full employment.
- 在实现充分雇用后的两年内,向与投资项目相关的新雇员支付的薪金总额。

Incentives may be awarded for investment projects in the manufacturing sector and for projects concerning the provision of so-called service center services (i. e., provision of ICT services primarily to users outside of Serbia). The incentives may not be awarded for investment projects in the traffic sector, software development (unless if the development serves the purpose of product improvement, manufacturing process or service center services), catering, games of chance, trade, synthetic fiber development, coal and steel, mining, tobacco, weapons and ammunition, ship construction, airports, public utility sector and sectors of energy, broadband networks, fishery and aquaculture.

激励可以授予给制造业的投资项目和与服务中心服务相关的项目（即主要向塞尔维亚以外的用户提供信息、通信和技术服务）。但激励不可授予给交通行业、软件开发（除非该项开发的目的是用于产品改进、生产过程或服务中心服务）、餐饮、赌博、贸易、合成纤维开发、煤炭和钢铁、采矿、烟草、武器和弹药、船舶建造、机场、公用事业和能源行业、宽带网络、渔业和水产养殖。

Under Article 8 of the Investment Decree, the maximum amount of investment incentives that may be awarded to an investor is equal to 50% of the justifiable costs of realization of the investment project for "large" enterprises, 60% for "medium" enterprises and 70% for "small" enterprises (as such are categorized under the Investment Decree and state aid rules). If the investment exceeds EUR 50 million, the maximum amount of investment incentives for the part exceeding EUR 50 million is equal to 25% of such justifiable costs, and 17% for the part of justifiable costs exceeding EUR 100 million.

根据《投资法令》第8条，可以给予投资者的投资激励的金额上限，对于大型企业为其完成投资项目而产生的合理费用的50%，对于中型企业为合理费用的60%，对于小型企业则为70%（分类的根据是《投资法令》和国家援助规则）。如果投资超过5000万欧元，则对超过5000万欧元部分的投资激励金额上限为合理支出的25%，超过1亿欧元的部分激励金额上限则为合理支出的17%。

The total amount of the incentives that may be awarded under the Investment Decree depends on the investment project and the location of where such is to be executed. All municipalities in Serbia are sorted into four groups (with additional fifth group for so-called "devastated areas"), depending on the level of their economic development, as compared to the Republic average, and areas that are less developed entitle the investor to a higher amount of incentives.

根据《投资法令》，可授予的激励总额取决于投资项目以及项目执行的具体位置。根据经济发展水平，塞尔维亚的所有城市可分为四组（另有所谓的"灾区"属于第五组），在与塞尔维亚的平均水平相比欠发达的地区投资，投资者能获得更高的激励金额。

Besides from the direct Government incentives, greenfield investments may also qualify for other incentives under different regulations applicable in the Republic of Serbia, depending on the type and amount thereof.

除了政府的直接激励，绿地投资还可能有资格申请塞尔维亚的不同法规规定的其他激励，这具体取决于投资的类型和金额。

As an example, Serbian Corporate Income Tax Law (CIT Law) stipulates an incentive in the form of a 10-year corporate income tax relief in Article 50a of the CIT Law, on a pro-rata basis defined in the CIT Law, if (i) more than RSD 1 billion (approx. EUR 8 474 576.27) is invested in the fixed assets intended to be used for carrying out the prevailing line of business or other lines of business defined in the foundation deed or other document of the taxpayer, and if (ii) the taxpayer hires at least 100 employees on an indefinite period of employment during the investment period, so that following the completion of the investment, the taxpayer has additional 100 employees actually working at its premises.

例如，《塞尔维亚企业所得税法》（以下简称《企业所得税法》）第 50a 条规定了一项按照《企业所得税法》规定的比例以 10 年期的企业所得税减免为形式的激励，获得此激励需满足以下条件：（i）超过 10 亿第纳尔（约 8 474 576.27 欧元）的金额被用于开展主要业务或由创立契约或纳税人的其他文件规定的其他业务的固定资产，并且若（ii）在投资期间，纳税人至少雇用了 100 名雇用期不固定的雇员，使得在其投资完成后，纳税人实际上有至少 100 名雇员在其营业地工作。

Further, certain customs reliefs are defined under Customs Relief Decree allowing for a non-tariffed (with exception of VAT) import into Serbia of business-related equipment by a foreign investor, subject to specific terms.

此外,《关税减免法令》的具体条款还规定了一些关税减免,允许外国投资者在免征关税(增值税除外)的情况下向塞尔维亚进口与业务相关的设备(受限于特定条款的规定)。

In view of the above, proper and timely consultations with legal and financial consultants is of crucial importance when planning a greenfield investment in Serbia, as this serves to ensure the most efficient utilization of available benefits granted to foreign investors.

鉴于以上规定,在对塞尔维亚进行绿地投资作出规划之时,与法律和财务顾问进行及时、适当的协商至关重要,唯有如此,方能确保最有效地利用给予外国投资者的各种福利。

3.3 公司法方面(corporate law aspects)

When analyzing the potential of conducting a greenfield investment in Serbia, one of the first issues the investor faces is the question of establishment of a local entity through which the relevant investment is to be implemented. In general, foreign investors establish a local company in Serbia in the form of a limited liability company (srp. društvo sa ograničenom odgovornošću), as the most versatile form of incorporation.

分析在塞尔维亚进行绿地投资的可能性时,投资者面临的首要问题之一是设立一个可借以实施相关投资的本地实体。一般而言,外国投资者会在塞尔维亚建立一家有限责任公司(塞尔维亚语为 društvo sa ograničenom odgovornošću)作为本地公司,这也是最通用的公司形式。

Accordingly, in order to ensure appropriate implementation of its greenfield investment, a foreign investor should in advance decide on various questions related to the set-up of its local subsidiary and its business operations.

因此,为了保证绿地投资的适当实施,外国投资者应事先决定与其当地子公司的设立及其业务经营有关的各种问题。

First of all, a foreign investor wishing to establish a company in Serbia has to submit the registration application to the Serbian Business Registers Agency (BRA), which must be followed with documents necessary for the company's incorporation, as outlined below:

首先,希望在塞尔维亚设立公司的外国投资者必须向塞尔维亚商业登记机构（BRA）提交登记申请，并附有公司设立必须的下述文件：

- Notarized Foundation Deed of the company, made in line with the requirements of the Serbian Company Law;
- 符合塞尔维亚公司法要求的经过公证的公司创立契约；
- Commercial register excerpt for the company's founder;
- 公司创始人的商业登记摘录；
- Decision on appointment of the managing director(s) and decision on appointment of supervisory board chairman and members (i. e., only if the company is to have a two-tier management structure);
- 关于任命管理董事的决定和关于任命监事会主席和成员的决定（仅在公司具有双层管理结构时）；
- Certificate from the commercial bank confirming that the initial founding capital has been paid in by the founder; and
- 商业银行确认初始创始资金已由创始人支付的证明；及
- Registration application form with proof of payment of the official registration fees.
- 有正式登记费用的支付证明的登记申请表。

3.3.1 商业登记摘录（Commercial register excerpt）

The company's founder needs to submit an original of its registration certificate (i. e., commercial registry extract), issued and notarized in accordance with the laws of the country in which the company's founder has its seat, as well as apostilled, if applicable.

公司的创始人需要提交登记证书原件（即商业注册摘录），此类文件根据公司创始人所在国家或地区的法律而颁发和公证，并且如适用的话，还应经过认证。

Based on our previous experience, a so-called "full legalization" procedure must be followed for the documents issued by the competent authorities in China. Namely, any document issued in China must be (i) legalized for the use abroad in accordance with Chinese laws, and then (ii) certified by diplomatic-consular authority of Serbia in China, before it may be used in Serbia as a public document.

根据我们以往的经验，中国主管机关签发的文件必须经过"完全合法化"

程序。也就是说,在中国签发的任何文件必须:(ⅰ)根据中国法律,在国外对其加以使用的行为被合法化,并且(ⅱ)经塞尔维亚驻中国外交领事机构认证后,才能在塞尔维亚作为公共文件使用。

As general information, the Republic of Serbia has an embassy in Beijing and a general-consulate in Shanghai that may perform the above certification of documents.

一般来说,塞尔维亚在北京设有大使馆,在上海设有总领事馆,皆可以进行上述文件的认证。

3.3.2 经公证的创立契约(Notarized foundation deed)

Foundation Deed is the crucial document for every limited liability company in Serbia. Before the legal counsels may prepare and finalize the foundation deed of the limited liability company, the company's founder must decide on several issues, most important of which are: the corporate governance structure; the prevailing business activity; which is to be registered with the BRA; other issues such as: business name, the seat of the new company, and the amount of initial founding capital.

在塞尔维亚,创立契约是每个有限责任公司的重要文件。在法律顾问准备并定稿有限责任公司的创立契约之前,公司的创始人必须决定几个问题,其中,最重要的是:公司管理结构;登记于塞尔维亚商业登记机构的主要业务活动;其他问题,例如,商号、新公司所在地以及初始创始资本金额。

• 公司管理结构(Corporate Governance Structure)

The company's founder may opt between the one-tier governance system (i.e., the General Assembly and one or more Managing Directors) or a two-tier governance system (i.e., the General Assembly, the Supervisory Board and one or more Managing Directors).

该公司的创始人可以选择一层管理体系(即股东大会和一名或多名管理董事)或双层管理体系(即股东大会、监事会和一名或多名管理董事)。

Each of the above stated corporate governance structures has its own benefits, as well as flaws, and proper choice should always be made in consultation with the local legal advisor of the company's founder.

上述公司管理结构各有其利弊,应在向公司创始人的当地法律顾问进行咨询后作出适当的选择。

• 主要业务活动(The Prevailing business activity)

Only the prevailing business activity of the company is registered with BRA. However, the company may engage in other business activities as well, without any registration requirements, as outlined in the company's business strategy, internal documents and/or Foundation Deed.

公司的主要业务活动应在塞尔维亚商业登记机构登记。但是，公司也可以按照公司的业务战略、内部文件和/或创立契约参与其他业务活动，对此，并无登记的要求。

It should be noted that some business activities are subject to licensing, and cannot be performed without a specific approval by the competent authority.

应该指出的是，某些商业活动需要获得许可，未经主管机关的特别批准不得进行。

• 商号、公司所在地以及初始创始资本（Business name of the company/Seat of the company/Initial founding capital）

A limited liability company's business name is the name under which such company conducts its business activities. This name must not be interchangeable with another company's business name and must not cause any confusion regarding the company or its business activities.

有限责任公司的商号是该公司开展业务活动的名称。此名称不得与其他公司的商号互换，亦不得对公司或其业务活动造成任何混淆。

Seat of the company is an integral part of the company's establishment process. Accordingly, it is common for a newly established company, seeking to implement a greenfield investment in Serbia, to temporarily lease commercial premises from third party providers until it is finally decided where the new business facility will be constructed.

公司所在地是公司成立过程中不可或缺的一部分。因此，新设公司寻求在塞尔维亚实施绿地投资时，通常会暂时从第三方供应商处租赁商业房地，直至其最终决定新营业设施的建设地点。

As a general rule, the monetary portion of a limited liability company's registered capital must amount to a minimum of RSD 100 (less than EUR 1). The initial founding capital does not need to be contributed prior to the company's establishment, but only within a timeframe of up to 5 years from the establishment date, and as specified in the company's foundation deed. However, it is common to pay in the initial founding capital prior to the incorporation in order to ensure that the new company will have sufficient funds to perform business activities immediately upon its establishment.

一般来说，有限责任公司注册资本的货币部分必须至少达到100第纳尔（少于1欧元）。初始创始资本不需要在公司成立之前缴纳，但应自公司成立之日起5年内缴足，还应当遵循公司创立契约的相关规定。但是，在公司注册成立之前支付初始创始资本是通常的做法，这是为了确保新公司在成立后即有足够的资金开展业务活动。

3.3.3 任命管理董事/监事会成员的决定 [Decision on appointment of the managing director(s)/supervisory board members]

A Decision on Appointment of the Managing Director(s) indicates the overall number of the Managing Directors in the company and possible limitations to their representation power.

关于任命管理董事的决定表明了公司管理董事的总数以及对其代表权可能的限制。

It should be noted that only the co-signature limitation by other directors, representatives of the company, procura holders, etc., may be registered on the website of the BRA, and thus be considered obligatory towards third parties.

应该注意的是，只有经其他董事、公司代表、公司持有人等以共同签名的方式作出的限制才能在塞尔维亚商业登记机关网站上进行登记，并因此被视为对第三方具有拘束力。

If the company has a two-tier corporate governance structure the supervisory board members must be appointed as well. The supervisory board must have at least 3 members, whereby the overall number of its members must be uneven.

如果公司具有双层管理结构，则还须任命监事会成员。监事会须至少具有3名成员，其成员总数必须为非偶数。

3.3.4 设立公司的费用与成本（Fees and costs of incorporation）

The total administrative fees for filing a company registration application for a limited liability company with the BRA are approx. EUR 60. Costs of notarization/certification before a court or a public notary should usually not exceed EUR 500. Moreover, the costs of certified translation of documents provided in a foreign language depend on the quantity and are usually charged EUR 10-12 per page.

向塞尔维亚商业登记机关提交有限责任公司的登记申请的总管理费约为60欧元。在法院或公证人处进行公证、认证的费用通常不应超过500欧元。此外,对外语文件的翻译核证费用取决于其数量,通常每页会收取10—12欧元的费用。

3.3.5 登记后的活动 (Post-registration activities)

Once registered, the company should produce a company stamp, open its permanent bank account and submit, promptly upon registration of the company, all necessary documents and applications (i.e., lease agreement for the business premises, initial tax application, etc.) to the relevant authorities within the legally prescribed deadlines. In general, the post-registration activities are usually done by a tax/accounting consultant with local expertise in this area of business.

一经登记,公司应制作公司印章、开立其永久银行账户,并在公司登记后在法定时限内立即向有关机关提交所有必要的文件和申请(即营业地的租赁协议、首次税务申报等)。一般而言,登记后的工作通常由在当地该业务领域具有专业知识的税务、会计顾问完成。

3.4 对塞尔维亚的绿地投资:不动产法律方面 (Greenfield Investments Into Serbia: Real Estate Law Aspects)

One of the most important choices in the course of implementation of a greenfield investment in Serbia is choosing the appropriate location for the site of the future business facility. In this regard, besides from finding a suitable location, and negotiating on its acquisition, several legal issues should also be taken into account.

在塞尔维亚实施绿地投资的过程中,最重要的选择之一是为未来的营业设施进行合适的选址。在这方面,除寻找合适的地点并就其收购进行谈判外,还应当考虑若干法律问题。

In general, it should be noted that the *Constitution of the Republic of Serbia* guarantees property rights to investors. It provides that all forms of ownership enjoy equal protection, which ownership may be taken away or limited solely for the purpose of public interest determined by law, with at least a market fee consideration being paid therefor.

《塞尔维亚共和国宪法》保障投资者的财产权。该法规定，所有形式的所有权均受平等保护，所有权仅可因法律规定的公共利益而被剥夺或限制，并至少向权利人支付该财产的市价作为对价。

3.4.1 外国人对不动产的收购（Real property acquisitions by foreigners）

Pursuant to the Serbian Property Law, foreign nationals may acquire real property in Serbia, subject to reciprocity. While foreign individuals may acquire flats and residential buildings, foreign legal entities may only acquire real property that is necessary for the conduct of their business activities in Serbia. The respective acquisition may be subject to, inter alia, issuance of a confirmatory statement on reciprocity by the Ministry of Justice and in case of acquisition of property for business reasons by foreign legal entities, issuance of the affirmative opinion of the Ministry of Trade.

根据《塞尔维亚财产法》，外国公民可以在互惠条件下收购塞尔维亚的不动产。虽然外国自然人可以收购公寓和住宅建筑，但外国法人实体只能收购在塞尔维亚开展业务活动所必需的不动产。相关收购可能会受到司法部发布的关于互惠的确认声明的约束，以及在外国法律实体因商业原因而收购财产的情况下，还会受到贸易部的批准意见的约束。

Further, certain limitations may be imposed depending on the type of real property in question. As an example, agricultural land may be acquired only by Serbian nationals, or, as of late, by EU citizens, in accordance with the provisions of Stabilization and Association Agreement between Serbia and the EU (i. e., with an area of up to 2 hectares).

此外，根据所涉的不动产的类型，这些不动产可能会被施加某些限制。例如，农用地只能由塞尔维亚公民收购，或根据塞尔维亚和欧盟之间的《稳定和结盟协定》的规定，近来亦可由欧盟公民收购（欧盟公民收购面积最多2公顷）。

In practice, the ownership over a real property, which is necessary for the implementation of a greenfield investment, is acquired by the locally established subsidiary, which is considered a domestic legal entity and may therefore enjoy all of the proprietary rights without any limitations reserved for foreigners.

在实践中，由当地设立的子公司收购实施绿地投资所必需的不动产的所有权，该等子公司被视为国内法人实体并因此可不受限于任何对外国人的限制并享有全部所有权。

Generally Speaking, prior to entering into any real estate transactions, it is prudent to conduct a due diligence analysis of the property and the seller of the respective property.

一般来说,在进行任何不动产交易之前,较为谨慎的做法是对相应财产及其卖方进行尽职调查分析。

3.4.2 建设用地(Construction land)

According to the *Constitution of the Republic of Serbia* and the *Serbian Law on Planning and Construction*, construction land in urban areas is either state owned or private property. In reality, almost all construction land in urban areas is owned by the state.

根据《塞尔维亚共和国宪法》和《塞尔维亚规划和建设法》,城市地区的建设用地是国有或私有财产。实际上,几乎所有的城市建设用地都归国家所有。

The disposal, barter and lease of construction land in public property regime is granted mostly through auction or a tender procedure. However, in certain cases, real property may be sold or leased by direct negotiation. Exceptionally, local municipalities may lease construction land for a price under market value or even without compensation, with prior consent of the Government of the Republic of Serbia. Publicly-owned construction land cannot be leased unless a planning document, based on which location conditions and construction permit are issued, has been produced.

在公共财产管理体制内,建设用地的处置、互易和租赁主要通过拍卖或招标程序进行。但是,在某些情况下,不动产可以通过直接谈判的方式出售或出租。在特殊情况下,在征得塞尔维亚政府事先同意的情况下,地方市政当局可以以低于市场价的价格或甚至无需补偿的价格租赁建设用地。在未作出规划文件(区位条件和施工许可将根据规划文件发布)的情况下,不得出租公有建筑用地。

With regard to acquisition of a privately owned construction land, there are no limitations to the negotiation and sale/purchase process. However, care should be observed whether such land is encumbered by any pre-emption rights, mortgages, easements, etc., before deciding to proceed with acquisition thereof.

关于对私有建筑用地的收购,在谈判和买/卖过程中并无限制。但是,在决定收购之前，应注意这些土地是否受到任何优先购买权、抵押权、地役权等的限制。

3.4.3 设施建设（Facility construction）

Subject to acquiring a proper land plot for implementation of the planned greenfield investment, there are certain administrative procedures that must be observed before starting the construction of the projected facility.

如已收购了合适的土地用于实施计划的绿地投资，在开始建设规划设施之前，必须遵守某些行政程序。

There are several types of permits and approvals that need to be obtained from the competent authorities in order to complete the construction process (e.g., location terms, construction permit, use permit, etc.). These permits and approvals usually concern not only the facility planned for construction, but also the accompanying infrastructure, e.g., roads and railroads, electricity supply, sewage, water retention pools, ancillary facilities, etc. It is common for foreign investors to schedule meetings with representatives of local authorities to request assistance with these types of issues, in line with their scope of authorizations.

为了完成施工项目，需要从主管机关获得几种类型的许可和批准（例如区位条款、施工许可证、使用许可证等），这些许可和批准通常不仅涉及计划建设的设施，还涉及附随的基础设施，例如道路和铁路、电力供应、污水处理设施、蓄水池、附属设施等。外国投资者通常与地方主管机关的代表安排会议，以请求主管机关在其权限范围内协助解决这些类型的问题。

Pursuant to the applicable provisions of the Serbian Law on Planning and Construction the "one-stop shop" system of issuance of construction permits is in force. The main goal is to achieve that construction permits are issued promptly, especially since filling and issuance of all construction related permits is done electronically, which significantly reduces the time in which the construction permits are issued.

根据《塞尔维亚规划和建设法》的适用规定，"一站式"施工许可证签发制度已在实施中。其主要目标是使施工许可证能够及时签发，特别是由于所有与施工相关的许可证的填写和签发都通过电子的方式完成，施工许可证签发的时间显著缩短。

Besides from dealing with the administrative aspect of the real property construction, the investor must also find and hire the general contractor that will perform the construction of the relevant facility. In this process, it is usual to have several rounds of negotiations with potential contractors, as well as to closely negotiate on terms and provisions of the construction agreement, which is often based on FIDIC model – agreements. Serbian Law on Obligations specifically regulates the construction agreements and their contents; thus, input of a local legal counsel is of crucial importance in this process.

除了处理不动产建设的行政相关事宜,投资者还必须找到并雇用进行相关设施建设的总承包商。在这个过程中,通常会与潜在的承包商进行几轮谈判,并就施工协议(通常基于国际咨询工程师联合会模板协议,即FIDIC模板协议)的条款和规定密切地进行谈判。《塞尔维亚责任法》具体规定了施工协议及其内容;因此,在这个过程中,当地法律顾问的参与至关重要。

Depending on the circumstances of the case, the investor may also require assistance from other professional service providers (e. g., project designers, expert supervisors, etc.), which must work in compliance with the applicable provisions of the relevant Serbian regulations.

根据案件的具体情况,投资者还可能需要其他专业服务提供者(例如项目设计者、专家监督员等)的帮助,这些服务提供者必须遵守塞尔维亚相关法规的适用规定进行工作。

3.4.4 完工后的活动(Post-completion activities)

Once the facility has been constructed, negotiations with utility service providers are usually instigated, in order to ensure appropriate functioning of the newly constructed building. Specific utility regulations should be observed in this regard, as most of the utility contracts are pre-determined and do not offer great scope of possibilities for amendments thereto.

一旦设施建成,通常会启动与公用事业服务提供商的协商,以确保新建建筑物的正常运作。在这一方面,应该遵守具体的公用事业规定,因为大多数公用事业合同都是预先确定的,并不具有很大的修改可能性。

Other activities may be necessary as well once the construction has been completed, including but not limited to observing of safety, environmental and other applicable regulations.

一旦施工完成，可能还须开展其他活动，包括但不限于遵守安全、环保和其他适用的法规。

3.5 监管法方面（Aspects on Regulatory Law）

In parallel with establishment of a local company, there are several regulatory legal aspects that also need to be observed by a newly established company in Serbia.

在塞尔维亚的新设公司也需要遵守一些监管方面的法律法规。

Each company has a prevailing business activity in which it pre-dominantly engages. The company may also engage in other activities that are not prohibited by law, irrespective of whether they are determined by its Foundation Deed or statutes. However, some activities are subject to limitations and/or may require specific approvals by competent authorities in Serbia (e.g., defense industry, mining, energy and oil sector, etc.).

各公司均有其主营业务，还可以从事或依公司章程决定或依法规且法律不禁止的其他活动。但是，某些活动会受到限制和/或可能需要塞尔维亚主管机关（例如国防工业、采矿、能源和石油行业等）对其进行具体批准。

Besides from potential obligation to obtain approval for conduct of certain business activities, it is also necessary to take into account that some activities require specific standards of care and that there is an obligation for companies engaging in such activities to act in accordance with mandatory laws.

除了履行为进行某些业务活动需获得批准的潜在义务，还须考虑某些商业活动需要特殊的注意标准，并且参与此类活动的公司有义务按照强制法的规定行事。

As an example, if the production process of the implemented greenfield investment may influence the environment and/or creates waste, provisions of the Environmental Protection Law and the Serbian Waste Management Law must be followed. Special environmental impact assessment studies may be required, as well as the obtainment of a so-called Integrated Pollution Prevention and Control Permit from competent authorities. Further, waste management is generally subject to attainment of specific permits (e.g., for collection, transport, housing, treatment, disposal) or a so-called integral permit (srp. integralna dozvola), which is issued to one operator who performs several types of waste management activities. There are special procedures which must be observed for disposal of certain types of waste such as batteries, rubber, oils, etc. Failure to observe the provisions of the Waste Management Law may lead to fines for commercial offences.

例如，如果实施绿地投资的生产过程可能会对环境产生影响和/或产生废弃物，则必须遵守《塞尔维亚环境保护法》和《塞尔维亚废弃物管理法》的规定。可能需要进行特殊环境影响评估调查，以及获得主管机关签发的综合污染预防和控制许可证。此外，废弃物管理通常需要获得特定的许可证（例如，用于收集、运输、存储、处理和清除废弃物的许可证），或所谓的综合许可证（塞尔维亚语为 integralna dozvola），综合许可证会签发给一个执行多种废弃物管理活动的操作员。处理某些类型的废弃物（如电池、橡胶、油等）必须遵守特殊的程序。如不遵守《塞尔维亚废弃物管理法》的规定，则可能会因涉嫌商业违法行为而受到罚款。

Other specific business activities may entail various other requirements under applicable Serbian regulations, as the case may be.

视具体情况，其他业务活动也可能须遵守各项塞尔维亚法规的要求。

Moreover, general regulatory aspects should be taken into account, such as the observance of mandatory AML regulations. On 31 December 2018, the Central Register of Ultimate Beneficial Owners (Central Register) has been established with the BRA.

此外，还应当考虑一般性的监管问题，例如，须遵守强制性的《塞尔维亚反洗钱法规》。2018 年 12 月 31 日，塞尔维亚商业登记中心建立了载有最终受益所有人的中央登记簿（简称中央登记簿）。

Serbian companies, institutions, as well as branches and representative offices established by foreign investors in Serbia, are among the entities designated by the Serbian Law on Central Register as entities whose legal representatives have a duty to register their Ultimate Beneficial Owners (UBO) with this Central Register. The Central Register is established as an online portal of the BRA and registration thereon must be executed by official electronic certificate of the legal representative of the required entity.

塞尔维亚的公司、机构以及外国投资者在塞尔维亚设立的分支机构和代表处，均为《塞尔维亚中央登记法》中所指定的实体，这些实体的法人代表有义务在中央登记簿上登记其最终受益所有人（UBO）。中央登记簿是塞尔维亚商业登记局（BRA）的网站建立的，相关登记必须由需要登记的实体法定代表人使用官方电子认证完成。

A required entity may be fined if it fails to register data on its UBOs timely (i. e. within 15 days from the change occurring or from the moment of establishment of the required entity). The monetary fine may be applied if the required entity does not keep accurate and up to date records on determining its UBOs. Any person with intent to conceal information on a UBO, who fails to register required information, registers inaccurate information, or changes or erases truthful information on a UBO, can be held criminally liable and sanctioned by up to 5 years imprisonment.

被要求登记的实体如未能及时登记关于最终受益所有人的信息（即自变动发生之日起或实体设立之日起的 15 日内进行登记），则可能会因此而受到罚款。如被要求登记的实体未保存关于确定最终受益所有人的准确信息或最新信息，则可能受到罚款。任何有意隐瞒最终受益所有人相关信息的自然人，包括未对相关信息进行登记、登记信息不准确，或变更或删除真实信息，可能须承担刑事责任，最高可被判处 5 年监禁。

3.6 雇佣法方面（Aspects on Employment Law）

One of the most significant elements in the implementation of a greenfield investment is the hiring of required personnel. The general law applicable to employment relations in Serbia is the Labor Law, which in detail regulates the rights and obligations of both employers and employees.

在塞尔维亚开展绿地投资的过程中，最重要的因素之一是雇佣所需要的人员。在塞尔维亚，适用于雇佣关系的一般性法律是《塞尔维亚劳动法》，劳动法详细规定了雇员与雇主各自的权利和义务。

Employment relations are further regulated by collective agreements, internal labor regulations of the employers, and employment contracts. Neither of these may prescribe terms and conditions which are less favorable to employees than the terms and conditions prescribed by the Labor Law.

雇用关系由集体协议、雇主的内部劳动规章和雇用合同进一步规范。集体协议、雇主的内部劳动规章和雇用合同均不得规定相较于《塞尔维亚劳动法》的规定而言，对员工更为不利的条款和条件。

3.6.1 雇用合同；雇用外国人（employment contract; employment of foreigners）

An employment contract in Serbia must be concluded in writing, by and between an employee and his/her employer, before the employee actually starts working, and can either be concluded for a definite or an indefinite period (if this is not explicitly stated in the contract, it is deemed that the contract is concluded for an indefinite period).

在塞尔维亚，在雇员实际开始工作之前，必须由雇员和雇主之间以书面形式签订雇用合同，雇用合同的期限可以为固定的，亦可以为不固定的（如果未在合同中明确其期限，则视合同为无固定期限的合同）。

Every foreigner who works in Serbia must possess a work permit, either a personal work permit or a work permit, including employment work permit, work permit for special cases of employment or self-employment work permit. There are certain exceptions to this rule, the most important one being that foreigners who reside in Serbia for less than 90 days within a 6 month period, for example, who are shareholders, representatives or members of corporate bodies who have not entered into an employment relationship, are not required to have a work permit.

在塞尔维亚工作的外国人须持有工作许可证，个人工作许可证或某类工作许可证，包括雇用工作许可证、特殊情况工作许可证或自营职业工作许可证。这一规则存在一些例外，其中最重要的是，6个月内在塞尔维亚居住不满90天的外国人如尚未与公司建立雇用关系的股东、代表或公司机构的成员，不需要有工作许可证。

There are two basic categories of work permits:

工作许可有两种基本类别：

i. Personal work permit-destined to foreign citizens that arrive and enter the work market in Serbia freely-request for issuance of the work permit is submitted by the foreign citizen;

i. 个人工作许可证：该证适用于自由抵达塞尔维亚劳动力市场的外国公民，在这种情况下，由外国公民自行提出签发工作许可证的请求；

ii. Work permit-related to foreign citizens that are assigned to Serbia or are professionally engaged in Serbia to work for an employer, or as an entrepreneur.

ii. 工作许可证：该证适用于被分派到塞尔维亚或专门在塞尔维亚为某雇主或企业家工作的外国公民。

In any case, work permits are issued for the period of validity of the appropriate residence permit. Work permit for specific cases of employment are in general issued up to a maximum one year, unless the law or international treaty prescribe otherwise. Work permit for assignment and intercompany movement, in case where there is no international treaty in place between the country of assignment and Serbia may be extended for one more year, provided that business activity performed is of general interest for the Republic of Serbia and approved by the Ministry of Labour.

在任何情况下，工作许可证都会在居留许可证的有效期内签发。除非法律或国际条约另有规定，否则，特殊情况工作许可证最多可签发一年的有效期。在分派国与塞尔维亚之间没有国际条约的情况下，适用于工作分派和跨公司调动的工作许可的期限可另行延长一年，但其所进行的商业活动须符合塞尔维亚的普遍利益并经劳动部批准。

It should be noted that as of beginning of 2019, Serbian Ministry of Labour announced that the signing of a treaty on temporary employment between the Republic of Serbia and the People's Republic of China is planned. Such a treaty would improve the rights and the status of Serbian and Chinese nationals in both respective jurisdictions.

应该注意，截至2019年年初，塞尔维亚劳工部宣布，塞尔维亚共和国计划与中华人民共和国签署临时就业条约。该条约将改善塞尔维亚和中国的公民在两个司法管辖区的权利和状态。

3.6.2 管理董事（managing director/directors）

It is necessary for a managing director to either have a management or an employment contract in place with the local company. The former contract does not constitute an employment relation between the company and the managing director (s) and, therefore, the mandatory norms of the *Labor Law* do not apply.

管理董事须与当地公司签订管理或雇佣合同。前一类合同不构成公司与管理董事之间的雇用关系，因此，对其不能适用《塞尔维亚劳动法》的强制性规范。

Further, according to a recent change in interpretation of the employment and tax regulations, a contract executed with a managing director must always include remuneration.

另外，由于近来对雇用和税务规定的解释发生变化，公司与管理董事签署的合同须包含报酬事项。

3.6.3 试用期；固定期限的雇佣（probationary employment period; fixed term employment）

An employment contract may stipulate a probationary period of employment, which cannot last longer than six months. In the course of this probationary period, both the employer and the employee may terminate the contract with a notice period of at least 5 working days.

劳动合同可以规定试用期，但不得超过六个月。在试用期内，雇主和雇员均可以至少提前5个工作日作出通知终止合同。

An employment contract can be entered into for a definite term for the purpose of carrying out specific tasks, the maximum term of which is up to 24 months. Under specific circumstances, the definite term may be longer, for example, work of a foreign employee for the duration of his/her work permit; to work on a specific project with a predefined term, then until the end of such project; to work for a newly established company, then for a term of up 36 months.

为完成特定的工作而签署固定期限的雇用合同，其最长期限为24个月。在特定情况下，这一固定的期限可能更长，例如，外国雇员可在其工作许可证规定的期间内工作；在具有预定期限的特定项目中，雇员可为其工作直至该项目结束；雇员为新设公司而工作，其最长工作期限可为36个月。

3.6.4 工作时间；年假与带薪休假（working hours; annual and paid leave）

Regular working hours are 40 hours per week. This includes a break of at least 30 minutes per day. At the employer's request, the employee may be required to work overtime in the case of force majeure, a sudden increase in the volume of work or, if necessary, to complete an unplanned task within a specific period.

常规工作时间是每周40小时，其中包括每天至少30分钟的休息时间。在发生不可抗力、工作量骤增，或者如需在特定时期内完成计划外任务的情况下，应雇主要求，雇员可能需要加班。

The employee may not work for more than 12 hours per day (including regular hours and overtime) and may not have more than 8 hours of overtime work per week. An employee is entitled to a minimum of 20 days of annual paid leave, in addition to public holidays. The exact duration of such annual leave is established by the employer's labor regulations or the employment contract, based on criteria including the employee's years of service, as well as the position's general working conditions. The employee is entitled to additional paid leave in certain cases (e. g., wedding, childbirth, etc.).

雇员每天的工作时间不得超过12小时（包括正常工作时间和加班时间），每周加班时间不得超过8小时。除公共假期外，员工有权享受至少20天的带薪年假。年假的确切期限由雇主的劳动规章或雇佣合同基于雇员服务年限以及职位的一般工作条件等因素加以确定。在某些情况下（例如，结婚、生育等），雇员有权享受额外的带薪休假。

3.6.5 集体协议；工会（collective agreement; labor unions）

The employees are guaranteed the right to organize into trade unions. A registered trade union has the right to be informed by the employer of any economic and labor-related issues that are relevant for the status of the employees. The employer is obligated to provide technical conditions and space necessary for the activities of trade unions, as well as to provide them with access to necessary information.

员工组织工会的权利受到保护。已登记的工会有权接收雇主对与雇员状况相关的任何经济和劳工问题的通知。雇主有义务提供工会活动所需的技术条件和空间，并为他们提供必要的信息。

Trade unions in general negotiate with the employer on the terms of the collective agreement, which must provide more beneficial rights for the employees than the ones defined under the Labor Law. Provisions of the collective agreement apply to all employees with the employer.

一般而言，工会就集体协议的条款与雇主进行谈判，相较于《塞尔维亚劳动法》的规定，集体协议必须为雇员提供更多权利和权益。集体协议的规定适用于所有雇员。

The employer may not terminate the employment contract or in any other way discriminate its employee due to his/her activities as employee representative, trade union member, or because of his/her participation in trade union activities.

雇主不得因雇员担任雇员代表、工会会员或其参与工会活动而终止雇用合同，或以任何其他方式差别对待其雇员。

3.7 其他方面的法律 (Other Legal Aspects)

Besides from the issues described above, which present a general overview of major elements regarding the implementation of greenfield investments in Serbia, there is a number of other legal aspects that need to be observed.

上文概述了有关在塞尔维亚实施绿地投资的主要问题,除此之外,还有许多其他方面的法律问题需要加以注意。

Such issues are usually case-specific and generally concern, but are not limited to, different tax issues, commercial and market considerations, dealings with foreign and local suppliers/distributors, etc., which require a case-by-case legal analysis and support of local legal counsel in Serbia.

这些问题通常具有个案差异,通常涉及但不限于不同的税务问题、贸易和市场方面的考虑、与外国和本地供应商/分销商的交易等,这需要在塞尔维亚当地的法律顾问逐案进行分析并予以支持。

4. 沃尔夫·泰斯律师事务所参与的成功案例 (Successful Examples Supported by Wolf Theiss Office)

Wolf Theiss office supported various enterprises and reputable companies with regard to their greenfield investments into Serbia, resulting in a number of successful investment stories to which our office happily contributed. Below you may find a brief overview of several successful investment projects implemented in Serbia in recent years, in which we had the opportunity and pleasure to provide our legal assistance.

沃尔夫·泰斯律师事务所为各类企业和享有盛誉的公司就向塞尔维亚进行绿地投资提供支持,由此而产生了许多的成功投资案例,我们十分有幸为此作出了贡献。下文中您可以看到近年来在塞尔维亚实施的几个成功投资项目的简述,我们有幸为这些项目提供了法律服务。

4.1 哈金森公司 (Hutchinson SA)

Hutchinson, a member of Total group, is one of the leading manufacturers of automotive systems in the sector of body and precision sealing systems, fluid management systems, vibration control systems and other necessary automotive components.

哈金森公司是道达尔集团的成员之一,在汽车系统领域,该公司是车身和精密密封系统、流体管理系统、振动控制系统和其他必要汽车零部件的领先制造商之一。

Within the general intention of expansion of its business operations in Europe, Hutchinson chose Serbia as the best destination for its greenfield investment, with planned construction of production facilities that would supply the global needs of the group's clients.

为扩大其在欧洲的业务运营,哈金森公司选择塞尔维亚作为其绿地投资的最佳目的地,并规划建设生产设施,以满足集团客户的全球性需求。

Extensive negotiations were instigated with the government of the Republic of Serbia concerning the applicable incentives that would be awarded for the relevant investment, in which process we provided the necessary legal support to Hutchinson. The town of Ruma, less than 60km away from Belgrade, was chosen as a perfect place for the realization of the investment, and the investment was qualified as an investment of great importance for the Republic of Serbia.

哈金森公司与塞尔维亚政府就相关投资适用的激励措施进行了大量谈判,在此过程中,我们向哈金森公司提供了必要的法律支持。距贝尔格莱德不足60公里的鲁马镇被哈金森公司选为实现其投资的理想场所,此次投资对塞尔维亚而言十分重要。

The investment itself was pre-dominantly funded from Hutchinson group funds, being transferred directly into equity of the local subsidiary. Once the initial phases of the project have been implemented, the extension of the investment and manufacturing capacities was financed through loans granted by commercial banks.

该投资主要由哈金森公司资金资助,这些资金被直接转为当地子公司的股本。一旦项目的初始阶段落地,将由商业银行以贷款的形式为投资项目的扩展和生产能力的提高提供资金。

Client faced various legal challenges concerning the establishment of its local subsidiary, in the form of a limited liability company, engaging of a general contractor for construction of the production facility, hiring of new employees necessary for the production process, etc., in the process of which a close cooperation and support from a highly-qualified legal counsel proved crucial.

客户在设立本地子公司时面临各种法律难题,例如,以有限责任公司的形式设立公司、聘请总承包商来建设生产设施、雇用生产过程所需的新员工等,经验证明，在这个过程中，聘请一位与公司密切合作并向公司提供支持的高素质法律顾问是至关重要的。

Overall, the above investment resulted in over 600 new employees working in a new and modern production center established in Ruma, which has already been expanded on several occasions, confirming Serbia's overall greenfield investment potential.

总体而言，经由上述投资，共计600多名新员工在鲁马新建现代化生产中心工作，该中心已经多次扩建，这证实了塞尔维亚的绿地投资的整体潜力。

4.2 苏伊士集团财团和I-Environment投资有限公司（Consortium of Suez Groupe Sas and I-Environment Investment Limited）

In order to ensure harmonization with modern waste processing trends, the City of Belgrade's authorities initiated a specific Public Private Partnership (PPP) project for the provision of services for the treatment and disposal of residual municipal solid waste. The aim of the project, which was of national and local importance, was to remediate the existing waste facilities and to develop a comprehensive modern waste treatment complex that will generate energy from the waste produced in the city area.

为了确保与现代的废物处理趋势保持一致，贝尔格莱德市当局启动了一个特定的公私合作（PPP）项目，以提供处理和处置残余城市固体废弃物的服务。该项目对国家和地方均具有重要性，其目的是修复现有的废弃物设施，并开发一个综合的现代废弃物处理设施群，以从城市地区制造的废弃物中产生能量。

As the first of its kind in the region, the project attracted significant attention from foreign bidders, including the Consortium of France's Suez Groupe SAS and I-Environment Investment Limited, which we supported with a qualified legal counsel in the bidding process.

作为该地区的首个此类项目，该项目引起了外国竞标者的极大关注，其中包括法国苏伊士集团财团和I-Environment投资有限公司，我们在招标过程中担任其有资质的法律顾问。

Due to the specific business activity in question, provision of a hands-on support in all aspects of the project was necessary, including especially regulatory issues, environmental protection, waste management, and energy law, as well as procedural matters relating to PPP and public procurement laws in Serbia.

针对具体的业务活动，我们须在项目的各个方面为其提供实际支持，包括监管问题、环境保护、废弃物管理和能源法，以及与公私合作有关的程序性事项和塞尔维亚的政府采购法方面的支持。

The implementation of the investment itself required skilled navigation of yet untested procedural matters relating to PPPs and public procurement in Serbia. Several rounds of negotiation and drafting of project documentation, including a state-of-the-art PPP contract were involved in the process, also involving a high level real estate due diligence of a sizable area of the city and a detailed examination of all required administrative permits and licenses for implementation of the investment and construction of the relevant waste treatment complex.

投资本身的实施，需要对有关塞尔维亚公私合作和政府采购的未经检验的程序性事项熟练掌握。该过程涉及多轮谈判和项目文件的起草，包括最先进的公私合作合同，另外，还涉及对城市大规模地区的房地产进行高水平的尽职调查，并对与实施投资和建设废物处理设施群相关的所有必备的行政许可和执照进行详细审查。

Accordingly, joint efforts described above resulted in signing of the PPP contract with the City of Belgrade on 29 September 2017, after two years of tendering process, ensuring thus the implementation of this landmark project in Serbia.

因此，经过两年的招标和上述各方的共同努力，2017年9月29日与贝尔格莱德市的公私合作合同签署完成，确保这一具有里程碑意义的项目在塞尔维亚的开展。

While the final financing details are still being worked upon, it is estimated that the total investment size is approx. EUR 345 million, with majority of the funds being provided by the investors themselves. However, as one of the landmark projects in Serbia, and while having in mind the infrastructural importance thereof, a significant part of the financing funds for the project are obtained through loans approved by the international credit institutions, such as the European Bank for Research and Development, International Finance Corporation and the Austrian Development Bank. Such funds will be used by the special purpose vehicle established in the form of a limited liability company to ensure the modernization of existing processes, as well as clean utilization and processing of waste for the entire region.

虽然最终的融资细节仍待确定,但预计总投资规模约为 3.45 亿欧元,其中,大部分资金由投资者自行提供。然而,作为塞尔维亚具有里程碑意义的项目之一,并考虑到其基础设施的重要性,该项目的许多融资资金通过国际信贷机构,如欧洲研究和开发银行、国际金融公司和奥地利开发银行批准的贷款而获得。这些资金将由以有限责任公司形式设立的特殊目的公司使用,以确保现有工艺现代化,以及确保该地区的能源清洁利用和废物处理。

5. 总结(Conclusion)

There is a growing trend of China-based investors deciding to implement their greenfield investments in Serbia. Namely, more and more often the Chinese companies pick Serbia as a perfect destination for their "breach" into the European market, allowing big possibilities for the expansion of their global business operations.

中国投资者决定在塞尔维亚实施绿地投资的趋势有所增长。也就是说,越来越多的中国公司选择塞尔维亚作为他们"进入"欧洲市场的完美目的地,这为这些公司扩大其全球范围的业务经营提供了巨大的可能性。

In recent years, we had several opportunities to cooperate with Chinese investors seeking to establish themselves in Serbia, a pre-dominant part of which came from automotive, electronic appliances and other industries.

近年来,我们有机会与寻求在塞尔维亚进行业务发展的中国投资者合作,这些投资者主要来自汽车、电子电器及其他行业。

Serbian Wolf Theiss office has been engaged in the implementation of a greenfield investment by a Chinese automotive parts manufacturer, as a local legal counsel and is engaged in all aspects of the relevant investment. A local limited liability company has been established by the investor in Serbia, which will enable a local presence for easier realization of the investment.

塞尔维亚沃尔夫·泰斯律师事务所作为当地法律顾问全方位参与了一家中国汽车零部件制造商的绿地投资相关事宜。在塞尔维亚,该投资者已设立了一家有限责任公司,这有助于其在当地的投资目的的实现。

Due to the existence of a relatively well-developed automotive industry in Serbia, one of the most important challenges is choosing a proper location for the implementation of the investment and construction of the new production facility, which would allow the investor to best use its strategic position on the market.

由于塞尔维亚具有相对发达的汽车工业，最重要的挑战之一是为投资的实施和新生产设施的建设选择合适的位置，这有助于投资者能够在市场上充分利用其战略地位。

Further, discussion on the specifics of employment-related issues at an early phase is crucial, in order to ensure adequate organization of work processes and long-term employee satisfaction, which is necessary for the establishment of an uninterrupted production process. The need for qualified personnel also entails the setting-up of a proper hiring process, in line with the applicable local regulations.

另外，在较早的阶段即对具体雇用问题进行讨论至关重要，这有助于确保工作流程的充足配置和长期员工的满意度，而这对于维持连续生产而言是必要的。如需要招聘有资质的相关人员，还需要根据当地适用的法规建立合适的招聘流程。

Moreover, in parallel, a negotiation process with the government of the Republic of Serbia aiming to receive investment incentives should be conducted, in order to ensure the best terms for implementation of the planned investment project. The financing method has not been finally decided upon, even though it is most likely that equity financing will be chosen for the initial phases of project implementation.

与此同时，应与塞尔维亚政府进行磋商，以获得投资激励，从而确保实施计划投资项目的最佳条件。融资方案尚未最终确定，但在项目实施的初始阶段投资者很可能选择股权融资。

These and other legal challenges involve significant cooperation with our Chinese clients, with whom we jointly engage and approach any potential obstacles that may arise in the course of a successful realization of their greenfield investment in Serbia.

在这种种法律难题中，我们与我们的中国客户进行了密切合作，我们共同积极应对了可能出现在绿地投资的过程中的任何潜在障碍。

— 作者简介 —

Aleksandar Ristić is a qualified Serbian attorney with almost 5 years of professional experience, specialized in dispute resolution, real estate, M&A, and other commercial and corporate law matters. Aleksandar specializes in supporting clients with their investments into Serbia, in which respect he is leading several high-profile investment projects and provides qualified advice in all necessary legal areas. Aleksandar is fluent in English and Serbian. Recently he has been assisting a number of worldwide leading producers of parts for the automotive industry with establishment of their production facilities in Serbia. He also has extensive experience with representing clients in commercial litigation and complex insolvency/restructuring cases in Serbia, and has so far represented several high-profile clients in various 'piercing of the corporate veil' cases, which are very rare in Serbia. He is a graduate of the 2015 class of the University of Belgrade School of Law and received his LL. M. at the University of Belgrade in 2018.

Aleksandar Ristić 拥有塞尔维亚律师资格，具有近5年的专业经验，专门从事争议解决、房地产、并购和其他商业及公司法业务。Aleksandar 专攻于在对塞尔维亚投资方面为客户提供法律支持，他正在负责牵头多个备受瞩目的投资项目，并在项目涉及的所有必要法律领域，为客户提供高质量的法律顾问服务。Aleksandar 精通英语和塞尔维亚语。最近，他协助许多全球领先的汽车工业零件制造商在塞尔维亚建立了生产工厂。他在代表客户处理塞尔维亚的商事诉讼和复杂的破产/重组案件方面也具有丰富的经验。迄今为止，他已经代表了数位知名客户处理各种"揭开公司面纱"的案件，这在塞尔维亚非常少见。Aleksandar 是贝尔格莱德大学法学院2015届毕业生，并于2018年在贝尔格莱德大学获得了法学硕士学位。

股权并购在斯洛文尼亚：在家电行业开展投资
Equity in Slovenia
Investing in the Home Appliance Industry

点 评

本文分享的是 2018 年中国家电生产商海信收购斯洛文尼亚白色家电和电子产品制造商戈兰尼的案例。在海信收购戈兰尼的过程中，本文作者为海信在交易的各方面提供法律咨询。鉴于交易的复杂性、交易价值、所涉司法管辖区的数量以及戈兰尼对斯洛文尼亚的重要程度，该交易可被视为 2018 年斯洛文尼亚最重要的交易之一。

海信收购戈兰尼时，戈兰尼的股票仍在卢布尔雅那和华沙证券交易所上市，因此拟议交易特别需要遵守斯洛文尼亚法律中关于要约收购斯洛文尼亚上市公司的一系列要求，包括若收购方获得目标公司所有投票权的 1/3 以上则可能触发强制要约收购义务（1/3 以下的可发出自愿要约）；要约人应在收购意向公布后的 10 至 30 日内公布收购要约；在收购要约发布之前，招股说明书必须经斯洛文尼亚证券市场管理局批准；需要由具有中央证券存管公司成员资格的经纪公司（只有某些银行和经纪公司具有这种地位）以要约人的名义和账户进行收购要约（以及与之相关的其他法律行为）；法定的要约承诺期限为 28 至 60 日等。

在公司治理层面，斯洛文尼亚公司法相较中国公司法也存在较为明显的差异。就私人有限责任公司而言，斯洛文尼亚公司法仅要求该类公司拥有一名或多名管理人员（董事）并仅对公司管理事宜进行了非常基本的规定，私人有限责任公司的股东在确定公司的管理结构及管理规则方面拥有较大的自由裁量权。就股份公司而言，允许股份公司选择设置单层管理结构或双层管理结构，单层管理结构系指由执行董事和非执行董事组成的董事会，双层治理结构系指管理委员会和监事会。因而在投资后的公司管理过程中可结合斯洛文尼亚公司法等相关规定，选择适宜的公司形式及管理结构。

斯洛文尼亚作为欧盟成员国，除需遵守欧盟的相关规定之外，斯洛文尼亚也建立了自己的外商直接投资审查制度。此外，斯洛文尼亚与外国直接投资相关的立法包括《推动外国直接投资和企业国际化法案》《外国直接投资金融刺激法令》等。

1. 投资项目简介（Introduction of Investment Project）

In 2018, Wolf Theiss advised Chinese home appliance producer Hisense Co., Ltd. and its group (Hisense) on its acquisition of Slovenian white-goods and electronics manufacturer Gorenje, d. o. o. (previously Gorenje, d. d.; Gorenje). This was the first direct investment of a Chinese investor into a Slovenian public company and by value one of the largest transactions in Slovenia in 2018.

在2018年，沃尔夫·泰斯律师事务所为中国家电生产商海信有限公司及其集团（以下简称海信）提供法律咨询服务，助力海信收购斯洛文尼亚白色家电和电子产品制造商戈兰尼（前名称为Gorenje, d. d.，简称Gorenje[1]）。这是中国投资者首次直接投资斯洛文尼亚的上市公司，此次投资亦是2018年斯洛文尼亚资金规模最大的交易之一。

Gorenje is one of the leading white-goods manufacturers in Europe. In financial year 2017, its consolidated revenues amounted to EUR 1.3 billion and Gorenje group as a whole employed around 11 000 employees. Gorenje is present in more than 90 countries globally while its production facilities are located in Slovenia, Serbia and the Czech Republic. At the time of the transaction, Gorenje group consisted of more than 80 subsidiaries and joint venture companies in more than 30 countries around the world. Some of the Slovenian subsidiaries were involved in the non-core business, such as waste management, construction engineering and production of bicycles.

戈兰尼是欧洲一流的白色家电制造商之一。在2017财年，其综合收入达13亿欧元。戈兰尼集团共雇用了近11 000名员工，在全球90多个国家开展业务，它的生产基地位于斯洛文尼亚、塞尔维亚和捷克共和国。在本次交易发生时，

---

[1] "股份公司"，斯洛文尼亚语为"delniška družba"，缩写为"d. d."；"私人有限责任公司"，斯洛文尼亚语为"družba z omejeno odgovornostjo"，缩写为"d. o. o."。

戈兰尼在全球 30 多个国家拥有 80 多家子公司和合资公司。部分斯洛文尼亚的子公司负责废弃物管理、建筑工程和自行车生产等非核心业务。

Gorenje's shares were at the time of the transaction listed on Ljubljana and Warsaw stock exchanges. The shares were held by approximately 12 000 shareholders with the biggest ten shareholders holding around 70% of all shares. Among the biggest shareholders were Kapitalska družba, d. d. (an investment management entity fully owned by the Republic of Slovenia; "Kapitalska družba" in Slovenian) holding 16.37%, International Finance Corporation (member of the World Bank Group) holding 11.80%, Panasonic Coproration holding 10.74%, Home Products Europe B. V. holding 5.00%, BNP Paribas Securities Services S. C. A. holding around 4% and certain other investors who held shares through fiduciary accounts with banks. Gorenje also held around 0.5% of treasury shares.

在交易时，戈兰尼的股票仍在卢布尔雅那和华沙证券交易所上市。约 12 000 名股东持股该公司，其中，最大的 10 名股东合计约持有公司 70% 的股份。戈兰尼最大的股东包括：持股 16.37% 的 Kapitalskadružba, d. d（一个由斯洛文尼亚共和国全资拥有的投资管理实体；斯洛文尼亚语为"Kapitalska družba"）、持股 11.80% 的一家国际金融公司（世界银行集团的成员）、持股 10.74% 的松下公司、持股 5% 的一家欧洲家居用品有限公司、持股约 4% 的法国巴黎银行证券服务有限公司以及一些通过银行信托账户持股的其他投资者。戈兰尼还有约 0.5% 的库存股。

In November 2017, Gorenje initiated a search for a new strategic partner stating that they are searching for a strategic partner that would support Gorenje in its future growth and which could also result in such strategic partner entering into a shareholding structure of Gorenje. In March 2018, Gorenje received five non-binding bids for strategic partnership following which it allowed three companies to conduct due diligence of Gorenje. The process of selection of a future strategic partner concluded in May 2018 with receipt of binding bids for strategic partnership, whereby Gorenje chose Hisense as the best bidder. According to the takeover prospectus, Hisense in its binding bid offered to publish a takeover offer for the shares of Gorenje at EUR 12 per share (almost twice the share price on the stock exchange at the time).

2017 年 11 月，戈兰尼开始寻找新的战略合作伙伴，以促进公司未来的发展，该战略合作伙伴也可以参股戈兰尼。在 2018 年 3 月，戈兰尼收到了五份不具约束力的战略合作伙伴投标，戈兰尼允许其中的三家公司对其进行尽职调查。至 2018 年 5 月，戈兰尼结束寻找战略合作伙伴，并认为海信是最佳投标人，同时，戈兰尼收到了针对战略合作具有约束力的投标。在收购说明书中，海信提出以每股 12 欧元的价格（在当时，几乎是股票交易所市价的两倍）收购戈兰尼的股份。

Since Gorenje was a listed company with a relatively dispersed shareholding, the main step of the transaction was a voluntary takeover offer published by Hisense in May 2018. Nevertheless, Hisense did not acquire shares of Gorenje only through a takeover offer, but had already prior to the publication of the takeover offer acquired 32.96% stake in Gorenje by way of private share purchases, thereby stopping just short of exceeding the mandatory takeover offer threshold under Slovenian takeover law, which is set at 1/3 of all voting rights in the target. In the course of the following takeover offer, additional 62.46% of the shareholders tendered their shares to Hisense. Therefore, following the takeover offer, Hisense held the total of 95.42% of all shares of Gorenje.

由于戈兰尼是一家股份相对分散的上市公司，海信于 2018 年 5 月发出自愿收购要约，这是本次交易的主要环节。然而，海信并非仅通过要约收购的方式收购戈兰尼的股份，在收购要约公布之前，海信已私下收购了戈兰尼 32.96% 的股份。斯洛文尼亚收购法规定，如收购方持有目标公司的投票权达到了 1/3，则应发出强制性收购要约，而海信恰在达到上述限制前停止收购。在接下来的要约收购中，另有股东向海信转让了 62.46% 的股份。经过要约收购，海信持有了戈兰尼 95.42% 的股份。

Given the success of the takeover offer and the high shareholding stake acquired in its process, Hisense was in a position to trigger the squeeze-out of the remaining minority shareholders, which it finalised in October 2018. This enabled Hisense to become the sole shareholder of Gorenje.

鉴于要约收购成功，且海信因此持有戈兰尼绝大部分的股份，海信处于能够将剩余少数股东排除在外的地位，2018 年 10 月，排除计划最终执行完毕，海信由此成为戈兰尼的唯一股东。

The total value of the transaction including the private purchases of stocks, takeover offer and the squeeze-out of minority shareholders exceeded EUR250 million. No share capital increase took place in the course of the transaction.

本次交易通过私下购买股票、要约收购和排除少数股东完成，交易的总价值超过了 2.5 亿欧元。在交易的过程中，股本并未增加。

Following the acquisition of all shares, the delisting of Gorenje's shares from Ljubljana and Warsaw stock exchanges took place and was completed in the second half of 2018.

在海信收购戈兰尼的全部股份后，戈兰尼的股票在卢布尔雅那和华沙证券交易所退市，退市于 2018 年下半年完成。

As the last step in the process of acquisition, following the squeeze-out and the delisting, Hisense adopted a decision to convert Gorenje from a joint stock company into a private limited liability company—the change took effect in March 2019.

在排除其他股东和戈兰尼股票退市之后，海信决定将戈兰尼股份公司转变为私人有限责任公司，这是本次交易的最后一步，该变更于 2019 年 3 月生效。

In the process of acquisition of Gorenje, Wolf Theiss, acting as a lead counsel, advised Hisense on all legal aspects of the transaction.

在收购戈兰尼的过程中，沃尔夫·泰斯律师事务所作为首席律师团队，为海信在交易的各方面提供法律咨询。

Among others, Wolf Theiss advised with respect to the following: competitive bidding process, transaction structuring, due diligence (in Slovenia, the Czech Republic, Serbia, and Poland), capital markets laws (in Slovenia and Poland), the takeover offer and the process of takeover, and competition/anti-trust filings with competent authorities.

其中，沃尔夫·泰斯律师事务所的法律咨询涵盖以下方面：竞标，交易架构，尽职调查（在斯洛文尼亚、捷克共和国、塞尔维亚和波兰），资本市场法律（在斯洛文尼亚和波兰），要约收购，向主管机关进行竞争与反垄断申报。

Wolf Theiss further advised Hisense with respect to the squeeze-out of minority shareholders, delisting and conversion from a joint stock company into a private limited liability company.

沃尔夫·泰斯律师事务所还为海信排除少数股东、退市和将股份公司转变为私人有限责任公司等环节提供咨询。

Given the complexity of the deal, the deal value, the number of jurisdictions involved and the importance of Gorenje for Slovenia, the transaction could be considered the most important transaction in Slovenia of 2018.

鉴于交易的复杂性、交易价值、所涉司法管辖区的数量以及戈兰尼对斯洛文尼亚的重要程度，该交易可被视为2018年斯洛文尼亚最重要的交易之一。

2. 交易结构（Transaction Structure）

The structure of the transaction was somewhat unusual in that Gorenje commenced a search for a strategic partner—whereby it noted that such strategic partner may also enter into the shareholding structure of Gorenje—and led the whole bidding process, while it did not issue any new share capital that such strategic partner could subscribe nor sell any of its treasury shares to such partner. Instead, through the bidding process, Gorenje merely selected who they thought would be the best strategic partner, whereby such best bidder would then have to acquire the shares from the existing shareholders. Since Gorenje was at the time a listed company with a dispersed shareholding (no majority shareholder) the majority stake in Gorenje could only be acquired through a takeover offer.

本次交易的结构较为罕见，虽然戈兰尼开展竞标，尝试寻找战略合作伙伴，并提出战略合作伙伴可以参股戈兰尼，但戈兰尼并未发行任何新股供其认购，亦未向其出售任何库存股。相反，戈兰尼通过竞标仅选择了他们认为最为合适的合作伙伴，且最佳合作伙伴须收购现有股东的股份。由于戈兰尼当时是一家股权分散（并无多数股东）的上市公司，因此，海信只能通过要约收购的方式获得戈兰尼的多数股份。

Against this background, it is worthwhile looking at the structure of the acquisition of Gorenje by Hisense from a chronological perspective. The whole transaction can be chronologically divided in the following phases:

基于这样的背景，从时间角度研究本次交易的结构十分有意义。按时间顺序，整个交易可以分为以下几个阶段：

- Early process for the selection of a strategic partner of Gorenje (i.e. the submission of a non-binding bid, invitation to the second phase of the transaction, due diligence exercise);
- Submission of a binding bid which was followed by a decision of Gorenje to se-

lect Hisense as the preferred strategic partner;

• Private acquisition of shares of Gorenje in the amount not exceeding the mandatory takeover offer threshold;

• Voluntary takeover offer;

• Obtainment of required approvals from the competent competition/anti-trust authorities;

• Squeeze-out of minority shareholders;

• Delisting of Gorenje's shares from Ljubljana and Warsaw stock exchange;

• Reduction of share capital by withdrawal (cancellation) of treasury shares;

• Conversion from a joint stock company into a private limited liability company and a resulting change of a corporate governance system.

• 戈兰尼在前期选择战略合作伙伴（即：提交无约束力的投标、邀请参与第二阶段的交易、尽职调查）；

• 提交有约束力的投标，随后，戈兰尼决定首选海信作为战略合作伙伴；

• 私下收购戈兰尼的股份，且金额不超过强制要约收购的门槛；

• 自愿要约收购；

• 获得竞争/反垄断主管机构的必要批准；

• 排除少数股东；

• 戈兰尼股票在卢布尔雅那和华沙证券交易所进行退市；

• 通过提取（撤销）库存股减少股本；

• 从股份公司转变为私人有限责任公司，从而改变公司治理制度。

2.1 戈兰尼选择战略合作伙伴的前期程序（Early Process for the Selection of a Strategic Partner of Gorenje）

In November 2017, Gorenje commenced its search for a strategic partner that would support Gorenje in the long-term sustainable growth and development. Gorenje noted at the time that this may also result in such strategic partner becoming a shareholder of Gorenje. The search for a strategic partner came after Panasonic, who had been previously considering expanding the scope of its partnership with Gorenje (following the establishment of a commercial partnership with Gorenje and subscription of EUR 10 million of Gorenje's newly issued share capital in 2013), decided not to proceed with such plans.

2017 年 11 月，戈兰尼开始寻找战略合作伙伴，以支持戈兰尼的长期可持续成长和发展。戈兰尼当时指出，战略合作伙伴也可以成为戈兰尼的股东。在寻找战略合作伙伴之前，松下一直在考虑扩大与戈兰尼的合作范围（松下在 2013 年与戈兰尼建立了商业合作伙伴关系并认购戈兰尼新发行的 1000 万欧元股本），但最终，松下决定不再推进此类计划。

In December 2017, Gorenje's financial adviser reached out to potential interested companies. In March 2018, Gorenje received five non-binding bids for a strategic partnership, following which it invited three companies to conduct due diligence in Gorenje.

2017 年 12 月，戈兰尼的财务顾问与有意向的公司进行了接洽。在 2018 年 3 月，戈兰尼收到了五份不具约束力的战略合作投标，之后，戈兰尼邀请了三家公司对其进行尽职调查。

2.2 有拘束力的投标和选择海信作为战略合作伙伴（Binding Bid and Selection of Hisense as the Strategic Partner）

On 8 May 2018, Gorenje received three binding bids for a strategic partnership and requested two of the offerees to improve their offers. Already the next day, on 9 May 2018, Gorenje announced that it chose Hisense as the best bidder, whereby it took into account the "*strategic elements which were the basis for the commencement of the process of searching for a strategic partnership*", the feasibility of the transaction and the price offered to the shareholders.

2018 年 5 月 8 日，戈兰尼收到了三份具有约束力的战略合作要约，戈兰尼要求其中两份作出改善。在第二天，即 2018 年 5 月 9 日，戈兰尼宣布，"鉴于作为合作基础的战略要素"、交易的可行性和投标人对股东作出的报价，海信是本次竞标的最佳投标人。

Hisense, in its binding bid, submitted to the management of Gorenje a written commitment in which it committed itself to publish a takeover offer at EUR 12 per share under a condition that it is selected by Gorenje as its strategic partner. Such offered price carried a considerable takeover premium as the market price of Gorenje's shares at the time the binding bid was made stood at around EUR 6.50. Hisense obliged itself to publish a takeover intention (a legally required step before the publication of a takeover offer) in 15 days and a takeover offer within the time limits prescribed by the law.

海信在投标时,向戈兰尼管理层提交了一份书面承诺,保证在戈兰尼选其作为战略合作伙伴的前提下,将以每股 12 欧元的价格发出收购要约。由于在发出约束性投标时,戈兰尼股票的市场价格约为 6.50 欧元,因此,这一报价可带来相当大的收购溢价。海信有义务在 15 日内公布收购意向书(在收购要约公布之前必须采取的步骤),并在法律规定的时限内公布收购要约。

2.3 在公布收购要约前的股份收购 (Acquisition of Shares Prior to the Publication of the Takeover Offer)

Hisense had, through its newly established company (Hisense Luxembourg Home Appliance Holding S. à r. l.), already during the period following the selection as the best bidder and before the publication of the takeover offer (on 29 May 2018) been acquiring shares of Gorenje in private deals. In this manner, it, among other, acquired the 11.80% stake held by International Finance Corporation (IFC) and a 5% share held by Home Products Europe B. V..

在海信被选为最佳投标者至收购要约公布之前(2018 年 5 月 29 日)的期间,海信已通过其新成立的公司即海信卢森堡家电控股有限责任公司,以私下交易的形式收购了戈兰尼的股份。此外,它还通过这种方式收购了原本由国际金融公司(IFC)持有的戈兰尼 11.80%的股份,以及由欧洲家居用品有限公司持有的 5%的股份。

The important consideration in this step was for Hisense not to exceed the statutorily prescribed threshold above which it would be required to publish a mandatory takeover offer. Slovenian takeover law stipulates that in case an acquirer acquires more than 1/3 of all voting rights in the target it is obliged to publish a mandatory takeover offer. Gorenje only issued one class of shares which all carried equal voting rights. Hisense (through Hisense Luxembourg Home Appliance Holding S. à r. l.), who had acquired a total of 32.96% of shares of Gorenje prior to the publication of the voluntary takeover offer, did therefore not exceed such threshold.

在这一步中,海信不能超过法定的公开强制要约收购门槛是需要考虑的重要事项。斯洛文尼亚收购法规定，如收购方获得目标公司所有投票权的 1/3 以上，则有义务公开进行强制性的要约收购。戈兰尼只发行了一类股票，此类股票均具有相同的投票权。海信通过海信卢森堡家电控股有限公司在自愿收购要约公布之前仅收购了戈兰尼全部股份的 32.96%，因此，并未超过该限制。

2.4 自愿收购要约（Voluntary Takeover Offer）

This step consisted of multiple phases. As mentioned above, Hisense committed itself to, within 15 days from the submission of the binding bid, publish a takeover intention and to then publish a takeover offer within the statutorily prescribed time limits. Hisense published a takeover intention already on 11 May 2018.

该步骤包括多个阶段。如上所述，海信承诺自提交有约束力的投标之日起 15 日内公布收购意向，随后，海信在法定的期限内公布了收购要约。在 2018 年 5 月 11 日，海信公布了收购意向。

Slovenian takeover law requires the offeror to publish a takeover offer in 10 to 30 days from the publication of the takeover intention. Accordingly, Hisense Luxembourg Home Appliance Holding S. à r. l. published a takeover offer on 29 May 2018.

斯洛文尼亚收购法规定，要约人应在收购意向公布后的 10 至 30 日内公布收购要约。因此，海信卢森堡家电控股有限公司在 2018 年 5 月 29 日公布了收购要约。

The takeover offer was technically made by Ilirika d. d. , a Slovenian stock brokerage house, who published the takeover offer in the name and for the account of Hisense Luxembourg Home Appliance Holding S. à r. l. . This was necessary as the Slovenian takeover law requires the takeover offer and other legal acts associated with it to be made on behalf and for the account of the offeror by a brokerage company having the status of a member of the central securities depository company (only certain banks and brokerage houses have such status).

斯洛文尼亚股票经纪公司 Ilirika d. d. 专业地发出了收购要约，并以海信卢森堡家电控股有限公司的名义和账户公布该要约。这是必要的，因为根据斯洛文尼亚收购法规定，要由具有中央证券存管公司成员资格的经纪公司（只有某些银行和经纪公司具有这种资格）以要约人的名义和账户进行收购要约以及从事与之相关的其他法律行为。

The offer was open for acceptance for 29 days, from 29 May 2018 until 26 June 2018. The statutorily prescribed period for which the takeover offer needs to be open for acceptance is at least 28 days, while the maximum is 60 days.

该要约的承诺期限为29日，即自2018年5月29日开始，至2018年6月26日结束。法定的要约承诺期限为最少28日，最多60日。

The takeover offer was not conditioned on any success threshold, meaning that Hisense was required to acquire the shares tendered in the takeover offer regardless of (how small) the number of so tendered shares. Nevertheless, the takeover offer was well received as shareholders holding 62.46% of all shares of Gorenje decided to tender their shares to Hisense in its course. On 29 June 2018, Slovenian Securities Market Agency (Agencija za trg vrednostnih papirjev) issued a decision declaring the takeover offer successful and the tendered shares were consequently registered in the name of Hisense Luxembourg Home Appliance Holding S. à r. l.. Following the takeover offer, Hisense became 95.42% shareholder of Gorenje.

收购要约不以任何条件的成就为前提，这意味着在要约收购中，无论投标的股份为多少，海信均须全部收购。不过，收购要约得到了积极的回应，戈兰尼的股东决定向海信投标公司62.24%的股份。2018年6月29日，斯洛文尼亚证券市场管理局（斯洛文尼亚语：Agencija za trg vrednostnih papirjev）发布了一项决定，宣布要约收购成功，且投标的股份将被登记在海信卢森堡家电控股有限公司的名下。在要约收购后，海信成为持有戈兰尼95.42%股份的股东。

Among the major shareholders who sold their shares to Hisense in the course of the takeover offer were Panasonic and Kapitalska družba.

在要约收购的过程中，向海信出售股份的大股东为松下和Kapitalska družba。[1]

Throughout the whole time in which Hisense's takeover offer was open for acceptance, a possibility remained that a competing takeover offer may be published by any other interested acquirer. Namely, the selection of Hisense as the best bidder in the course of the search for a strategic partner of Gorenje could not legally prevent the pos-

---

[1] Kapitalska družba是一家斯洛文尼亚的公共有限责任公司。该公司通过资产管理为养老金与残疾保险金提供资金，其唯一创始人及股东为斯洛文尼亚国家。——译者注

sibility that any other party (either a participant in the bidding process who, just as Hisense, had an opportunity to conduct a due diligence of Gorenje, or a third party, who was not involved in the bidding process) could launch a competing takeover offer for Gorenje's shares. Nevertheless, this risk did not materialize.

在海信收购要约的承诺期限内,任何其他有意的收购方均可发出有竞争力的收购要约。也就是说,在戈兰尼寻找战略合作伙伴的过程中,虽然海信被选为最佳投标者,但这不能合法地阻止任何其他投资方针对戈兰尼的股份发起竞争性的收购要约。竞标过程中,参与竞标者如海信,以及任何参与竞标过程的主体或并未参与竞标过程的第三方均有机会对戈兰尼进行尽职调查。然而,这种风险并未出现。

2.5 竞争主管机关的批准(Approvals from the Competition Authorities)

The takeover of Gorenje could only be successfully completed once it was approved by the competent competition authorities. Both Gorenje and Hisense were present in certain same relevant markets, in particular in the EU and in Eastern Europe. The merger filings were therefore filed with the European Commission and certain national competition authorities outside of the EU.

只有经由竞争主管机关批准,海信才能成功完成对戈兰尼的收购。戈兰尼和海信处于特定的相关市场,特别是在欧盟和东欧。因此,我们还向欧盟委员会和欧盟以外的一些国家竞争主管机关提交了合并申报。

The European Commission noted in its decision issued in the simplified procedure that both Gorenje and Hisense are producing and supplying home appliances, such as refrigerators and stoves. However, the Commission did not find the transaction non-compliant with the EU competition protection rules since the market shares of both companies on the EU market were limited and also numerous competitors would remain present on the market even after the transaction.

欧盟委员会在简易程序中发布了一项决定,该决定指出,戈兰尼和海信均生产、供应家用电器,如冰箱、炉灶等。然而,欧盟委员会未发现该交易不符合欧盟竞争保护规则,因为两家公司在欧盟市场上份额有限,即使在交易完成之后,该市场上仍然存在众多竞争者。

2.6 排除少数股东（Squeeze-out of Minority Shareholders）

Slovenian company law allows for a squeeze-out of minority shareholders by a majority shareholder if such majority shareholder holds 90% or more of the share capital of the company. In addition, Slovenian takeover law provides that in a case of a squeeze-out that follows a successful voluntary takeover offer in which the takeover offer was accepted by shareholders holding at least 90% of all shares with voting rights to which the offer was addressed (i. e. shares with voting rights that were not already held by the majority shareholder at the time it published the takeover offer), the majority shareholder has to conduct a squeeze-out by providing consideration offered in the takeover offer, provided that a shareholders' resolution on a squeeze-out is adopted within three months of the issuance of the decision declaring that the takeover offer was successful by the Securities Market Agency. In such case, the majority shareholder does not need to determine the fair reimbursement of the minority shareholders (as is otherwise required under the company law in a squeeze-out) thereby also avoiding the need for an engagement of a company valuation specialist and an auditor.

斯洛文尼亚公司法规定，如果多数股东持有公司90%或以上的股份，则多数股东可排除少数股东。此外，该法还规定，在自愿要约收购成功以后，即收购要约为持有公司90%以上具有投票权的股份的股东所接受之后（即在发布收购要约时，具有投票权的股份并未被多数股东持有），多数股东必须通过给付收购要约中报出的对价，来实施排除少数股东的程序，但前提是股东自证券市场机构宣布要约收购成功之日起三个月内对此作出决议。在这种情况下，大股东不需要确定对少数股东的公平补偿（公司法在排除时另有要求），从而也避免了聘用公司评估专家和审计师。

In line with the rules described above, Hisense at the shareholders' meeting of Gorenje on 17 September 2018 as a 95.42% shareholder of Gorenje proposed an adoption of a resolution on the squeeze-out of minority shareholders at the price offered in the takeover offer. Hisense was required to offer such price since it, in the takeover offer, acquired 62.46% of shares of Gorenje, out of the total of 67.04% of shares of Gorenje that it had not yet held prior to the publication of the takeover offer. This meant that Hisense acquired 93% of the shares to which its voluntary takeover offer was addressed. The squeeze-out was effective as of 26 October 2018, when the shareholders' resolution on the squeeze-out was registered in the Slovenian companies register.

2018年9月17日，海信依据上述规则，作为持有戈兰尼股份95.42%的股东，在股东大会上提出以收购要约中的报价排除少数股东的决议。海信必须按照收购要约报价，这是因为，在作出收购要约之前，未被海信持有的戈兰尼股份占比67.04%，而通过要约收购，海信获得了戈兰尼62.46%的股份。这意味着海信收购的股份占自愿收购要约所针对的股份的93%。2018年10月26日，股东大会关于排除少数股东的决议被登记于斯洛文尼亚公司登记簿，自此，排除少数股东的决议生效。

2.7 戈兰尼股票自证券交易所退市（Delisting of Gorenje's Shares from Stock Exchanges）

At the same shareholders' meeting, Hisense also proposed a resolution on the delisting of Gorenje's shares with a ticker symbol GVRG from Ljubljana and Warsaw stock exchanges. The listing of Gorenje's shares was no longer necessary as they were all held by Hisense. In addition, both delistings had to be completed before Gorenje could eventually be converted from a joint stock company into a limited liability company. The proposed resolution on delisting was adopted and the shares were later delisted from both stock exchanges. Whereas the delisting procedure in Slovenia was a rather simplistic and straightforward process, the delisting in Poland from the Warsaw stock exchange encompassed a several stage approval process with a substantially longer timeline.

在此次股东大会上，海信还提出了戈兰尼股票（代码为GVRG）自卢布尔雅那和华沙证券交易所退市的决议。由于海信已持有戈兰尼的全部股份，戈兰尼的股票无须再继续上市。此外，股票退市应在戈兰尼由股份公司转变为有限责任公司之前完成。拟退市的决议案获得通过，随后，戈兰尼的股票在两个证券交易所摘牌。斯洛文尼亚的退市程序相当简单直接，而在波兰华沙证券交易所退市则须经过几个阶段的批准程序，因此，需要的时间亦长得多。

2.8 通过注销库存股减少股本（Reduction of Share Capital by Deletion of Treasury Shares）

As already noted above, Gorenje was at the time of the transaction also holding some of its own shares (treasury shares), which represented about 0.5% of total share capital of Gorenje.

如上所述，戈兰尼在交易时还持有一些自有股（库存股），占戈兰尼总股本的 0.5% 左右。

With a view to increase the profitability of Gorenje's equity, the shareholders' resolution on reduction of share capital of Gorenje by way of withdrawal of treasury shares was adopted at the shareholders' meeting on 17 September 2018.

为了提高戈兰尼股本的盈利能力，在 2018 年 9 月 17 日的股东大会上，股东通过了以撤回库存股的方式减少戈兰尼股本的决议。

2.9 从股份公司转变为私人有限责任公司（Conversion from a Joint Stock Company into a Private Limited Liability Company）

Lastly, on 7 February 2019, Hisense as the sole shareholder of Gorenje adopted a shareholder's resolution to convert the corporate form of Gorenje from a joint stock company to a private limited liability company. The change was registered with the court register soon thereafter on 11 March 2019.

最后，在 2019 年 2 月 7 日，海信作为戈兰尼的唯一股东，通过了由股份公司转型为私人有限责任公司的决议。此后不久，该变更于 2019 年 3 月 11 日被登记于法院。

In many similar cases of takeovers of Slovenian joint stock companies, the acquirers decided to convert the target from a joint stock company into a private limited liability company. The decision of Hisense was driven by multiple reasons, in particular a lesser and more flexible regulation of limited liability companies under Slovenian corporate law, which allows for a simpler and more cost-efficient management.

在许多收购斯洛文尼亚股份公司的类似案例中，收购方均决定将目标公司从股份公司变更为私人有限责任公司。海信的决定基于多种原因，特别是斯洛文尼亚公司法对有限责任公司的监管较少且更加灵活，这使有限责任公司的管理更加简单，更能节约成本。

2.10 公司治理结构的变化（Changes to the Corporate Governance Structure）

As already mentioned, Slovenian corporate law allows shareholders of private limited liability companies a bigger freedom in determining the corporate governance structure than in cases of joint stock companies.

如前所述，根据斯洛文尼亚公司法，在确定公司的治理结构方面，私人有限责任公司相较于股份公司的股东拥有更多自由。

At the time of the transaction, Gorenje employed a two-tier corporate governance structure with a management board and a supervisory board. This is one of the two corporate governance structures available to joint stock companies in Slovenia. Namely, in addition to the two-tier structure, Slovenian company law also allows joint stock companies to opt for a one-tier structure with a board of directors that consists of executive and non-executive directors. Slovenian company law also provides rather detailed rules under which such boards operate.

在本次交易中,戈兰尼采用了双层公司治理结构,即公司管理层包括管理委员会和监事会。这是在斯洛文尼亚股份公司可以采用的两种公司治理结构之一。也就是说,除了双层结构,斯洛文尼亚公司法还允许股份公司选择单层结构,该类公司的管理层是由执行董事和非执行董事组成的董事会。斯洛文尼亚公司法提供了相当详细的规则,以便此类公司的董事会据以操作。

However, in case of a private limited liability company, Slovenian company law only requires such company to have one or more managers/directors and only provides the very basic rules applicable to the management of the company. Beyond this requirement, the shareholder(s) of a private limited liability company have a significant discretion in determining the corporate governance structure of the company and the rules which govern it (such can already be determined in the articles of association).

但是,斯洛文尼亚公司法仅要求私人有限责任公司设置一名或多名经理(董事),并且该法仅制定了十分基本的公司管理规则。此外,私人有限责任公司的股东在确定公司的治理结构及管理规则(可以在公司章程中确定)方面拥有较大的自由裁量权。

When converting Gorenje from a joint stock company into a private limited liability company, Hisense decided to adopt a corporate governance structure consisting of individual directors and a committee of directors as a collective body consisting of all directors. Two of the directors are named as chief managing directors and can represent the company each individually, while the other directors can represent the company together with one chief managing director. Certain high level decisions are reserved for the committee of directors, such as determination of Gorenje's operational plans and investment programs and preparation of annual financial budget plans and final accounting plans.

在将戈兰尼从股份公司转变为私人有限责任公司过程中，海信决定采用由董事个人和董事委员会组成的公司治理结构，作为公司董事的集体机构。其中，两名董事被任命为首席董事总经理，可以单独代表公司，而其他董事可以与一名首席董事总经理共同代表公司。某些重要事项只能交由董事会决定，例如确定戈兰尼的运营计划和投资程序，以及编制年度财务预算计划和决算计划。

3. 项目融资方式（Project Financing Method）

The transaction was financed with Hisense's own funds.

本次交易由海信自有资金融资。

In accordance with Slovenian takeover law, Hisense had, prior to the publication of the takeover offer, deposited on the special account of KDD –Centralna klirinško depotna družba (Slovenian Central Securities Clearing Corporation) an amount required for the settlement of the purchase price for the shares tendered in the course of the takeover offer.

在收购要约公布之前，海信已根据斯洛文尼亚收购法，将用于支付股份购买价格的金额存入了斯洛文尼亚中央证券清算公司（Centralna klirinško depotna družba）[1]的特别账户。

In addition, as required under Slovenian company law, Hisense had to provide, prior to the squeeze-out of minority shareholders, a statement of a bank in which the bank accepted to be jointly and severally liable for the settlement of the purchase price for the shares acquired through the squeeze-out (bank guarantee).

此外，根据斯洛文尼亚公司法的要求，海信在排除少数股东之前，须提供一份银行的声明，表明银行愿对排除程序中海信支付购股份购买价格的义务承担连带责任（银行担保）。

---

[1] 这是一家专门从事证券交易清算和结算的公司，其主要业务包括证券的集中托管、结算和相关的金融服务，其在斯洛文尼亚的金融市场中扮演着核心角色，确保了市场的透明度、效率和稳定性，降低交易对手风险，提高市场效率，对斯洛文尼亚金融市场的健康运作至关重要。——译者注

4. 交易文件中的核心条款（Key Terms in Transaction Documents）

With the exception of initial private purchases of shares, the transaction was conducted in a form of a public takeover offer and a following squeeze-out.

除了首次私下购买股份，该交易是以公开收购要约和后续排除的方式进行的。

Therefore, the main transaction document in the transaction was a takeover offer and the accompanying prospectus, which were both market standard. The takeover offer was made for all shares not yet held by Hisense at the time of its publication and was not conditional on any success threshold. The prospectus had to be approved by the Slovenian Securities Market Agency in advance of the publication of the takeover offer, as mandated by Slovenian takeover law.

因此，收购要约和随附的招股说明书是本次交易中的主要文件，二者均符合市场标准。收购要约针对要约发布时海信尚未持有的全部股份，且不以任何条件的成就为前提。根据斯洛文尼亚收购法，在收购要约发布之前，招股说明书必须经斯洛文尼亚证券市场管理局批准。

The squeeze-out was conducted based on a shareholders' meeting resolution. Since the squeeze-out was performed within three months following the closing of the takeover offer the takeover law required Hisense to offer to the minority shareholders the same compensation (i. e. price) per share as offered in the takeover offer.

本次排除基于股东大会的决议进行。由于本次排除是在收购要约结束后的三个月内进行的，因此，收购法要求海信按照收购要约的报价向少数股东提供每股相同的补偿（即价款）。

5. 项目的主要问题（Main Legal Issues of the Project）

On 31 May 2020, by adopting a third legislative package to contain the consequences of the COVID-19 epidemic, Slovenia introduced a screening mechanism for foreign direct investments (FDI), which shall be applied until 30 June 2023. The government is currently drafting a bill that will adopt the FDI screening mechanism as a permanent measure. The newly adopted foreign direct investment mechanism targets investments made by foreign investors (i. e. any foreign citizen or entity including EU/

EEA/Swiss citizen or entity) in Slovenia.

2020年5月31日，斯洛文尼亚通过了第三个一揽子立法，以遏制COVID-19的后果，并引入了外商直接投资监管机制（FDI），该机制一直适用到2023年6月30日。政府目前正在起草一部法案，将外商直接投资监管机制作为一项永久性措施。新采用的外商直接投资监管机制针对外国投资者（即任何外国公民或实体，包括欧盟/欧洲经济区/瑞士公民或实体）在斯洛文尼亚的投资。

A relevant investment according to the new screening mechanism is any investment aiming to establish or to maintain lasting and direct links between the foreign investor and the economic entity established in Slovenia through direct and indirect acquisition of at least 10% participation in capital or voting rights in a Slovenian target company. Such investments may include takeovers, mergers, greenfield investments and even acquisition of real estate (acquisition by a foreign investor of real estate essential to critical infrastructure or in the vicinity of such infrastructure is also subject to the FDI screening). If the investment poses a threat to the security and public order of Slovenia, especially in cases where it may have an effect on any areas considered as risk factors which including: (i) critical infrastructure, (ii) critical technologies and dual use items, (iii) supply of critical inputs, (iv) access to sensitive information, (v) the freedom and pluralism of media, and (vi) certain programs and projects in the interest of the European Union), the Ministry of Economic Development and Technology may conduct a screening procedure and can decide to authorize, condition, prohibit or unwind a particular foreign direct investment.

根据新的监管机制，相关投资是指旨在通过直接和间接收购斯洛文尼亚目标公司至少10%的资本或投票权，在外国投资者和在斯洛文尼亚设立的经济实体之间建立或保持持久和直接联系的任何投资。此类投资可能包括收购、兼并、绿地投资，甚至收购房地产（外国投资者收购关键基础设施所必需的房地产或此类基础设施附近的房地产也需接受外商直接投资监管）。如果投资对斯洛文尼亚的安全和公共秩序构成威胁，特别是在投资可能对被视为风险因素的任何领域产生影响的情况下，这些领域包括：（i）关键基础设施，（ii）关键技术和双重用途项目，（iii）关键投入的供应，（iv）敏感信息的获取，（v）媒体的自由和多元化，以及（vi）涉及欧盟利益的某些计划和项目），经济发展和技术部可启动监管程序，并可决定批准、限制、禁止或取消特定的外商直接投资。

The decision to engage in a screening procedure is based particularly on a preliminary evaluation of the following points: (i) whether the foreign investor is directly or indirectly controlled by third country (non-EU) governments including national authorities or third country (non-EU) armed forces, including through ownership structure or significant funding; (ii) whether the foreign investor has already been involved in activities affecting security or public order in an EU member state; and (iii) whether there is a serious risk that the foreign investor engages in illegal or criminal activities. A decision to prohibit or unwind an individual foreign direct investment in the screening procedure has the consequence that the relevant merger agreement, takeover procedure or acquisition agreement is declared null and void. The screening procedure can apply even to foreign direct investments made up to 5 years before the adoption of the screening mechanism.

启动筛选程序的决定主要是基于对以下几点的初步评估：（i）外国投资者是否直接或间接受第三国（非欧盟）政府（包括国家当局）或第三国（非欧盟）武装部队控制，包括通过所有权结构或重大融资；（ii）外国投资者是否已经在欧盟成员国参与影响安全或公共秩序的活动；（iii）外国投资者是否有从事非法或犯罪活动的严重风险。禁止或取消外商直接投资进入筛选程序的决定将导致相关合并协议，收购程序或收购协议被宣布为无效。该外商投资监管机制甚至可以适用于监管机制生效前5年内的外商直接投资。

The respective FDI must be notified to the Ministry of Economic Development and Technology no later than 15 days after the day of the execution of the respective agreement or the publication of the takeover offer.

相关外商直接投资必须在相关协议签署或收购要约公布之日后15日内通知经济发展和技术部。

The requirements with respect to takeover law were described above under Chapter 2.4. and the requirements with respect to delisting under Chapter 2.7.

上文第2.4部分述了有关收购法的要求，第2.7部分概述了对退市的要求。

Subject to that, the only other regulatory approvals that were required in the course of the transaction related to securities markets and competition/anti-trust law. One of the main challenges of Slovenian law in this respect is that Slovenian takeover law does not allow for the takeover offer to be conditional on the outcome of the merger control proceedings (i. e. the obtainment of the required merger control clearances). Therefore, it is essential that the applications for merger clearances are submitted at the very early stage in order for the clearances to be obtained in time before the implementation of the takeover.

在此情况下，交易中须进行的唯一其他监管批准是证券市场和竞争/反垄断法的批准。在这方面的一个主要难题是，斯洛文尼亚收购法不允许收购要约以合并控制程序的结果为条件（即获得所需的合并控制许可）。因此，必须在早期阶段提交合并许可申请，以便在实施收购之前及时获得许可。

Furthermore, in the course of the takeover offer, the question emerged whether Kapitalska družba was at all allowed to tender shares of Gorenje it held. Kapitalska družba is a holding company owning shares in a number of companies and is fully owned by the Republic of Slovenia. In 2015, the Parliament of the Republic of Slovenia adopted a document titled Strategy of Management of the Capital Investments of the State (Strategija upravljanja kapitalskih naložb države, Strategy) determining, among other things, which of the state's (direct or indirect) shareholdings in Slovenian companies may be sold and which have to remain state-held. In this respect, the *Strategy* divides the state's shareholding investments in Slovenian companies into three groups: strategic, important and portfolio investments.

在要约收购的过程中，还出现了一个问题，即 Kapitalska družba 是否能自由投标持有的戈兰尼股份。Kapitalska družba 是一家控股公司，持有众多公司的股份，该公司的全部股份由斯洛文尼亚共和国持有。2015年，斯洛文尼亚共和国议会通过了一份题为"国家资本投资管理战略"的文件（斯洛文尼亚语：Strategija upravljanja kapitalskih naložb države；以下简称《战略》），该文件确定了哪些国家（直接或间接）持股的斯洛文尼亚公司可以被出售，哪些必须始终由国家所有。《战略》将国家对斯洛文尼亚公司的持股投资分为三类：战略投资、重要投资和组合投资。

The Strategy identified the stake of Kapitalska družba in Gorenje as "important", meaning that Kapitalska družba shall maintain its 16.37% shareholding which was already below the so called "25% + 1 share" shareholding threshold, envisaged in the *Strategy* as the minimum direct or indirect shareholding of the stake in the companies designated as "important" (this threshold is important as it allows such shareholder to prevent adoption of certain shareholders' resolutions that need to be adopted with a 75% majority). Therefore, there was a concern on part of Kapitalska družba whether it is allowed to tender its shares in the course of the takeover offer.

根据《战略》,Kapitalska družba 在戈兰尼的股份属于重要投资,这意味着 Kapitalska družba 应维持其 16.37%的持股,该《战略》认为,在被指定为"重要"的公司中,直接或间接持股的最低比例应为"25%+1 股",而 Kapitalska družba 的持股已低于该比例的限制(这一限制十分重要,因为这使此类股东能够阻止通过一些须经 75%多数赞成的股东决议)。因此,在要约收购的过程中,需要考虑 Kapitalska družba 是否可以出售其股份。

The situation became clearer when the Ministry of Finance noted that the *Strategy* is merely a political document while the role of the management of the holding entities to which the *Strategy* applies is to maximise the value of such entities for its owner (i.e. the state). In the view of the Ministry of Finance, it was therefore up to the management of Kapitalska družba to make a decision on the disposal of its shareholding in Gorenje, whereby it had to take into account the value of the investment in case it decided to sell or hold.

当财政部指出《战略》仅仅是一份政治性文件,且《战略》对相关持股实体的规定是为了使此类实体对所有者(即国家)的价值最大化时,情况就变得明朗了。因此,财政部认为,Kapitalska družba 管理层可决定是否出售其持有的戈兰尼股份,但在作出决定时须考虑投资的价值。

Presumably due to the relatively high offered price and the fact that it would otherwise become a minority shareholder in a highly concentrated ownership structure of Gorenje, Kapitalska družba eventually decided to tender its shares in Gorenje in the takeover offer. The Government of the Republic of Slovenia (also acting as the sole shareholder of Kapitalska družba) did not oppose the sale.

可能是由于海信报价相对较高,以及若不出售股份,Kapitalska družba 将在所有权结构高度集中的戈兰尼公司成为少数股东,Kapitalska družba 最终决定在要约收购中出售其持有的全部戈兰尼股份。斯洛文尼亚共和国政府(也是 Kapitalska družba 的唯一股东)对此并不反对。

─ 作者简介 ─

Klemen Radosavljević is a Partner who joined Wolf Theiss in 2008. Klemen graduated from the University of Ljubljana and obtained a master of laws (LL. M.) degree from the London School of Economics and Political Science. Klemen is admitted to the bar in Slovenia and has extensive experience in the areas of corporate/M&A, banking & finance, and regulatory law (banking and insurance regulation and competition law). Klemen has advised on various complex transactions in Slovenia with respect to a number of industry sectors (automotive, pharmaceutical, finance, insurance, food and beverage, transportation). He also regularly advises international and domestic corporations on various aspects of Slovenian and EU competition law.

Klemen Radosavljević 于 2008 年加入沃尔夫·泰斯律师事务所，现为该律所合伙人。Klemen 毕业于斯洛文尼亚的卢布尔雅那大学，并在伦敦政治经济学院获得 LL. M. 学位。Klemen 拥有斯洛文尼亚执业律师资格，并在公司并购、银行金融和监管法（银行及保险监管和竞争法）领域拥有丰富的工作经验。Klemen 为斯洛文尼亚若干工业部门（汽车、制药、金融、保险、食品、饮料和运输）的多种复杂交易提供法律顾问服务。同时，他经常就斯洛文尼亚和欧盟竞争法的各个部分向国际和国内公司出具法律意见。

股权并购在希腊：在物流运输领域开展投资
Equity in Greece
Investing in the Logistics and Transportation Industry

点 评

希腊位于巴尔干半岛的东南端，三面环海，因地中海位于亚、欧、非三洲之间，希腊作为地中海沿岸国家海岸线绵长，发展物流运输行业具有得天独厚的地理优势。海洋运输行业作为希腊的支柱行业之一，具有政策支持、技术积累及历史传统三方面的明显优势。希腊海洋运输行业持续处于世界领先地位，由此也带动了其他类型物流运输业的发展。

本文作者在文中分别介绍了对希腊著名港口比雷埃夫斯港及前雅典国际机场海利尼肯机场的股权收购项目，并从项目概况及背景、参与方、涉及的主要法律问题及项目最新进展等角度，对收购希腊物流运输行业企业的各类事项进行了详细剖析。

希腊的外商投资环境整体来看是在逐渐优化的。尤其对于比雷埃夫斯港的收购项目促成了部分法律的修订，例如税收方面的优惠政策及投资程序方面的简化措施等提高了投资效率，为外国投资者在希腊进行投资创造了更有吸引力的条件。虽然希腊设立了"企业希腊"（Enterprise Greece）等促进外国投资活动的机构作为外国投资者的联络点，并意图提升外国投资者的市场准入并帮助阐明投资的要求和限制。但政治风险仍是对希腊进行投资不可忽视的一环，在比雷埃夫斯港及海利尼肯机场的股权收购项目中，均出现了工会反对、工人罢工等干扰性活动；另外鉴于历史文明原因，在物流运输行业进行投资的过程中，可能还会出现相关土地或建筑物涉及文物或遗址保护的问题。

1. 比雷埃夫斯集装箱码头项目 (Piraeus Container Terminal Project)

1.1 项目概述 (Overview of the Project)

1.1.1 位置 (The location)

The port of Piraeus (the "Port" is ranked by Lloyd's List as one of the world's top container ports. It was ranked the seventh largest port in Europe in 2018 and is the second largest port in the Mediterranean.

比雷埃夫斯港被《劳埃德船舶日报》列为世界顶级集装箱港口之一。在2018年，它被评为欧洲第七大港口，也是地中海的第二大港口。

1.1.2 私有化方案 (Privatization method)

On 5 March 2014, pursuant to the third economic adjustment programme between Greece and the European Institutions, the Greek Government sought expressions of interest for the purchase of 67% of the shares in the Piraeus Port Authority S. A. (PPA).[1] As part of this process, the management of the Port was transferred from PPA to the Hellenic Republic Asset Development Fund (HRAD), which acquired 74.138% shares in PPA pursuant to decision 195/27.10.2011 of the Inter-Ministerial Restructuring and Privatizations Committee of the Hellenic Republic.

2014年3月5日，根据希腊与欧洲机构之间的第三个经济调整计划，希腊政府寻求购买比雷埃夫斯港务局股份公司（PPA）67%的股份。作为该过程的一部分，港口的经营管理将自PPA转交由希腊共和国资产开发基金（HRAD）负责，该基金根据希腊共和国部长级重组和私有化委员会的第195/27.10.2011号决定，收购了PPA 74,138%股份。

COSCO Group (Hong Kong) Limited (COSCO) was declared as the preferred investor in the Port on the basis of its offer of €22 per share. A transfer of 67% of the shares in the Port then took place from HRAD to COSCO in two phases. In the first phase on August 2016, 51% of the shares were transferred for a purchase price of €280 500 000. This made COSCO the controlling shareholder of PPA. The remaining 16% of the shares are to be held in an escrow account for release within five years of the first phase and after completion of a mandatory Port investment program which re-

---

[1] Kaptanis I. et al., "Greek Port Regulations", *Greek Law Digest*, July 2016.

quires COSCO to invest € 300 000 000.[1]

凭借每股22欧元的报价，中国远洋运输集团（香港）有限公司（以下简称中远集团）被宣布为该港口的首选投资者。其后，通过两个阶段，HRAD将港口67%的股份转让给中远集团。在第一个阶段，中远集团于2016年8月以280 500 000欧元的购买价格获得港口51%的股份。这使中远集团成为PPA的控股股东。余下16%的股份将被存入托管账户，并将在第一个阶段的五年之内且在强制性港口投资方案（该方案要求中远集团投资300 000 000欧元）完成之后被转让给中远集团。

1.2 项目背景（Project Background）

The PPA was established in 1930 as a state-owned entity. After 1999, the PPA has been formed into a state-owned stock company for the purpose of owning and maintaining the infrastructure and superstructure of the Port and providing Port services.

PPA成立于1930年，是一个国有实体。1999年后，PPA成为一家国有股份公司，从而拥有和维护港口的基础设施和上层建筑，并提供港口服务。

In 2002, the PPA and the Hellenic Republic entered into a concession contract which granted PPA the right of exclusive use and management of the Port for a period of 40 years, in return for a yearly concession fee of 1% of the Port's gross turnover for the first three years and 2% thereafter.[2] The contract was subsequently extended to 45 years in order to cover COSCO's 35 year concession.

2002年，PPA和希腊共和国签订了特许经营合同，希腊政府授予PPA在40年内独家使用和管理港口的权利，为此，PPA须在前三年支付港口总营业额的1%作为特许经营费，此后，PPA须支付的特许经营费为港口总营业额的2%。合同的期限后来被延长至45年，以涵盖中远集团为期35年的特许经营权。

In 2003, following the flotation of the Port, PPA was listed in the Athens stock exchange as an Société anonyme (S. A.) and 25% of the shares were sold to private investors. The Greek state retained 75% of PPA's shares and also retained a part of the

---

[1] Hellenic Republic Asset Development Fund, "Asset Development Plan", January 2017, p. 7.
[2] Psaraftis H. & Pallis A., "Concession of the Piraeus container terminal: Turbulent times and the quest for competitiveness", *Maritime Policy & Management*, January 2012, p. 29-30.

management of the Port.[1]

2003年，在港口发行股份以后，PPA在雅典证券交易所上市，成为股份公司，其25%的股份被出售给私人投资者。希腊共和国保留了PPA 75%的股份，并保留港口的部分管理权。

In 2004, the Hellenic Republic, as the majority shareholder of PPA, decided to enter into discussions with various terminal operating companies including Cosco Pacific, HPH, DP World, APM Terminals, Mediterranean Shipping Company (MSC and TIL) and foreign governments (China and Korea), regarding the provision of a concession regarding the terminals' container station (namely, SEMPO). The Ministry of Merchant Marine announced that it was interested in investing in the Port and particularly in SEMPO.[2]

2004年，希腊共和国作为PPA的大股东，决定与各码头运营公司如中远太平洋、和记黄埔港口、迪拜环球港务集团、马士基码头公司、地中海航运公司及其子公司和外国政府（中国政府和韩国政府）就码头集装箱站（即集装箱码头SEMPO）的特许权进行讨论。商船部宣布其有意向港口投资，尤其是向SEMPO投资。

1.3 投标（Tender）

In 2007, the Hellenic Republic and the PPA agreed to proceed with the Project by means of an international tender.

2007年，希腊共和国和PPA同意通过国际招标开展该项目。

At that time, the Port had two container terminals: Pier Ⅰ established in 1898 was the original container terminal and Pier Ⅱ established in 1906 was a large and modern terminal with a potential for expansion. A new Pier Ⅲ is proposed and this would be located next to Pier Ⅱ.[3]

当时，港口有两个集装箱码头：Ⅰ号码头建立于1898年，这是最早的集装箱码头，1906年建成的Ⅱ号码头是一个具有扩建潜力的大型现代码头。正在提议建设一个新的Ⅲ号码头，它将位于Ⅱ号码头附近。

---

[1] Ibid.
[2] Ibid., p.30-31.
[3] Benefit, "Case Studies: Piraeus Container Terminal", accessed on 29 March 2019, <http://www.benefit4transport.eu/wiki/index.php?title=Case_Studies:_Piraeus_Container_Terminal>.

In February 2008, the PPA decided to retain operation of Pier Ⅰ but to arrange an international tender for the concession of Pier Ⅱ, on the condition that (i) part of the income received from the investor or private operator would fund construction of Pier Ⅲ and (ii) the capacity of Pier Ⅱ would be increased from 1.7m TEU to 2.7m TEU p.a., mainly through the upgrade of the equipment and an increase in the container density.[1]

2008年2月，PPA决定继续运营Ⅰ号码头，对Ⅱ号码头的特许权进行国际招标，条件是（i）投资者或私人运营商获得的部分收入将资助Ⅲ号码头的建设；（ii）Ⅱ号码头的容量将从每年170万标准箱增加至每年270万标准箱，这主要通过设备升级和增加集装箱密度来实现。

The selection and the evaluation of the offers made by potential investors was based on the experience and track record of the operator, its financial solvency and the ability to provide guarantees for the amount of 2 000 000 TEUs per annum until the sixth year of the concession period and 3 700 000 TEUs until the eighth year and thereafter of such period. One of the main criteria for the concession was the percentage of gross revenue to be offered by the operator to PPA. COSCO offered 21% for the first 8 years and 24.5% thereafter, while the second ranked bidder offered 19.0%.

潜在投资者做出选择和评估报价的依据是运营商的经验、业绩记录和财务偿付能力，以及其在特许期的第六年时保证达到每年2 000 000标准箱的吞吐量且在该期间的第八年及以后保证达到每年3 700 000标准箱的吞吐量的能力。运营商向PPA提供的总收入百分比是特许权的主要标准之一。在前8年，中远集团的报价为21%，8年后的报价为24.5%，而排名第二的竞标者的报价为19.0%。

The duration of the contract to COSCO is 30 years from the date of the commencement of COSCO's operation of Pier Ⅱ, with a mandatory extension for an additional term of 5 years, subject to the satisfaction of the contractual obligations for the construction of the new Pier Ⅲ.

对于中远集团而言，合同期限为30年，从中远集团开始运营Ⅱ号码头之日起算。合同具有5年的强制延长期限，但前提是中远集团须满足建造Ⅲ号新码

---

[1] Benefit, "Case Studies: Piraeus Container Terminal", 2019.

头的合同义务。

1.4 参与方（Parties Involved）

PPA is the public sector counter-party in the public-private partnership with COSCO.[1] PPA is formed as a Societe Anonyme operating under the supervision of the Hellenic Republic, for the purpose of managing the Port. The Greek State and PPA have entered into a concession agreement (Law 3654/2008), pursuant to which PPA acquired the exclusive right to use and exploit the land, buildings and infrastructure of the Port, and also has the right to enter into sub-concession agreements with third party operators.

PPA 是与中远集团达成公私合作关系的公共部门参与方。PPA 成立后作为一家股份公司，在希腊共和国的监督下开展经营，其目的是管理港口。希腊政府和 PPA 签订了特许权协议（第 3654/2008 号法律），根据该协议，PPA 获得了使用和开发港口土地、建筑物和基础设施的专有权，并同时有权与第三方运营商签订特许权协议。

Cosco Pacific Limited is a container leasing company based in Hong Kong and is listed on the Hong Kong stock exchange. It has credit rating of AAA with 57% of its share capital being owned by independent investors and 43% by China Cosco Holdings (CCH). CCH also owns Cosco Container Lines and China Cosco Bulk Shipping Group. Cosco Holdings is a state-owned enterprise and the largest shipping firm in China with 53% of its share capital to be held by COSCO.[2] COSCO is active in various sectors, including shipping, logistics, finance and manufacturing.

中远太平洋有限公司是一家总部设在中国香港特区的集装箱租赁公司，该公司在香港特区证券交易所上市。其信用评级为 AAA，57%的股本由独立投资者持有，43%的股本由中国远洋控股（CCH）持有。CCH 还拥有中远集装箱运输有限公司和中国远洋散货运输集团的所有权。CCH 是一家国有企业，也是中国最大的航运公司，其 53%的股本由中远集团持有。中远集团活跃于航运、物流、金融和制造业等各个领域。

---

[1] Ibid., p.33.

[2] Van der Putten F. P., "Chinese Investments in the Port of Piraeus, Greece: The Relevance for the EU and Netherlands", Netherlands Institute of International Relations, February 2014.

Piraeus Container Terminal SA (PCT) is a wholly owned subsidiary of COSCO. PCT signed the concession agreement on 25th November 2008 to develop and operate Pier II and Pier III at the Port, which has been ratified by Law 3755/2009 (Government Gazette. 52/A/30.3.2009) as amended by Law 4072/2012 (Government Gazette 86/A/11.4.2012).[1]

比雷埃夫斯集装箱码头公司（PCT）是 COSCO 的全资子公司。在 2008 年 11 月 25 日，PCT 签署了特许权协议，以在港口开发、运营 II 号和 III 号码头。协议经第 3755/2009 号法律（政府公报.5/A/30.3.2009）批准，并经第 4072/2012 号法律修订（政府公报 86/A/11.4.2012）。

1.5 公私合作（Public-private Partnership，PPP）

In general, PPP is a government service or private business venture financed and operated through a partnership between a government and a private company.[2] The PPP enables the public sector to use the expertise of the private sector with regard to certain facilities, such as port infrastructures.[3]

一般而言，公私合作（PPP）是指通过政府和私营公司之间的合作来获得资金和运营的政府服务或私营企业。PPP 使公共部门能够利用私营组织在某些设施（例如港口基础设施）方面的专业知识。

The principal reason for using a PPP is the potential for investing and updating infrastructures without the need for large public investment and in particular it allows the retention of cash flow which in the case of the Port can be used for the new container terminal (Pier III). The use of a PPP also provides a solution in relation to the restrictions arising from the EU Competition Directive, which has led to the EU raising concerns in relation to the alleged preferential treatment given to Global Container Shipping Company MSC, one of the Port's biggest and most active clients.[4]

采用 PPP 的主要原因是可以在不需要大量公共投资的情况下投资和更新基础设施，特别是，它能够保持现金流，在港口的案例中，这可以用于新的集装

---

[1] Cosco Pacific, "Annual Report 2012".
[2] Siousiouras D., "Dealing with the need of Greek ports expansion: a public-private partnership opportunity".
[3] Ibid.
[4] Benefit, "Case Studies: Piraeus Container Terminal", 2019.

箱码头（Ⅲ号码头）。PPP 的采用也提供了应对欧盟竞争指令限制的解决方案，该措施导致欧盟对所谓的给予 MSC 全球集装箱运输公司（该港口最大的和最活跃的客户）的优惠待遇产生顾虑。

The basis of the agreement is a contract executed in 2008, which conferred the management, but not the ownership, of two of the Port's container terminals for a period of thirty-five years. [1]

该协议的基础是 2008 年签订的合同，该合同授予对港口两个集装箱码头的管理权而非所有权，管理权的期限为 35 年。

1.6 特许权协议的主要条款（Main Terms of the Concession Agreement）

The parties entered into a contract in the form of a standard concession agreement. However, the subject concession agreement covered to a great extent the provision of investments in new facilities. In this regard, the contract has been described as a hybrid, having elements of a brown-field operating concession (i. e., contract for the purchase or lease of existing production facilities to be utilised for new production activity) and a green-field investment contract (i. e., agreement involving a parent company which develops its operations from the ground). [2]

双方以标准特许权协议的形式订立合同。但是，主特许经营权协议在很大程度上涵盖了对新设施的投资。就此而言，该合同被称为一个"混合物"，其具有"棕地"经营特许权（即购买或租赁现有生产设施用于新生产活动的合同）和绿地投资合同（即外国母公司新建设施以开展业务的协议）的要素。

The potential investments include the construction of Pier Ⅲ (in the first 6 years of the 30 year concession period), covering also various upgrades to the Port. The estimated cost of upgrading Pier Ⅱ and the construction of Pier Ⅲ was approximately € 500 000 000. Part of the cost would be covered by the Port's operating cash flow and the remaining costs by equity and corporate debt in the form of bonds or senior loans secured on assets of the parent company, instead of project non-recourse financing. [3] It should be noted that, the concession agreement does not contain a renewal

---

[1] Maráczi F., "The Geopolitical Significance of Piraeus Port to China", October 2017.

[2] Benefit, "Case Studies: Piraeus Container Terminal", 2019.

[3] Ibid.

clause or an extension option or a provision related to the period after the end of the concession.

潜在的投资包括建造Ⅲ号码头（在30年特许期的前6年），还包括对港口的各种更新。更新Ⅱ号码头和建造Ⅲ号码头的预计费用约为500 000 000欧元。部分费用将由港口的经营现金流支付，其余费用将通过由母公司资产担保的、以债券或高级贷款为形式的股权和公司债支付，而非通过无追索权项目融资。应该注意的是，特许协议不包含续约条款、延期选择或与特许权结束后的期间有关的条款。

The total concession fee for the whole period was €4 000 000 000 and its structure includes:

整个期间的特许经营费总额为4 000 000 000欧元，其分配结构包括：

(i) a fee in the amount of €50 000 000;

(ii) receipt of a percentage of gross revenue that increases from 21.0% (during the first year to the eighth year) up to 24.5% (from the ninth year inwards) and which is payable monthly;

(iii) a leasing fee linked to the length of the quay (€1800 per meter) payable annually; and

(iv) a leasing fee linked to the container yard area (€4.00 per m^2) payable annually.[1]

(i) 50 000 000欧元的费用；

(ii) 按月支付的总收入白分比，该款项从第一年到第八年占比21.0%增加到从第九年开始的24.5%；

(iii) 按年支付的与码头长度（每米1800欧元）相关的租赁费；和

(iv) 按年支付的与集装箱堆场面积（每平方米4.00欧元）相关的租赁费。

The market risk arising from the concession is mitigated by including a percentage of gross revenues in the concession fee, although this is mainly placed with the operator as a result of throughout guarantees and fixed lease payments provided in the agreement. The financial risk is again carried out by the operator due to the planned construction programme and the limited margin for the reduction of operating costs.

---

[1] Benefit, "Case Studies: Piraeus Container Terminal", 2019.

由于协议中规定了全程担保以及固定的租赁付款，特许经营权带来的市场风险主要由运营商承担，但该风险可以通过在特许经营费用中包含总收入的一定百分比来降低。由于已规划完成的施工方案以及降低运营成本带来的利润有限，运营商还承担着财务风险。

In addition, COSCO will bear the financial risk of a force majeure event up to an insured amount to be placed by COSCO. The Greek State has undertaken to compensate COSCO for any cost to be incurred by a force majeure event which exceeds such insurance coverage. The risk of loss of business due to industrial action is also covered by the operator. However, there is a provision for the extension of the concession agreement to forty-two years, in the event that the terminal operations are disrupted by PPA. [1]

此外，COSCO将承担不可抗力事件的财务风险，最高可达COSCO的保险金额。希腊国家承诺赔偿COSCO因超出此类保险范围的不可抗力事件而产生的任何费用。运营商也承担因产业行为而导致的业务损失风险。但是，协议中有一项规定，即如果码头经营受到PPA的干扰，则特许权将延期至42年。

The contract does not contain operational performance requirements and there are no penalties for non-performance. However there are penalties in case of a breach of the obligation to maintain the assets in good condition and to finish the investment programme within the agreed period. [2]

合同不包含经营履行要求，且未规定对不履行协议的处罚。但是，如果违反维持资产状况良好的义务或未在约定的期限内完成投资方案，则会受到处罚。

In March 2009, the Greek Parliament ratified the contract by implementing law 3755 of 2009, incorporating provisions that were not included in the tender or the contract itself, but only in the law that ratified the contract. In this regard, the legal provisions of the ratification included, among other things, that COSCO would benefit from certain income tax exemptions, while VAT and depreciation obligations would be lower than those imposed on other Greek corporations of the same nature. [3]

在2009年3月，希腊议会通过实施2009年第3755号法律批准了该合同，

---

〔1〕 Benefit, "Case Studies: Piraeus Container Terminal", 2019.

〔2〕 Ibid.

〔3〕 Bentis A. et al., "China's Image in Greece 2008-2018", Institute of International Economic Relations, p. 38.

在第 3755 号法律中（且仅在该法律中）纳入了未包括在招标中或合同中的条款。对此，法律规定包括 COSCO 将从特定的所得税豁免中受益，且相比同等性质的其他希腊公司，其增值税和折旧义务更低。

1.7 主要法律问题（Main Legal Issues）

The global economic crisis, the resultant imposition of capital restrictions, the opposition of the labour unions and the changes of the governing parties in Greece created delays for the completion of the project in a more efficient manner.[1]

全球经济危机以及由此产生的资本限制、工会反对和希腊执政党的更迭，都阻碍了该项目更加有效的完成。

The Federation of Permanent Employees of Greek Ports and the Federation of Cargo Handlers undertook strikes which led to the close of the terminal for a period of two months. The unions succeeded in making the PPA to offer to new staff hired after the concession similar salaries and working conditions to existing staff. This restricted the flexibility of the PPA during the progress of the project and made it difficult to reduce the terminal's operating costs.[2]

希腊港口固定员工联合会和货物装卸工人联合会进行了罢工，导致该码头关闭了两个月。工会成功地使 PPA 向聘用于特许经营后的新员工提供与现有员工相当的工资和工作条件。这限制了 PPA 在项目进展期间的灵活性，并使港口经营成本难以降低。

In its decision 2015/1827 published in March 2015, the following state aid provisions made to the Piraeus Container Terminal SA were considered by the European Commission to be incompatible with the European Union's internal market regulations: accrued interest to be exempt from income tax; VAT tax refund; the transfer of future losses without any time restriction; violation of European Union's anti-dumping regulations and exemption of financing agreements from stamp duty.

在 2015 年 3 月公布的 2015/1827 号决定中，欧盟委员会认为对比雷埃夫斯集装箱码头股份公司的国家援助条款与欧盟内部市场规定有以下不符：应计利息免征所得税；增值税退税；未来损失转移无任何时间限制；违反欧盟反倾销

---

[1] Benefit, "Case Studies: Piraeus Container Terminal", 2019.
[2] Benefit, "Case Studies: Piraeus Container Terminal", 2019.

条例和免除印花税的融资协议。

Pursuant to the decision, Greece should cancel and recover the non-compatible with the Treaty on the Functioning of the European Union Article 108 (3) state aid from the beneficiary. In June 2015, Greece filed an action for annulment of the European Commissions' decision but this was rejected by the European General Court.

根据该决定，希腊应取消并自受益人处追回与《欧盟运作条约》第 108 (3) 条不符的国家援助。2015 年 6 月，希腊提起请求撤销欧盟委员会决定的诉讼，但欧洲总法院驳回了这一诉求。

A number of pre-conditions were required to be met under the Greek law regime for a licence to be granted for the construction of the main and ancillary harbour structures. One prerequisite was that the Committee of Port Planning and Development was required to assess and confirm the technical planning of the project. In addition, compliance with the environmental requirements of Law 4014/2011 required verification by the competent authorities. Upon satisfaction of such pre-conditions, the Minister of Shipping and Island Policy issued the required permits so that operations could commence.[1]

根据希腊法律制度，为获得建造主要和附属港口建筑物的许可证，须满足许多先决条件。其中的一项先决条件是港口规划和开发委员会须评估和确认项目的技术规划。此外，第 4014/2011 号法律中环境要求的遵守情况须经过主管机关的核查。在满足这些先决条件后，航运和岛屿政策部签发了所需的许可证，港口得以开始经营。

As a result of the project there have been improvements in the legal framework for foreign investments which have improved investment environment in Greece. For example legislative decree number 2687/1953 (as amended), provides for beneficial property rights, preferential tax treatment and easier access to staff work permits.

由于该项目，希腊关于外国投资的法律框架得到了改善，这改善了该国的投资环境。例如，第 2687/1953 号法令（修订版）规定了利好的财产权、税收优惠待遇和更易获批的员工工作许可。

Pursuant to law 4146/2013 which relates to the "Creation of a Business-Friendly Environment for Strategic and Private Investments" there has been a simplification in

---

[1] Ibid.

the institutional framework for private investments, and this has increased the efficiency and transparency of the investment procedures. The Greek government also established "Enterprise Greece", which is an agency promoting foreign investment activity and is a point of contact for foreign investors, with the aim of increasing market accessibility and helping to clarify investment requirements and restrictions.[1]

根据有关"为战略和私人投资创造有利商业环境"的第 4146/2013 号法律，私人投资的体制框架已经简化，提高了投资程序的效率和透明度。希腊政府还成立了"企业希腊"（Enterprise Greece），这是一个促进外国投资活动的机构，也是外国投资者的联络点，该机构旨在提升市场准入并帮助阐明投资的要求和限制。

1.8 最新进展（The Latest Developments）

The Master Plan submitted by COSCO in respect of the next steps regarding the Port's development was approved only in part by the Port Planning and Development Committee of the Ministry of Shipping Affairs due to planning and environmental issues and the Committee rejected plans which included the building of hotel facilities, parking, storage areas, a shopping mall and a logistics centre.

由于规划和环境问题，COSCO 提交的关于港口开发后续步骤的总体规划仅部分得到了航运事务部港口规划和发展委员会的批准，委员会拒绝了包含建设酒店设施、停车场、仓储区、购物中心和物流中心的规划。

In addition, the Ministry of Infrastructure and Transport rejected the application by PPA for a licence in relation to the unification of the Port in respect of the construction of logistics facilities. This shipyard permit was also rejected by the Ministry of Financial Affairs.

此外，基础设施和运输部拒绝了 PPA 有关整合港口物流设施建设的许可证申请。该船厂许可证也被财政部拒绝。

The Port concession is considered to have been a successful project. In 2018 the amount of container transhipments increased by 19.4%（4 409 205 TEU）compared with 2017（3 691 815 TEU）, while the profit recorded by COSCO increased by

---

[1] Santander Trade Portal, "Greece: Foreign Investment", accessed on 29 March 2019, https://en.portal.santandertrade.com/establish-overseas/greece/foreign-investment.

57.6%（USD 1 000 000 000）. It is anticipated that the net economic benefit of the investment in the Port will continue to grow and peak in 2022 at €106 300 000 as a result of the increase in the Port's business activity and operational efficiency.[1]

港口特许经营被视为一个成功的项目。2018年的集装箱转运量（4 409 205标准箱）较2017年（3 691 815标准箱）增加19.4%，而COSCO记录的利润增加了57.6%（1 000 000 000美元）。由于港口业务活动的增加和运营效率的提高，预计港口投资的净经济效益将继续增长，并将在2022年达到峰值106 300 000欧元。

2. 海利尼肯机场项目（Hellinikon Airport Project）

2.1 项目概述（Overview of the Project）

2.1.1 位置（The location）

The former Athens International Airport based at Hellinikon in Attica (Hellinikon Airport) was the international airport of Athens, Greece from 1938 to 2001, after which it was replaced by the Athens International Airport. The Hellinikon Airport is located in the Elliniko-Argyroupoli municipality in Attika, which is part of the South Athens regional unit, approximately 7km south east of the city of Athens and covers an area of approximately 6000 hectares.

位于阿提卡海利尼肯的前雅典国际机场（现为海利尼肯机场）是1938—2001年希腊雅典的国际机场，此后，该机场被雅典国际机场取代。海利尼肯机场位于阿提卡的埃利尼—科阿吉鲁波利市，是雅典南部地区的一部分，其位于雅典市东南约7公里处，占地面积约6000公顷。

2.1.2 私有化方案（Privatization method）

The property rights over Hellinikon will be transferred by the Hellenic Republic to the Hellenic Republic Asset Development Fund and thereafter the ownership will be transferred to Hellinikon S.A. which will also have the surface rights to the Hellinikon Airport and will undertake management of 100% of the property for 99 years. The privatization of Hellinikon Airport will be completed through the sale of all the shares in

---

[1] Foundation for Economic & Industrial Research, "The Economic Impact of the Privatisation of the Piraeus Port Authority", 2016.

Hellinikon S. A. to third party investors.〔1〕

海利尼肯机场的产权由希腊共和国转让给希腊共和国资产开发基金，其后，所有权将转让给海利尼肯股份公司，海利尼肯股份公司也拥有海利尼肯机场的地面所有权，并在 99 年内对全部财产进行管理。海利尼肯机场的私有化将通过向第三方投资者出售海利尼肯股份公司的全部股份来完成。

2.1.3 当前状态（Current status）

The international tender process for Hellinikon commenced in 2011 and the contract for the purchase of the shares in Hellinikon S. A. was approved by the Greek Parliament and executed in November 2014. Pursuant to the contract, the completion of the transfer of the shares was to take place within two years from execution of the contract, although the required conditions precedent for the transactions have not yet been met as of today's date.〔2〕

海利尼肯项目的国际招标程序开始于 2011 年，购买海利尼肯股份公司股份的合同由希腊议会批准，并于 2014 年 11 月签署。根据合同，股份转让将在合同签署后的两年内完成，不过，截至今日，交易尚未达到所要求的先决条件。

2.2 项目背景（Project Background）

The Hellinikon project covers various investments in different sectors. The land on which the old airport was located will be developed into a multipurpose park and will include houses, commercial facilities, work areas, healthcare institutions, social welfare facilities, sports fields, tourist attractions and cultural areas. Part of the project involves the upgrade of the coast of Hellinikon, through the construction of a marina complex which will include a shopping mall, hotel and campus for students.〔3〕 The project also includes the construction of an integrated tourist resort, which will include a five star hotel and a casino.

海利尼肯项目涉及不同领域的各类投资。旧机场所在的土地将被开发为多功能公园，该公园内将含有房屋、商业设施、工作区、医疗机构、社会福利设施、运动场、旅游景点和文化区。该项目的一部分涉及通过建造一个包含购物

---

〔1〕 Hellenic Republic Asset Development Fund, "Asset Development Plan", January 2017, p. 4.
〔2〕 Ibid.
〔3〕 Hellenic Gaming Commission, "Hellinikon Intergrated Resort Casino-Greece", August 2018.

中心、酒店和校园的码头综合设施来实现对海利尼肯海岸的升级。该项目还包括建设含有一家五星级酒店和一家赌场的综合旅游度假区。

The construction of a 200 569 hectares park (namely, the Metropolitan Park) constitutes the main pillar of the project. The ultimate goal of the Project is to develop the locality, increase the touristic and commercial development and at the same time preserve and promote the historical and cultural heritage of Hellinikon. This includes a focus on important cultural landmarks, such as the Olympic Games venues.[1]

建造一个 200 569 公顷的公园（即大都会公园）是该项目的主要支柱。该项目的最终目标是促进当地发展、增加旅游和商业发展机会，同时保护和推动海利尼肯的历史文化遗产。这包括对重要的文化地标的关注，如奥运场馆。

In July 2011, one of the conditions for the third economic adjustment programme, that the Greek State and the European institutions had entered into, was the undertaking of the Greek Government to take the necessary steps towards the privatisation of certain state-owned assets.

2011 年 7 月，希腊政府承诺采取必要步骤以实现某些国有资产的私有化，这是希腊政府和欧洲机构签订的第三个经济调整方案的条件之一。

Hellinikon was included in the privatization program launched by the Greek Government pursuant to Law 3986 of 2011 and, in order to expedite and facilitate the privatisation program, pursuant to this Law the Greek Government established the Hellenic Republic Asset Development Fund (HRADF). Ownership of state-owned assets included in the privatisation plan was transferred to HRAFD which was tasked with managing and completing the privatisation process.[2]

海利尼肯项目被囊括在希腊政府根据 2011 年第 3986 号法律发起的私有化方案中，为了加快和促进私有化方案，希腊政府根据该法建立了希腊共和国资产发展基金（HRADF）。私有化方案中涉及的国有资产的所有权将转移到 HRAFD，HRAFD 的任务是管理和完成私有化的进程。

The privatisation process was undertaken by transferring the shares of Hellinikon

---

[1] The Hellinikon Project, "The Hellinikon contract-Background", https://thehellinikon.com/the-vision/meet-the-investors/assessed on 28 March 2019.

[2] Ibid.

S. A. from the Greek State to HRADF. Pursuant to Greek Laws 1902, 1903 and 1905 (all of 2014), the Council of State confirmed the legality and validity of the transfer of the shares. Previously the transfer had been challenged by, amongst other actions, an appeal which was submitted to the Hellenic Council of State, against the ministerial decision which ratified the transfer of shares of Hellinikon S. A. to HRADF.[1]

私有化进程是通过将海利尼肯股份公司的股份从希腊国家转移到 HRADF 来进行的。根据 2014 年颁布的希腊第 1902、1903 和 1905 号法律，希腊国务委员会确认了股份转让的合法性和有效性。此前，股份转让受到了其他诉讼的质疑，该诉讼已被提交给希腊国务委员会，该诉讼反对批准将海利尼肯股份公司的股份转让给 HRADF 的部长级决定。

2.3 投标（Tender）

On December 2011, an invitation of interest to potential investors for the Project was published in the media, with a submission deadline by the 17th of April 2012. The following companies expressed their interest in relation to the Project at this first stage:

2011 年 12 月，媒体发布了对项目潜在投资者感兴趣的邀请函，投标的截止日期为 2012 年 4 月 17 日。在第一阶段，下述公司表达了其对项目有意：

Elbit Cochin Island Ltd of Israel; Gazit Group USA Inc. of United States of America; Kaglow Holdings Ltd. of Cyprus; L&R London and Regional Group Holdings Limited of United Kingdom; Lamda Development S. A. of Greece; LSGIE SA of Spain; Qatari Real Estate Investment Company QSC of Qatar; Sovinyon/Air Services International Limited FZE/Varangis Qatar LLC a joint venture from Qatar; and Trump Acquisition LLC. of the United States of America.[2]

以色列埃尔比特科钦岛有限公司；美国加齐特集团公司；塞浦路斯 Kaglow 控股有限公司；英国 L&R 伦敦及英国区域集团控股有限公司；希腊兰达开发股份公司；西班牙 LSGIE 股份公司；卡塔尔的卡塔尔 QSC 房地产投资公司；卡塔尔的一家合资企业——索温尼恩/FZE 航空服务国际有限公司/Varangis 卡塔尔有限责任公司；和美国的特朗普收购有限责任公司。

The following four companies were shortlisted as potential investors satisfying the

---

[1] The Hellinikon Project, "The Hellinikon contract-Background", March 2018.
[2] Ibid.

pre-selection requirements and were qualified for the next phase of the process: (i) Elbit Cochin Island Ltd, (ii) L&R London and Regional Group Holdings Limited, (iii) Lamda Development S. A. (Lamda) and (iv) Qatari Real Estate Investment Company QSC.

以下四家公司入围满足预选要求且符合本过程下一阶段资质的潜在投资者：(i) 埃尔比特科钦岛有限公司，(ii) L&R 伦敦及英国区域集团控股有限公司，(iii) 兰达开发股份公司（以下简称兰达）和 (iv) 卡塔尔 QSC 房地产投资公司。

At the end of the tender process, Lamda was the only candidate that submitted a binding offer and that offer was unsealed on March 2014. The financial advisors of HRADF, Citigroup and Piraeus Bank, submitted two positive opinions on the financial offer submitted by Lamda and the investment consortium Global Investment Group.[1]

在招标过程结束时，兰达是唯一提交具有约束力的要约的候选人，该要约的启封时间为 2014 年 3 月。HRADF、花旗集团和比雷埃夫斯银行的财务顾问就兰达和国际投资集团（一家投资财团）提出的财务报价提交了两份积极意见。

2.4 参与方（Parties Involved）

The background of the parties that expressed an interest in the project is as follows:
表示对项目有意的参与方的背景如下：

Lamda is a listed company and part of the Latsis Group. The company is mainly involved in projects for the development, investment and management of real estate assets in Greece and Europe.

兰达是一家上市公司，也是拉齐斯集团的一部分。该公司主要参与希腊和欧洲房地产资产的开发、投资和管理项目。

Global Investment Group is an international investment consortium, which is composed of the Fosun Group, the Eagle Hills Group and the Latsis Group. The venture was formed together with Lamda in order to develop the Hellinikon site.

国际投资集团是一家国际投资财团，由复星集团、鹰山集团和拉齐斯集团组成。该合资企业与兰达一并成立，以便开发海利尼肯项目。

Fosun Group is a leading international investment group from China that invests in

---

[1] Ibid.

tourism, trade, financial services, energy and real estate construction. Fosun had previously made investments in Greece including in Club Med Greece. [1] This conglomerate had also acquired a 9.5% stake in Folli Follie in May 2011 for a consideration of € 84 590 000. In June 2010, Fosun Group signed an agreement with Latsis Group to invest the amount of 200 000 000 United States dollars for the development of Hellinikon. [2]

复星集团是中国领先的国际投资集团,其投资于旅游、贸易、金融服务、能源和房地产建设领域。复星集团此前曾在希腊投资,包括希腊地中海俱乐部。该集团还在2011年5月以84 590 000欧元的价格收购了芙丽芙丽9.5%的股份。在2010年6月,复星集团与拉齐斯集团签署协议,以投资2亿美元用于开发海利尼肯项目。

Hellinikon S. A. was established in 2011 with the purpose of undertaking the management, administration and development of Hellinikon. In 2012, pursuant to Law 4062 of 2012 (Art. 7, para. 1), the use, management and administration of the area (6 205 667.31 m^2) was assigned by the two former owners, the Agios Kosmas National Youth Sports Centre (EAKN) and the Agios Kosmas (Attica) Olympic Sailing Centre (Marina), to the company. [3]

海利尼肯股份公司成立于2011年,其目的是进行海利尼肯的经营、管理和开发。在2012年,根据2012年第4062号法律(第7条第1款),两名前所有者将该地区(6 205 667.31平方米)转移给该公司进行利用、经营和管理,该地区的前所有者即阿吉奥斯·科斯玛斯国家青年体育中心(EAKN)和阿吉奥斯·科斯玛斯(阿提卡)奥林匹克帆船中心(游艇停靠区)。

Hellinikon Global I S. A. is a wholly owned subsidiary of Lamda and was formed as a special purpose vehicle for the acquisition of the shares in Hellinikon S. A. Lamda will retain at least 33.34% of the shares in Hellinikon Global I S. A. for three years

---

[1] The Hellinikon Project, "Meet the investors", assessed on 28 March 2019, https://thehellinikon.com/the-vision/meet-the-investors/.

[2] Enterprise Greece, Invest & Trade, "Fosun Group Inks Deal in Greece", assessed on 29 March 2019, https://www.enterprisegreece.gov.gr/en/news/news/fosun-group-inks-deal-in-greece.

[3] The Hellinikon Project, "The Hellinikon contract-Background", March 2018.

from the actual date of transfer of the shares.[1]

海利尼肯Ⅰ号国际股份公司是兰达的全资子公司,该公司作为特殊目的公司而成立,用于收购海利尼肯股份公司的股份。兰达将自实际转让股份之日起的三年内,保留海利尼肯Ⅰ号国际股份公司至少33.34%的股份。

2.5 主要条款（Main Terms）

Pursuant to the contract for the transfer of the shares in Hellinikon S. A., by HRADF to Hellinikon Global I S. A., the investors were required to deposit € 915 000 000 in instalments during a period of 10 years, from 2016 to 2026. In addition, the development plan requires the investment of € 7 200 000 000 over a period of 25 years.[2]

根据 HRADF 向海利尼肯Ⅰ号国际股份公司转让海利尼肯股份公司股份的合同,投资者需在 2016 年至 2026 年的 10 年间分期存入 915 000 000 欧元。此外,开发规划要求在 25 年内投资的金额达 7 200 000 000 欧元。

As part of the commitment of the Hellenic Republic towards the European institutions pursuant to the financial aid program, HRADF was required to raise US $ 4 950 000 000 through the privatisation program.

作为希腊政府根据财政援助计划对欧洲机构作出承诺的一部分,HRADF 须通过私有化方案筹集 4 950 000 000 美元。

Fosun Group and its partners have to invest 1/3 of the total bid to acquire a 99 year lease of Hellinikon.[3] According to the Lamda's offer, the purchase price for the shares of Hellinikon S. A. was € 915 000 000 and the available budget for the completion of the infrastructure project was € 1 500 000 000. The total estimated amount required for the completion of the project was estimated to be € 2 400 000 000. However, revised estimates suggest that the total amount would increase to € 8 000 000 000.

复星集团及其合作伙伴必须投资投标总价的 1/3,以获得海利尼肯 99 年的

---

[1] The Hellinikon Project, "Meet the investors", assessed on 28 March 2019, https://thehellinikon.com/the-vision/meet-the-investors/.

[2] Foundation for Economic & Industrial Research, "The Economic Impact of the development of the Hellinikon area-Executive Summary", September 2016, p. 10.

[3] Michael Cole, "China's Fosun Buys Into Bottom Of Greek Market With $ 1.26B Real Estate Deal", *Forbes Asia*, March 2014, assessed on 25 March 2019, https://www.forbes.com/sites/michaelcole/2014/03/30/chinas-fosun-buys-into-bottom-of-greek-real-estate-with-1-26b-deal/#3dc6008e64d2.

租期。根据兰达的报价,购买海利尼肯股份公司的价格为 915 000 000 欧元,可用于完成基础设施项目的预算为 1 500 000 000 欧元。完成该项目所需的预计总额约为 2 400 000 000 欧元。但是,经修订的预期数额表明,总额将增加到 8 000 000 000 欧元。

The transfer of the shares in Hellinikon S. A. and the start of the project are subject to the satisfaction of certain conditions precedent under the contract, including:

海利尼肯股份公司股份的转让和项目的开始均以合同中某些先决条件的满足为前提,包括:

the ratification of the contract by the Greek Parliament; the approval of the Integrated Development Plan through a Presidential Decree; distribution of the right of ownership among joint owners; transfer of rights in the property to Hellinikon S. A.; relocation of the public and state bodies which use Hellinikon premises; establishment of a committee to manage and operate all communal areas; an operating license for the casino's operation; no pending judicial proceedings in respect of applications for annulment relating to any other administrative decisions; and no material change in conditions (reduction by more than 5% of the area). [1]

希腊议会批准合同;通过总统令批准综合开发计划;在共同所有人中分配所有权;将财产权转让给海利尼肯股份公司;搬迁占用海利尼肯场地的公共和国家机构;成立管理和运营全部公共区域的委员会;赌场运营的营业执照;不存在关于申请撤销任何其他行政决定的待决司法程序;和条件未发生重大变化(减少的面积超过该区域的 5%)。

Pursuant to the agreement between the parties, Lamda undertook to make every possible effort in order to complete 80% of its obligations under the contract within a period of 12 years from the date of the transfer of the shares and HRADF would retain its rights in the future economic benefits of the project. [2]

根据参与方之间的协议,兰达承诺尽一切努力自股份转让之日起的 12 年内完成合同规定的 80% 的义务,且 HRADF 将在项目未来经济利益方面保留其权利。

---

[1] The Hellinikon, "Contractual pre-conditions for the commencement of the Development of Hellinikon", January 2018, assessed on 25 March 2019 https://thehellinikon.com/en/author/conconcept-pl-us/.

[2] The Hellinikon Project, "The Hellinikon contract-Background", March 2018.

The obligations imposed on Lamda included a number of sub-projects of public benefit, such as:

对兰达赋予的义务包括许多关乎公共利益的子项目,例如:

construction and maintenance of the Metropolitan Park; development of green areas and open spaces of 600 000 m^2; other public benefit uses of 300 000 m^2; public transport infrastructures; facilities for recyclable materials; facilities for domestic waste and transit/temporary area for recyclable products; re-construction of a part of Posidonos Avenue; pedestrian and bicycle facilities; cultural and sports facilities in the Metropolitan Park; the renovation of the buildings in Hellinikon; and the development of approximately 1 km of the water front. [1]

大都会公园的建设和维护;绿地和60万平方米空地的开发;30万平方米的其他公益用地;公共交通基础设施;可回收材料的设施;放置生活垃圾的设施和可回收物的中转/临时安置区;波西多诺斯大道的部分重建;供行人和自行车使用的设施;大都会公园的文化和体育设施;海利尼肯建筑物的翻新;以及约1公里滨水区的开发。

A critical point for the commencement of the project development is the restructuring of the ownership rights on the property between the various owners. Hellinikon is owned by the Greek State and the use, management and exploitation of the property is vested in Hellinikon S. A.. Pursuant to the contract, 30% of the property rights will be transferred from the Greek State to HRADF, in order to be distributed between the indivisible joint owners. After the completion of this step, HRADF will transfer all of its property rights to Hellinikon S. A. [2]

开始项目开发的关键点是在各业主之间重新确定财产所有权。海利尼肯由希腊国家所有,该财产的使用、管理和开采归属于海利尼肯股份公司。根据合同,30%的产权将由希腊国家转移至HRADF,以便在不可分割的共同所有者间进行分配。完成该步骤后,HRADF将其所有的产权转让给海利尼肯股份公司。

The relevant documentation in respect of the process and steps of the tender and the draft contract were submitted to the Greek Court of Auditors in order for the court to

---

[1] The Hellinikon Project, "The Hellinikon contract-Background", March 2018.

[2] The Hellinikon, "Contractual pre-conditions for the commencement of the Development of Hellinikon", January 2018.

assess the legal compliance of the pre-contractual process. The court confirmed the validity of the process and its decision was subsequently confirmed by three subsequent decisions (Laws 1183, 1184 and 1185 of 2015) by the greater composition of the Court.[1]

有关招标程序和步骤的文件以及合同草案已提交至希腊审计法院,以评估合同前置程序的法律合规性。该法院确认了该程序的有效性,随后,该法院通过规模更大的机会,以三项决议(2015年第1183、1184和1185号法律)确认了该决议。

Pursuant to the decisions under Laws 1902, 1903 and 1905 of 2014, the Council of State decided that the transfer of shares was in compliance with Greek legislation. Accordingly, the sale and purchase contract of the shares was executed between HRADF, Hellinikon Global I S. A. and Lamda, acting as guarantor of Hellinikon Global I S. A.

根据在2014年基于第1902、1903和1905号法律作出的决议,国务委员会作出了股份转让符合希腊法律的决定。因此,HRADF和海利尼肯Ⅰ号国际股份公司签署了海利尼肯的股份买卖合同,并由兰达担任海利尼肯Ⅰ号国际股份公司的担保人。

After review and consultation, The Council of Economic Policy confirmed and approved the asset development plan submitted by HRADF, which included, amongst other things, the execution, on 7th June 2016, of a Memorandum of Understanding (MOU) between HRADF, Hellinikon Global I S. A. and Lamda, setting out the basic structural and economic parameters of the project and pursuant to which they agreed to sign an amendment to the original contract. Pursuant to the MOU, and after a further confirmation of the draft amended contract by the Court, the parties executed the contract on 19 July 2016.[2]

经过审查和磋商,经济政策委员会确认并批准了HRADF提交的资产开发计划,其中包括在2016年6月7日由HRADF、海利尼肯Ⅰ号国际股份公司和兰达之间签订的合作备忘录,该备忘录列出了项目的基本结构和经济变量,据此,各方同意签署对原始合同进行的修订。根据该合作备忘录,在法院进一步

---

[1] The Hellinikon Project, "The Hellinikon contract—Background", March 2018.
[2] Ibid.

确认经修订的合同草案之后，各方于 2016 年 7 月 19 日签署了合同。

The contract was accordingly unanimously ratified by a majority of the Greek Parliament (more than 260 out of 300 Deputies) and was enacted pursuant Law 4422 of 2016, which was published in the Government Gazette at 181/A/on 27 September 2016.

因此，该合同得到希腊议会多数议员的一致批准（300 名议员中超过 260 名赞成），并根据 2016 年第 4422 号法律颁布（该法律 2016 年 9 月 27 日公布于 181/A/号政府公报）。

The Greek authorities subsequently required certain provisions, relating to urban planning law, to be amended after the initial master plan had been approved and the contract executed. In this regard, after the amended agreement was signed, in July 2016, a further amendment to the plan was considered to be necessary and was submitted to HRADF for approval.[1]

希腊主管机关随后要求在初步总体规划获得批准且合同签订后修改某些与城市规划法相关的规定。在这一方面，在经修订的协议签署后，2016 年 7 月，该计划被认为须进行进一步修改，同时被提交给 HRADF 审批。

The updated plan, which included an environmental impact study, was reviewed by a number of administrative authorities, including the Experts Committee (as required by Law 4062 of 2012), the Central Council for the Exploitation of Public Property and the Council of State. The plan was accordingly ratified through a Presidential Decree on March 2018.

更新的规划包括环境影响研究，该研究由包括专家委员会（根据 2012 年第 4062 号法律的要求）、公共财产开发中央委员会和国务委员会在内的若干行政主管机关审查。据此，总统令于 2018 年 3 月批准了该规划。

After the confirmation of the urban planning studies, through a joint ministerial decision, the exact structure of the project and all the potential expansion options or restrictions to the development plan were set out in greater detail. This included the plans concerning construction of the main park, the public areas and the transportation network.[2]

---

[1] The Hellinikon, "Contractual pre-conditions for the commencement of the Development of Hellinikon", January 2018.

[2] Ibid.

在确认城市规划研究之后，通过联合部长决议，该规划更详细地载明了项目的确切结构以及所有关于发展规划的潜在扩展机会或限制。这包括关于主要公园、公共区域和交通网络建设的规划。

2.6 主要法律问题（Main Legal Issues）

There has been a significant movement against the project from local and non-local communities. In March 2011, the Greek trades unions sent a letter to the Greek Government and the European Institutions declaring their opposition against the privatization of the Hellinikon. In addition, a considerable number of demonstrations, social and sports events and strikes took place against the completion of the Project.

本地和非本地的社区发起了对该项目的重大反对运动。在2011年3月，希腊贸易工会致函希腊政府和欧洲机构，宣布反对海利尼肯的私有化。继而发生了大量示威活动、社会和体育活动以及罢工反对项目完成。

Further obstacles, that created unexpected delays, included the Greek forestry authorities declaring 3.7 hectares of Hellinikon land as protected woodland. HRADF submitted an appeal against this decision and the Piraeus Technical Committee for Examining Disputes concluded that area was classified as "artificial planting" and not forest land. In addition, the Archaeological Council concluded that thirty hectares of Hellinikon land would be classified as an archaeological site of special interest and would be protected and preserved as an antiquity. The decision is of advisory effect but it requires the land in question to be maintained free of buildings or other constructions. This required an amendment to the investment agreement, in order for the competent authorities to have supervisory control of the relevant parcels of land at Hellinikon. [1]

造成意外延误的其他障碍包括希腊林业主管机关宣布海利尼肯3.7公顷的土地为受保护的林地。HRADF提出上诉反对该决定，比雷埃夫斯争端审议技术委员会议定：该地区应被归类为"人工种植区"而非林地。此外，考古委员会得出的结论认为，海利尼肯30公顷的土地将被列为关乎特殊利益的考古遗址，并将作为文物受到保护和维护。该决定具有咨询效力，但它要求有关土地不受

---

[1] Keep Talking Greece, "CAS rules 5% of Hellinikon investment of 'archaeological interest', blocks very high buildings", October 2017, assessed on 20 March 2019, https://www.keeptalkinggreece.com/2017/10/04/hellinikon-investement-arhaeology/.

楼房或其他建筑物的影响。这使投资协议需要修改，以便主管机关对海利尼肯的相关土地进行监督控制。

In addition, during 2019 the municipality of Alimos submitted a legal action to the Council of State against the decision for the creation of a public sector body that will collect user fees from the exploitation of Hellinikon.

此外，在2019年，阿里莫斯市政府向国务委员会提起诉讼，反对设立一个因开发海利尼肯而收取使用费的公共部门机构的决定。

2.7 最新进展（The Latest Developments）

The Agency for the Management of Common Spaces in the Metropolitan Axis of Hellenikon—Agios Kosmas, which is the agency formed in order to supervise and coordinate the public spaces that will be incorporated into Hellenikon, held its first meeting on January 2019. The meeting was attended by representatives of all involved parties in order to proceed with the implementation of the project. The agency also coordinated the preparation of the publication for the tender in respect of the casino which constitutes a condition precedent for the transfer of the shares under the contract.[1]

阿吉奥斯·科斯玛斯是位于海利尼肯城市中心的公共空间管理局，该机构系为监督和协调将被纳入海利尼肯项目的公共空间而成立，在2019年1月，其举行了第一次会议。有关各方的代表出席了该会议，以继续实施该项目。该机构还协调了有关发布赌场招标的准备工作，这是合同中约定的转让股份的先决条件。

An amendment to the Greek legislation setting out the licensing requirements for casino operations in Greece was submitted in the Greek Parliament in order to facilitate and open the way to the international tender for the casino, which will allow the winning bidderto enter into concession agreements with third parties for the development also of non-gambling.

载明赌场经营许可条件的希腊立法修正案已被呈递给希腊议会，以便为赌场的国际招标提供便利、扫清障碍，这将允许中标者与第三方就开发与禁止赌博签订特许权协议。

---

[1] "8 billion euro Hellinikon Project is set to move ahead", *Greek City Times*, January 2019, assessed on March 19, https://greekcitytimes.com/2019/01/19/8-billion-euro-hellinikon-project-is-set-to-move-ahead/.

— 作者简介 —

Nigel Bowen-Morris is a partner specialising in ship finance, non-contentious shipping, general banking and corporate work and is the managing partner of Stephenson Harwood LLP's Piraeus office, which he established in 1996. He advises international banks and financial institutions on asset secured loans to the shipping industry in Greece and the Eastern Mediterranean region. Bowen-Morris has worked continuously in Greece for over 20 years and is a member of the Piraeus Bar Association, the Law Society of England and Wales and the Roll of Solicitors of Ireland.

Nigel Bowen-Morris 于 1996 年创办了 Stephenson Harwood LLP 律师事务所的比雷埃夫斯办公室，是该办公室的管理合伙人，专注于从事船舶融资、无争议航运、一般银行业务和公司业务。在希腊和地中海东部地区的航运业资产担保贷款业务方面，他为国际银行和金融机构提供法律顾问服务。Bowen-Morris 已经在希腊从事了二十多年的法律工作，是比雷埃夫斯市律师协会、英格兰和威尔士律师协会的会员，并且是爱尔兰地区的注册律师。

Konstantinos Antoniou is a finance associate with broad experience in banking, finance and capital markets law. He specialises in shipping finance, particularly in relation to advising leading banks on bilateral and syndicated transactions, including the financing and refinancing of second-hand vessels and new buildings.

Konstantinos Antoniou 是一位在金融和资本市场法律方面具有丰富经验的金融律师。他专注于从事航运融资业务，特别是就双边交易及企业联合交易向知名大型银行提供法律顾问服务，交易方向包括二手船只及新建建筑物的融资及再融资。

Stephenson Harwood LLP is a law firm with over 1100 people worldwide, including more than 180 partners. Our headquarters are in London, with 10 offices across Asia, Europe and the Middle East. In addition we have forged close ties with other high quality law firms and an integrated local law capability in Singapore and the PRC.

The Piraeus ship finance team is a core arm of the international ship finance practice. Lawyers regularly advise on facilitating loans from German, English, Swiss, Scandinavian and other European banks to shipping companies in Greece, as well as those located in Turkey, Bulgaria, Italy, Croatia, Israel and Libya. The team also acts for Turkish banks in the context of shipping financings being offered to Turkish shipping groups. Lawyers are also instructed on a broader range of finance-related work, including bank lending, commercial and trade agreements and insolvency and restructuring. In addition, we undertake a broad range of Greek law instructions.

Stephenson Harwood 律师事务所是一家拥有 1100 多名员工的全球性律师事务所，其中有 180 多名合伙人。律师事务所总部设在伦敦，在亚洲、欧洲和中东地区设有 10 家办公室。此外，该所还与位于新加坡和中国的多家头部律师事务所建立了密切的合作关系，拥有丰富的当地法律资源。

比雷埃夫斯市的船舶融资律师事务团队是国际船舶融资业务的核心部门。团队律师经常就德国、英国、瑞士、斯堪的纳维亚和其他欧洲地区银行提供的贷款相关业务出具法律意见，该贷款服务主要是向希腊以及土耳其、保加利亚、意大利、克罗地亚、以色列和利比亚的船运公司提供。该团队同样还向土耳其银行提供法律服务，服务事项主要是关于银行为土耳其航运集团提供航运融资方面的业务。该所业务同样涉及金融领域，包括银行贷款、商业和贸易协定以及破产和重组等方面业务。此外，该所多次就希腊法律出具法律意见。

投资在匈牙利：绿地投资
Investments in Hungary
Green Field Investments

点 评

在投资层面，2015 年后，匈牙利政府通过了新的立法及相关规则，要求欧盟或欧洲经济区以外的投资者如欲收购某些提供战略服务的匈牙利公司（如大数据、能源、军用级产品等）须经过筛查，主管的部长在批准或禁止拟议投资方面拥有广泛的自由裁量权。根据本文作者的阐释，该立法目前主要影响上述被视为具有战略意义的行业，以及欧盟或欧洲经济区以外的公司通过收购或设立公司从而直接或间接持有匈牙利公司至少 25% 的投票权的行为，其他行业受到的影响较小。但在受限行业亦可考虑在所有权或投票权不超过 25% 门槛的前提下实施投资。在欧盟严格审查外商投资的趋势下，匈牙利政府于 2020 年 5 月 25 日通过了一项新法令以审查外商投资。新审查法令针对对某些匈牙利公司的投资规定了新的批准要求。该法令于 2020 年 5 月 26 日生效，而先前的外商直接投资审查机制不受其影响。

公司经营层面，匈牙利公司法规定只有董事总经理手写的个人签名或联合签名才能在合同或活动中被视为公司的有效代表，没有任何适格代表签名的公司公章在匈牙利不具有法律效力。这一规定与中国的实践存在较大差异，建议在经营过程中加以留意。

1. 简介（General Introduction）

Hungary has become a well-known attractive target for green field investments in the last twenty years. Located in the geographical heart of Europe, Hungary offers outstanding infrastructure for new projects and is considered a bridge between the eastern and western part of the continent. The Hungarian government is constantly striving to create a favorable atmosphere for foreign direct investment, most notably by providing state aid projects through subsidy schemes and tax exemptions which, depending on the actual area of Hungary where the project is located, can receive government funding up to between 30%–50% intensity in exchange for creating and sustaining new jobs and ensuring local infrastructural development. Additionally, the Hungarian government took major steps introducing new labor law policies and supporting educational efforts and policies that allow the constant training and flow of highly qualified workforce for new investment opportunities. Meanwhile, recent efforts of the government allowed for a swifter and more flexible practice of re-location of employees to Hungary to combat any lack of available workforce for the manufacturing industry.

在过去二十年间，匈牙利已成为对绿地投资而言极具知名度和吸引力的目标国家。匈牙利位于欧洲的地理中心，是欧洲大陆东西部之间的桥梁，能为新项目提供优良的基础设施。匈牙利政府一直致力于为外国直接投资创造有利的环境，特别是通过补贴计划和免税的方式提供国家资助，根据项目实际所在区域的不同，匈牙利的各个项目可以获得比例在30%—50%的政府资助，匈牙利政府以此创造和维持新的就业机会，并确保当地的基础设施发展。此外，为了获得新的投资机会，匈牙利政府还采取了重要举措，引入新的劳动法政策，并支持教育方面的努力和政策的展开，不断培训高素质劳动力，并能持续流动。同时匈牙利政府近来致力于帮助外国员工在匈牙利能够更加快捷、更加灵活地重新定居，以解决制造业缺乏可用劳动力的问题。

Hungarian-Chinese relations are historically good and for over ten years, Hungarian governments fully committed themselves to the development of the strengthening relationships with Asia. This newly implemented "Eastern Opening" policy further strengthened since theeconomic crisis of 2008. As a result, Chinese foreign direct investment into Hungary increased significantly after the country joined the European Union in 2004. According to Chinese statistics, in 2010, 89% of the whole Chinese capital flow to the Central and Eastern European region went into Hungary. As of 2019, infrastructure development and the financing of Hungarian public debt are some of the most important areas where further Chinese involvement is highly expected in Hungary.

中国与匈牙利的关系历来友好，在过去的十多年间，匈牙利政府充分致力于巩固与亚洲的关系。自 2008 年国际经济危机以来，新实施的"东部开放"政策进一步强化。因此，在 2004 年匈牙利加入欧盟以后，中国对该国的对外直接投资激增。根据中方的数据，在 2010 年，中国流入欧洲中部和东部地区的全部资金中高达 89% 进入匈牙利。至 2019 年，基础设施发展和匈牙利公债融资是匈牙利高度期待中国进一步参与投资的领域。

The direct, mostly green field, investments of Chinese companies in Hungary cover key industries such as manufacturing, telecommunications, chemical industry, trade, whole sales or retails, banking, hotels and catering, logistics and real estate. According to available Hungarian statistics, more than 5000 Chinese companies operate in Hungary, including several multinationals, as well as small businesses operating in the service or retail sector. The number of Chinese-controlled foreign affiliates has increased steadily since 2011.

中国企业在匈牙利的直接投资主要是绿地投资，涵盖制造业、电信、化工、贸易、批发或零售、银行、酒店和餐饮、物流和房地产等重要行业。根据匈牙利的统计数据，超过 5000 家中国企业在匈牙利营业，其中包括几家跨国公司，以及在服务或零售业开展经营的小企业。自 2011 年以来，中国控股的外国子公司数量稳步增长。

One of the largest investments by Chinese companies in Hungary was a green field manufacturing plant development by a Chinese heavy industry enterprise. Wolf Theiss assisted the client with respect to all the relevant legal aspects, including the company establishment, negotiating construction and lease agreements, HR and employment matters, regulatory and state aid as well as tax counselling. we aim to provide all potential investors with information of notable legal requirements which a green field investment project may face when considering Hungary as its place of operation.

中国重工业企业开发的绿地制造工厂是中国公司在匈牙利规模最大的投资之一。沃尔夫·泰斯律师事务所协助客户处理所有相关法律问题，包括公司的设立、建筑和租赁协议的谈判、人力资源事宜、监管和国家援助以及税务咨询。本文旨在介绍绿地投资项目的投资人在考虑将匈牙利作为其经营地时可能面临各类重要的法律要求。

2. 投资项目简介（Introduction of the Investment Project）

Our client, a large Chinese enterprise, engaged in manufacturing mold machines and components, mechanical parts for various industries and equipment for the oil and gas industries, decided to establish its first permanent entity in Europe in 2015. After having analysed several opportunities, the client decided to commit its European hub in Hungary, considering the local availability of highly skilled workers, the country's membership in the European Union and its excellent geographical location which enables the company to serve its primary European partners and the regional markets directly from a European site instead of being compelled to rely solely on supply lines maintained from China.

我们的客户是一家大型中国企业，从事制造模具机器和零部件、各种行业的机械零件以及石油和天然气行业的设备，该企业决定 2015 年在欧洲建立其第一个常设机构。在对数个项目作出分析后，我们的客户考虑到匈牙利当地有技能纯熟的工人，且该国为欧盟成员，同时，该国优越的地理位置将使公司能够直接为其主要欧洲合作伙伴和区域市场提供服务，而不必完全依赖来自中国的供应，因此客户决定将在欧洲投资的中心设立在匈牙利。

Although the client actively monitored the Hungarian market and investigated joint venture or other local partnership opportunities with potential Hungarian or European partners, eventually it made a decision to proceed with setting up its own exclusively owned legal entity with the sole participation of the Chinese parent company. Wolf Theiss was already involved in this at an early stage of the investment and actively assisted the client in order to understand and choose the most suitable company form and understand the general legal and business environment in Hungary.

尽管客户积极对匈牙利市场进行跟踪调查，并与潜在的匈牙利或欧洲合作伙伴调查合资或其他本地合作机会，但其最终决定在中国母公司的单独参与下建立自己的独资法人实体。沃尔夫·泰斯律师事务所在投资的早期阶段即已参与其中，并积极协助客户了解并选择最合适的公司形式、了解匈牙利的总体法律和商业环境。

As a prudent investor, client had also considered other methods of establishing its business in Hungary, notably, the acquisition of an already operating local vehicle. The reason why this option was worth taking into account was the possibility of skipping certain required processes such as setting up a local company, acquiring relevant licenses and government approvals as well as purchasing and creating essential infrastructure to significantly decrease the time to start with production. Faced with the challenge of deciding the most effective and risk-averse strategy of entering the Hungarian market, client requested Wolf Theiss to outline possible pros and cons between a green field investment and an actual strategic acquisition of an already existing Hungarian manufacturing company. With its practical experience in both fields, Wolf Theiss provided much appreciated advise on the structural differences of the two scenarios, amongst other the potential cost of a full fledged corporate due diligence, the added complexity of acquiring an active business and the added rounds of negotiation regarding the sale and purchase agreement, which these deals always carry within themselves.

作为审慎的投资人，客户还考虑了在匈牙利开展业务的其他方法，尤其是收购已营业的本地公司。这种选择值得考虑是因为客户可以借此省去一些必要的流程，例如设立本地公司、获取相关的许可证和政府的批准，以及购买和建设必要的基础设施，从而显著节约时间以尽快开始生产。为确定进入匈牙利市场最有效且最能规避风险的策略，客户要求沃尔夫·泰斯律师事务所在绿地投资与实际收购匈牙利现有制造公司之间进行比较，概述各自利弊。凭借在这两个领域的实务经验，沃尔夫·泰斯律师事务所对两种方案结构性的差异提供了值得赞赏的建议，这些差异包括以下方面：充分进行企业尽职调查的潜在成本、收购活跃业务所带来的额外复杂性以及关于买卖协议的多轮谈判的增加，这些情况常常发生在交易的过程中。

Having received the much required input to weigh their options, client eventually backed away from the acquisition route because the targets which had been considered were older companies, carrying decades of corporate history, which client saw as a risk it did not intend to take. Therefore, the final choice fell on the establishment of a completely new company and entering the Hungarian market in a more gradual manner, which also provided for a more relaxed timeline for the completion of each individual part of this complex investment project.

在获得必要的信息以权衡各种选择之后，我们的客户最终放弃了收购路线，这是由于客户曾考虑的一些目标公司都是老公司，它们承载了数十年的经营历史，客户认为这是他们不愿承担的风险。因此，客户最终决定建立一个全新的公司，并以更加和缓的方式进入匈牙利市场，这也为完成复杂投资项目的各个部分提供了更加宽松的时间。

3. 交易结构（Transaction Structure）

As for the incorporation of the local vehicle, the client eventually proceeded with establishing a limited liability company (korlátolt felelösségü társaság in Hungarian) which is deemed to be an ideal corporate form for foreign investments in medium or large operating companies.

客户最终设立了一家有限责任公司（匈牙利语为 korlátolt felelösségü társaság）作为当地的经营载体，该类公司被认为是外资向中型或大型经营公司投资的理想形式。

In the course of the preliminary discussions, client had also considered other company forms, such as a private company limited by shares (zártkörüen müködö részvénytársaság in Hungarian), which is also suitable for large scale and complex businesses with multiple shareholders. Ownership or holdings of shares in such a company form are evidenced by share certificates. Such certificates need to be produced in a printed or an electronic form. A series of shares can also be produced in a printed or an electronic form. Any private company limited by shares can issue various types of shares (ordinary shares, preference shares, employees' shares, interest-bearing shares, shares granting pre-emption rights and redeemable shares) granting different rights. Shares are registered. This vehicle eventually turned out to be unnecessarily complex and would have required more extensive administrative (creating and updating shares) and more demanding equity requirements (the minimum registered capital of a company limited by shares is 5 000 000 Hungarian forints, approx. 16 000 euros, while in a limited liability company the minimum registered capital is only 3 000 000 Hungarian forints, approx. 10 000 euros) and as a result, client chose to establish a limited liability company as mentioned above.

在初步讨论的过程中，客户还考虑了其他公司形式，例如私人股份有限公司（匈牙利语为 zártkörüen müködö részvénytársaság），该形式适用于拥有众多股东和复杂业务的大型公司。在此类公司中，股票是拥有或持有股份的证明，且

投资在匈牙利：绿地投资

股票需以印刷或电子的形式制作，系列股票也可以以印刷或电子的形式制作。股份有限公司均可发行各类股票（如普通股、优先股、员工股、计息股、授予优先权的股份和可赎回股份）并授予不同的权利。股票会被登记。此类公司最终会变得不必要的复杂，它受制于更广泛的行政管理（在股票的制作与更新方面）和更加苛刻的股权要求（股份有限公司的最低注册资本是 5 000 000 匈牙利福林，约 16 000 欧元，而有限责任公司的最低注册资本仅为 3 000 000 匈牙利福林，约 10 000 欧元），因此，客户基于上述原因选择成立有限责任公司。

The procedure for setting up a limited liability company is relatively simple and quick. By using the statutory, Hungarian only template deed of foundation, attached as an annex to the Hungarian Act on Company Registry, a Hungarian limited liability company can be incorporated within one business day after having received the company's local tax number, which usually takes one to two business days. In case the deed foundation is not drafted on the basis of the statutory template, the shareholder or founder can relatively freely define the structure of thecompany and the other terms and conditions of the operation. Having an individualized deed of foundation also implies a longer registration timeline—as the court of registration has to scrutinize the document more thoroughly and comprehensively. Nevertheless, registration in this case usually can take place within 8-10 days from filing with the court.

有限责任公司的设立程序相对简单、快捷。匈牙利公司登记法案附有公司创立的契约模板，通过使用这一匈牙利唯一的法定契约模板，匈牙利境内的有限责任公司可以在收到公司当地税号后的一个工作日内成立，而收到税号通常仅需一到两个工作日即可。如果契约并非基于法定模板起草，则股东或创始人可以相对自由地确定公司的结构和其他关于公司经营的条款和条件。个性化的契约意味着登记时间更长，这是因为登记法院必须更加彻底、全面地审查文件。不过，在这种情况下，登记通常可在提交法院后的 8—10 天内进行。

In this particular case, client decided not to use the statutory template, most importantly because client preferred to be more comfortable with a bilingual, Hungarian-Chinese deed of foundation. Such bilingual document is legally possible to use and generally admissible with the court of registration, although, the Hungarian version will prevail in case of any discrepancy or contradiction. Therefore, the Chinese translation of the Hungarian wording of the deed of foundation (and that of the other corporate documents in general) was of paramount importance for the client. In this respect we could effectively assist the client and ensure the appropriate translation of different legal documents to Chinese by local professional translator.

在本项目中，客户决定不使用法定模板，最重要的原因在于，客户更乐于使用双语（匈牙利语和中文）订立契约。这种双语文件可以合法使用，并且一般可被登记法院接受，但是，如果在两种语言之间出现任何差异或矛盾，将以匈牙利语的版本为准。因此，以匈牙利语订立契约（以及其他公司文件）的中文翻译对客户来说至关重要。在这一方面，我们可以有效地协助客户，并确保由当地专业的翻译人员将不同的法律文件恰当地翻译成中文。

One unique issue the client and Wolf Theiss faced during the incorporation process was that the Chinese company could not provide a company registry or commercial excerpt which would certify its existence and incorporation in China as requested by Hungarian company law. We understood that Chinese companies rather have operation permit or business licence that is issued by the competent governmental authority in one original copy and contains the basic legal details of the entity. Therefore, for the purpose of the Hungarian registration process, we used a copy of such business licence prepared by a local Chinese notary. This solution was acknowledged by the Hungarian companies' court.

在注册成立的过程中，客户和沃尔夫·泰斯律师事务所遇到了一个独有的问题，即中国公司无法提供公司登记或商业摘录，以按照匈牙利公司法的要求证明公司在中国境内的设立和存续。我们了解到，中国公司具有由主管政府机关出具的经营许可证或营业执照正本，且该许可证或执照包含该实体机构的基本法律信息。因此，为完成匈牙利的登记程序，我们使用了经中国公证处公证的该营业执照的副本。这一解决方案得到了匈牙利公司法院的认同。

Majority of the documents required for the company establishment were signed in China. As the prevailing Hungarian laws require certain formalities for corporate documents, notarization of the signatures became necessary. Nevertheless, pursuant to the applicable bilateral Chinese-Hungarian treaty, Chinese notarial deeds and acts are acknowledged and admissible in Hungary without the additional requirements of apostille or legalisation by the Hungarian consulate. This allowed the client to further expedite the company set up.

公司成立的大部分必备文件均在中国签署。现行的匈牙利法律要求公司文件须经某些正式手续,因此,文件上的签名要进行公证。不过,根据适用的中匈双边条约,中国经公证的契约和行为在匈牙利得到承认和受理,无须匈牙利领事馆进行额外的公证或认证。这使客户能够进一步加速公司的成立。

With respect to the managing directors of the Hungarian company, client expressly preferred to appoint Chinese nationals already employed by client. As Hungarian company laws do not define any restrictions based on the nationality or citizenship of the directors, we were able to assist client with realizing such appointments.

客户明确倾向于由已雇用的中国公民担任匈牙利公司的董事总经理。由于匈牙利公司法未对董事总经理的国籍或公民身份作出任何限制,因此,我们能够协助客户完成此类任命。

Besides the Chinese directors, the client also requested the appointment of a local Hungarian manager who permanently resides in Hungary and therefore would be fully available to handle the daily operations of the company. As full proficiency in the Chinese language and engineering expertise were also preferences expressed by client, we involved a local company to provide employment recruiting services in the project. Following several rounds of interviews client eventually succeeded in choosing the right person to fill the position who was then effectively appointed as an additional director as well.

除中国董事总经理外,客户还要求任命一位在匈牙利永久居住的当地管理人员,以充分处理公司的日常运营。由于客户还明示偏好熟练掌握中文和工程专业知识的候选人,我们亦邀请了当地公司在项目中提供就业招聘服务。经过几轮面试,客户最终成功确定了合适人选,以填补公司另一董事职位。

Client also had to investigate the actual legal framework pertaining to legal representatives of a company in Hungary. Having chosen the limited liability company as its preferred company form, Wolf Theiss informed client that the management of a limited liability company in Hungary is commonly carried out by one or more managing directors. Managing directors may be appointed for either a definite or an indefinite period of time, hence client had to carefully consider the relevant periods of the project and the particular expertise of the managing directors appointed by the company to oversee the operations. Client also had the chance to appoint various other types of representatives such as an authorised officer (in Hungarian: procurist) or to provide certain distracted powers of representation to employees; however at the time of the project, client remained focused on the management level.

客户还须研究关于匈牙利公司法定代表人的实际法律框架。在将有限责任公司确定为首选的公司形式后,沃尔夫·泰斯律师事务所告知客户,匈牙利的有限责任公司通常由一名或多名董事总经理进行管理。董事总经理的任期可为确定的,亦可为不确定的,因此,客户须仔细考虑项目的期限,以及负责监督公司业务的董事总经理所需的特殊专业知识。客户也可以任命其他类型的代表,如授权主管(匈牙利语为 procurist),或向员工授予某些分散的代表权;但在项目落地时,客户仍将关注重点放于管理层。

In the process of creating its local management, client had to decide on the number of individuals to be appointed (since at least one managing director had to be appointed with effect as of the date of incorporation) as well as the type of representation to be provided with. According to Hungarian law, managing directors, depending on the decision of the founding company, are entitled to represent (i.e. sign on behalf of and make legally binding statements) the company individually or jointly, with another managing director or an authorised officer. Another major consideration regarding the managing directors was the underlying legal relationship of their mandate, as under Hungarian law managing directors can carry out their duties as such based on a civil law mandate or employment contract, which required careful planning from tax and employment law perspectives.

在建立当地管理层的过程中,客户须决定将任命的人数(截至公司设立之日,至少应有一名董事总经理的任命生效)以及将授权的代表人类型。根据匈牙利法律,董事总经理可根据将成立的公司的决定单独或联合,即与另一位董事总经理或授权主管代表公司,代表公司签署并订立具有法律约束力的声明。对董事总经理授权的基本法律关系是另一个需要考虑的事项,因为根据匈牙利的法律,董事总经理履行其职责既可以基于民法意义上的授权,也可以基于雇用合同的约定,因而从税法和雇用法的角度进行仔细规划十分必要。

Together with the questions that arose in connection with the appointment of managing directors, client had to consider if it required any additional methods or bodies to represent supervisory functions on a local level. This topic was also something to consider with respect to any future developments and the plans to expand the operation, as the requirement to establish a supervisory board for a Hungarian limited liability company only becomes mandatory, if the annual average of the number of full-time employees employed by the business association exceeds two hundred. A further aspect of this expansion lies in the fact that employees have the right to partake in the supervisory board's operation in case the works council has not waived its right to participate in the supervisory board. In this case the representatives of the employees shall comprise of one-third of the members of the supervisory board.

除任命董事总经理外,客户还须一并考虑的问题是,是否需要通过其他方法或设立其他机构来代表公司在地方行使监督职能。公司的未来发展和扩大经营计划也是需要考虑的事项,这是因为,如果商业协会雇用的全职员工年均超过200人,那么,设立监事会将是匈牙利的有限责任公司须遵守的法定强制性要求。扩张带来的另一个问题在于,如果工会没有放弃参与监事会的权利,则雇员有权参与监事会的运作。在这种情况下,监事会1/3的成员应由雇员代表构成。

As mentioned earlier, a major question which client had in terms of the representation related risks under Hungarian law was due to the fact that managing directors can represent the company based on either a civil law mandate or an employment contract. Hence, client wanted to secure the best position in terms of being able to pursue any claims for damages potentially attributable to any representatives of the company. Luckily, client was happy to accept its options under the general statutory regulations, which provide that any damages caused by representatives of the company is, if attributable, deemed as a breach of contract and damages arising therefrom may be claimed.

如前所述,根据匈牙利法律,客户在公司代表方面可能面临着风险,原因在于董事总经理可以根据民法上的授权或雇用合同代表公司,因此,如公司代表给公司造成损害,客户希望在向其索赔时能够占据最有利的地位。幸运的是,客户十分乐于接受一般法的规定,根据该规定,公司代表造成的任何损害,如可归责于该代表,即可被视为违约,公司可就此种损害要求赔偿。

An interesting and very unique aspect of the Chinese client was the question of using official company stamps as a method of representation for the Chinese parent company. However, under Hungarian corporate law only the hand-written individual or joint signature of the managing directors can be considered as sufficient in order to validly represent the company in any contract or undertaking. Consequently, company stamps in Hungary (while they usually contain the logo, name and basic details including address, registry number of the respective company) have no legal effect without any of the signatures of the relevant representative. Therefore, the liberty of using an easily attachable company stamp was not possible for Hungary. Therefore, the quality and physical availability of local managing directors became an even greater consideration for client.

中国客户通常使用公司公章作为中国母公司的代表。但是，根据匈牙利公司法，只有董事总经理手写的个人签名或联合签名才能在任何合同或活动中被视为公司的有效代表。因此，在匈牙利，不具适格签名的公司公章没有法律效力，虽然它们通常包含标识、名称和基本信息如地址、相应公司的登记号等。因此，在匈牙利，公司印章不能轻易使用。当地董事总经理的品质和实际能力是客户更加关注的问题。

One further issue which had to be handled in the course of setting up the company was the mandatory opening of a local bank account for the company. The local bank account is legally required for the registration proceeding as the initial registered capital, which cannot be less than 3 000 000 Hungarian forints (approx. 10 000 euros) — must be paid in by the founder to such account and evidenced by the bank when filing for registration of the company. In addition, the confirmation by the bank on the safe remittance of the amount is mandatory and has to be attached to the registration package and filed with the companies' court. Nevertheless, such bank account opening is always subject to the bank's own internal KYC and Anti-Money Laundering procedures which takes time and could even require that the competent representatives travel to Hungary in order to personally sign the necessary documents and provide the required identification details to the bank. In our case, client would have preferred to open the necessary bank account with the Hungarian branch office of a large Chinese bank, however the estimated timeline for the process seemed to cause undesired delays to the setting up of the company. Therefore, eventually the client opted for another local bank that could handle the bank account opening flexibly and more expeditiously and ensured the safe and timely set up.

在设立公司的过程中，依法开立本地银行账户是必须处理的另一个问题。

为完成登记程序，必须依法开立银行账户，因为创始人须将初始注册资本即不得少于 3 000 000 匈牙利福林（约 10 000 欧元）存到该账户，并在提交公司登记申请时由银行对此加以证明。此外，银行须确认金额已安全汇付，并附在汇总的登记文件中提交给公司法院。不过，开立这种银行账户始终受银行内部实名认证规则（KYC）和反洗钱程序的约束，这会花费一定的时间，甚至可能要求主管代表前往匈牙利亲自签署必要的文件，并向银行提供所需的身份证明信息。在本案中，客户原希望在中国大型银行的匈牙利分支机构开设必要的银行账户，但这可能会导致公司成立出现预期之外的延迟。因此，客户最终选择了另一家本地银行，该银行可以更加灵活、迅速地处理银行开户事宜，确保银行账户安全、及时设立。

4. 融资（Financing）

In terms of financing, the client's initial intention was to use its own equity and resources for the investment project. Nevertheless, we also discussed and assessed with client at the early stage of the investment planning the available state funds and incentives provided by Hungary for foreign investors. Hungary offers a wide range of subsidies to foreign investors, such as subsidies based on individual government decision and subsidies for asset investment and job creation projects and development tax allowances. Client had a great variety of tenders to choose from, including EU co-financed tenders as well as local governmental funding. EU funds are available for asset acquisition, infrastructural development, new construction, renovation, service development, job creation and financing of human resource expenses.

关于融资，客户的初衷是将自己的股权和资产用于投资项目。不过，在投资规划的早期阶段，我们也与客户讨论并评估了匈牙利为外国投资者提供的可用国家资助和激励措施。匈牙利向外国投资者提供广泛的补贴，例如，由政府单方决策的补贴、资产投资补贴、创造就业项目以及发展税收的补贴。客户具有多种选择，包括欧盟共同出资的补给以及地方政府资助。欧盟的补给可用于资产收购、基础设施开发、新建建筑、改造、服务开发、创造就业机会和人力资源等项目。

Client eventually decided to only apply for Hungarian state funding. For this purpose we assisted the client in the course of negotiating with the competent governmental entity, namely the Hungarian Investment Promotion Agency (HIPA) which provides a wide range of services from management consultancy through information packages on the business environment to assistance with incentive applications.

客户最终决定只申请匈牙利国家资助。为此，我们协助客户与匈牙利投资促进局（HIPA）进行磋商，该机构作为政府主管实体，提供多种类的服务，包括以信息汇总的形式提供关于业务环境的管理咨询和协助申请激励措施。

In our case the main focus of the collaboration with HIPA was to obtain a certain amount of state incentive for the envisaged investment, as well as assistance with location searches and site evaluations for the service and manufacturing center. After several rounds of negotiations, during which Wolf Theiss actively assisted the client, HIPA provided a tailor-made incentive offer and introduced a couple of suitable real properties mainly in industrial parks in different locations around the country. HIPA also provided the client with valuable information on the labour market and the general availability of skilled workers to address the client's needs.

在本案中，与HIPA合作的重点是为拟进行的投资争取国家激励，并协助寻找、评估建设服务和制造中心的地点。在沃尔夫·泰斯律师事务所积极协助客户进行了数轮谈判后，HIPA提供了特定的激励性报价，并在全国各地的工业园区内推介合适的房产。为满足客户的需求，HIPA还提供了有关劳动力市场以及熟练工人供应的有价值的信息。

On the basis of several factors including volume of the investment, number of work places created by the investment, development status of the preferred region, HIPA offered a significant amount of cash incentive as well as tax allowances which was well received by the client. Furthermore, with HIPA's active assistance, the client also succeeded in finding a suitable industrial property close to Budapest where the plant could be established.

基于若干因素包括投资额、投资创造的工作场所数量、首选地区的发展状况等，HIPA提供了大量的现金激励和税收减免，这些都得到了客户的好评。此外，在HIPA的积极协助下，客户还成功地在布达佩斯附近找到了合适的工业选址，在那里可以建立工厂。

5. 租赁契约（Lease Agreement）

Already, during the initial discussions concerning the investment itself, client was contemplating on the possibilities of acquiring real estate and developing its own property or rather entering into a lease agreement with respect to an already fully completed structure that can be refurbished and customised to its operational needs. Finally, client settled on the lease of a property located within the industrial area in middle Hungary easily accessible from Budapest. This was a particular challenge, given the fact that the location chosen for the project was originally constructed and was actually used for manufacturing of combat vehicles. Therefore, Wolf Theiss had to take a deep dive in the contractual provisions of the lease agreement as creating the necessary manufacturing conditions required substantial fit-out efforts.

在投资的初步讨论阶段，客户考虑是收购房地产来自己进行开发，还是签订租赁协议以租用全部完工且可以根据经营需求翻新和定制的建筑物。最后，客户决定租赁位于匈牙利中部工业区内的房产，从布达佩斯可轻易到达该地区。但该选址最初为制造战斗机而建造并已实际投入使用，因此，为营造必要的生产条件需要进行大量的装修，沃尔夫·泰斯律师事务所为此深入研究了租赁协议的合同条款。

Additionally, we had to make sure, that the lease and its continuity was guaranteed for the entirety of the project and also provide chances for the extension of the lease in case client decided to expand its manufacturing activity in Hungary or the European region.

此外，我们必须确保租约持续涵盖整个项目期，且当客户决定扩张在匈牙利或欧洲地区的生产经营时，我们还须确保能为其争取延长租赁期限。

Drafting and negotiating a lease agreement also revealed matters falling within the competence of our regulatory and projects team's area of expertise. In particular, our respective team took considerable credit in reaching an agreement and setting up of the conditions of private cable connection and usage for client, which practically enabled the business to access electricity directly, through its own infrastructure and without additional forwarding costs-drastically reducing costs and preventing loss of profit.

我们的监管和项目团队具有起草租赁协议并就其进行谈判的专业能力。本所的各个团队协助客户达成协议，并为客户的私人电缆连接和使用创造条件，这实际上使企业能够通过其自己的基础设施直接接入电力资源，而无需额外的转接成本，从而大幅地减少了客户的成本和利润损失，本所也因此获得了较高的声誉。

Another major success in terms of business and legal negotiation which our firm helped client to achieve was regarding the base rates and the corresponding underlying items which made up the utility costs payable by client. Wolf Theiss had a major role in identifying costs which, according to law or the interpretation of the agreement with other service providers, cannot be taken into account when calculating the utility costs, again for the sake of helping client achieve a more lean and effective operation.

在帮助客户完成业务和进行法律谈判时，我们的另一重大成果是考虑客户应付的效用成本，这笔费用根据基本费率和相应标的物核算。根据法律或与其他服务供应商订立的协议，在计算效用成本时无须将一些花费考虑在内，我们在确定这些成本上发挥了重要作用，这同样帮助客户更加精益有效地开展营业。

6. 雇用事宜（Employment Matters）

One further issue we handled for this particular investment project was the employment matters in relation to the employees, especially the Chinese employees of the newly established limited liability company.

我们还为该投资项目处理了另一个问题，即雇员的雇用事宜，特别是新成立的有限责任公司的中国雇员雇用事宜。

In general, foreign nationals could also be employed by a Hungarian company. Since 1 January 2009, citizens of EU member states and their family members can be employed in Hungary without a work permit. In this case, the employer is required to report the employment data of EU citizens to the competent employment center. No residence permit is necessary for EU citizens who plan to spend more than 3 months in the country for employment purposes. Nevertheless, they are required to report the details of their extended stay to the Office of Immigration and Nationality and to apply for a residence card. Non-EU citizens may start working in Hungary after obtaining all permits and documents necessary for their employment in Hungary.

一般来说，匈牙利公司可以雇用外国公民。自 2009 年 1 月 1 日起，欧盟成员国的公民及其家人可以在没有工作许可证的情况下在匈牙利就业。在这种情况下，雇主须向主管就业中心报告欧盟公民的就业数据。以就业为目的计划在匈牙利停留 3 个月以上的欧盟公民，无需办理居留许可证。不过，他们若延长逗留期限，须向入境和国籍办公室报告，并申请居留卡。非欧盟公民在获得就业所需的全部许可证和文件之后，可以在匈牙利工作。

As a general rule, third country nationals are allowed to work in the territory of Hungary provided that they obtained either:

通常，第三国国民可以在匈牙利工作，但前提是他们应获得以下任一证件：

(i) residence permit for employment purposes, or

以就业为目的的居留许可证，或

(ii) work permit.

工作许可证。

Different application rules apply in the above cases, and the employee has also different rights under the different permits.

上述两种证件适用不同的申请规则，雇员也因不同的许可证而具有不同的权利。

If employees would stay in Hungary for a longer period of time (i. e. formore than 3 continuous months) for employment purposes (i. e. employment with the Hungarian company), they would be obliged to apply for residence permit for employment purposes, which would entitle them both to stay and to work in Hungary for the Hungarian company.

如雇员出于就业的目的（即在匈牙利公司就业）在匈牙利停留更长的时间（即超过连续的3个月），则雇员有义务申请以就业为目的的居住证，这将使他们有权利在匈牙利继续居留，并在匈牙利公司工作。

Contrary to the above, the work permit entitles the employee "only" to work in Hungary for the defined employer. Work permit should be applied for, generally, if the employment in Hungary would not exceed 90 days in a period of 180 days. The right of stay in this case has to be proved by other document(s).

与上述相反，工作许可证仅使雇员有权利在匈牙利为特定的雇主工作。一般来说，如雇员在匈牙利为期180天内就业的时间不超过90天，则雇员应申请工作许可证。在这种情况下，居留的权利应当由其他文件证明。

Due to the complex and mechanized nature of the technologies transferred to and implemented in Hungary, pursuant to the client's business plans, several Chinese nationals were brought to Hungary in order to effectively launch the operation of the service and manufacturing center and also to assist the training process of the newly hired local Hungarian employees who are expected to gradually take over the day-to-day tasks of the plant.

由于该项目在匈牙利实施的机械化技术较为复杂，根据客户的业务计划，一些中国雇员将被带到匈牙利，以便有效地开展服务制造中心的工作，他们也会协助培训新雇用的匈牙利员工，使他们能逐步接管工厂的日常任务。

The application process for the residence and work permits in Hungary is a relatively complex procedure which eventually also necessitated the active involvement of Wolf Theiss. Therefore, we actively assisted the client with respect to collecting the necessary information, including the position or job for which the Chinese nationals were to be hired pursuant to the Hungarian statistical nomenclature, description of the Chinese nationals professional qualifications required for carrying out the activity, the foreseeable date of the beginning and ending of the relationship, the place of work etc. and the required documents enclosed to the application forms (for instance, template agreement with the required content, certified copy and official translation of the document certifying the qualification or education of the employee, certifications for the financial background, for the employee's Hungarian accommodation and the access to comprehensive health insurance services). As in certain cases, the employee is required to appear before the authority in person when submitting the application, Wolf Theiss also accompanied the affected persons to the offices of the authority.

在匈牙利，居住和工作许可证的申请程序相对复杂，该过程需要沃尔夫·泰斯律师事务所积极参与。因此，我们积极协助客户收集必要的信息，包括：根据匈牙利的职位或工作名称聘用中国公民，说明中国雇员所需具备的专业技能资格，雇用关系预计开始和结束的日期，工作地点等，以及附于申请表的所需文件（例如，包含必备内容的模板协议、雇员资质和教育背景的证书副本及其官方翻译、财务情况证明，以使雇员能够在匈牙利居住，并获得全面的健康保险服务）。在某些情况下，员工必须亲自到现场提交申请，沃尔夫·泰斯律师事务所也会陪同这些员工前往当局办公室。

7. 其他地方法规考虑因素（Other Local Regulatory Considerations）

A major aspect client also had to consider was any potential limitations in the local laws or regulations of Hungary with respect to investment capital from China. The nature of this matter was twofold as on one side, Wolf Theiss had to investigate whether any foreign exchange control regime enforced by the National Bank of Hungary had an impact on the project and secondly, whether any limitations on Chinese foreign direct investment had to be investigated in order to limit potential risk arising out of any local legislation preventing the project altogether. Luckily, at the time of the implementation of the project, neither of these concerns proved to be an issue.

客户还须考虑匈牙利当地的法律或法规是否对中国资本的投资设置了任何潜在限制。这是个一体两面的问题,一方面,沃尔夫·泰斯律师事务所必须调查匈牙利国家银行实施的外汇管制制度是否会对项目产生影响;另一方面,还须调查是否存在对中方对外直接投资的限制,这些调查是为了控制地方立法阻止项目开展而产生的潜在风险。幸运的是,在项目实施之时,这些顾虑都被证实不存在问题。

It was confirmed however, that client's fears were mostly unfounded as the Hungarian Forint is a freely convertible currency, accordingly, money market instruments and negotiable instruments do not require notification or permission in Hungary. As a result, many of the problems associated with settlement of financial arrangements (e. g. closing of a share sale; transferring the statutory minimum registered capital) between a Hungarian and a foreign entity (in this case Chinese) are not considered an issue in Hungary.

然而事实证明,客户通常不须为此担忧,因为匈牙利福林可以自由兑换,相应地,在匈牙利,货币市场票据和流通票据不需要任何通知或许可。因此,匈牙利和外国实体(此处指中国企业)之间有关财务安排(例如,股份出售交割;法定最低注册资本变动)的许多问题在匈牙利不被视为问题。

Whilst payments can be fulfilled in both domestic and in foreign currency, transactions are normally carried out in the domestic currency Forint. Foreign companies may open foreign exchange bank accounts (where such accounts are registered and interest bearing) in any convertible currency or may deposit amounts Forint in a registered bank account in Hungary.

虽然在匈牙利,支付款项既可以用国内货币,也可以用国外货币,但通常交易会通过匈牙利境内货币(匈牙利福林)开展。外国公司可以以任何可兑换的货币开立外汇银行账户（此类账户已注册并计息），也可以将匈牙利福林存入已注册的匈牙利银行账户。

Another top priority for client was to get a full and comprehensive picture of the legislation impacting Chinese investment in Hungary. At the time of the project (2015), Hungary had no major restriction of foreign direct investments, only the bilateral regulation for Chinese investments. Therefore, client was not required to apply for any additional approvals.

客户还须充分、全面地了解对中方在匈牙利投资有影响的立法。在2015年项目开展之时，匈牙利未对外国直接投资作出重大限制，仅对中国投资进行双边监管。因此，客户无需申报任何其他批准。

Since then however, following the trend emerging around EU member states, new legislation was passed by the Hungarian Government setting out the rules to enable screening of foreign acquisitions of certain Hungarian strategic companies engaged in providing strategic services (e.g., big data, telecommunication, energy, military grade products) with respect to investors coming outside of the European Union or the European Economic Area. This practically means, that any Chinese investor (given that the business intended to be established falls within one of the industrial areas covered by this new legislation) must seek prior consent from the competent Hungarian ministry for carrying out its proposed acquisition or upon setting up its new venture in Hungary. The given minister, based on the legislation, has a wide range of discretion whether to approve or to prohibit the contemplated investment.

然而此后，继欧盟成员国出现的趋势，匈牙利政府通过了新的立法，并制定了一些规则用以监管欧盟或欧洲经济区以外的投资者对匈牙利某些提供战略性服务的公司进行的并购行为，这些战略性服务如大数据、能源、军用级产品等。实际上这意味着，任何中国投资者（鉴于拟建立的企业属于新法规所涵盖的工业领域之一）必须事先征得匈牙利主管部门的同意，方能开展拟议收购或在匈牙利建立新企业。根据立法，主管的部长在批准或禁止拟议投资方面拥有广泛的自由裁量权。

Nevertheless, we note that such legislation currently only affect the respective industrial sectors that are considered strategic as mentioned above and acquisitions or company establishments resulting in the acquisition or incorporation of entities in which at least 25% of the voting rights are directly or indirectly held by companies having their seat outside of the European Union or the European Economic Area. This means, that most of the industries in which Hungary receives its most notable green field investors remain untouched and free of any restrictions created by this new policy. Additionally, investors may also consider strategic partnerships and a joint venture cooperation in certain industries affected by the restriction, provided that their ownership or voting rights remain under the mentioned 25% threshold. Hence with careful planning and the help of experienced counseling, the risk of these investmentrestrictions can be almost completely negated or kept at a low level.

不过，我们注意到，该立法目前仅影响上述被视为具有战略意义的行业，以及欧盟或欧洲经济区以外的公司通过收购或设立公司从而直接或间接持有匈牙利公司至少25%股份的行为。这意味着在匈牙利，最受绿地投资人青睐的多数行业不受影响和限制。此外，在受限的行业，投资者还可以考虑进行战略合作和合资合作，但须以所有权或投票权不超过上述25%的限制为前提。凭借精心的策划和丰富的经验，本所的咨询服务可以协助客户完全规避这些风险，或尽量予以控制。

An additional matter, which client experienced in the course of setting up its operation in Hungary was in connection with the requirements of having CE markings on machinery used for the production. CE markings are standardized labels on products, which certify that an item meets EU requirements in terms of product safety, health and quality as set out in various EU Directives. The CE marking is intended primarily for the national control authorities of the member states, simplifying the task of essential market surveillance of regulated products. Applying for and receiving these markings (based on a quality control procedure-through which the CE marking is issued for the relevant product) the manufacturer or the importer will have the ability to circulate (i. e., sell, import, trade) the respective goods freely within the EU. It is interesting to note, that once received, CE markings are usable in all EU member states, hence client, when Wolf Theiss was assisting client in obtaining relevant CE markings for its manufacturing machinery, not only received the permission to use its machines at their Hungarian site, but has also opened up the possibility of using or distributing them across other EU member states.

在匈牙利，用于生产的机器须标有 CE 标志，这是客户在准备开业的过程中遇到的另一个问题。CE 标志是产品的标准化标签，用于证明产品已按照指令符合欧盟关于产品安全、健康和质量的要求。CE 标志主要用于成员国的内部控制，它简化了对管制产品的市场监督工作。在经申请获得这些标记后（基于质量控制程序，CE 标志将被颁发给通过该程序的相关产品），制造商或进口商可以在欧盟内部自由流通（即销售、进口、交易）商品。值得一提的是，CE 标志一经获得，即可在欧盟全部成员国内使用，因此，在沃尔夫·泰斯律师事务所帮助客户获得生产器械的 CE 标记后，客户不仅可在匈牙利使用该器械，也可在其他欧盟成员国使用或分销该器械。

— 作者简介 —

Márk Chiovini is a member of the Corporate and M&A team in Budapest. He specialises in corporate law, company filing procedures, domestic and cross-border M&A transactions, joint ventures and legal due diligence processes. He also deals with real estate sale and acquisitions, project developments and lease negotiations, and assists a wide range of Hungarian and international clients on consumer protection, regulatory, administrative law and general commercial matters. He also has competition law experience, in particular in merger control filings, cartel investigations, compliance analysis and unfair commercial practices. He completed his legal studies at the Eötvös Loránd University, during which he was a member of Bibó István College for Advanced Studies. He has also completed legal studies at the University of Padua, Italy within the framework of an Erasmus scholarship.

Márk Chiovini 在布达佩斯办公室的公司并购团队工作。他擅长的领域是公司法、公司备案程序、境内和跨境并购交易、合资企业和法律尽职调查程序等。同时，他还处理房地产销售收购、项目开发和租赁谈判业务，并在消费者权益保护、监管、行政法和一般商业事务方面为众多匈牙利和其他国际客户提供法律服务。他还拥有竞争法方面的工作经验，尤其是在合并控制申报、卡特尔调查、合规分析和反不正当竞争领域。他在罗兰大学获得了法律学位，在此期间他是 Bibó István 高等研究学院的成员。在伊拉斯谟奖学金项目的资助下，他还取得了意大利帕多瓦大学的法律学位。

Péter Ihász is a member of the Corporate and M&A team. He assists clients mainly in the course of the establishment of companies, their day-to-day operation, as well as during negotiations concerning general commercial and corporate issues. Péter also participates in legal due diligence processes as well as domestic and cross-border M&A transactions. In addition, his areas of interest include international and Hungarian commercial and private trusts, asset management and IP law.

Péter Ihász 在公司并购团队工作。他主要在公司设立、公司日常法律事务领域为客户提供法律服务,同时还辅助客户进行公司事务相关的日常商业谈判。Péter 同时还参与法律尽职调查程序以及境内和跨境的并购交易。此外,他所涉及的领域还包括匈牙利国内以及国际上的商业和私人信托、资产管理和知识产权法相关业务。

股权并购在荷兰：在物流产业开展投资
Equity in Netherlands
Investing in the Logistics Industry

点 评

　　荷兰作为欧洲的门户和交通枢纽，其得天独厚的地理位置、高效的服务业和先进的基础设施，这些成就了荷兰在欧洲乃至全世界领先的物流产业。本文简要介绍了荷兰物流产业的投资优势和相关行业的监管框架，并结合2019年中国投资者在荷兰的收购案例，分析在荷兰开展并购交易时可能涉及的相关法律问题。

　　在荷兰开展并购交易时，需要特别注意交易是否触发反垄断申报义务。中国投资者并购荷兰当地的企业需提前谨慎地评估反垄断申报所带来的影响。就本文分析的案例而言，中国投资者仅通过投资取得少数股权，未触及相关竞争法申报的门槛。这种投资思路，也值得借鉴。

　　针对项目融资方案，该案例提供了在荷兰常见的一种融资方式，即通过卖方贷款方式融资。在此种融资方式下，标的股份的出售方向购买方提供资金贷款，购买方应仅将贷款资金用于支付股份购买价格。而后，购买者必须在特定期限内偿还卖方贷款及利息。这种交易模式能够大大减轻购买者的资金压力，从而促进交易进程，提高交易的成功率。当然，这种模式不能随便使用，需要在专业法律顾问的指导下谨慎开展。

　　另外，由于中国投资者境外投资的国内前期审批较多，为了避免因此承受压力或者彼此失去信任，中国投资者应在收购的早期阶段对中国主管部门或母公司批准交易的具体进展向卖方及时坦诚地沟通。在跨境交易中，精通中文并了解文化差异的顾问机构是交易成功的必要保证，在交易中，本文作者不仅为客户在民法和税法方面提供法律服务，还承担着弥合文化差异的工作。

　　同时，《欧盟外商投资审查条例》（第2019/452号条例）建立了欧盟外商直接投资监管框架（以下简称条例）对在欧盟成员国（包括荷兰）设立机构的公司的外商直接投资（FDI）进行监管。荷兰作为欧盟成员国之一，该条例在荷兰法律体系中具有直接效力，但仍需在荷兰国内法中加以阐述。据此，荷兰立法者起草了关于建立外商直接投资一般审查机制的立法提案，即《经济和国家安全审查法案》，此审查机制适用于在荷兰被认为负责重要的经济流程或活跃于敏感技术（包括双重用途技术）市场上的一个或多个企业内导致控制权发生变化的交易。《荷兰投资、兼并与收购安全审查法案》（Wet veiligheidstoets investeringen, fusies en overnames）已于2023年6月1日生效，平等地适用于荷兰籍与非荷兰籍的投资者。

1. 荷兰的物流产业（Logistics in the Netherlands）

For many centuries, the Netherlands has been a center for world trade. With two significant European cargo main ports: Schiphol airport and Port of Rotterdam. The Netherlands is a key logistics hub for the through-transportation of goods to the European hinterland, making it an attractive location for foreign investors.

几个世纪以来，荷兰一直是世界贸易的中心。荷兰拥有两个重要的欧洲货运主要港口：史基浦机场和鹿特丹港。该国是货物运输通往欧洲腹地的重要物流枢纽，这使其成为一个对外国投资者充满吸引力的地方。

Global trade is expanding and the transportation of goods around the world continues to increase. Therefore, there is a need for logistics to be as sustainable and efficient as possible. Many new measures have been implemented to reduce the CO_2 emissions produced by the sector, such as hybrid delivery vehicles for urban areas and ships using quayside electricity whilst in port.

全球贸易正在扩大，世界各地的货物运输量继续增加。因此，物流需要变得尽可能可持续和高效。荷兰采取了许多新措施来减少各产业的二氧化碳排放，例如城市地区使用混合动力运输车辆，港口使用岸边电力船舶。

Through sustainable innovation, the Dutch logistics sector is expected to take a leading position in recent years. Logistics also plays a crucial role for virtually all other sectors according to the data, from the transportation of raw materials, right through to finished products. With a value added of 55 billion euros per year and 813 000 employees, the logistics sector is a strong driver of the Dutch economy. Within the logistics sector, and according to the industry research report of Mordor Intelligence, it was expected that the size of the freight and logistics market in the Netherlands would reach 73.7 billion US dollars by 2024, and it is expected to grow at a compound annual growth rate of 4.65% during the forecast period from 2024 to 2029, reaching 92.52 billion US dollars by 2029.

通过可持续创新，荷兰物流业近些年一直处于领先地位。物流对几乎所有其他行业起着至关重要的作用。有数据表明，从原材料的运输到成品，荷兰物流业增加了 550 亿欧元/年的产值和 813 000 名员工的就业，是荷兰经济的强大推动力。在物流业方面，根据 Mordor Intelligence 的行业研究报告，2024 年荷兰货运和物流市场的规模将达到 737 亿美元，并预计在 2024—2029 年的预测期间将以 4.65% 的复合年增长率增长，到 2029 年将达到 925.2 亿美元。

1.1 荷兰在全球物流业中发挥关键作用的重要因素（Important Factors that the Netherlands Play a Key Role in the Global Logistics Industry）

1.1.1 连接全球的生产者和消费者（Connecting producers and consumers in worldwide）

The Netherlands play a key role in the globalised economy, by connecting producers and consumers worldwide via sophisticated logistics. Success is based on a combination of cutting-edge infrastructure, excellent service providers and a coastal location at the heart of Europe. Because of its strategic location on the European coast, the Netherlands provide excellent access to the European market of more than 500 million consumers.

荷兰通过复杂的物流系统连接着世界各地的生产者和消费者，在全球化经济中发挥着关键作用。先进的基础设施、优秀的服务提供商和位于欧洲中心沿海地区的区位奠定了其成功的基础。基于在欧洲海岸的战略位置，荷兰为超过 5 亿消费者提供了进入欧洲市场的良好途径。

1.1.2 鹿特丹港和阿姆斯特丹史基浦机场（The port of Rotterdam and Amsterdam Airport Schiphol）

Key factors are the Port of Rotterdam, Europe's largest port (and fourth largest worldwide) and Amsterdam Schiphol Airport, a major European airfreight and passenger hub. Excellent logistics service providers and an extensive network of roads, railways, inland waterways and pipelines support both. This powerful combination has made the Netherlands the "Gateway to Europe" accounting for significant quantities of European roadtransport and water-transport.

还有一个关键因素是鹿特丹港——欧洲最大的港口（全球第四大港口），和阿姆斯特丹史基浦机场，欧洲主要的空运和客运枢纽。优秀的物流服务提供商和密集的公路、铁路、内陆水道和管道网络都为鹿特丹港和阿姆斯特丹史基浦机场提供了很好的支持。这种强大的组合使荷兰成为"通往欧洲的门户"，占据了欧洲陆路和水路运输相当重要的一部分。

1.1.3 高等级的基础设施（Highly ranked infrastructure）

According to the World Economic Forum (WEF), the quality of the Netherlands' infrastructure is among the best in the world, within Europe, the infrastructure of Netherlands was ranked first by the WEF. Reflecting excellent facilities for maritime, air, road and railroad transport, ranked 2nd, 3rd, 2nd and 6th, respectively in 2019.

根据世界经济论坛，荷兰是欧洲乃至世界上基础设施质量最好的国家之一。其海运、空运、公路和铁路运输的优良设施，在2019年分别排名第二位、第三位、第二位和第六位。

1.1.4 广泛应用的信息技术（Extensive use of information technology）

The Netherlands also makes extensive use of Information Technology to deliver optimised supply chain solutions in sectors where time is critical, such as food and flowers.

荷兰还广泛地利用了信息技术，在时间因素十分关键的领域（如食品和鲜花）提供经过优化的供应链解决方案。

1.1.5 可持续性是重要议题（Sustainability as an important topic on the agenda）

In addition, the Netherlands is pioneering developments in environmentally sustainable logistics operations and silent logistics.

此外，荷兰在环境可持续的物流运营和减噪物流方面也处于领先地位。

1.2 关于物流行业的法规要求（Regulatory Requirements Regarding the Logistics Sector）

For transportation companies performing road transport, licenses may be required.

The Dutch Carriage of Goods by Road Act (Wet Wegvervoer Goederen, WWG) provides for rules concerning road transportation companies established in the Netherlands. The WWG appoints the Dutch Road Haulage Organization for National and International Transport (NIWO) as the authority having the power to grant licenses, authorizations and attestations to more than 14 000 transport companies that are engaged with the road transport of good in the Netherlands.

从事道路运输的运输公司需要许可证。《荷兰道路货物运输法》规定了在荷兰设立道路运输公司的相关规则。该法还授权荷兰国家和国际公路运输组织作为有权授予许可、授权和证明的机构，该机构为超过 14 000 家在荷兰主营道路货物运输的运输公司授权并开具证明。

The WWG makes an important distinction between "professional (road) transport" and "owner-operator (road) transport". If the performed transport can be characterized as owner-operator transport, there are less regulatory requirements applicable than in case of professional transport.

《荷兰道路货物运输法》对"专业（道路）运输"和"所有者—运营商（道路）"运输进行了重要区分。如果从事的运输可以归类为所有者—运营商运输，则与专业运输相比，其适用的监管要求将更少。

2. 交易结构 (Transaction Structure)

2.1 项目简介 (Introduction of the Investment Project)

In 2019, one of our Chinese clients invested in a Dutch private company with limited liability. It acquired a minority interest of 20% of the shares in the capital of the target company. The target company and its subsidiaries together form a group of companies that is active in logistics, focusing on road and rail transport for the chemical industry and food industry.

2019 年，我们的一位中国客户投资了一家荷兰私营有限责任公司即"目标公司"，并收购了占目标公司股本 20% 的少数股权。目标公司及其子公司共同活跃于物流行业，主营化学工业和食品工业的公路和铁路运输。

2.2 交易文件 (Transaction Documents)

In connection with the transaction, the seller and our client entered into a share purchase agreement (SPA). Said SPA governs the rights and obligations of the seller and our client with respect to the sale and transfer of the shares in the capital of the target company. The seller (who was prior to completion of the transaction the sole shareholder), sold and transferred 20% of its shares to our client. As a result, two shareholders (the majority shareholder being the seller in the transaction; the minority shareholder being our client) hold the target company. Said shareholders entered into a shareholders agreement (SHA) governing their rights and obligations with respect to the target company.

就交易而言，卖方与我们的客户订立了股份购买协议（SPA）。上述 SPA 约定了卖方和我们的客户在目标公司出售和转让股份方面的权利和义务。卖方（在完成交易之前是唯一股东）将其 20% 的股份出售并转让给我们的客户。因此，公司股份由两名股东持有。大股东是交易中的卖方，少数股东是我们的客户。上述股东签订了一份股东协议（SHA），约定了他们在目标公司中的权利和义务。

Under Dutch law, it is common practice that parties enter into a non-disclosure agreement (NDA) with respect to their intentions regarding the envisaged transaction. A NDA creates a legal obligation between the parties securing that certain information (e.g. the envisaged transaction) remains protected/confidential. Such NDA is usually the first transaction document to be entered into between parties.

根据荷兰法律的规定，通常的做法是，各方就其设想的交易意图订立保密协议。保密协议在双方之间产生法律义务，以保证某些信息（例如，交易的预想设计）始终受到保护并被各方保密。此类保密协议通常是缔约方之间签订的第一份交易文件。

Following the signing of an NDA, parties often enter into a term sheet. The term sheet governs the initial intentions of parties with respect to the transaction (e.g. the purchase price for the shares). Our client was not represented by Dutch legal advisors during the negotiations of the term sheet. As a result, our client was bound to certain disadvantageous clauses in the transaction documentation (e.g. less voting rights with respect to the target company) pursuant to the term sheet. It is therefore essential that professional legal advisors are engaged in an early stage.

签署保密协议后，各方通常会签署交易意向书。交易意向书规定了交易方的初始意向（例如股份购买价格）。在交易意向书谈判期间，我们的客户没有聘请荷兰的法律顾问。因此，根据交易意向书，我们的客户必须遵守交易文件中的某些不利条款（例如，在目标公司较少的投票权）。因此，让专业法律顾问尽早参与交易是十分必要的。

2.3 尽职调查（Due Diligence）

Simultaneously with the drafting of the transaction documents as described above, the professional advisors of our client, also the financial and tax advisors, conducted a due diligence regarding the target company and the business carried out by it. The purpose of such an investigation is identifying key issues relating to the transaction. Following identification of certain issues, we have sought protection against those issues in the transaction documents. In general, potential risks can be limited/covered by means of (i) lowering the purchase price, (ii) including specific conditions precedent or conditions subsequent, (iii) including warranties and (iv) including specific indemnifications.

在起草上述交易文件的同时，我们的客户的专业顾问，即财务和税务顾问，对目标公司及其开展的业务状况进行了尽职调查。此类调查的目的是确定与交易相关的关键风险问题。在确定某些风险问题后，我们在交易文件中寻求对这些风险问题的保护条款。一般而言，潜在风险可以通过（i）降低购买价格，（ii）约定特定先决条件或后续条件，以及（iii）约定保证和（iv）约定特定赔偿等方式来限制或者涵盖。

2.4 竞争法申报（Competition Law Filings）

2.4.1 荷兰竞争法（Dutch competition law）

Under Dutch law, certain mergers, acquisitions, public bids and other transactions that may bring about a so-called concentration have to be notified to governmental entities. The Dutch Competition Act (DCA) provides a system of merger control for operations that affect the Dutch economy. It largely copies and partially incorporates the system of European merger control, and prohibits concentrations that create or strengthen a dominant position resulting in a significant restriction of effective competition on the Dutch market or a part thereof. The provisions regarding merger control set forth in the DCA apply to mergers, acquisitions, public bids and all other transactions that may bring about a concentration. In accordance with this act, concentrations shall be deemed to arise where:

根据荷兰法律的规定，某些合并、收购、公开招标和其他可能导致所谓经营者集中的交易必须向政府部门报告。荷兰竞争法（DCA）针对影响荷兰经济的交易设置了合并控制制度。它基本上照搬并部分纳入欧洲合并控制制度，禁止产生经营者集中或加强其支配地位从而严重限制荷兰市场或其中部分市场的有效竞争的行为。DCA 中载明的有关合并控制的规定适用于合并、收购、公开招标以及可能导致集中的所有其他交易。根据该法案，以下情况应认为属于经营者集中行为：

i. Two or more previously independent undertakings merge;

i. 两个或两个以上之前相互独立的企业进行合并;

ii. One or more persons or legal entities already controlling at least one undertaking, or one or more undertakings acquire, whether by purchase of securities or assets, by contract or by other means, direct or indirect control of the whole or parts of one or more other undertakings; or

ii. 一个或多个自然人或法人实体已经控制至少一个企业，或者一个或多个企业通过购买股权或资产、合同或其他方式，直接或间接控制一个或多个其他企业的全部或部分；或

iii. A full-function joint venture is established. According to section 27 of the DCA, a full-function joint venture is established when two or more undertakings form an economic entity that operates independently from its parents on a lasting basis. Two criteria are essential here, independence and a lasting basis. Without fulfilling these requirements joint ventures fall under the "cooperative joint ventures" definition, which means that they have to be treated under section 6 of the DCA (the cartel prohibition) which is equivalent to article 101 Treaty on the Functioning of the European Union (TFEU).

iii. 设立一个全功能合资企业。根据《荷兰竞争法》第 27 条，当两个或多个企业组成一个经济实体并独立于其母公司持续经营的，即设立了一个全功能的合资企业。此处有两项关键标准：独立性与持续性。未满足前述要求的合资企业符合"合作经营企业"的定义，意味着该等企业适用《荷兰竞争法》第 6 节（卡特尔禁令），即相当于《欧盟运行条约》（TFEU）第 101 条。

For a joint venture to operate on a lasting basis it needs to be created for a long period. Joint ventures that are set up for only a single project, such as the construction of a new warehouse, are usually not considered lasting. For a joint venture to have a sufficient degree of independence, it needs to perform the normal market functions in its commercial activities that other market parties also carry out in that specific market. A sufficient degree of autonomy can only be reached if the joint venture has a management dedicated to its day-to-day operations and access to sufficient resources, including finance, staff, and assets (tangible and intangible) in order to conduct the joint venture's business activities. Ultimately, the joint venture needs to deal with its parents' companies at arm's length on the basis of normal commercial conditions. If the joint venture achieves more than 50% of its turnover with third parties, this will typically be an indication of full-functionality.

一个拟持续经营的合资企业需要长期设立。仅为单个项目设立的合资企业，如新建仓库，通常不被视为具有持续性。一个具有充分独立性的合资企业，需要在商业活动中履行其他市场主体也会履行的正常市场职能。而只有当合资企业管理层致力于日常经营与获取充足的资源，包括财务、员工和资产（有形和无形），以开展合资企业的业务活动时，才具有全部的自主权。最终，合资企业需要在正常商业条件的基础上，在保持一定独立性的情况下处理和母公司的关系。如果合资企业50%的营业额来自第三方，这通常表明了其具备全功能。

A concentration that meets certain thresholds as regards the turnover of the undertakings concerned will have to be notified to the Dutch Authority for Consumers & Markets (ACM). A concentration remaining below the threshold turnover levels may be effectuated without a notification to the ACM.

企业营业额达到某些规模的经营者集中行为，必须向荷兰消费者与市场管理局（ACM）报告。没有达到营业额规模的经营者集中，则无需报告。

Section 29 DCA provides that a concentration must be notified to the ACM if the combined turnover of all undertakings concerned exceeds €150 million in the calendar year preceding the concentration; and at least two undertakings concerned each achieved a turnover of at least €30 million in the Netherlands in that year.

根据DCA第29条规定，如果所有相关企业在参与集中前一年的年度营业额总计超过1.5亿欧元；并且至少有两家相关荷兰企业在该年度分别实现了至少 3000 万欧元的营业额，则经营者集中必须向 ACM 报告。

A concentration that has been effectuated without having been duly notified or without the parties observing the appropriate waiting period will be regarded as being null and void under the laws of the Netherlands.

根据荷兰法律的规定，未经按时报告或当事方未经适当等待期限而实施的经营者集中将被视为无效。

In addition, the ACM has wide powers to impose fines and orders in the context of concentration control. Failure to notify a concentration will usually lead to a fine upon discovery by the ACM. Both companies and directors involved can be fined in this regard. Fines for companies may run up to 10 per cent of the worldwide turnover in the year preceding the year of the fine.

此外，ACM 拥有广泛的权力，可以对集中控制的情形进行罚款和下达指令。未能报告集中通常会导致 ACM 对之罚款。涉及的公司和董事都可能因此被罚款。对公司的罚款可能高达前一年全球营业额的 10%。

In the case of our client, the transfer of 20% of the shares, did not trigger an obligation to notify the ACM, because our client did not acquire (shared) control of the target company and it did not concern a full-function joint venture.

就我们的客户而言，转让 20% 的股份并没有触发向 ACM 报告的义务，因为我们的客户没有获得（共享）对目标公司的控制权，亦不涉及（成立）一个全功能的合资企业。

2.4.2 欧洲竞争法（European competition law）

Under the EU Merger Regulation, any concentration with an EU dimension must be notified to the European Commission. The concept of concentration covers mergers, acquisitions of control and full-function joint ventures. So under the *EU Merger Regulation*, only full function joint ventures are examined. Cooperative joint ventures escape the application of the EU concentration control regulation, but they can be supervised and appraised under other fields of competition law (mainly the cartel prohibition). The difference between a full-function joint venture and a cooperative joint venture is that the first operates autonomously and independently from its parent companies on a lasting basis. A joint venture is not full-function (which means cooperative) if it only takes over one specific function within the parent companies' business activities without its own access to or presence on the market. A joint venture may also be cooperative if it purchases from its parent companies, but adds little value to the products or services at hand.

根据《欧盟合并条例》，任何具有欧盟规模的集中必须通知欧盟委员会。集中的概念包括合并、控制权收购和（成立）全功能合资企业。根据《欧盟合并条例》，仅全功能合资企业须被审查。合作企业规避了欧盟集中控制法规的适用，但它们会在其他竞争法领域（主要是企业合并禁令）被监督和评估。全功能合资企业和合作经营企业之间的区别在于前者持久性地独立于其母公司自主经营。"合资企业"如果仅接管母公司商业活动中的特定功能，且自身不接触或不出现于市场的，不具备全功能（即合作经营）。"合资企业"如果从母公司处采购却几乎没有给该产品或服务增值的，仍然仅是合作经营企业。

In the transaction at hand, there was no question of any (full function) joint venture at all, simply because there was no acquisition of (shared) control by our client through the transfer of 20% of the shares in the share capital of the target company. The acquisition of (shared) control is an absolute prerequisite for the application of the concentration control regime of the EU Merger Regulation. The EU Merger Regulation only applies to cases where companies will gain control in another undertaking, or will create a joint venture in which they exert control. Control can be established both *de facto* and *de jure*. Control may exist for example if two undertakings each hold 50% of the shares in a joint venture, which provides both parties with the right of veto. On the other hand, in the event of the acquisition of a minority share, a company may well not acquire control at all. In that case, the underlying share transaction does not constitute a concentration or a full function joint venture at all; hence, it will not be subject to the EU merger control regime.

在本次交易中，不涉及（全功能）合资企业的问题是因为我们的客户通过转让20%的股本并未获得或共享对目标公司的控制权。获得（共享）控制权是适用《欧盟并购条例》的集中控制规定的绝对先决条件。《欧盟并购条例》仅适用于企业获得另一企业控制权的情形，或设立一家在其中行使控制权的合资企业的情形。控制权可从事实和法理两方面构建。比如，当两家企业在一合资企业中各持有50%股权，从而双方均享有否决权的情形下，控制权便可能存在。

另外，在获得少数股权的交易中，企业很可能根本无法获得控制权。该情形下，潜在的股权交易根本无法构成集中或全功能合资企业，因此，也不会受欧盟并购控制规定的约束。

3. 项目融资方案（Project Financing Method）

In this specific case the purchase price was paid by our client as a lump sum. Our client financed the purchase price via an intra-group arrangement (i.e. the money came from one of its non-Chinese group companies). Please note that intra-group financing is a commonly used finance arrangement in the Netherlands. Besides, intra-group financing also many transactions involving Chinese buyers are financed via bank credit facilities. We do see that it is quite difficult for Chinese buyers to have a transaction funded through China. To avoid this, transactions can also be financed via bank credit facilities or through intra group finance arrangements.

在这个具体案例中，购买价款由我们的客户一次性支付。我们的客户通过集团内部安排（即资金来自其中一家非中国集团公司）为支付购买价款提供资金。请注意，集团内部融资是荷兰常用的融资方式。此外，集团内部融资以及涉及中国买家的许多交易都是通过银行信贷融资提供的。我们确实看到中国买家很难直接以中国境内融资安排的方式获得交易资金。为避免这种情况，交易还可以通过银行信贷或通过集团内部融资安排获得资金。

Another finance method with respect to transactions in the Netherlands is the use of a vendor loan. In such case, the seller lends an amount to the purchaser. The purchaser shall use such loan solely for paying the purchase price for the shares. The purchaser has to repay the vendor loan including interest within a certain term.

在荷兰交易的另一种融资方法是使用卖方贷款，在这种情况下，卖方向购买者提供资金贷款，购买者应仅将此类贷款用于支付股份购买价格。购买者必须在特定期限内偿还卖方贷款及利息。

4. 交易文件中的关键条款（Key Terms in Transaction Documents）

4.1 股份购买协议（SPA）

With respect to the SPA, the following terms are of great importance (please note that this is not an exhaustive list, but just some examples):

以下条款为 SPA 中非常重要的条款（请注意，以下并非详尽列举，仅提供部分示例）：

Payment of the purchase price: it goes without saying that the manner in which the purchaser will pay the purchase price for the shares should be written down very precisely. Earn-out arrangements are also quite common in the Netherlands; these are payment arrangements, which are linked to the post-closing performance of sellers (in many cases the sellers/managing directors of target companies stay also after closing).

支付购买价款：不言而喻，购买者支付股份购买价格的方式应该被非常准确地写进 SPA。在荷兰，按照被收购主体的业绩情况进行分期支付收购价款的安排也很常见；这些付款安排与卖方交割后的业绩挂钩（在许多情况下，目标公司的卖方/董事总经理也在交割后留任）。

In addition, a clause regarding so-called leakage can be needed (i. e. prohibiting the target company to make any-dividend-distributions in the period between signing of the transaction documents and executing the deed of transfer/closing).

此外，可能需要一个关于所谓防泄露的条款（即在签署交易文件和执行转让/交割契据期间，禁止目标公司进行任何股息分配）。

Completion actions: It is common practice in the Netherlands to include a clause in the SPA, stipulating what party needs to complete which actions at (or prior to) the day the deed of transfer is executed, namely, closing of the transaction. For example, the signing of a notary letter or the delivery of waiver letters of banks regarding their rights pursuant to the release of a right of pledge on the relevant shares etc.

交易完成：在荷兰，通常会在 SPA 中约定当事人在转让契据执行即进行交易交割当日（或之前）需要完成的行动的条款。例如，签署公证书或提交由银行出具的解除相关股份质押的豁免函等。

Limitation of liability: in the event that one of the parties to the SPA is in breach of its contractual obligations contained therein, the other party may hold the defaulting party liable.

责任限制：如果 SPA 的一方违反协议约定的合同义务，另一方可要求违约方承担责任。

In this respect, it is common practice to include wording pertaining to the limitation of liability; usually certain thresholds are included in the share purchase agreement. These limitations usually only apply to breaches of the warranties; typically in case of damages under the indemnifications, the liability of the seller is unlimited (obviously, this also depends on the negotiations).

对此，通常的做法是加入与责任限制有关的条款，也会在 SPA 中约定限额。这些限制通常仅适用于违反保证的行为；通常在赔偿损失的情况下，卖方的责任是无限制的（显然，这也取决于谈判）。

Upon signing of the SPA, the shares are not transferred yet. Under Dutch law, the transfer of shares is effectuated by means of the execution of a notarial deed of transfer. Said execution is required for the closing of the transaction.

签署 SPA 后，股份尚未转让。根据荷兰法律的规定，股份转让是通过执行公证转让契据来实现的。所以，整个交易的交割也需要执行前述程序。

4.2 股东协议（SHA）

With respect to the SHA, the following terms are (amongst others) of vital importance：

以下条款（以及其他）为 SHA 中的关键条款：

Important resolutions: certain resolutions should be adopted by the shareholders with a special majority of the votes. In the Netherlands most resolutions of the general meeting are adopted by a normal majority. In case a client only holds a minority stake in a company it is therefore of great importance that certain, essential resolutions only can be adopted if the minority shareholders consent as well. Essential resolutions are (amongst others): the winding up or liquidation of the company, amendment of the articles of association, any sale of all or a substantial part of the business of the company and making participations in the capital of other companies.

重要决议：股东应以特别多数票通过决议。在荷兰，股东会的大多数决议都以正常多数通过。如果客户只持有公司的少数股权，那么 SHA 应加入只有少数股东也同意才能通过重要决议的条款，这一点非常重要。（除其他决议外）重要的决议是指公司的解散或清算、公司章程的修订、公司全部或大部分业务的出售以及参与对其他公司的投资。

Information rights: in principle each shareholder should be informed by the board of managing directors regarding the business of the company. In the SHA this right of information can be made more concrete and broadened (e. g. the obligation of the company to submit to the shareholders a quarterly report which shall inter alia consist of a balance sheet, profit and loss account and cash flow statements).

知情权：原则上，董事会管理成员应通知每位股东公司业务经营情况。在SHA中，这种知情权利可以更具体和更广泛（例如，公司有义务向股东提交季度报告，其中应包括资产负债表、损益表和现金流量表）。

Transfer of shares: we included wording pertaining to the restriction of transferring shares in the target company. It is common practice in the Netherlands to incorporate share-transferring restrictions (e. g. in the form of an offering requirement whereby the offering shareholders should offer the shares first to the other shareholder). The pricing mechanism is always one of the topics regarding which parties need to negotiate.

股份转让：我们约定了有关限制转让目标公司股份的措辞。在荷兰，通常采用股份转让限制机制（例如以要求出售股份的股东应首先向另一股东发出要约的形式来进行限制）。定价机制始终是交易相关方需要协商的主题之一。

Tag/drag along: we included wording pertaining to the event that a shareholder envisages to sell all its shares in the target company to an interested buyer. In such an event, the minority shareholder has the right to sell and transfer all the shares it holds in the target company to the interested buyer as well under the same conditions (i. e. the tag along). The drag along is also always included; this means that if a (majority) shareholder wants to sell its shares in a target company that then the other (minority) shareholders are forced to sell their shares as well against the same conditions.

随售/拖售权：我们会在协议中设计如果股东设想将其全部持有目标公司的股权出售给感兴趣的买方的条款。在这种情况下，小股东有权按照相同条件将其持有目标公司的全部股权出售并转让给感兴趣的买方（即行使随售权）。拖售权也是经常被设置在协议中的条款，这意味着如果股东（即大股东）希望转让其持有的目标公司的股权，其他股东（即小股东）也将被迫按照相同条件转让其持有的目标公司的股份。

Good/Bad leaver provisions: in many cases if the managing directors of the target company hold shares as well, provisions are included to cover the situation that the employment or management agreement with such managing director is terminated. It is common practice that in such a case the managing director/shareholder is forced to sell its shares in the company against a certain price. The price depends on the question what the reason for termination of the employment/management agreement was.

正常/不良离职条款：在许多情况下，如果目标公司的董事总经理也持有股份，则条款会涉及与该董事总经理的雇用或管理协议终止的情况。在这种情况下通常的做法是，董事总经理/股东必须以一定的价格出售其在公司的股份。价格取决于终止雇用/管理协议的具体原因。

In this specific case, parties agreed the establishment of an advisory board of the target company. However, the implementation of a board of supervisory directors would have been more favorable for our client. This because, under Dutch law, an advisory board is no formal corporate body. Since the advisory board is not arranged for in the DCC, the only relevant provisions are included in the shareholders agreement.

在这个具体案例中，各方同意成立目标公司的顾问委员会。但是，设置监事会对我们的客户更有利。这是因为根据荷兰法律的规定，咨询委员会不是正式的公司机构。而《荷兰民法典》（DCC）没有对咨询委员会作出规定，因此相关条款仅包含在股东协议中。

5. 主要法律问题（Main Legal Issues）

One of the main legal issues during the negotiations with respect to the transaction documents was the non-compete clause in the SHA. It is common practice in the Netherlands to include a non-compete clause in the SHA, prohibiting engaging in competing business. Our client wanted to have the possibility to engage in competing business with a specific competitor. We had extensive discussions regarding the manner a breach of the non-compete should be dealt with. Finally, we agreed upon a clause that our client would lose its voting rights with respect to the shares (by converting its shares into so-called depository receipts) in the event the non-compete clause was breached. Further, in case of a breach of a non-compete clause often it is agreed between parties that such shareholder loses its information rights (as a shareholder).

在交易文件的谈判期间，主要法律焦点之一是 SHA 中的不竞争条款。在荷兰，通常的做法是在 SHA 中加入不竞争条款，禁止从事竞争性业务。我们的客户希望可以与特定竞争对手进行竞争。我们就以何种方式处理违反不竞争条款行为的议题进行了广泛的讨论。最后，我们一致同意，即如果违反不竞争条款,我们的客户将失去其股份中的投票权(通过将其股份转换为所谓的存托凭证)。此外,如果违反不竞争条款,则双方同意该股东丧失其作为股东享有的知情权。

6. 税务问题(Tax Issues)

In case of a share purchase also different tax aspects need to be taken into account. When a (Chinese) legal entity acquires the shares in the Dutch ("BV", in Dutch "Besloten Vennootschap", it means private limited liability Company), we will identify the tax risks for the buyer in the tax due diligence and subsequently negotiate a (full) tax indemnity in relation to any (joint and a several) liability for Dutch corporate income tax (CIT) in the SPA. Next to identifying potential tax exposures and obtaining contractual protection in connection to the acquisition, also funding and legal structuring should be reviewed.

在购买股份的情况下,还需要考虑不同的税务问题。当(中国)法人实体收购荷兰私营公司(BV,荷兰语为 Besloten Vennootschap)的股份时,我们将在税务尽职调查中确定买方的税务风险,并随后就 SPA 中的荷兰企业所得税(CIT)的任何(连带和分别的)责任产生的(全额)税务赔偿开展谈判。然后确认潜在的税务风险并确保可获得与收购相关的合同保护,以及审查融资和法律结构。

A Dutch BV is subject to CIT on its worldwide income. In general, the change of the shareholder does not influence the CIT position of the Dutch BV. Please note that there are some anti-abuse provisions on which the change of a shareholder might have an impact, specially in the field of loss compensation. CIT is levied at the following rates:

荷兰私营公司的全球收入应缴纳企业所得税(CIT)。一般而言,股东的变动不会影响荷兰私营公司的 CIT 头寸。请注意,股东的变更可能会对一些反滥用条款产生影响特别是在损失赔偿领域。CIT 按以下税率征收:

表 1 2020—2022 年企业所得税（CIT）征收税率

Annual taxable profit（in €）年度纳税利润（欧元）	Rate 2020 2020 年税率	Annual taxable profit（in €）年度纳税利润（欧元）	Rate 2021 2021 年税率	Annual taxable profit（in €）年度纳税利润（欧元）	Rate 2022 2022 年税率
0—200 000	16.5%	0—245 000	15%	0—395 000	15%
≥200 000	25%	≥245 000	25%	≥395 000	25%

An important item that needs to be reviewed in a due diligence process from a CIT perspective is the transfer pricing of the Dutch target BV. In case the Dutch target BV is involved in various intercompany transactions, it must have transfer pricing documentation in its files. In principle, the Dutch tax authorities could adjust the applied pricing should the terms and conditions agreed upon between related parties not be at arm's length. Such adjustments could potentially result in a higher taxable income, and will be secondly adjusted (dividend withholding tax).

从 CIT 的角度来看，需要在尽职调查过程中审核的重要方面是荷兰的私营目标公司的转移定价安排。如果荷兰的私营目标公司涉及各种公司间交易，则必须在其文件中包含转移定价文件。原则上，如果关联方之间达成的条款和条件不符合公平原则，荷兰税务机关可以调整适用的定价。此类调整可能会导致较高的应税收入，并将进行二次调整（股息预扣税）。

Following the same legal provisions, the Dutch BV should include in its administration information and documentation in which the intercompany transactions are documented and where the arm's length character of the intercompany transactions is substantiated. If this requirement is not met, the burden of proof in relation to the arm's length remuneration for the intercompany transactions shifts from the Dutch tax authority to the Dutch target company.

根据相同的法律规定，荷兰私营公司应在其运营管理中保存记录公司间交易的信息和文件，以及证明公司间交易符合公平交易特征的信息和文件。如果不满足此要求，则公司间交易的公平报酬的举证责任从荷兰税务机关转移到荷兰目标公司。

In case the Dutch target BV does have employees, as an employer it must withhold a monthly wage tax from salaries and other taxable remuneration paid to their employees. In addition, employers must pay social security contributions calculated on the total gross salaries of employees, including directors. In a due diligence process the risks regarding the wage tax and social security contributions will be identified.

如果荷兰私营目标公司确实有雇员,作为雇主,必须从支付给雇员的工资和其他应税报酬中扣除相应的税款。此外,雇主必须支付按雇员(包括董事)的总薪资计算的社会保障缴款。尽职调查过程中将识别与工资税和社会保障缴款相关的风险。

A Dutch BV that is engaged in performing services (i. e. providing cross-border transport services), qualifies as taxable person for Value Added Tax (VAT). A VAT is imposed on supplies of goods and services made by taxable persons for VAT at every stage of the production and distribution process. In order to prevent accumulation of the tax at subsequent stages, the general principle of the VAT mechanism is that entrepreneurs are entitled to deduct the VAT paid on the purchase of goods and services, which they use for taxable business purposes (input VAT), from the VAT due on supplies of goods and services made to third parties (output VAT). In a due diligence process the risks regarding the VAT will be identified.

作为一家从事提供服务(即提供跨境运输服务)的荷兰私营公司,该公司是增值税的缴纳主体。增值税是对销售货物或者提供服务的主体在生产和分销过程的每个阶段征收的。为了防止在后续阶段积累税收,增值税机制的一般原则是企业有权从向第三方提供的商品和服务支付的增值税(销项增值税)中扣除因购买商品和服务而支付的且用于纳税业务目的的增值税(进项增值税)。尽职调查过程中应识别与增值税相关的风险。

In general, the Dutch tax authority can make corrections to the declared and assessed corporate income tax position of the Dutch target company for 5 years. As a tax liability of the Dutch BV is not influenced by the change in shareholder, in a due diligence process it is therefore necessary to assess the Dutch BV's tax position of at least the last 5 years.

一般而言,荷兰税务机关可以对荷兰目标公司5年来经申报和评估的企业所得税税率进行更正。由于荷兰私营公司的税务责任不受股东变动的影响,因此在尽职调查过程中,有必要评估荷兰私营公司至少在过去5年的税务状况。

Apart from the due diligence process and negotiating warranties/indemnities, it is also important to assess the international tax position after the acquisitions of the shares. Including if the shareholder structure is optimized from a tax perspective that future dividend distributions are exempt from dividend withholding tax in the Netherlands, and if a future disposal of the shares in the Dutch BV is also exempt from Dutch taxation. or If the potential Dutch tax benefits can be further utilized by the acquiring group now a Dutch presence is available in the group or not.

除了尽职调查程序和对保证/赔偿条款进行谈判，在收购股份后评估国际税务状况也很重要。即股权结构是否从税收的角度优化，使未来的股息分配在荷兰免除股息预扣税，未来出售荷兰私营公司的股份是否也免除荷兰税收，或者因为现在该集团中已经有荷兰公司的存在，收购集团是否可以进一步利用潜在的荷兰税收优惠。

China and the Netherlands have concluded a tax treaty to avoid double taxation. Besides avoiding double taxation, the treaty mainly provides a lowered tax rate of 10% (or 5%) on income paid by a company in one state to a company in the other, such as dividends. Based on Dutch domestic law, dividends distributed by Dutch companies are in principle subject to dividend withholding tax at a rate of 15%. In most cases however, Dutch companies are exempt from dividend withholding tax when a tax treaty is concluded with the state in which the recipient is situated (such as the treaty with China) and the shareholder in China is engaged in business activities. We also provide post-acquisition tax advice regarding for example supply chain optimization.

中国和荷兰缔结了一项税收条约，以避免双重征税。除了避免双重征税，该条约还主要规定了一个较低的所得税率10%（或5%），以适用于一个国家的公司向另一个国家的公司支付的如股息等收入。根据荷兰国内法律，荷兰公司分配的股息原则上须缴纳15%的股息预扣税。但是，在大多数情况下，当与收款人所在国签订税收协定，例如与中国的条约，并且中国的股东从事商业活动时，荷兰公司可免除股息预扣税。我们还提供有关供应链优化的收购后税务建议。

7. 荷兰外商直接投资规则（Foreign Direct Investment Rules in the Netherlands）

The EU foreign investment screening regulation [Regulation (EU) 2019/452] establishing a framework for the screening of foreign direct investments into the European Union regulates foreign direct investment (FDI) in companies which have an establishment in a member state of the EU, including the Netherlands. The Regulation has direct effect in the Dutch legal system, but it nevertheless requires elaboration in Dutch national law.

《欧盟外商投资审查条例》（第2019/452号条例）建立了欧盟外商直接投资监管框架，对在欧盟成员国（包括荷兰）设立机构的公司的外商直接投资（FDI）进行监管。该条例在荷兰法律体系中具有直接效力，但仍需在荷兰国内法中加以阐述。

7.1 欧盟第2019/452号条例的内容（Content of EU Regulation 2019/452）

The regulation supports EU Member States in screening investments that can affect national security or the public order. The Regulation also provides for a number of criteria and areas that EU Member States can draw on in establishing national FDI legislation and in determining whether an investment is likely to affect national security or the public order.

该条例支持欧盟成员国审查可能影响国家安全或公共秩序的投资。该条例还规定了欧盟成员国在制定国家外商直接投资立法和确定投资是否可能影响国家安全或公共秩序时可以借鉴的一些标准和范围。

7.2（未来）荷兰外商直接投资制度的内容 [Content of the (future) Dutch FDI regime]

The Dutch Minister for Economic Affairs (or its implementing bodies) is expected to act as the enforcement body of FDI-legislation. The Dutch legislator has drafted a legislative proposal (The proposal is Economy and National Security Screening Bill, hereinafter "Bill") regarding the creation of a general screening mechanism for FDI. This screening mechanism applies to transactions that cause a change in control within one or more undertakings in the Netherlands that are considered responsible for vital economic processes or that are active on the market for sensitive technology (including dual use technology). Any change in control in those types of companies by foreign investors has to be notified to the Minister for Economic Affairs. The Minister will subsequently take a screening decision within eight weeks. This term can be extended to six months. The Minister can, in case of threats to national security, choose to allow a notified transaction under specific terms, or (if this is deemed insufficient to remedy the threats), to prohibit the notified transaction. Any action that infringes the screening decision is considered void.

预计荷兰经济事务部（或其执行机构）将充当外商直接投资法的执行机构。荷兰立法者正在起草关于建立外商直接投资一般审查机制的立法提案（《经济和国家安全审查法案》，以下简称法案）。此审查机制适用于在荷兰被认为负责重要的经济流程或活跃于敏感技术（包括双重用途技术）市场上的一个或多个企业内导致控制权发生变化的交易。外国投资者在这类公司中控制权的任何变化都必须告知经济事务部。该部随后将在八周内作出审查决定。这个期限可以延长至六个月。在国家安全受到威胁的情况下，该部可以选择允许按照特定条款进行公开交易，或者（如果认为这不足以补救威胁）禁止公开交易。任何违反审查决定的行为均被视为无效。

The Bill is at the moment still in the legislative process. Once the Bill will go into force it will be retroactively applicable to investments made since 2 June 2020. The Dutch government admits that retroactive intrusion in the ownership of companies is a harsh measure and will therefore only be used in circumstances in which the public threat of an investment outweighs the intrusiveness of the act.

该法案目前仍在立法过程中。一旦该法案生效，它将追溯适用于自2020年6月2日以来的投资。荷兰政府承认，该法案追溯适用于公司所有权的做法是一项严厉的措施，因此只有在特定投资的公共威胁超过该法案的侵犯性标准的情况下才会适用。

The Bill focuses on three areas when deciding whether national security is at stake：

在判断特定交易是否危及国家安全时，该法案着重于考量三个方面：

- Critical infrastructure (vital infrastructure is the term used in the Bill). The relevant areas are specified on the website of the National Coordinator for Counterterrorism and Security (NCCS) but can be further elaborated by a governmental decree;

●关键基础设施领域（关键基础设施是本法案中使用的术语）。有关领域在荷兰国家安全和反恐协调局（NCCS）的网站上有详细说明，但政府可以通过颁布法令的形式对该领域的范围作出进一步解释；

● Critical processes (vital processes is the term used in the Bill). The relevant areas are specified on the website of the NCCS but can be further elaborated by a governmental decree; and

●关键流程（关键流程是本法案中使用的术语）。有关领域已在NCCS网站上明确，但可能为政府法令进一步解释；以及

● Critical technology (sensitive technology is the term used in the Bill). This includes the dual use of strategically important products that are subject to export checks under Regulation (EU) 428/2009.

●关键技术（敏感技术是本法案中使用的术语）。其包括具有战略意义的产品的双重使用，这些产品必须根据欧盟法规（EU）428/2009进行出口检查。

The Bill does not discriminate between sensitive investments from within the national territory, the European internal market or third countries: the Dutch regime can apply to all investments regardless of the source.

该法案并未区分来自本国、欧洲内部市场或第三方国家的敏感投资：荷兰的外商投资审查机制可以适用于所有投资，无论其来源。

7.3 上述提及的内容对物流市场的影响（The Influence of the Aforementioned Information on the Market of Logistics）

The area of logistics concerns the stream of goods and the distribution of these goods. This means that the market of logistics is a wide market encompassing all kinds of different sectors. This could put investors in the area of logistics in the crosshairs of a sector that is considered to be part of essential infrastructure or to incorporate essential processes or sensitive technology. For instance, in the Netherlands both the harbor of Rotterdam and the airport of Schiphol comprise vital infrastructure.

物流领域涉及货物流和这些货物的分配。这意味着物流市场是一个广泛的市场，包括各种不同的部门。这可能使物流领域的投资者成为被视为重要基础设施一部分或纳入关键流程或敏感技术的部门的焦点。例如，在荷兰，鹿特丹港和史基浦机场都是重要的基础设施。

8. 其他问题与解决方案（Other Issues and Relevant Solutions）

Other issues which we come across when assisting our Chinese clients are:

The fact that in many transactions time is of the essence; a swift follow-up/turn-around of the different versions of the transaction documentation is key. In case of Chinese buyers, specific approvals are required. Especially in case of auction processes, this may prejudice the possibility to buy the target company since for local purchasers have less mandatory internal approvals.

在服务中国客户时遇到的其他问题是：

在许多交易中，时间至关重要；对不同版本的交易文件的快速跟进或者传递是关键。如果是中国买家，则需要某些经特别批准的手续。特别是在拍卖过程中，这可能会降低购买目标公司的可能性，因为本地购买者具有较少的强制性内部批准。

To avoid frustration/lost of trust it is key to be transparent at an early stage already regarding specific approvals from for example Chinese authorities or the parent company.

为了避免焦虑或者彼此失去信任，必须在收购的早期阶段对中国相关主管机关或母公司批准交易的具体进展保持及时、坦诚沟通。

In our experience it is essential to have someone who can speak Chinese and understands the cultural differences; in almost all transactions we are not only advising on civil law and tax law, but we are also bridging cultural gaps.

根据我们的经验，有一个能说中文并了解文化差异的人是（交易中）必不可少的；在几乎所有的交易中，我们不仅在民法和税法方面提供法律服务，还进行弥合文化差异的工作。

— 作者简介 —

Jeroen Pop is Corporate/M&A partner at AKD. Together with Ivo Vreman, he is heading the China Desk of AKD. Over the years, Jeroen has been involved in commercial contracting (such as distribution agreements, agency agreements, supply agreements etc.), joint ventures, M&A deals, cross border restructurings and investments and Jeroen advises on corporate governance. Jeroen mainly works in an international environment with a focus on Asia.

Jeroen Pop 是 AKD 律师事务所的合伙人，工作领域为公司/并购。他和 Ivo Vreman 一起负责管理 AKD 中国办公室。多年来，Jeroen 一直专注于商业领域的合同制定业务（如分销协议、代理协议、供应协议等）、合资企业、并购交易、跨境重组和投资业务，并为公司治理提供法律顾问服务。Jeroen 主要专注于国际市场业务，并重点关注亚洲地区的法律业务。

Ivo Vreman specialises in providing tax advice to companies with international operations. Ivo's practice has a broad focus and he advises on matters such as international restructuring, mergers, takeovers, setting up joint ventures and the tax implications of inter-company transactions.

Ivo Vreman 专注于为开展国际业务的公司提供税务咨询。Ivo 的工作领域非常广泛，在跨境重组、合并、收购、合资企业设立以及公司间交易的税务安排等领域提供法律顾问服务。

Joost Houdijk specializes at AKD in European and Competition law. Joost advises and litigates on cartels and abuse of a dominant position. He regularly assists companies with filing notifications for mergers and acquisitions with the European Commission and the Dutch Authority for Consumers and Markets (ACM). In addition to competition law, Joost's field of work also covers EU law on free movement, EU transportation law and consumer protection law.

Joost Houdijk 是 AKD 的律师，隶属于欧盟和竞争法团队。他就卡特尔安排和滥用支配地位问题提供咨询和诉讼服务，还经常协助企业向欧盟委员会和荷兰消费者与市场管理局（ACM）提交兼并申报。除竞争法外，Joost 还擅长外国直接投资（FDI）监管，执业领域还包括欧盟自由流动法、欧盟运输法和消费者保护法。

AKD Benelux lawyers（AKD） is the independent and internationally focused legal and tax advisor for any business dealing with the Benelux countries, with 450 lawyers, civil law notaries, tax advisors and staff. AKD combines expertise in all legal practice areas with sector knowledge and understanding of the clients' business, both nationally and internationally. Outside the Benelux, AKD partners with an extensive network of highly reputable law firms to form fully integrated, experienced and multidisciplinary teams. With this collaborative approach, AKD can comprehensively assist her clients in doing business around the globe. AKD has a dedicated China desk, including native speakers. The Desk helps Chinese clients to navigate the Benelux. At the same time, AKD's China Desk advises Dutch companies on expanding to China.

AKD 比荷卢经济联盟律师事务所（以下简称 AKD 律师事务所）是一家独立的、国际化的事务所，拥有 450 名律师、民法公证人、税务顾问和员工为所有与比荷卢联盟国家有交易往来的企业提供法律顾问服务。AKD 律师事务所将其在不同领域的法律实践经验与丰富的行业知识储备和对国内外客户业务的充分了解结合起来。在比荷卢联盟国家区域之外，AKD 律师事务所与其他知名律师事务所建立广泛紧密的合作关系，形成完全一体化、经验丰富和跨领域跨学科的专业团队。通过这种合作方式，AKD 律师事务所可以为客户提供全球范围内的全面法律服务。AKD 律师事务所在中国设立了一个办公室，该办公室中也有母语为中文的律师。该办公室可以为中国客户提供比荷卢联盟国家范围内的业务引导。与此同时，AKD 律师事务所的中国办公室也同样为想要将业务范围扩大到中国的荷兰公司提供法律顾问服务。

投资在德国：并购德国工程服务公司
Investments in Germany
Acquisition of a German engineering services company

点评

德国是世界领先的工程机械制造强国，德国企业在机械和机械工程领域具备深厚实力和竞争优势，对中国企业产生了巨大的吸引力。

本文作者具备为中国企业在德国航空工程领域投资提供法律服务的经验，对中国投资者在德国投资需要关注的事项进行了详细的阐释。相较于常规的投资并购流程，在德国投资还涉及德国当地的一些特殊要求，值得赴德投资时注意，具体包括：

其一，有限责任公司的股份出售/转让协议涉及公证程序。公证的范围涵盖各方之间的全部商业协议，如未能涵盖全部商业协议，则可能导致经过公证的协议（包括股份转让协议）无效等严重后果。德国公证规则还要求参加公证的人员应能理解公证协议的内容，否则可能影响协议的签署，这对各方参与公证人员的语言能力等提出了一定要求。

其二，德国当地的审批程序，较为常见的是外国投资控制和经营者集中申报程序。德国的外国投资控制分为特定行业和跨行业的外国投资控制制度，前者适用于对国家安全至关重要的行业，且适用于欧盟国家和非欧盟国家的投资者；后者适用于某些与民用安全有关的行业，若来自非欧盟且非欧洲自由贸易区国家的投资者直接或间接获得该德国目标公司至少10%的投票权，则该交易适用跨行业外国投资控制制度。但是，无论德国目标公司处于哪一行业，如果非欧盟和非欧洲自由贸易区收购方对公司的任何收购导致买方直接或间接获得德国目标公司至少25%的投票权，都可能受到跨行业外国投资控制审查。近年来，德国立法机构采取行动加强了主管部门在外国投资控制方面的权力，加大了对于未履行申报义务或者未获得审批的交易的处罚力度,本文作者在文中进行了详细论述。因此投资者需根据交易具体情况就可能涉及的程序进行关注并做好相关安排,避免因未能履行相关程序影响交易进程。德国作为欧盟国家,经营者集中申报程序同样分为德国层面和欧盟层面,在实施投资前需要确认是否可能触发经营者集中申报程序,以及可能触发何种层面的申报程序。

1. 简介（Introduction）

1.1 德国工程行业（The German Engineering Sector）

Germany is synonymous for cutting-edge engineering, not only in terms of mechanical and electronic engineering, but also of chemical, pharmaceutical and civil engineering. Mechanical engineering products and products from electrical and optical manufacturing processes are particularly successful all over the world. The phrase "Made in Germany" combines German virtues such as reliability and adherence to schedules with a commitment to quality and sustainability.

德国是尖端工程的代名词,这不仅体现在机械和电子工程方面,还体现在化学、制药和土木工程方面。德国的机械工程产品以及电气和光学制造产品享誉世界。"德国制造"一词包含着德国的优秀品质,这些品质包括可靠性、严格遵守日程,以及对质量和可持续性的保证。

Germany's strong power in terms of mechanical and machinery engineering does not only appear in the automotive industry, Germany's most prominent industry sector, but also in the aerospace industry, which has achieved great success over the last two decades. Since the mid-1990's, industry revenues have more than quadrupled-to over EUR 40 billion in 2019. The German aerospace industry employs around 114 000 workers, half of which are engineers or highly qualified professionals. Germany's mix of a solid manufacturing power, ready availability of talents, and cost efficiency are unique competitive advantages to develop cutting-edge technologies for the growing aviation demand.

德国在机械和机械工程方面的强大实力不仅体现在德国最突出的工业领

域——汽车行业中，还体现在航空航天行业中，后者在过去的二十年中取得了巨大的成功。自20世纪90年代中期以来，航空航天行业收入增长了三倍多，到2019年已超过400亿欧元。德国航空航天行业雇用了大约114 000名工人，其中一半是工程师或高素质的专业人员。德国拥有强大的制造能力、随时可用的人才以及低成本高效率，这些成为满足不断增长的航空需求而开发尖端技术的独特竞争优势。

As China seeks to expand its national footprint in the aerospace industry and to catch up to global champions such as Airbus and Boeing, German engineering companies with knowledge in the aerospace sector have become attractive to Chinese strategic investors. Hence, this article will provide insights on a corresponding acquisition project as well as on particularities foreign and Chinese investors typically face when acquiring German companies.

随着中国寻求扩大其在航空航天领域的国家影响力并追赶空客和波音等全球领军企业，在航空航天领域有丰富知识储备的德国工程公司已经对中国投资者产生吸引力。因此，本文将对相应的收购项目以及外国和中国投资者在收购德国公司时通常面临的细节问题提供见解。

1.2 中方对德投资（Chinese Investments in Germany）

With the integration of global economy and political support of China itself ("going out policy"), annual investments by Chinese companies in European countries soared from virtually zero in the mid-2000's to EUR 72 billion in 2016, up 188% from EUR 25 billion in 2015.

随着全球经济的一体化和中国自身的政策支持（"走出去政策"），中国公司在欧盟国家的年度投资额从2000年中期几乎为零，猛增至2016年的720亿欧元，比2015年的250亿欧元增长了188%。

Germany is the second largest recipient of Chinese foreign direct investment in Europe, with investments in the period from 2000 to 2015 adding up to almost EUR 8 billion. In 2016, foreign direct investments experienced a dramatic rise to an unprecedented height of around EUR 11 billion in only one year. This increase was mainly driven by individual major transactions, like the takeover of the leading robot manufacturer *Kuka* by *Midea* for EUR 4.6 billion.

德国是中国对欧直接投资的第二大接受国，2000年至2015年的投资总额接近80亿欧元。2016年，中国对欧直接投资在短短一年内急剧增长，达到约110亿欧元的空前水平。增长主要是由个别重大交易推动的，例如 Midea 以46亿欧元收购了领先的机器人制造商 Kuka。

Germany's advanced manufacturing capabilities were the biggest attraction for Chinese investors with automotive and industrial equipment accounting for around two thirds of total Chinese investments since 2000. But also the healthcare sector, IT equipment, finance and business services as well as consumer products are waking interest in more recent years. The focus of Chinese investors has shifted from the acquisition of insolvent companies to strategic investments into multinational companies with ownership of leading technology.

德国先进的制造能力对中国投资者最具吸引力。自2000年以来，对汽车和工业设备的投资额约占中国在德国投资总额的三分之二。但是近年来，保健、IT设备、金融和商业服务以及消费品领域也引起了中国投资者的兴趣。中国投资者的重心已从收购资不抵债的公司转向战略性地投资拥有领先技术的跨国公司。

M&A acquisitions and greenfield projects are the main ways to invest in Germany and Europe, with the majority of investments being made through M&A acquisitions. Further, instead of mega mergers, most deals in Germany were small and medium sized takeovers, with state-owned companies accounting for a higher share of investments than in the European average.

并购和绿地投资项目是在德国乃至在欧洲投资的主要方式，其中大部分投资是通过并购进行的。此外，在德国投资的大多数交易都是中小型收购而非大型并购，国有公司在投资中所占比例高于欧洲平均水平。

After 2016, Chinese foreign direct investments in Europe experienced a sharp decline. In Europe, the volume of Chinese direct investments decreased by 45% to EUR 26 billion in 2018 compared to EUR 48 billion in 2017. In 2019, investments of only EUR 14 billion were made. In 2020, Chinese foreign direct investments in Europe further decreased to only 1.3 billion, presumably also a consequence of the ongoing COVID-19 pandemic.

2016年之后，中国对欧直接投资急剧下降。中国对欧直接投资总额从2017年的480亿欧元下降到2018年的260亿欧元，下降了45%。2019年投资总额仅为 140 亿欧元。2020 年中国对欧直接投资进一步下降至 13 亿欧元。这一下降可能也是受到新冠疫情的影响。

Germany accounted for around 26% (EUR 3.8 billion) of China's total foreign direct investments in Europe in 2019, declining for the third consecutive year after 2016 (not taking into account the share acquisition of 9.7% in Daimler by Chinese carmaker Geely). In 2020, the volume of Chinese investments in Germany was just EUR 316 million. Besides, some divestments of shares previously bought in Europe appeared since 2018.

2019 年，德国占中国对欧直接投资总额的 26%左右（38 亿欧元），继 2016 年之后连续三年下降（不考虑中国汽车制造商吉利收购戴姆勒 9.7%的股份）。2020 年，中国在德国的投资额仅为 3.16 亿欧元。此外，自 2018 年以来在欧洲出现了一些撤资的现象。

One of the reasons for this trend is that the German government is more and more critical towards Chinese investments in sensitive technology and critical infrastructure, with the 2018 failed acquisitions of mechanical engineering company Leifeld and state grid operator 50 Hertz by Chinese investors serving as illustrative examples. The regulatory framework for foreign investments into Germany and the EU therefore becomes tighter in recent years.

出现这种趋势的原因之一是德国政府对中国在敏感技术和关键基础设施方面的投资要求越来越严格，中国投资者在 2018 年对德国机械工程公司 Leifeld 和国家电网运营商 50 赫兹的收购失败就是例证。因此，近年来，德国和欧盟的外国投资监管框架变得更加严格。

At the same time, Chinese foreign exchange control has tightened and a stricter approval process of outbound investments has been implemented in China. A volatile international trade environment, which refers to the trade conflict between China and the USA as well as to Brexit, also contribute to the slowdown of investments in the last years.

同时，中国的外汇管制收紧，国家实施了更严格的境外投资审批程序。动荡的国际贸易环境，例如国家之间的贸易冲突、英国脱欧，也都导致了过去几年投资的放缓。

2. 交易（The Transaction）

2.1 交易概况（Outline of the Transaction）

In 2017, one of our clients is a Chinese state-owned enterprise (SOE) active in the aerospace industry and invested in a German Company active in the aerospace engineering sector. The target's shareholder and seller of the shares is a European group with a focus on services and IT. The acquisition was for 100% of the shares in the target, a limited liability company under German law (GmbH-Gesellschaft mit beschränkter Haftung). The target company has subsidiaries both within Germany and internationally. It supplies testing equipment and provides engineering services to producers of aircrafts as well as suppliers to the aerospace industry.

2017年，我们的客户是一家航空航天业的中国大型国有企业（SOE），投资了一家活跃在航空工程领域的德国公司。目标公司的股东（股份的卖方）是一家专注于服务业和IT业的欧洲集团。此次交易目的是收购目标公司100%的股份，目标公司是一家根据德国法律成立的有限责任公司（有限责任公司，德语为Gesellschaft mit beschränkter Haftung，GmbH）。目标公司在德国境内和全世界范围内均设有子公司。它为飞机制造商和航空航天工业的供应商提供测试设备和工程服务。

2.2 交易文件（Transaction Documents）

At the very beginning of discussions between our client and the seller, the parties entered into a non-disclosure agreement. As in other jurisdictions, entering into a non-disclosure agreement is warranted in Germany to oblige the party receiving information to treat it confidentially, but also under corporate laws and for other compliance reasons (e.g. in terms of antitrust or data protection compliance).

在我们的客户与卖方讨论之初，双方签订了保密协议。与其他司法管辖区一样，在德国必须签署保密协议，以使接收信息的一方有义务根据德国公司法和其他合规原因（例如在反垄断或数据保护合规性方面）对信息进行保密处理。

Once an agreement on the very key parameters of the sale was achieved, the parties signed a term sheet of no more than two pages, containing only key parameters of the deal such as the valuation, transaction structure, process and timeline going forward. In M&A processes that are not competitive auction processes orchestrated by a financial advisor or investment bank, entering into a non-binding pre-contractual agreement is customary. The purpose is to fix at the least the parameters in an agreement that the parties consider so essential that they need to be agreed on to further invest into the project.

就本次交易的关键参数达成一致后，双方签署了一份不超过两页的投资条款清单，其中仅包含交易的关键参数如估值、交易结构、流程和未来时间表等。如果并购不是由财务顾问或投资银行策划的竞争性拍卖，则通常还会签订无约束力的合同前协议，其目的是至少确定协议各方认为至关重要的参数，以便于进一步推进该投资项目。

As our client acquired all shares in the target and as the target did not need to be carved out of a corporate group, the single key transaction document that needed to be negotiated was the share purchase agreement.

由于我们的客户收购了目标公司的所有股份，并且目标公司不需要从公司集团中剥离出来，因此需要协商的唯一关键交易文件就是股份购买协议。

2.3 在德国就股份购买协议进行公证（Notarization of Share Purchase Agreements in Germany）

A particularity of German corporate law is that agreements pertaining to the sale/transfer of shares in a limited liability company need to be notarized by a notary public and this applied to the case of our client. Notarization under German law is not only a fairly unique procedure but also entails a number of practical challenges with respect to the transaction documentation.

德国公司法的一个特点是，涉及有限责任公司的股份出售/转让协议需要由公证人进行公证，我们客户的情况也是如此。根据德国法律，公证是一个较为特殊的程序，而且在交易文件方面也存在许多实际挑战。

Notarization means that the notary public reads out loud every single word of the share purchase agreement, including its annexes (for certain types of annexes, reading them out loud can be omitted, such as lists, maps etc.), in the presence of the parties or their representatives, typically lawyers on the basis of a power of attorney. Notaries that are familiar with M&A transactions will read 20 to 30 pages in an hour if no negotiations take place or major revisions need to be made to the documents during the notarization process. Hence, notarization of an entire set of transaction agreements can often take multiple hours, a full day or even longer.

在德国，公证是指公证人在当事方代表或者授权律师在场的情况下，大声朗读股份购买协议的每个单词，包括其附件（对于某些类型的附件朗读可以省略，例如列表、地图等）。在公证过程中如果不需要进行谈判或对文件进行重大修改，熟悉并购交易的公证员将在一小时内阅读20至30页。因此，整套交易协议的公证通常可能需要几个小时、一整天甚至更长的时间。

Only representatives that have been present (and awake) during the entire notarization can sign the notarial deed that includes the transaction documents. It is not possible for the parties' principals to join the notarization and sign the deed at the last moment.

只有在整个公证过程中在场（并且保持清醒）的代表才能签署包括交易文件的公证书。交易双方的负责人不能在最后时刻加入公证过程并签署契约。

The concept of notarization also entails that the notarial deed has to capture the entire commercial agreement of the parties. If, for instance, the parties agree to terminate shareholder loans, enter into new managing director service agreements, transitional services agreements or similar, such agreements need to be included in the deed to the extent that the parties have already achieved an agreement on their terms. In our case, this meant that it was not sufficient to simply notarize the SPA but that the SPA needed to have, for example, agreements attached that provided a pre-agreed transfer of software and IP rights. In practice, a German SPA often has numerous attachments that include agreed forms of agreements that the parties will enter into in the future. Non-compliance with this requirement (e. g. conclusion of side letters, regardless of whether written, oral or implied) has drastic consequences: The entire notarized agreement is null and void, including the transfer of shares.

在德国，公证的概念还说明公证书必须涵盖各方的全部商业协议。例如，如果双方同意终止股东贷款，订立新的董事总经理服务协议、过渡性服务协议或类似协议，则在双方已就协议的条款达成一致的情况下，需要将这些新签订的协议体现在公证书中。在我们的案例中，这意味着仅对SPA进行公证是不够的，SPA 需要附带提供预先约定的软件和知识产权转让协议等。在实践中，德国的 SPA 通常具有许多附件，其中包括各方将在未来签订协议的各类形式。不遵守这一要求（例如无论是否以书面、口头或是默示方式签署附函）都会产生严重后果：所有经过公证的协议无效，包括股份转让协议。

A further important aspect is that under German notarization rules, all persons present in the notarization need to be able to understand the content of the agreements being notarized. Practically, this means that the agreements may only be in a language all participants have sufficient command of. Usually, this limits the available languages to German and English. If any language is included in the transaction documents that not all persons present in the notarization understand, it is mandatory that the relevant parts are accompanied by a translation (which may only be a convenience translation but not the governing language). For the senior executive of our client that attended the notarization, this meant that he was ultimately not allowed to sign the agreements as the notary was not convinced of his level of English being sufficient to grasp the contents of the SPA and other transaction documents. A practical way to solve this is to have, for example, a German lawyer also attend the entire notarization so that he/she is able to sign on the basis of a power of attorney as a back-up solution.

另一个重要方面是，根据德国公证规则，所有参加公证的人都必须能够理解所被公证协议的内容。实际上，这意味着协议只能使用所有参与者都能理解的语言。协议的可用语言通常被限制为德语和英语。如果交易文件使用的语言不能被所有出席公证的人理解，则相关部分必须附带翻译（该翻译只是为了方便理解，而非作准语言）。对于参加公证的高级主管来说，如果公证人不相信他的英语水平足以掌握 SPA 和其他交易文件的内容，这意味着他最终将无法签署协议。解决此问题的一种实用方法是，比如作为备用解决方案之一，让一名德国律师也参加整个公证，通过授权委托，他/她就能在协议上签字。

Representing corporate parties to an agreement on the basis of a power of attorney is standard in Germany. Yet, under German notarization rules, special standards apply with respect to the form and evidence of documents to be provided. The general standard applicable to a representative of a corporation in a notarization is that the notary has to be "convinced" that the person present in the notarization is duly authorized to represent the corporation.

在德国，根据授权委托书代表各方签订协议是标准做法。但是，根据德国公证规则，对于所提供的文件的形式和证据要适用特殊标准。适用于公证中公司代表的一般标准是，公证人必须"确信"参与公证中的人员已被正式授权，可以代表公司。

For a Chinese limited liability company, this means that if the legal representative attends the notarization, he/she will have to present a legalized copy of the company's business license (showing that he/she is the legal representative) including a translation of the business license into German, such translation to be prepared by a Chinese-German translator that is officially appointed by a German court.

对于中国的有限责任公司，这意味着如果法定代表人参加公证，那么他/她将必须出示公司营业执照的合法副本（以表明他/她是法定代表人），其中要包括公司营业执照的德语译本，译本由德国法院正式任命的中德双语翻译提供。

If the legal representative does not attend himself/herself, the person representing the company on the basis of a power attorney will additionally have to present a power of attorney (in English and/or German) that has been signed by the legal representative at a notary public. The power of attorney needs to be legalized or have an apostille attached (depending on where the notarial certificate is made).

如果法定代表人未亲自出席，则根据授权委托书代表公司的人员还必须出示一份由法定代表人签署的经公证的授权委托书（使用英语、德语或英德双语）。授权委托书应为合法的或有加注认证（这取决于公证书的发证地）。

Lastly, one should point out that notarization costs a fee that is calculated on the basis of the value of the transaction that is notarized. A transaction in the 2-digit million Euro range can cost up to the maximum amount of approx. EUR 100 000 of notarization fees. The notarization fees are customarily borne by the buyer but, of course, it is possible to negotiate a cost-sharing with the seller. In our project, we achieved that the notary's fees were to be borne by the parties equally.

最后，应该指出，公证的费用是根据公证过的交易的价值计算得出的。一笔上千万欧元范围内的交易可能会花费最高约 100 000 欧元的公证费。公证费通常由买方承担，买方可以与卖方协商分担费用。在我们承办的项目中，我们实现了公证费由各方平均承担。

2.4 尽职调查（Due Diligence）

In parallel with discussions on the commercial and legal terms of the transaction, our client carried out financial, tax and legal due diligence. As our client was familiar with the target company, its business and employees through being a customer for several years, some customary due diligence areas were omitted (e.g. HR, technical due diligence). In the legal due diligence, we identified several risk areas in the field of regulatory issues (federal security clearances in the context of working for state-owned aircraft manufacturers and their suppliers) and IP (ownership of copyrights in software that is essential to the business).

在讨论交易的商业和法律条款的同时，我们的客户进行了财务、税务和法律方面的尽职调查。由于我们的客户作为目标公司多年的合作伙伴，对其业务和员工都很熟悉，因此我们在一些常规领域省略了尽职调查（例如人力资源和技术尽职调查）。在法律尽职调查中，我们确定了在监管（在为国有飞机制造商及其供应商工作时的联邦安全许可）和知识产权（对企业至关重要的软件著作权）方面的几个风险领域。

In order to ensure that some issues were rectified prior to the acquisition of the target company by our client, the SPA included corresponding closing conditions. As other risks identified were difficult to quantify, our client did not request a purchase price deduction for such issues but relied on representations and warranties as well as specific indemnities for identified risks.

为确保在我们的客户收购目标公司之前弥补某些疏漏，SPA 包含了相应的交割条件。由于其他确定的风险难以量化，我们的客户并未因此类风险而要求降低购买价格，而是选择使用陈述和保证以及针对确定风险的特定赔偿条款来控制风险。

3. 监管备案（Regulatory Filings）

3.1 德国的外国投资控制（German Foreign Investment Control）

One major issue foreign investors are regularly confronted with when acquiring German companies is German foreign investment control. In more recent years, this particularly applies to Chinese investors.

外国投资者收购德国公司时经常遇到的一个主要问题是德国对外国投资的控制。近年来，这尤其适用于中国投资者的情况。

Under German foreign investment control law, the Federal Ministry of Economic Affairs and Energy (the "Ministry") may review acquisitions of German companies by a foreign acquirer. Two different regimes need tobe distinguished: a sector-specific foreign investment control regime and a cross-sectoral foreign investment control regime.

根据德国的外国投资控制法，联邦经济事务和能源部（即下文中"主管部门"）可以审查外国收购方对德国公司的收购。在此，需要区分两种不同的审查制度：特定行业的外国投资控制制度和跨行业的外国投资控制制度。

3.1.1 特定行业的外国投资控制（Sector-specific foreign investment control）

The sector-specific foreign investment control regime applies to direct or indirect acquisitions of at least 10% of voting rights by a foreign acquirer if the German target company is active in an especially security-critical industry, such as the production or development of war weapons and military equipment, or IT security products for the processing of classified government information. The sector-specific foreign investment control applies to both acquisitions by investors from EU countries and acquisitions by investors from non-EU countries. Acquisitions subject to the sector-specific foreign investment control require an approval by the Ministry. Under German law, closing of the intended transaction is subject to the condition of such approval and thus, the underlying legal transaction is provisionally ineffective until the approval is granted. The SPA will therefore usually contain a corresponding closing condition.

如果德国目标公司主要业务是对安全至关重要的行业（例如，战争武器的生产或开发，或用于处理机密政府信息的军事设备或IT安全产品），当外国收购方直接或间接收购该目标公司至少10%的投票权时，则适用特定行业的外国投资控制制度。该制度既适用于来自欧盟国家的投资者的收购，也适用于来自非欧盟国家的投资者的收购。适用特定行业外国投资控制制度的收购需要获得主管部门的批准。根据德国法律，预期交易的交割完成取决于获得批准的条件是否满足，在获得批准之前，基础法律交易暂时无效。因此，SPA通常将包含相应的交割条件。

In addition, the provisions on "gun-jumping" prohibit behavior that can be interpreted as an anticipated closing, e.g. the exercise of voting rights in the target by the buyer, the granting of profit claims of the target for pre-closing periods or the provision of information to the buyer that the Ministry classifies as being important for essential security interests of the Federal Republic of Germany or for public security and order in Germany. A violation of the gun-jumping prohibition can be criminal behavior and fined or sanctioned with a prison sentence of up to five years.

此外，属于"抢跑"的禁止行为可以被解释为完成预期成交行为，例如，买方行使目标公司的表决权，要求获得目标公司在交割完成前期间取得的利润，或向买方提供主管部门认为对德国基本安全利益或公共安全秩序具有重要意义的信息。违反"抢跑"禁令的行为可能构成刑事犯罪，将被处以罚金或最高5年的监禁。

If the sector-specific foreign investment control regime is applicable, the buyer is obliged to report the acquisition in writing to the Ministry. Such reporting must include the acquirer and the German target company, and outline the fields of business in which the acquirer and the German target company are active. If the Ministry does not initiate a formal review procedure within two months from the receipt of the buyer's written notification, the acquisition is deemed to have been approved.

如果适用特定行业的外国投资控制制度，则买方有义务以书面形式向主管部门报告收购情况。该等报告必须包括收购方和德国目标公司，并概述收购方和德国目标公司活跃的业务领域。如果主管部门在收到买方的书面通知后的两个月内未启动正式的审查程序，则视为收购已获批准。

The Ministry may, however, decide to initiate a formal review procedure prior to the expiration of this two-month period. Such review then considers whether the respective acquisition poses a threat to essential security interests of the Federal Republic of Germany. If a review procedure is opened, the acquirer is obliged to submit further documents and the Ministry may expressly approve, restrict or prohibit the acquisition within four months after the full set of documents has been submitted.

但是，主管部门可能决定在这两个月期限到期之前启动正式的审查程序。此类审查将考虑相应的收购是否将对德意志联邦共和国的基本安全利益构成威胁。如果启动了审查程序，则收购方有义务进一步提交文件，而主管部门可在提交全套文件后的四个月内明确批准、限制或禁止此收购行为。

3.1.2 跨行业外国投资控制（Cross-sectoral foreign investment control）

Even if the intended transaction is not subject to the sector-specific foreign investment control regime, it may still be subject to the cross-sectoral foreign investment control regime.

即使预期交易不受特定行业外国投资控制制度的约束，也仍可能受跨行业外国投资控制制度的约束。

A transaction is subject to the cross-sectoral foreign investment control, and the parties to the transaction are obliged to notify the Ministry of the transaction, if an investor from a non-EU and non-EFTA country directly or indirectly acquires at least 10% of the voting rights in a German target company being active in certain civilian security-relevant sectors ("Notifiable Acquisition"). Such sectors, so-called "critical infrastructure" industries, include energy, water, food, telecommunications, cloud computing services, transport, finance, insurance, healthcare and media. In response to the COVID-19 pandemic, the catalogue of critical infrastructure industries was particularly extended to also cover inter alia personal protective equipment and certain pharmaceuticals including relevant raw materials and active ingredients.

如果德国目标公司活跃在某些与民用安全有关的行业，若来自非欧盟且非欧洲自由贸易区国家的投资者试图直接或间接获得该德国目标公司至少10%的投票权，则该交易适用跨行业外国投资控制制度，交易各方有义务将交易情况通知主管部门即须申报交易。前述行业即"关键基础设施"行业，包括能源、水、食品、电信、云计算服务、运输、金融、保险、医疗保健和媒体。作为新冠疫情的应对举措，"关键基础设施"行业还将个人防护设备和特别药品（包括相关原材料和活性成分）也包括进去。

As with acquisitions subject to the sector-specific foreign investment control, the consummation of notifiable acquisitions is subject to the condition precedent of clearance the Ministry or the time-periods for review having expired. The prohibition on gun-jumping also applies to notifiable acquisitions.

与特定行业外国投资管制一样，负有申报义务的交易的完成也必须经主管部门批准，或等待审查期限到期。禁止"抢跑"的规定也适用于须申报的交易。

Moreover, irrespective of the German target company's business activities, any acquisition of a company by a non-EU and non-EFTA acquirer in which the buyer directly or indirectly acquires at least 25% of voting rights in a German company may be subjected to a cross-sectoral foreign investment control review. However, in these cases, no approval or notification requirement applies. The Ministry may, within two months after gaining knowledge of the signing of the transaction agreement (five years after signing at the latest), initiate a formal in-depth review of the transaction. This review may potentially result in restrictions or even a prohibition of the transaction for reasons of public order or security.

此外，无论德国目标公司处于哪一行业，如果非欧盟和非欧洲自由贸易区收购方对公司的任何收购行为将导致买方直接或间接获得德国目标公司至少25%的投票权，都可能受到跨行业外国投资控制审查。在这些情况下，无需通知主管部门也无需经其审批。但是主管部门在获悉有关交易协议签署情况后两个月内（最迟在签署后的五年内），可以对交易进行正式的深入审查。此审查可能会导致交易基于公共秩序或安全原因被限制甚至禁止。

As an acquisition could potentially be prohibited even five years after signing of the transaction agreement, investors often voluntarily apply to the Ministry for a binding certificate of non-objection prior to the intended acquisition in order to obtain more deal certainty. If the Ministry does not initiate a formal in-depth review within two months after receipt of such an application, the certificate is deemed to have been issued.

即使在签署交易协议的五年后，收购也可能会被禁止，所以投资者通常会在计划收购之前自愿向主管部门申请签发具有约束力的无异议证书，以使交易更加确定。如果该部门在收到此类申请后的两个月内未启动正式的深入审查，则视为无异议证书已签发。

Foreign investments can be restricted or prohibited if the acquisition "potentially impairs" public order or security. This criterion replaced the previous requirement of an actual threat to the public order or security. The scope of review not only covers the public order or security of the Federal Republic of Germany but also of other EU member states and in relation to certain EU projects and programs. A factor that is relevant for many Chinese acquirers is that in determining whether an acquisition "potentially impairs" public order or security, the Ministry may (among other factors) particularly take into account whether the buyer is controlled by a state, government or military forces, including by way of financing or ownership of the buyer.

如果投资"可能会损害"公共秩序或安全就可能被限制或者禁止。这一标准取代了从前的标准,即实际威胁公共秩序或安全。审查的考量范围不仅包括德国还包括其他欧盟成员国的公共秩序或安全,并且涉及欧盟项目和计划。在判断一项收购是否"可能会损害"公共秩序或安全时,主管部门可能会特别考虑买方是否由国家、政府或军队控制,例如拥有买方所有权或者通过资金控制。这一点是中国收购方需要关注的。

If an in-depth review procedure is opened, the acquirer is obliged to submit further documents. The Ministry may either issue a certificate of non-objection or restrict or prohibit the acquisition within four months after the full set of documents has been submitted.

如果启动了深入审查程序,收购方有义务提交进一步的文件。主管部门可以在完整文件提交后的四个月内签发无异议证书或限制或禁止收购。

During the review period for acquisitions that do not qualify as Notifiable Acquisitions, the underlying legal transaction is effective, however, the transaction agreement is under the statutory condition subsequent that the Ministry prohibits the transaction, with the consequence that the contract has to be unwound in case of an actual prohibition by the Ministry.

对无需申报的交易进行审查的期间,基础交易是有效的,但是相关交易协议是受到主管部门可能会禁止交易这一法定后决条件影响的,如果交易被主管部门禁止,则交易协议必须被解除。

3.1.3 计算持股比例(Calculation of thresholds)

For the calculation of the thresholds of 10% and 25% for foreign investment control, the voting rights of shareholders (even on different levels of shareholdings) which are directly or indirectly affiliated or which have concluded any kind of agreement on the joint exercise of voting rights have to be attributed to each other. In addition, dilution rules do not apply under German foreign investment control law and therefore, the thresholds are to be applied on each level of shareholding, i.e. on a non-diluted basis.

在计算外国投资控制中10%和25%的持股比例时,应当将直接或间接有关联关系或已就联合行使表决达成任何协议的股东的投票权一并计算，即使相关股东持股水平的级别不同。此外，稀释规则不适用于德国外国投资控制法，因此，该等持股比例适用于各级别持股水平，即应在非稀释基础上计算。

3.1.4 德国外国投资控制法的近期发展（Recent developments in German foreign investment control law）

German foreign investment control law has been continually tightened in the past few years. In 2017, the German legislator considerably extended the review periods for the Ministry and introduced reporting obligations for the cross-sectoral foreign investment control for transactions taking place in critical infrastructure industries.

德国的外国投资控制法近年来持续收紧。2017 年，德国立法机构大幅延长了主管部门的审查时间，并对适用跨行业外国投资控制制度且发生在关键基础设施行业内的并购交易施加了强制报告义务。

Then, in the end of 2018, German lawmakers again saw a need for action and strengthened the power of the Ministry in terms of foreign investment control. While foreign investments in the area of critical infrastructures and foreign investments that fall under the sector-specific foreign investment control regime were subject to control by the Ministry once shares with voting rights of at least 25% are acquired, this threshold was lowered to 10% in the course of the amendment of German foreign investment control law in 2018. This means that non-EU and non-EFTA acquirers of at least 10% of the voting rights in a German company incritical infrastructure industries are now obliged to notify the Ministry and that acquisitions of at least 10% of the voting rights in a German company active in an especially security-critical industry by EU and non-EU buyers now require the Ministry's approval. At the same time, the area of critical infrastructures was extended by including, for example, media industry companies, the definition of which is relatively open and provides the Ministry with a broad discretion as to whether or not a critical infrastructure is concerned. In the course of the latest amendments in 2020, healthcare and infection protection as well as public communication infrastructures were added to the catalogue of critical infrastructure industries. Moreover, the gun-jumping prohibition backed by criminal sanctions was introduced and the requirement of obtaining prior approval was extended to transactions in civil security-relevant sectors.

随后，在 2018 年年底，德国立法机构再次意识到采取行动的必要性，并加强了主管部门在外国投资控制方面的权力。原先，在"关键基础设施"行业的外国投资和适用特定行业外国投资控制制度下的外国投资，一旦获得德国目标公司至少 25% 的投票权，就会受到主管部门的控制，而在 2018 年修订的德国外国投资控制法中，这一持股比例降至 10%。这意味着，在"关键基础设施"行业中，获得德国公司至少 10% 投票权的非欧盟和非欧洲自由贸易区的收购方，现在有义务通知主管部门交易情况；获得一家活跃在对安全至关重要的行业的德国公司至少 10% 投票权的欧盟和非欧盟的收购方，现在需要获得主管部门的批准才可进行交易。同时，德国立法机构对"关键基础设施"行业的定义进行了扩展，例如包括媒体公司，而媒体公司的定义是相对开放的，这为主管部门提供了判断是否涉及"关键基础设施"的广泛自由裁量权。最近的 2020 年法律修订，在"关键基础设施"中还增加了保健防疫和公共通信基础设施。此外交易获得批准前的"抢跑"行为需要承担刑事责任，且需要获得批准的交易扩大至民事安全相关行业。

According to the newly published draft of the upcoming 17th amendment of the Foreign Trade and Payment Ordinance, once again the scope of German foreign investment control will be further extended by adding industries like AI, robotics, semiconductors, biotechnology and quantum technology as a new category called "critical technology", such businesses to be treated in the same way as companies active in "critical infrastructure".

根据最新公布的《德国对外贸易和支付条例》第十七次修正案草案，德国对外国直接投资审查的行业范围将进一步扩大。人工智能、机器人技术、半导体、生物技术和量子技术等行业被列为一个新的类别，称为"关键技术"，这类行业中的公司将与被列入"关键基础设施"行业中的公司受到同等对待。

Also, on the EU level, the Regulation (EU) 2019/452 establishing a framework for the screening of foreign direct investments into the EU has entered into force in April 2019 and applies since 11 October 2020. The regulation provides for, inter alia, a cooperation mechanism (including reporting duties and information rights) between EU member states especially with focus on critical infrastructure and key technologies. The Ministry has thus established a national contact point within its authority that coordinates the exchange of information relating to investment screening procedures with other EU member states and the EU Commission. The broad thematic reach of the regulation may lead to a further tightening of the Ministry's administrative practice. Thus, the foreign investment control regime in Germany is sure to stay dynamic.

此外,在欧盟层面,用于筛查进入欧盟的外国直接投资的框架法规——欧盟第 2019/452 号条例已于 2019 年 4 月生效,并于 2020 年 10 月 11 日开始实施。该法规规定了欧盟成员国之间的合作机制(包括报告义务和信息权),尤其是针对关键基础设施和关键技术的合作机制。为此德国主管部门在国内设置了联络处,用以与其他欧盟成员国和欧盟委员会协调关于投资审查的信息交换。欧盟条例涵盖的方面非常广泛,这可能导致德国主管部门在行政实践中进一步加强控制。因此,德国的外国投资控制制度必将保持活跃。

This trend over the past years had a perceptible effect on M&A practice. The Ministry has initiated more in-depth foreign investment reviews and foreign investment control proceedings have overall taken longer and are conducted more intensively. Recent developments show that there is a willingness on the part of the German government to actually use its foreign investment control powers if national security interests are perceived to be jeopardized.

过去几年的趋势对并购实践产生了明显影响。主管部门已经启动了更深入的外国投资审查,外国投资控制程序总体上花费了更长的时间,并且开展得更加频繁。近几年的事态发展表明,如果国家安全利益被认为可能会受到危害,则德国政府将切实行使其对外国投资的控制权。

This willingness has been demonstrated by several (intended) acquisitions of German companies by Chinese investors, starting with the acquisition of robot manufacturer Kuka by the Chinese electrical appliances manufacturer Midea in 2017. The German government tried but failed to prevent the takeover as German foreign investment law did not provide for respective measures and, subsequently, the German legislator initiated the 2017 reform of the German foreign investment control law. Then, in 2018, the government tried to prevent the intended acquisition of 20% of the shares in 50 Hertz, one of the four German electricity transmission systems operators, by State Grid Corporation of China because of security concerns and in order to protect critical infrastructures. As the planned acquisition was below the 25% voting rights threshold, the government was only able to prevent the takeover by instructing KfW, a German state-owned bank, to purchase the shares in 50 Hertz (the respective threshold was subsequently lowered to 10% by the 2018 reform). Finally, also in 2018, the government announced to prohibit the intended acquisition of the German machine tool manufacturer for automotive, aviation, aerospace and nuclear industries Leifeld Metal Spinning by Chinese investor Yantai Taihai, which led Yantai Taihai to withdraw its application for a certificate of non-objection and to abort the transaction.

从2017年中国电器制造商美的收购机器人制造商库卡开始，在数次中国投资者对德国公司进行的（拟）收购中，德国政府都展示了其行使控制外国投资权的意愿。但是因为德国的外国投资控制法没有规定相应的措施，所以德国政府试图阻止收购但未能成功。随后，德国立法部门开始了2017年德国外国投资控制法的改革。然后，在2018年，出于安全考虑以及保护关键基础设施的目的，德国政府试图阻止国家电网公司收购德国四大输电系统运营商之一的50赫兹公司的20%股份。由于国家电网公司计划收购的股份是20%，低于投票权为25%的收购门槛，政府只能通过指示一家德国国有银行——德国复兴信贷银行（kfw）来收购50赫兹公司，从而阻止国家电网公司的收购（随后，通过2018年的改革，相应的收购门槛降低为10%的股份）。最终，同样是在2018年，德国政府宣布禁止中国投资者烟台台海公司对德国汽车、航空、航天和核工业机床工具制造商Leifeld Metal Spinning的收购计划，这导致烟台台海公司不得不撤回了其对无异议证书的申请并放弃交易。

Against the backdrop of the rather stringent German foreign investment law, it is crucial for (even smaller) Chinese-German M&A transactions to timely and carefully assess whether the intended acquisition triggers notification or approval requirements under German foreign investment control or whether the investor should apply for a certificate of non-objection prior to the acquisition. The assessment should include a detailed risk analysis evaluating the business of the German target company, the acquirer and potential security concerns. Such analysis should be taken into account with regard to the time schedule of a transaction.

在相当严格的德国外商投资法背景下，对于（甚至规模较小的）中德并购交易而言，及时仔细地评估拟进行的收购是否会触发德国外商投资控制法下的通知或批准要求，或者确认投资者是否应申请收购之前的无异议证书至关重要。评估应包括详细的风险分析，分析应当涉及对德国目标公司以及收购方的业务评估和潜在的安全隐患。上述分析应当配合交易时间表的安排来完成。

3.1.5 我们所承办案件的外国投资控制情况（Foreign investment control in our case）

In our case, the key customer of the target company was our client and the vast majority of turnover was generated through civilian applications of our Chinese client and no turnover was generated with military applications. As a result, the initial risk assessment was that the transaction would only fall under the cross-sectoral foreign investment control regime and that it may not be a very critical case. Accordingly, our client applied for a (voluntary) certificate of non-objection.

在我们所承办的案例中，目标公司的主要客户是我们的客户，绝大部分的营业额是通过我们中国客户的民用应用产生的，没有营业额是通过军事用途产生的。结果，最初的风险评估表明该交易仅受跨行业的外国投资控制制度所管辖，并且这可能不是一个非常棘手的案例。因此，我们的客户申请了一份（自愿）无异议证书。

A few weeks after the application was submitted, the Ministry informed our client that, in their view, the transaction was subject to the sector-specific foreign investment control regime and opened a formal in-depth review procedure. The reason for this view was that the Ministry had involved other federal ministries (as is required under internal rules) and that the Ministry of Defense had voiced concerns. These concerns were based on information available to the Ministry of Defense according to which certain classified technical information on the turbines for a military aircraft (the turbines produced by a customer of the target company) had accidentally leaked to the target company. As a result, according to the ministries' view, the target company was active as a supplier to the military sector and had available classified technical information. Unfortunately, the seller and the target company had not provided any information on this issue to the client, resulting in a false assessment of the risk associated with foreign investment control.

在我们提交申请几周后，主管部门通知我们的客户称，他们认为该交易受特定行业的外国投资控制制度的约束，并启动了正式的深入审查程序。形成这种观点的原因是，该主管部门让其他联邦部委也加入了审查工作（根据内部规则的要求），并且国防部对此表示了担忧。这些担忧基于国防部可获得的信息，根据这些信息，有关军用飞机涡轮机（目标公司的客户生产的涡轮机）的某些机密技术信息被意外泄露给了目标公司。因此,各部委认为,目标公司是专注于军事领域的供应商,并且拥有机密技术信息。不幸的是,卖方和目标公司没有向客户提供有关此问题的任何信息,从而导致对与外国投资控制有关的风险作出了错误的评估。

With our client being a Chinese state-owned aircraft manufacturer and with, in the ministries' view, the target company being a supplier to a company selling military aircrafts to the German army, it became clear that the ministries would voice concerns with respect to the security of the Federal Republic of Germany in the context of the transaction.

由于我们的客户是一家中国的国有飞机制造商,并且德国各部委认为,目标公司是向德国军队出售军用飞机的公司的供应商,因此很显然,各部委对交易可能会对德国联邦的安全问题所产生的影响表示担忧。

As is usual in such case, our client first had to prepare a comprehensive information package for the ministries' review, including, for example, a translation of the SPA into German, detailed information on the target company's and our client's shareholding structure and business activities. On the basis of such submission, our client requested in-person meetings with the ministries and representatives of the target company. A meeting was eventually held at the Ministry in Berlin. In the meeting, it became obvious that the ministries' concerns were not only based on tangible concerns with respect to national security and that there was a general feeling of discomfort with a Chinese state-owned enterprise acquiring the target company.

通常,在这种情况下,我们的客户首先需要准备一份全面的信息清单以供各部审查,例如包括 SPA 文件的德语译本,有关目标公司以及我们客户的股权结构和业务活动的详细信息。在提交上述文件之后,我们的客户要求与各部委和目标公司的代表进行面对面的会谈。最终在位于柏林的主管部门处举行了一次会议。在会议上,显而易见的是,各部委的担忧不仅是基于对国家安全的切实关切,而且对中国国有企业收购目标公司总体感到不适。

In order to address the ministries' concerns, our client decided to offer that prior to closing of the acquisition of the target company, the "military business" of the company (effectively comprising only few documents and one employee that was in charge for the turbine-customer) would be carved-out from the target company and that information and data safeguards would be implemented between the target company and the carved-out military business.

为了消除各部委的担忧，我们的客户决定在收购项目交割之前将"军事业务"（实际上只包含很少的文件和一名负责涡轮客户的员工）从目标公司中移除，并且将在目标公司和已移除的军事业务之间实施信息和数据保护措施。

After several rounds of discussions with the ministries which have taken several months, this compromise was fixed in a so-called "public law agreement" between the Ministry and our client. This is a rather usual arrangement to fix commitments by the acquirer in cases in which the Ministry voices concerns. On the basis of the public law agreement, foreign investment clearance was finally granted.

在与各部委进行了数轮讨论之后（耗时数月），这种妥协已在部委与客户之间的所谓"公法协议"中得以达成。在主管部门对项目存在担忧的情况下，这是一种比较常见的用于落实收购方承诺的措施。根据公法协议，主管部门最终批准了此次外国投资。

3.2 合并控制（Merger Control）

A second main issue investors regularly face when investing in German companies is German and EU merger control. The purpose of such merger control is to prevent adverse effects on competition on the respective markets that may arise from the intended transaction. As opposed to foreign investment control, merger control is non-discriminatory, i.e. it applies in the same way to German or other investors.

投资者在投资德国公司时经常会遇到的第二个主要问题是德国和欧盟的合并控制。这种合并控制的目的是防止预期交易对所涉的各个市场的竞争产生不利影响。与外国投资控制相反，合并控制是非歧视性的，即对德国或其他国家投资者同等适用。

As merger control clearance is usually a condition for closing of the transaction and possibly may even be a deal breaker, the necessity and prospects of a merger control filing should be assessed as early as possible. At the same time, the parties to the transaction should at the very beginning of the transaction be aware that especially in rather complex cases the merger control process can take several months.

由于合并控制许可通常是项目交割的条件，甚至可能会导致交易终结，因此应尽早评估合并控制文件的必要性和前景。与此同时，交易各方应在交易之初就意识到合并控制程序可能要花费几个月的时间,特别是在交易相当复杂的情况下。

Merger control applies to transactions in which the buyer acquires direct or indirect control (be it through contracts, voting rights or other means) over a German company. Most relevant in practice is the acquisition of shares. Under EU merger control law, control is inter alia acquired if a company acquires 50% or a majority of the shares of another company. German merger control law is applicable even in case of an acquisition of only 25% of the shares. Control may also be acquired if substantial parts of the assets of one company are acquired by another, due to contracts, or by other means allowing one company to exercise control over another.

合并控制适用于买方对德国公司取得直接或间接控制(通过合同、取得投票权或其他方式获得控制)的交易,在实践中使用频率最高的是股份收购。根据欧盟合并控制法,如果一家公司收购了目标公司不低于50%的股份,则收购方即可获得对目标公司的控制权。但即使收购方仅收购了目标公司25%的股份,德国合并控制法也同样适用。收购方也可以通过收购目标公司的主要资产的方式取得控制权,比如通过合同收购,或者通过其他允许收购方对目标公司行使控制权的方式。

However, merger control only applies for transactions which involve a certain economic impact. For determining whether a merger control notification is required, it is in the case of acquisitions necessary to determine the consolidated turnover in Germany and worldwide for both the German target (group) and the acquirer group. Under the existing merger control regime in the EU, a merger control notification is either required on the EU level or on the level of the individual EU member states such as Germany. It is theoretically possible that a merger control notification is required in any member state (or even in any country worldwide) in which the target and/or the acquirer have sales. As an EU filing takes priority over a filing in the member states, in principle no notification requirements in Germany apply if an EU merger control notification is necessary. However, even if an EU merger control filing is not required, a filing under German merger control law may still be necessary.

然而,合并控制仅适用于具有一定经济影响的交易。为了确定是否需要合并控制通知,在进行收购时,必须确定德国目标公司(集团)和收购方在德国和全球的合并营业额。根据欧盟现有的合并控制制度,在欧盟层面或在单个欧盟成员国(如德国)的层面上都需要合并申报。从理论上讲,在与目标公司和/或收购方有销售往来的任何成员国(甚至全球的任何国家)都有合并申报义务。由于欧盟的申请优先于成员国的申请,因此原则上,如果需要欧盟合并审查申报,则不需要德国的审查申报。然而,即使不需要欧盟的合并控制申请,仍可能需要根据德国合并控制法进行申请。

In general, the notification must be made prior to closing and following signing of the relevant agreements (or the announcement of a public bid or the acquisition of a controlling interest, whichever is earlier).

通常情况下,必须在相关协议签署之后和项目交割之前或宣布公开竞标或获得控制权时进行申报,以较早者为准。

3.2.1 欧盟合并控制(EU merger control)

A merger control notification to the EU Commission has to be made if the worldwide aggregate turnover as stated in the latest financial statements of all parties involved in the transaction exceeds EUR 5 billion and the EU-wide turnover of at least two parties to the transaction each exceeds EUR 250 million. Even if these prerequisites are not met, the acquirer is still obliged to make a merger control filing if (i) the worldwide aggregate turnover of all parties exceeds EUR 2.5 billion, (ii) the individual EU-wide turnover of at least two of the parties to the transaction exceeds EUR 100 million, (iii) the aggregate turnover of the parties exceeds at least EUR 100 million in each of at least three member states of the EU, and (iv) in each of these at least three of the member states at least two of the parties to the transaction have a turnover of at least EUR 25 million each.

如果所有交易参与方的最新财务报表中所记载的全球总营业额超过50亿欧元,且交易中至少有两个交易方在欧盟范围内的营业额分别超过2.5亿欧元,则收购方必须向欧盟委员会发送合并申报。即使不满足上述先决条件,如果满足如下条件,收购方仍有义务进行合并控制申请:(i)各方在全球范围内的总营业额超过25亿欧元;(ii)至少两个交易参与方在欧盟范围内的个体营业额超过1亿欧元;(iii)交易参与方在至少三个欧盟成员国中的总营业额超过1亿欧元;(iv)至少有两个交易参与方在前述至少三个欧盟成员国中的各自营业额不低于2500万欧元。

As an exception, even if all of the above requirements are met, an EU merger control notification is not necessary if both parties to the transaction achieve more than two thirds of their EU-wide turnover in one and the same member state.

作为例外，即使满足上述所有条件，但如果交易双方在同一欧盟成员国内取得了欧盟范围内营业额的三分之二以上，则无需欧盟合并审查申报。

Under certain conditions it is possible that cases be re-allocated from the EU level to the member state level or from the member state level to the EU level (at the initiative of the parties to the transaction) prior to or (on request of a member state but upon determination of the Commission) following a formal notification.

在某些情况下，有可能在提交申报之前（由交易方主动提出）或正式申报后（根据成员国的请求但须经欧盟委员会决定）将案件从欧盟层面重新分配到成员国层面，或从成员国层面重新分配给欧盟层面。

Prior to the actual filing of the merger control notification, even in rather simple cases the parties to the transaction have to gather extensive information serving as basis for a draft submission, which is usually prepared by the parties' lawyers. The draft then has to be submitted and discussed with the EU Commission. The actual filing triggers a review period of 25 business days (Phase I) during which the transaction must not be consummated. Unless the EU Commission has substantive competition law concerns, the parties would be free to close the transaction upon expiry of the review period. If the EU Commission had any substantive issues, it would start a Phase II review period which may take up to 125 working days. The Commission will restrict the transaction or even deny clearance if the intended transaction leads to a significant impediment of effective competition. If necessary, the parties may take remedies (e.g. consider a carve-out) in order to prevent a denial.

在实际提交合并申报之前，即使在相当简单的情况下，交易方也必须收集广泛的信息作为提交草案的基础，该草案通常由当事人各方的律师准备。随后，交易方必须提交该草案，并与欧盟委员会讨论。实际提交后，第一阶段会有25个工作日的审核期，在此期间不得完成交易。交易方可以在审核期满后自由完成交易，除非欧盟委员会有实质性的竞争法问题。如果欧盟委员会有任何实质性问题，将开始第二阶段审核，该审核最多可能需要125个工作日。如果意向交易严重阻碍了有效竞争，委员会将限制交易，甚至拒绝批准。如有必要，各方可以采取补救措施（例如考虑分拆交易），以防止委员会拒绝批准。

Depending on how quickly the required information can be compiled and on whether the EU Commission initiates a Phase II review, the process can take several months.

该过程可能需要花费几个月的时间，周期长短取决于所需信息的编辑速度以及欧盟委员会是否启动第二阶段审核。

3.2.2 德国合并控制（German merger control）

A merger has to be notified to the German Federal Cartel Office (in German: *Bundeskartellamt*) if in the financial year preceding the merger (i) the parties have an aggregate worldwide turnover of more than EUR 500 million, (ii) the turnover in Germany of at least one of the parties to the transaction exceeds EUR 50 million, and (iii) the turnover in Germany of another party to the transaction exceeds EUR 17.5 million.

如果在合并前的财政年度（i）交易双方在全球范围内的总营业额超过5亿欧元，(ii) 至少有一方在德国的营业额超过5000万欧元，(iii) 交易另一方在德国的营业额超过1750万欧元，交易方必须向德国联邦卡特尔局（德语为 Bundeskartellamt）进行申报。

Even if the above prerequisites are not met, the acquirer is, apart from a few special exceptions for members of a banking association, still obliged to make a merger control filing if (i) in the financial year preceding the merger the parties have an aggregate worldwide turnover of more than EUR 500 million, (ii) in the financial year preceding the merger the turnover in Germany of one of the parties to the transaction exceeds EUR 50 million, (iii) the consideration for the acquisition exceeds EUR 400 million, and (iv) the target company has substantial operations in Germany.

即使不满足上述先决条件，除银行协会成员的一些特殊例外：(i) 在合并前的财政年度中，交易方的全球总营业额超过5亿欧元；(ii) 在合并前的财政年度中，交易的其中一方在德国的交易额超过5000万欧元；(iii) 收购对价超过4亿欧元；以及 (iv) 目标公司在德国有显著经营活动，收购方仍然有义务进行合并申报。

In general, the thresholds for a merger control filing are thus not very high and merger control is often compulsory to be obtained if the Chinese acquirer has sales in Germany.

通常，合并审查申报的门槛不是非常高，如果中国收购方在德国有销售业务往来，则通常必须进行申报。

The procedure of a German merger control filing is similar to an EU filing. However, a German merger control filing usually requires less information to be submitted and it is not common to submit a draft to the Federal Cartel Office before the actual filing. After the actual filing, the Federal Cartel Office may start a Phase II review period if it had any substantive issues during the initial one-month review period (Phase I). During Phase II, which takes up to five months from receipt of the complete notification, the Federal Cartel Office has the right to lodge requests for information with the parties to the transaction but also with third parties. In addition, the Federal Cartel Office might ask for exploratory meetings with the parties. The Federal Cartel Office will restrict the transaction or even deny clearance if the intended transaction leads to a significant impediment of effective competition. If necessary, the parties may take remedies (e. g. consider a carve-out) in order to prevent a denial. In case of a denial of clearance, the German economics minister may, upon application, authorize a transaction prohibited by the Federal Cartel Office if, in the individual case, the restraint of competition is outweighed by advantages to the economy as a whole resulting from the transaction, or if the transaction is justified by an overriding public interest. Such ministerial authorization has, however, so far only been granted in very rare cases.

德国合并申报程序与欧盟的程序相似。然而，德国的合并申报通常要求提交的信息较少，在实际申请之前向德国联邦卡特尔局提交草案的情况并不常见。在实际提交之后，如果德国联邦卡特尔局在最初的一个月审查期内（第一阶段）发现任何实质性问题，则可以开始第二阶段审查期。第二阶段审查从收到完整的申报文件时起算可达5个月。德国联邦卡特尔局有权向交易各方以及第三方提出信息请求。此外，德国联邦卡特尔局可能会要求与双方召开探索性问询会议。如果有意进行的交易严重阻碍了有效竞争，则德国联邦卡特尔局将限制交易，甚至拒绝批准交易。如有必要，各方可以采取补救措施（例如考虑分拆交易），以防止交易被禁止。在拒绝批准交易的情况下，如果在个别交易中，整个交易给经济发展带来的益处超过了限制竞争的弊端，或者交易是基于巨大的公共利益，那么德国经济部长可应申请许可被德国联邦卡特尔局禁止的交易。然而迄今为止，这种部长级特权仅在极少数情况下才行使。

In rather simple cases, clearance may be granted within few weeks or even days, whereas cases in which a Phase II review is initiated may take several months.

对于简单的交易，可能会在几周甚至几天内被审核批准，而交易一旦被启动第二阶段审核，则可能需要花费几个月的时间。

The Federal Cartel Office charges a filing fee the amount of which depends on the value of the transaction and the difficulty of the matter but is otherwise in the discretion of the Federal Cartel Office up to a maximum amount of EUR 50 000 or, in extraordinarily complex cases, EUR 100 000. In practice, in smaller cases, the filing fee is often in the range of EUR 5000 to EUR 10 000.

德国联邦卡特尔局收取申请费，申请费的金额取决于交易的估值和项目的难度，由德国联邦卡特尔局根据不同项目酌情决定，一般最高限额为 50 000 欧元，但如果案例非常复杂，则为 100 000 欧元。实际上，较小的交易项目，申请费通常在 5000 欧元至 10 000 欧元。

3.2.3 营业额准入的计算（Calculation of turnover thresholds）

Since the parties' turnover is decisive for the presence or absence of a merger control filing obligation, its correct calculation is of great importance. In principle, the undertakings belonging to a party's group must first be identified. The party's group consists of the party's ultimate parent and all undertakings which are, directly or indirectly, solely or jointly, controlled by the ultimate parent. In principle, this can be presumed for all undertakings in which the ultimate parent, directly or indirectly, solely or jointly (i.e. together with one or more third-partyundertakings), (i) owns more than half the capital or business assets, or (ii) has the power to exercise more than half the voting rights (less for listed companies, typically around 30%), or (iii) has the power to appoint more than half the members of the supervisory board, the administrative board or bodies legally representing the undertakings, or (iv) has the right to manage the undertakings' affairs. This group of undertakings is not always limited to the companies within the scope of consolidation of the ultimate parent's consolidated financial statements but may also include companies which are not consolidated but only accounted for as equity (in particular joint ventures).

由于交易方的营业额对于是否存在合并审查申报义务具有决定性作用，因此正确地计算营业额非常重要。原则上，必须首先确定交易方所属的企业集团。企业集团包括最终母公司和由最终母公司直接或间接、单独或共同控制的所有企业。原则上，由所有最终母公司直接或间接、单独或共同（即与一个或多个第三方企业一起）控制的企业共同组成，(i) 拥有超过一半的资本或业务资产，或 (ii) 有权行使一半以上的投票权（对于上市公司而言，通常大约30%），或 (iii) 有权任命一半以上的监事会，行政委员会或机构成员在法律上能够代表经营者，或 (iv) 有权管理经营者事务。经营者集团并不总是限于最终母公司合并财务报表的合并范围内的公司，还可以包括未被合并但仅按权益入账的公司（特别是合资公司）。

The turnover which is decisive for the above thresholds is the consolidated turnover of the whole group in their last completed financial year prior to the implementation of the transaction. In principle, this turnover must be (i) generated from the sale of goods or services in the ordinary course of business of the undertaking (i.e. revenue/sales), (ii) net, i.e. exclude VAT and other taxes directly related to turnover as well as sales rebates and discounts, (iii) external, i.e. exclude turnover generated with group-internal sales, and (iv) geographically allocated (for the purposes of determining turnover generated in the EU and in Germany) on a sales-per-destination basis.

对上述申报门槛起决定性作用的是整个集团在实施交易之前的最后一个完整财政年度的合并营业额。原则上，该营业额必须是：（i) 在企业的正常经营过程中从商品或服务的销售中产生的（即收入/销售额），(ii) 净额，即不包括与营业额直接相关的增值税和其他税项，以及销售返利和折扣，(iii) 外部营业额，即不包括集团内部销售产生的营业额，以及 (iv) 按地理位置划分销售目的地的营业额，用于确定区分该营业额产生于欧盟和德国。

3.2.4 合并审查举例（Merger control in our case）

Our client, like many Chinese companies investing in Germany, ultimately is an SOE. As described above, the consolidated group turnover is decisive for merger control filing requirements, with the party's group consisting of the party's ultimate parent and all undertakings which are controlled by the ultimate "parent company". As a consequence, the turnover of every single Chinese SOE would theoretically have to be included in assessing whether the turnover thresholds are met. A merger control filing would thus become very likely for every acquisition by an SOE, even if the acquirer entity itself, as in our case, has a turnover of zero in the EU or a member state.

与许多在德国投资的中国公司相似，我们的最终客户是国有企业（SOE），如上所述，合并集团的营业额对于是否需要合并控制申请具有决定性作用，该交易方的集团由该方的最终母公司和由该最终母公司控制的所有企业组成。因此，从理论上讲，营业额的审查门槛计算应当包含每家中国国有企业的营业额。因此，当收购方为中国国有企业时，很有可能还是需要进行合并控制申请，即使是类似本案中的情形，即收购方公司本身在欧盟或欧盟各成员国中的营业额为零。

In fact, the EU Commission is tending towards this interpretation and makes the question whether the SOE involved in the transaction is part of a group comprising other SOEs dependent on whether the respective SOE has sufficient independent decision-making powers. The Commission takes, inter alia, into account the likelihood and the possible power of the state to influence the SOE's commercial strategy and conduct, personal ties and overlaps of directors of different SOEs, and existing precautions for the exchange of commercial information. In this way, the Commission tries to assess which SOEs belong to the economic unit of the SOE involved in the transaction. If the Commission's assessment concludes that the SOE involved in the transaction is not to be regarded as being independent, and therefore other SOEs' turnovers have to be aggregated, the likelihood of the transaction to reach the relevant thresholds (and thus the likelihood of a merger control filing obligation) increases significantly. In the majority of cases involving Chinese SOEs reviewed by the EU Commission, however, there was no need for the EU Commission to decide whether the turnover of other SOEs should be taken into account, because the individual turnover of the parties to the mergers was sufficient to establish the Commission's jurisdiction.

实际上，欧盟委员会倾向于这种解释，并根据参与交易国有企业是否具有足够的独立决策权，来决定交易中涉及的国有企业是否与其他国有企业共同组成一个集团。除此之外，欧盟委员会考虑了国家影响国有企业商业战略和行为的可能性、不同国有企业的董事之间的个人联系和重叠以及现有的商业信息交流预防措施。通过这种方式，欧盟委员会试图评估哪些国有企业属于参与交易的国有企业的经济单位。如果委员会通过评估得出的结论是交易中涉及的国有企业不应被视为独立的法人主体，那么其他国有企业的营业额必须被汇总计算进去，则该交易达到相关申报门槛的可能性（即因此需要进行合并控制申请的可能性）会显著增加。但在欧盟委员会审查的大多数涉及中国国有企业的合并案件中，不需考虑其他国有企业的营业额的问题，因为合并各方的独立营业额足以确立欧盟委员会的管辖权。

In our case, the relevant turnover thresholds for an EU merger control filing obligation were still not exceeded as the target company had an EU-wide turnover of less than EUR 100 million. Hence, an EU merger control filing was not necessary.

在我们的案例中,由于目标公司在欧盟范围内的营业额少于1亿欧元,尚未超过欧盟合并控制申请义务的相关营业额门槛。因此,无须进行欧盟合并控制申请。

On the German national level, the issue of state ownership has in the past received less attention. Most member states take heterogeneous views on how to handle state ownership in terms of merger control. The German Federal Cartel Office did not pay much attention to this issue until the acquisition of the locomotive business of German rail infrastructure company Vossloh by the Chinese rolling stock manufacturer CRRC (Zhuzhou) in 2020.

Under the Federal Cartel Office's practice at the time of our case, a German merger control filing was obsolete. Our client had no revenues/sales in Germany and the consideration for the acquisition was less than EUR 400 million.

国家对企业持所有权问题在德国过去受到的关注较少。大多数欧盟成员国对如何在合并控制中处理国家对企业持所有权持不同意见。在中国中车集团有限公司(株洲)(以下简称中车)收购德国铁路基建公司福斯罗火车业务一案之前,德国联邦卡特尔局对此类国企问题关注较少,并且在审查(最终)国有企业的合并时不评估国家对企业持所有权的因素。

根据我们合并申报时的法律实践,由于我们的客户在德国没有营业额或销售业务,并且收购对价不到4亿欧元,因此不需要在德国进行合并控制申请。

In the CRRC/Vossloh decision, the Federal Cartel Office applied a broad interpretation of the affiliated group of CRRC and stated that at least all companies in which the Chinese state holds the majority of shares should be included for purposes of the review. This resulted in an extensive information obligation on part of CRRC: The Federal Cartel Office requested information of at least those companies that are active in the relevant sector, including in upstream or downstream markets. In the substantive competition review, the Federal Cartel Office looked into the possibility of low-price and dumping strategies and the cost advantages especially in the context of the state involvement.

在中车收购福斯罗案的决定中，德国联邦卡特尔局对中车关联企业集团作了宽泛的解释，其指出，为了审查的目的，企业集团至少应包括中国国家持有多数股份的所有公司。这加重了中车负担的信息义务。德国联邦卡特尔局要求至少提供相关行业的公司的信息，包括上游或下游市场。在实质竞争审查中，德国联邦卡特尔局特别考察了在国家参与的背景下，企业实施低价倾销战略的可能性及其成本优势。

In light of this decision, Chinese SOEs with plans to acquire German companies should carefully assess German merger control filing requirements already at an early stage of the transaction. It seems conceivable that the Federal Cartel Office could in the future take a closer look at the acquirer, in particular in case of (Chinese) SOEs, and request extensive information also on other state-owned enterprises before deciding on the transaction.

鉴于这一先例，有计划收购德国公司的中国国有企业应该在交易的早期阶段就仔细评估德国的并购审查的申报要求。不难想象，德国联邦卡特尔局今后可能会更仔细地审视收购方，尤其是中国国有企业，并在做出决定前要求提供更多其他国有企业的信息。

4. 文化相关问题（Cultural Issues）

Apart from legal issues, difficulties that often have an impact on Chinese/German M&A transactions and that need to be overcome also often arise from cultural discrepancies. The impact of these discrepancies on the success of a transaction should not be underestimated and a lack of mutual cultural understanding can obstruct negotiations or even lead to a failure of the intended transaction. Illustrative examples from our experience are the differences between Chinese and Germans in terms of decision-making and their perspective on agreements.

除法律问题外，文化差异也常常引起困难，这些困难通常会影响中德并购交易亟须解决。这些差异对交易能否成功的影响不容小觑，缺乏相互的文化理解会阻碍谈判，甚至导致意向交易的失败。根据我们的经验，有借鉴性的案例是中国人和德国人之间的差异往往体现在问题决策以及他们对协议的看法上。

4.1 中国式决策（Chinese Decision-making）

While decision-making in Chinese privately-owned companies can be fairly simple (particularly if they are majority-owned and managed by its founder), it can also be very complex and non-transparent for SOEs. The various approval levels and processes that SOEs have to go through for important decisions are often not explained to the German counterparty and, from their perspective, take a very long time. Explaining the administrative processes that need to be adhered to on the Chinese side is thus a great way of building trust and gaining patience on the German side.

尽管中国民营企业的决策方式相当简单（特别是如果他们是多数股权持有方并且该公司由其创始人管理），但对国有企业而言却可能非常复杂。国有企业通常不会向德国交易方解释企业作出重要决策所必须经过的各种审批级别和流程，从德国交易方的角度来看，这需要很长时间。因此，解释中方需要遵守的行政程序是在交易中与德国交易方建立信任并让德方保持耐心的好方法。

4.2 中方对于交易协议的考虑视角（Chinese Perspective on Agreements）

For German parties, an agreement generally is to be strictly observed by the counterparty, also if the circumstances have changed since its conclusion. "Pacta sunt servanda" (Latin for "agreements need to be adhered to") is a concept that is deeply rooted in German culture.

通常对于德国交易方而言，双方都应严格遵守协议，即使自达成协议以来情况有所变化。"Pacta sunt servanda"（拉丁语，"协议必须被遵守"）是一个根植于德国文化的概念。

In contrast, from a German perspective, Chinese tend to see an agreement as fit for the moment it is entered into but something that needs to be adjusted if relevant circumstances change, hence as a "living" compromise of the parties.

相比之下，从德国的角度来看，中国人倾向于认为协议只是在签订之时的合意，如果协议签订之后相关情况发生变化，则需要对协议进行调整，因此双方之间的协议应当是动态变化的。

A similar issue arises in negotiation situations if the Chinese party offers a compromise but later has to retract such offer. Germans are used to the parties only offering compromises for which they clearly have a mandate (internally). In contrast, we have experienced that Chinese investors negotiate aspects of an agreement for which they hope to get internal approval, e. g. from superiors that may not always be available for discussions, and sometimes do not get it. As such situations are usually not explained to the German parties, they are often perceived as the Chinese side retracting agreements already made in bad faith. It is an important task for the advisors involved to mediate between the different negotiation styles and cultures in such situations.

在谈判中也会出现类似的问题,即中方先提出协议方案但后来不得不撤回该方案。而德国人习惯于交易方只提供他们明确有权(内部授权)作出的方案。相比之下,我们经历过,中国投资者在谈判协议的某些方面希望获得内部批准,例如来自并不总是能参与商议的上级领导的批准,有时甚至无法获得批准。由于中方通常不会向德国各方解释这种情况,因此德方通常将它们视为中方出于恶意撤回已经达成的协议。在这种情况下,法律顾问的一项重要任务是需要在不同的谈判风格和文化之间进行调解。

— 作者简介 —

Gleiss Lutz is the leading independent full service law firm in Germany. More than 350 lawyers (including 84 partners) provide creative, pragmatic and integrated advice to their clients on all aspects of business law concerning their most difficult legal issues, most important transactions and their "bet-the company" crises and disputes. With its strong international network, Gleiss Lutz advises not only leading German but also international companies and financial institutions from all over the world.

Gleiss Lutz 是一家在德国领先的律师事务所,能够提供独立全方位的法律服务。律所共有350多名律师(包括84名合伙人),能够就商事领域的各方面业务为客户提供创造性、务实和综合全面的法律顾问服务,服务范围涉及客户遇到的最棘手的法律问题、最重要的交易以及客户"赌上公司存亡"的危机情况和争议解决。凭借其强大的国际网络,Gleiss Lutz 不仅为德国知名企业提供法律顾问服务,同时也为世界各地的国际企业和金融机构提供法律顾问服务。

Dr. Michael Burian is partner and head of Gleiss Lutz' China and Asia Practices. **Dr. Anselm Christiansen** is a partner at Gleiss Lutz. **Jannik Hermes** is project associate. Their practices cover mergers & acquisitions as well as corporate law, with a focus on Asia-related cross-border transactions. They regularly advise Asian clients, especially Chinese companies, on German and European law issues. In addition, they advise German companies on their business activities in Asia.

Michael Burian 博士是 Gleiss Lutz 律师事务所的合伙人,是中国和亚洲区的相关业务的负责人。**Anselm Christiansen** 博士是 Gleiss Lutz 律师事务所的合伙人。**Jannik Hermes** 是法律咨询师。他们的执业领域涵盖公司并购和公司法相关业务，重点专注于亚洲地区相关的跨境交易。他们经常为亚洲客户，特别是中国公司，提供关于德国和欧洲法律的顾问服务。此外，他们还为德国公司在亚洲开展的业务提供法律顾问服务。

在开曼群岛和英属维尔京群岛构建投资：通过开曼群岛和英属维尔京群岛拓展"一带一路"

Investments in the Cayman Islands and the BVI Expanding the Belt and Road through the Cayman Islands and the BVI

点 评

本文作者细致地分析了选择开曼群岛和英属维尔京群岛（以下简称 BVI）构建"一带一路"投资的主要优势，包括公司法人实体设立速度较快、程序简便、成本较低，两地区拥有对商业和债权人友好的法律制度，政治和经济稳定，符合国际审慎监管、透明度、合作反洗钱和打击恐怖主义融资等标准，税收具有中立性和透明度等。我们在为客户提供境外投资架构搭建方案时，亦会根据具体项目中客户的需求，推荐是否需要在开曼群岛、BVI 设立相关公司管理层级。

本文作者进一步对开曼群岛私募股权基金的构建、使用豁免有限合伙企业的优点及需要注意的事项，以及开曼群岛私募股权投资结构等较为常见的架构事项进行了介绍，希望给读者一些启发。

1. 项目背景（Project Background）

The footprint of the Belt and Road Initiative (B&R) not surprisingly includes structuring projects using offshore jurisdictions such as the British Virgin Islands (BVI), the Cayman Islands (Cayman), Ireland, Luxembourg and Jersey, all of which are leading offshore and midshore jurisdictions, respectively.

"一带一路"倡议的足迹毫无疑问地遍及诸如英属维尔京群岛（BVI）、开在开曼群岛和英属维尔京群岛构建投资：通过开曼群岛和英属维尔京群岛拓展"一带一路"

曼群岛、爱尔兰、卢森堡以及泽西岛等地，在这些全球领先的离岸和中岸司法辖区的项目建设过程中都得到了落实。

In Asia, at the forefront of B&R activity have been projects in the Greater Bay area, Guangdong-Hong Kong-Macau Bay Area, including Hong Kong SAR, the Macau SAR, Guangzhou, Shenzhen, Huizhou, Zhongshan, Dongguan, Zhuhai, Foshan, Jiangmen and Zhaoqing. There have been many projects in the Greater Bay area delivering significant outcomes for Chinese society such as: focusing on promoting infrastructure connectivity; enhancing the level of market integration; building technology and expanding innovation; generally adding to an enhanced quality lifestyle for residents of the Greater Bay area including for day-to-day living, working and travelling; cultivating international cooperation; and supporting the establishment of major cooperation platforms.

在亚洲，"一带一路"倡议的前沿地区为中国粤港澳大湾区，包括香港特别行政区、澳门特别行政区、广州、深圳、惠州、中山、东莞、珠海、佛山、江门和肇庆等地。粤港澳大湾区的许多项目已经取得重大成果，为中国社会作出了贡献，例如，重点推进基础设施互联互通；提高市场整合水平；建设科技，扩大创新；为大湾区居民提供更优质的生活方式，包括日常生活、工作和旅行；促进国际合作；以及支持建立重大合作平台。

Whether through the establishment of investment vehicles such as private equity or hedge funds, holding company structures or downstream investment portfolio companies, structuring through a Cayman, BVI or other offshore or midshore entities is a well-trodden path.

无论是通过建立私募股权或对冲基金，还是通过控股公司结构或下游投资组合公司等投资工具，利用开曼群岛、BVI 或其他离岸、中岸实体搭建投资结构，都是很常见的做法。

2. 开曼群岛和 BVI 的投资优势（The Advantages on Investing in Cayman and the BVI）

Over 91 000 exempted companies; approximately 10 000 funds; 130 trust companies; and 300 active banks are established, registered or, respectively, licensed in Cayman. In the BVI there are over 400 000 business companies; over 900 mutual funds; and more than 1000 private trust companies.

超过 91 000 家豁免公司、约 10 000 家基金、130 家信托公司以及 300 家业务活跃的银行在开曼群岛设立、注册或持牌。在 BVI，有超过 40 万家商业公司、900 多个共同基金以及 1000 多家私人信托公司。

In order for Cayman and the BVI to assist China and for China to take advantage of the opportunities available in the evolving global economy, it is essential that the Chinese business community understands the beneficial role played by Cayman and the BVI in the global financial services sector.

为使中国能够抓住借助开曼群岛和 BVI 全球经济不断发展的机遇，让中国企业了解开曼群岛和 BVI 在全球金融服务业中发挥的有益作用十分关键。

The many reasons Chinese banks and financial institutions, State-Owned Enterprises (SOEs), private companies, government agencies and high net worth individuals make use of Cayman and the BVI, include:

中国的银行和其他金融机构、国有企业、私营企业、政府机构以及高净值人士投资开发开曼群岛和 BVI 的原因有很多，包括：

• the speed and simplicity of establishing entities and relatively low cost which is essential to keep pace with the need of the Chinese business community to set up investment and holding vehicles for new, fast-moving business transactions. In January 2019, both Cayman and the BVI introduced local substance requirements for nine specific business activities to comply with the recommendations by the (Organization for Economic Cooperation and Development (OECD)'s Harmful Tax Practices Group, however, both Cayman and the BVI do not generally impose a high degree of "local content" on their overseas clients. For example, general speaking, neither exempted Cayman nor BVI companies, need to hold a physical meeting of their directors or shareholders in Cayman or the BVI and they do not need to file audited financial statements in Cayman or the BVI.

• 在开曼群岛和 BVI 设立公司法人实体速度较快、程序简便、成本较低，这满足中国企业界为快速发展的新型商业交易设立投资和持有工具的需求。2019 年 1 月，开曼群岛和 BVI 都对 9 项具体的商业活动提出了"本地成分要求"以遵守经济合作与发展组织（以下简称经合组织）有害税务行为小组的建议，然而，开曼群岛和 BVI 一般不会要求其海外客户具有高程度的"本地成分"。例如，一般而言，开曼群岛豁免公司和BVI公司都不需要在开曼群岛或BVI召开董事会或股东大会，也不需要在开曼群岛或BVI提交经审计的财务报表。

● An English-based legal system and established judiciary (with final appeal to the Privy Council in the UK). The legal systems of Cayman and the BVI are ideally suited to undertaking finance and banking transactions due to their business and creditor-friendly legislation.

● 以英语为基础的法律体系和成熟的司法体系（诉讼最终可上诉至英国枢密院）。开曼群岛和BVI对商业和债权人友好的法律制度，非常适合从事金融和银行交易。

● Low country risk. Cayman and the BVI are politically and economically stable jurisdictions. Cayman has a sovereign debt rating of Aa3 from Moody's.

● 国家风险低。开曼群岛和BVI都是政治和经济稳定的司法管辖区。开曼群岛主权债务的穆迪评级为Aa3。

● Appropriate standards of regulation by the Cayman Islands Monetary Authority (CIMA) and BVI Financial Services Commission (FSC) which have been assessed by the International Monetary Fund and other international organisations, as being in compliance with international prudential regulatory, transparency, cooperation and anti-money laundering and combatting of terrorist financing (AML/CFT) standards. CIMA and FSC regulate investment funds, fund management companies, banks and trust companies, insurance business, fund administration and company management in Cayman and BVI, respectively.

● 开曼群岛金融管理局（CIMA）和BVI金融服务委员会（FSC）的监管标准适当，经国际货币基金组织和其他国际组织评估，符合国际审慎监管、透明度、合作反洗钱和打击恐怖主义融资（AML/CFT）等标准。CIMA和FSC分别监管开曼群岛和BVI的投资基金、基金管理公司、银行和信托公司、保险业务、基金行政管理和公司管理。

● Professional infrastructure and reputation. Cayman and the BVI are both well known for their established and experienced financial services sector and their substantial capacity—including in China's case, a substantial Cayman and BVI legal community based in several cities in China including Beijing, Shanghai and Shenzhen;

● 专业基础设施和声誉。开曼群岛和 BVI 都因其成熟和经验丰富的金融服务部门和强大的能力而闻名——包括在中方对外投资案例中,一个强有力的开曼群岛和 BVI 法律团体也长驻在北京、上海和深圳等多个中国城市。

● Recognition of corporate personality and integrity. The ability of Chinese clients to use separate group subsidiaries or, to operate through a segregated portfolio company, to maintain separate businesses and assets, often with their own ring-fenced financing, can be a major contributor to the successful management of business and jurisdictional risks in cross-border transactions;

● 对公司独立性和整体性的认可。中国客户能够通过独立的集团子公司,或者通过运营独立的投资组合公司,来维持公司业务和资产的独立性,还通常能够使用内部融资手段。这些可能都是在跨境交易过程中能够成功处理业务、控制司法风险的主要因素。

● Cayman insolvency law is simple and effective, enabling speed and certainty in relation to the enforcement of creditors' and contractual rights both pre and post insolvency;

● 开曼群岛的破产法简单而有效,可以快速、稳定地在破产前后实现债权人的合同权利。

● Tax neutrality means that a Cayman or BVI entity provides a tax-neutral platform so that investors from multiple jurisdictions are not subject to more taxation over and above that payable in each investor's home country. Cayman and the BVI each offer the opportunity to do this without foreign exchange controls and without significant restrictions on the payment of interest or dividends, the repayment of capital or the ability to repurchase shares or redeem or repurchase debt;

● 税收的中立性意味着开曼群岛或 BVI 的实体会提供一个税收中立平台,使得来自多个司法管辖区的投资者所缴纳的税款将不会超过在每个投资者本国应缴纳的税款。开曼群岛和 BVI 都提供了这样的机会,而且不会受到外汇管制,支付利息或股息、偿还资本、回购股份、赎回或回购债务等行为也未被施加重大限制。

● Transparency and beyond—Cayman and the BVI meet or exceed all globally-accepted standards for transparency and cross-border cooperation with law enforcement agencies in the world's major economies including China. This firm commitment to global transparency makes Cayman and the BVI an attractive and reliable partner for Chinese regulators and tax authorities. Cayman and the BVI were each an early adopter of automatic exchange of tax information with overseas authorities, including FATCA and the OECD's Common Reporting Standard. The Cayman Islands Tax Information Authority and the BVI International Tax Authority proactively collects tax information from a wide variety of Cayman and BVI entities and shares such information with over 100 other governments providing a level of transparency which assists them in the collection of their own taxes.

● 透明度：开曼群岛和BVI达到甚至超过了全球公认的透明度标准以及与世界主要经济体包括中国的执法机构开展跨境合作的标准。这种对全球公认透明度的切实承诺使开曼群岛和BVI成为对中国监管机构和税务机关有吸引力而且可信赖的合作伙伴。开曼群岛和BVI都是与海外政府相关部门，包括FATCA和经合组织共同报告标准自动交换税务信息的早期合作者。开曼群岛税务信息局和BVI国际税务局积极主动地从其辖区内的各种公司法人实体收集税务信息，并与100多个国家的政府共享此类信息，这能在一定程度上提高相关国家税务信息透明度，以协助其征收本国的税款。

2.1 国际认可的法律制度（Internationally Accepted Legal Systems）

Cayman and BVI structures are well placed to support B&R projects. Just one example of such projects are investment funds investing in venture capital transactions.

开曼群岛和BVI结构非常适合支持"一带一路"倡议项目。这类项目其中一例就是为风险投资交易设立的投资基金。

China's financial institutions and entrepreneurs are familiar with Cayman and BVI structures, which are based on common law and modelled on English company law principles. Such structures have a simple corporate management system, with internationally recognised shareholders' and creditors' rights such as shareholder limited liability, and creditor priority.

中国的金融机构和企业家熟悉开曼群岛和BVI的法律体系和公司架构，它们以普通法为基础，以英国公司法原则为模式。这种结构具有简明的公司管理体系，其公司股东和债权人的权利为全世界所认可，例如股东的有限责任和债权人的优先权。

Project entities are able to raise financing in traditional forms of debt instruments including listed or rated notes, warrants or via securitisations—all widely recognised in the international capital markets. Lenders can provide secured or unsecured credit with the comfort of knowing that such concepts as statutory and contractual ring fencing, preferred creditors and shareholders' liquidation preferences, are recognised and well understood by Cayman and BVI courts, which routinely hear complex international disputes. As Cayman and the BVI are British Overseas Territories, the final court of appeal in both jurisdictions is to the Privy Council in the UK, ensuring international investors' rights will be independently recognised and enforced.

项目实体能够以传统形式的债务工具（包括上市或评级的票据、认股权证或证券化）筹集资金，这些都在国际资本市场上得到广泛认可。放贷人可以放心地提供有担保或无担保信贷，因为他们知道，法定和合同"围栏"的风险隔离、优先债权人和股东的清算优先权等概念已得到开曼群岛和BVI法院的认可和充分理解，原因在于上述法院会经常审理复杂的国际争议。由于开曼群岛和BVI都是英国的海外领土，因此两个司法管辖区的最终上诉法院都是英国枢密院，以确保国际投资者的权利能得到独立承认和执行。

2.2 投资基金（Investment Funds）

Cayman investment funds, and in particular private equity funds structured as exempted limited partnerships or limited liability companies, are likely to be the investment vehicle of choice for raising capital from investors for a B&R project. Cayman is the leading jurisdiction for such structures with a market share of over 40%, enabling investors to structure:

开曼群岛投资基金，特别是作为豁免有限合伙企业或有限责任公司结构的私募股权基金，很可能成为向投资者筹集"一带一路"倡议项目资金的投资工具。开曼群岛是此类结构的主要司法管辖区，其市场份额超过40%，使投资者能够构建以下的投资框架：

Clear project investment objectives; drawdown mechanics for capital contributions; provisions for limited partner or limited company member representation on investment committees; market practice management fees; waterfall distribution; orderly winding up of the project through liquidation of the fund; a general partner's or project manager's exclusive right to manage the fund project; and a recognition of standard concepts such as carried interest or related performance and management fees for fund managers.

明确的项目投资目标;提取出资款项的机制;有限合伙人或有限公司成员在投资委员会中的代表性规定;市场实践管理费;基金收益瀑布型分配方式;通过资金清算有序地结束项目;普通合伙人或项目经理管理基金项目的专有权;以及对标准概念的认可,如基金经理的附带权益或相关业绩和管理费用。

In short, a structure that meets and delivers on the commercial expectations of all participants.

简言之,这一结构可以满足并实现所有参与者的商业期望。

One thing to note about B&R focused funds is the fund size-given the types of likely projects (from infrastructure to innovation) they are typically investing in, it is not surprising that fund sizes are significant in the RMB billion plus range. Again, given a likely project focus of infrastructure to innovation, such funds would be managed, by the People's Republic of China (PRC) or related entities including the PRC banks and SOEs, through the ownership by those principals of management shares and day-to-day management of the board of directors at the general partner level of a private equity fund.

"一带一路"倡议项目专项基金值得注意的一点是基金规模——考虑到他们通常投资的潜在项目类型(从基础设施到创新),该类基金规模会非常巨大,在10亿元人民币以上也不足为奇。再者,鉴于项目可能将重点放在基础设施、创新项目上,该等基金将由中国政府或包括中国银行和国有企业在内的相关实体进行管理,其方式是由该等主体持有管理股,并以普通合伙人的身份对私募股权基金的董事会进行日常管理。

3. 开曼私募股权基金结构 (Structure of Cayman Private Equity Fund)

3.1 从结构顶层开始——构建 (Establishment From the Top of the Structure)

As noted, Cayman investment funds focused on B&R would typically be structured as an open-ended or closed-ended exempted limited partnership (ELP). Depending on structuring needs, investment fund managers will often form an ELP to act as a private equity fund, investing in a portfolio or venture company; and/or form an alternative investment vehicle, a parallel fund or co-investment vehicle for international, including the PRC investors.

专注于"一带一路"倡议项目的开曼投资基金通常采用开放式或封闭式豁免有限合伙企业（ELP）的形式。根据结构需求，投资基金经理通常会组建一个 ELP 来作为私募股权基金，投资于投资组合或风险投资公司；还可能会为国际投资者包括中国投资者组建替代投资工具、平行基金或共同投资工具。

3.2 执行董事（Principals）

Project participants may come from different walks of life-bankers, property developers, SOEs or listed companies. Their varying backgrounds, investment profiles and strategies may have to be reflected in a shareholders or investment agreement at the general partner (GP) level which primarily ensures adequate control and management of the fund.

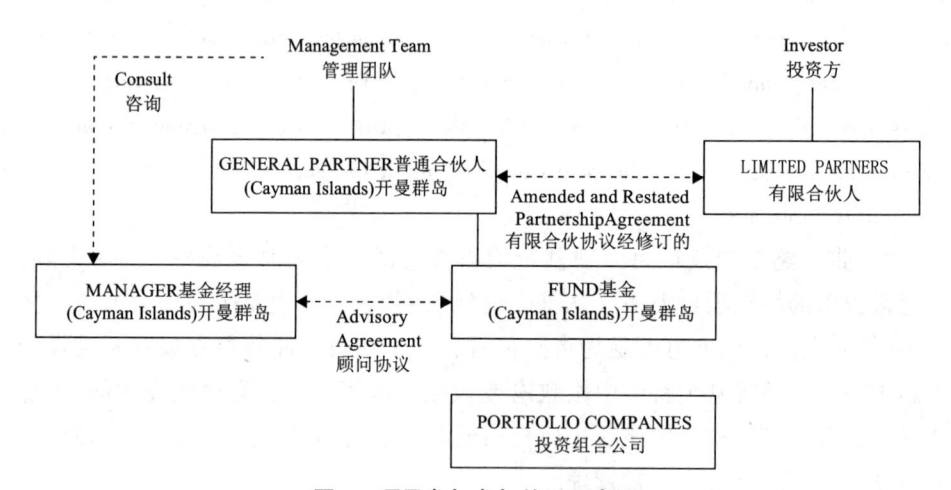

```
                Management Team                      Investor
                   管理团队                           投资方
Consult
 咨询
         ┌─────────────────────────┐         ┌─────────────────────┐
         │ GENERAL PARTNER 普通合伙人 │ ←─────→ │ LIMITED PARTNERS     │
         │ (Cayman Islands) 开曼群岛  │         │ 有限合伙人           │
         └─────────────────────────┘         └─────────────────────┘
                                Amended and Restated
                                PartnershipAgreement
                                有限合伙协议经修订的
 ┌─────────────────────────┐         ┌─────────────────────────┐
 │ MANAGER 基金经理         │ ←────── │ FUND 基金                │
 │ (Cayman Islands) 开曼群岛 │         │ (Cayman Islands) 开曼群岛 │
 └─────────────────────────┘         └─────────────────────────┘
                           Advisory
                           Agreement
                           顾问协议
                                      ┌─────────────────────────┐
                                      │ PORTFOLIO COMPANIES     │
                                      │ 投资组合公司            │
                                      └─────────────────────────┘
```

图 1　项目参与者与关系示意图

项目参与者可能来自不同的行业——银行家、房地产开发商、国有企业或上市公司。他们不同的背景、投资概况和策略可能需要反映在普通合伙人（GP）层面的股东或投资协议中，该协议主要确保能够对基金充分控制和管理。

The shareholders' agreement would document the principle commercial terms of the transaction representing the rights and privileges attaching to the shareholding or ownership stake of the respective principal.

股东协议将记录交易的主要商业条款，代表着各委托人的股权或对本金的所有权份额所附带的权利和特权。

Provisions would include: Voting rights; Return on capital investment including dividends or distributions; Transfer restrictions; Protective provisions; Liquidation or winding up preferences.

条款包括：投票权；资本投资回报，包括股息或分红；股权转让限制；保护条款；清算或清算优先权。

3.3 项目条款（Project Terms）

Where the structure is that of a private equity fund, the parties would document the project terms under the principle fund document. Where the fund is structured as a limited partnership that would be under a partnership agreement or limited liability company agreement in the case of an exempted limited liability company.

如果是私募股权基金的结构，双方将根据基金主文件记录项目条款；如果基金是有限合伙企业的形式，则应根据合伙协议记录项目条款；如果是豁免有限责任公司则依据有限责任公司协议记录项目条款。

Some of the principal terms of the partnership agreement would be as follows:

合伙协议的一些主要条款如下：

- Duration: typically the term or duration of the fund would be allied to the investment objectives or project timeline which obviously creates some certainty for investors.
- 期限：通常，基金的期限将与投资目标或项目时间表相关联，这显然能为投资者带来一些确定性。
- Economics: the project fund may set out an indicative distribution and payment waterfall which may include:
- 经济性：项目基金可能会设定一个指示性的分配方式和瀑布型支付方式，其中可能包括：

  i. *Return of realised capital and costs*: First, 100% to Limited Partners equal to capital contribution;

  ii. *Preferred return*: Second, 100% as commercially agreed, 6%-8%, on capital contribution;

  iii. *general partner catch up*: Third, 100% as commercially agreed 80/20 split: 80% limited partners and 20% to general partner represented by carried interest.

  i. 返还出资额：第一，支付有限合伙人100%出资额；

  ii. 优先收益：第二，按照商业协议约定，支付出资额的6%—8%；

ⅲ. 追赶收益：第三，按照商业协议约定，进行80%和20%的分割：80%支付给有限合伙人，20%以业绩提成的形式支付给普通合伙人。

● Management fee: commercially determined, 1%–2% per annum on limited partner's or investor's capital commitment or proposed investment is not untypical.

● 管理费：通常是根据有限合伙人或投资者作出的资本承诺或拟议的投资，每年收取1%—2%的管理费。

● Expenses: typically paid out of the fund's assets.

● 费用：通常从基金资产中支付。

● Withdrawal: on termination of the fund, with the agreement of the GP or operator of fund.

● 提款：基金终止后，经普通合伙人或基金管理人同意可以提款。

● Special terms: special arrangements may be made with particular investors through side letters setting out terms particular to their investment profile.

● 特殊条款：特殊安排可通过补充协议与特定投资者订立，其中应列明其具体的投资概况。

● There may be no restriction on types of distributable currency including RMB.

● 对于可分配货币种类（包括人民币）可以不设限制。

4. "一带一路"项目类型（Types of B&R Projects）

The ELP may be formed for any lawful purpose to be carried out and undertaken either in or from within the Cayman Islands or elsewhere upon the terms, with the rights and powers, and subject to the conditions, limitations, restrictions and liabilities mentioned in the Partnership Act.

ELP可根据《开曼群岛合伙企业法》中规定的条件、限制和责任，在开曼群岛或条款约定的其他地区以任何合法目的而成立。

The investment objectives of the ELP could be as broad as investing in projects in the Greater Bay Area or as narrow as an investment in a particular portfolio or venture capital company. In short, other than restricted by applicable law, the partnership structure does not seek to constrain the reach of B&R projects and with its imbedded flexibility is well placed to help with structuring project goals.

ELP的投资目标可以像投资粤港澳大湾区的项目一样广泛，也可以像投资某个特定的投资组合或风险投资公司一样具体。简言之，除了受适用法律的限制，合伙企业的结构并不会限制"一带一路"倡议项目，而且其固有的灵活性也有助于构建项目目标。

4.1 关键因素（Key Factors）

• An ELP must at all times comprise at least: (i) one or more general partners, at least one of which shall: (a) if an individual, be resident in the Cayman Islands; (b) if a company, be incorporated under the laws of Cayman Islands or registered as a foreign company under Part IX of Cayman Companies Act; or (c) if a partnership, be an exempted limited partnership registered pursuant to the Exempted Limited Partnership Act (the "Partnership Act") or registered as a foreign limited partnership from certain recognised jurisdictions pursuant to section 42 of the Partnership Act; and (ii) at least one limited partner.

• ELP 必须始终至少由以下人员组成：(i) 一名或多名普通合伙人，其中至少一名应：如果是个人，则为开曼群岛居民；如果是公司，则根据开曼群岛法律注册成立，或根据《开曼群岛公司法》第九部分注册为外国公司；或如果是合伙企业，则应是根据《开曼群岛豁免有限合伙法》（《开曼群岛合伙企业法》）注册的豁免有限合伙企业，或根据《开曼群岛合伙企业法》第42条在某些公认司法管辖区注册为外国有限合伙企业；以及 (ii) 至少一名有限合伙人。

• limited partners shall not be liable for the debts or obligations of the ELP save as provided in the partnership agreement, and as otherwise specified in the Partnership Act, in other words, investors take comfort from the fact that their exposure would be as they so determine under the commercial terms they agree.

• 有限合伙人不应对 ELP 的债务或义务承担责任，除非合伙协议另有规定，或者《开曼群岛合伙企业法》另有规定；换句话说，为使投资者感到安心，投资者的风险敞口将根据他们同意的商业条款确定。

• general and limited partners may be companies or partnerships.

• 普通合伙人和有限合伙人可以是公司或合伙企业。

• general partner or principals may take an interest as a limited partner, in other words, principals are able to invest in the fund.

• 普通合伙人或委托人可以作为有限合伙人享有权益，换言之，委托人可以投资该基金。

4.2 合伙制结构的优点（The Advantages of a Partnership Structure）

The ELP structure is internationally recognised and widely used.

ELP 结构已得到国际认可并被广泛使用。

There are no onerous official filing and publication requirements to establish the partnership or as a pre-condition to any effective change in filed information. Formation is by a general partner and at least one limited partner signing a partnership agreement (in simple form or otherwise) and the general partner filing with the registrar of exempted limited partnerships a short form registration statement containing basic details about the partnership. Partnership funds can be set up quickly with relative ease.

设立合伙企业或对合伙企业备案信息作任何有效变更都不需要繁琐的官方备案和公开发布。由普通合伙人和至少一名有限合伙人签署合伙协议（以简单形式或其他形式），并由普通合伙人向豁免有限合伙企业注册处提交一份包含合伙企业基本细节的简短登记声明，合伙基金即可相对容易且快速地设立。

On 7 February 2020, the Cayman Government published the Private Funds Act and the Private Funds (Savings and Transitional Provisions) Regulations, 2020 (PFL) which provides for the registration of closed ended funds (private funds) with CIMA. The Act, reflecting Cayman's commitment as a co-operative jurisdiction, is responsive to EU and other international recommendations and covers similar ground to existing or proposed legislation in a number of other jurisdictions. The PFL will generally apply to private funds set up as an ELP, company, unit trust or a limited liability company unless out of scope on the basis set out in the PFL.

2020 年 2 月 7 日，开曼群岛政府公布了《开曼群岛私募基金法》和《开曼群岛私募基金（保留及过渡性条款）条例（2020）》（PFL），其中规定封闭式基金（私人基金）需要在开曼群岛金融管理局登记。该法反映了开曼群岛作为一个合作司法管辖区的承诺，是对欧盟和国际上建议的回应，涵盖了与其他一些司法管辖区的现有或拟议立法类似的依据。一般来说，PFL 适用于作为 ELP、公司、单位信托或有限公司基金设立的私人基金，除非该私人基金超出 PFL 中规定的范围。

The Partnership Act benefits from the English common law principle that a partnership is not a separate legal person and conducts its business through its general partner. In all practical respects, however, the administrative ease and flexibility of the corporate form is provided, with the result that a limited partner of an ELP stands in most respects in a similar position to a shareholder in a Cayman exempted company.

《开曼群岛合伙企业法》遵循英国普通法原则，即合伙企业并非以单独的法人身份开展业务，而是通过其普通合伙人开展业务。然而，从任何实务的角度看，公司形式的行政便利性和灵活性均有提供，其结果是，在大多数方面，ELP 的有限合伙人与开曼群岛豁免公司的股东处于类似的地位。

The ELP structure, squarely places the management of the fund with the GP or principals behind the fund, usually the project manager. Those seeking project investment opportunities, subject to the express provisions of the limited partnership agreement that governs the management of the fund, (i) would not take part in the management of the fund and (ii) in their capacity as a limited partner, do not owe any fiduciary duty in performing any of their obligations under the partnership agreement to the partnership or any other limited partner.

ELP 结构明确地将基金的管理交由基金背后的普通合伙人或主要负责人来负责，通常为项目经理。那些寻求项目投资机会的人，在遵守管理基金的有限合伙协议的前提下，（i）不参与基金的管理，（ii）并且以有限合伙人的身份，在履行合伙协议规定的任何义务时，不对合伙企业或任何其他有限合伙人承担任何信托义务。

The establishment of the Cayman fund does not restrict the establishment of or investment in parallel investment funds to co-invest with the Cayman fund including RMB funds.

开曼基金的设立并不会限制设立或投资平行投资基金以共同投资开曼基金（包括人民币基金）。

4.3 经济实体法（Economic Substance Act）

Cayman introduced the International Tax Cooperation (Economic Substance) Act (2021 Revision) and the BVI enacted the Economic Substance (Companies and Limited Partnerships) Act, 2018 (together, the ES Act), respectively, which introduces certain reporting and economic substance requirements for "relevant entities" conducting "relevant activities". The ES Act in both Cayman and the BVI are responsive to global OECD *Base Erosion and Profit Shifting* regarding geographically mobile activities. It is worth noting that under the Cayman *ES Act* an entity that falls within the definition of an investment fund is not a relevant entity for the purposes of the ES Act and thereby falls outside the scope of the ES Act. The ES Act defines an "investment fund" as an entity whose principal business is the issuing of investment interests to raise funds or pool investor funds with the aim of enabling a holder of such an investment interest to benefit from the profits or gains from the entity's acquisition, holding, management or disposal of investments and includes any entity through which an investment fund directly or indirectly invests or operates. Investment fund business' is defined as *the business of operating* as an investment fund. Investment interests' means a share, trust unit, partnership interest or other right that carries an entitlement to participate in the profits or gains of the entity.

2021年《开曼群岛国际税务合作（经济实体）法》（2021年修订版）和2018年《BVI经济实体（公司和有限合伙企业）法》（合称《经济实体法》），两法分别对开展"相关活动"的"相关实体"提出了某些报告和经济实体要求。开曼群岛和BVI的《经济实体法》是对经合组织关于地理流动活动的全球税基侵蚀和利润转移的回应。值得注意的是，根据《经济实体法》，属于投资基金定义范围的实体不是《经济实体法》所指的相关实体，因此不属于《经济实体法》的管辖范围。《经济实体法》将"投资基金"主要业务定义为发放投资权益以筹集资金或集中投资者资金，目的是使这种投资权益的持有人能够从该实体的获取、持有、管理或处置投资的利润或收益中获益，并包括投资基金直接或间接投资或经营的任何实体。"投资基金业务"的定义是作为投资基金经营的业务。"投资权益"是指有权分享实体利润或收益的股份、信托单位、合伙权益或其他权利。

The result of this is that entities structured as an investment fund as well as an entity which the fund establishes to deploy capital, for instance, a typical Cayman SPV investing in a portfolio company, would also fall within the definition of an investment fund for the purposes of the *ES Act* and thereby falls outside the scope of the *ES Act*.

其结果是，构成投资基金的实体以及基金为配置资本而设立的实体，例如，一个典型的为投资组合公司设立的开曼特殊目的公司，也属于投资基金的定义范围，因此不属于经济实体法的范围。

4.4 基金关注点（Fund Focus）

For the principals and investors, the investment strategy is enabling in that may include one of achieving an absolute or positive return on investment mark to market notwithstanding that, for instance, the underline Greater Bay area project investment may well be subject to some volatility.

对于委托人和投资者而言，可行的投资策略可能包括获得绝对或正面的市场投资回报，尽管有些项目投资可能会受到某些波动影响，例如大湾区项目。

The fund focus could be narrower or more specific-for instance, investments in debt securities, including debt instruments, convertible securities, derivatives, listed and private equities and related funds and securities investment.

基金的关注点可以更窄或更具体，例如投资于债务证券，包括债务工具、可转换证券、衍生品、上市和私募股权以及相关基金和证券投资。

4.5 项目或投资公司（Project or Investment Company）

As noted, the project range of B&R is extensive-infrastructure, transportation, science, technology, innovation, real estate, healthcare, tourism to name a few-all ventures one would see coming from typical venture capital, small medium enterprises, and other enterprises. Therefore, the project fund would invest in projects that are commonly structured through a Cayman or BVI portfolio or holding company which indirectly holds the interests in the underlined B&R project.

如前所述，"一带一路"倡议项目范围非常广泛，包含基础设施、交通、科学、技术、创新、房地产、医疗保健、旅游等；类型包括典型的风险投资、中小企业和其他企业。因此，项目基金通常投资以开曼群岛或 BVI 投资组合而构建的项目，或间接持有"一带一路"倡议项目权益的控股公司并不意外。

5. 开曼私募股权投资结构（Structure of Cayman Private Equity Investment）

The project fund can seek an investment in a variety of ways ranging from hardware construction projects to software tech companies from AI to blockchain.

如图2，该项目基金可以从硬件建设项目到软件技术公司，从人工智能到区块链等多种领域寻求投资。

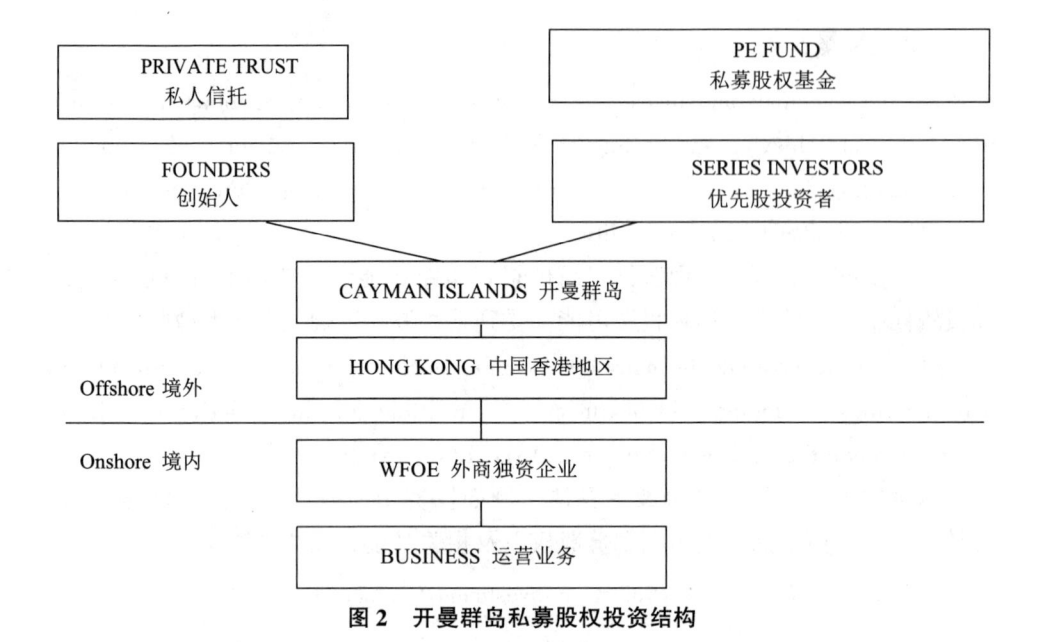

```
┌─────────────────────┐              ┌─────────────────────┐
│   PRIVATE TRUST     │              │      PE FUND        │
│     私人信托         │              │    私募股权基金      │
└──────────┬──────────┘              └──────────┬──────────┘
           │                                     │
┌─────────────────────┐              ┌─────────────────────┐
│     FOUNDERS        │              │   SERIES INVESTORS  │
│      创始人         │              │    优先股投资者      │
└──────────┬──────────┘              └──────────┬──────────┘
           │                                     │
           └──────────────┬──────────────────────┘
                          │
              ┌───────────────────────┐
              │ CAYMAN ISLANDS 开曼群岛 │
              └───────────┬───────────┘
                          │
              ┌───────────────────────┐
Offshore 境外 │ HONG KONG 中国香港地区  │
              └───────────┬───────────┘
─────────────────────────┼──────────────────────────
Onshore 境内              │
              ┌───────────────────────┐
              │  WFOE 外商独资企业     │
              └───────────┬───────────┘
                          │
              ┌───────────────────────┐
              │  BUSINESS 运营业务     │
              └───────────────────────┘
```

图 2 开曼群岛私募股权投资结构

Most leading PRC companies started their life as a portfolio company, which would include the BAT companies—Baidu, Alibaba and Tencent, which prior to being listed Cayman Chinese operating companies, formed part of an investment portfolio of an investment fund. Now B&R project funds are benefiting from the very same Cayman offshore structures to construct their own B&R investment. The benefits are equally as compelling: in short, a tried and tested structure that secures one's investment pre and post proposed exit.

大多数领先的中国公司都是以投资组合公司起家的，其中包括 BAT 三巨头公司——百度、阿里巴巴和腾讯。在上市之前，这些公司都是投资基金项目下投资组合的一部分。现在，"一带一路"倡议项目基金在进行投资时，也受益于开曼群岛与投资组合相似的离岸资本结构。这样做的好处同样一目了然：简言之，这是一个可以在投资前后都可确保双方交易安全性的交易架构，且久经考验。

5.1 开曼群岛或 BVI 的投资组合公司所具备的优势（The Benefits that Cayman or BVI Portfolio Companies Provide）

In no particular order and by no means an exhaustive list：

Voting rights; Conversion of Shares; Transfer of Shares/Restrictions on Transfers; Right of First Refusal; Right of Pre-emption; Redemption Rights; Repurchase Rights; Variation of Rights Provisions; Tag Along Provisions; Drag Along Provisions; Put Option; Call Option; Protective/Restrictive Provisions; Appointment of Directors; Dividends and Distributions; Winding Up.

以下列举内容没有特别的顺序，也非穷尽式列举：

投票权；股份转换；股份转让/转让限制；优先受让权；优先认股权；股份赎回权；股份回购权；更改权利之条款；随售权；拖售权；出售权；买入权；保护/限制性条款；委任董事权；股息及分发；清盘。

The above shopping list is a list of provisions one would usually see baked into the relevant transaction documents. The Cayman model is the best for delivery of those protections and rights that investors and project principals are seeking with the BVI model also popular.

上述清单是相关交易文件中通常会出现的一系列条款。开曼群岛模式是投资者和项目负责人寻求的保护交付和权利的最佳之选，BVI模式也很受欢迎。

5.2 投票权（Voting Rights）

These voting rights range from no voting rights or decision-making capability to the more typical "one member, one vote" to weighted voting where investors, in particular, significant project parties, would want their voting power to represent their economic investment i. e. a number of votes per share held that enables the exercise of voting power independent of other shareholders that can influence decision making. The point of voting rights is that it represents the right to be heard and counted disproportionately or otherwise.

这些投票权包括无表决权或决策能力，更典型的投票权如"一员一票"和加权表决权。投资者，特别是重要项目的参与方，希望他们的表决权代表他们的经济投资，即每股拥有的投票数，使他们能够独立于可影响决策的其他股东行使表决权。投票权的意义在于，它代表了不成比例地或以其他方式表达意见并发挥效力的权利。

There are no prescribed Cayman or BVI laws as such that constrain the parties in commercially determining their arrangements for the allocation of voting rights per share or relative to an investment.

开曼群岛或 BVI 没有法律规定以限制各方设置其每股表决权或与投资相关的分配安排。

5.3 股份转换（Conversion of Shares）

Typically, a project investor would in the first instance want preferred shares or shares that represent an economic interest. Such preferred shares reflect the fact that at the outset the investor's investment is at risk-it is always at risk pre-exit. The investor's rights pre-exit would focus on economic returns or rights in the event that the investor seeks a return on capital prior to, say, an initial public offering ("IPO") of the portfolio company's shares. However, in the event the company does get to IPO then the investor would want IPO shares—at that point it would have the right to convert its preferred shares into IPO or ordinary shares.

一般来说，项目投资者首先想要的是优先股或体现经济利益的股票。这种优先股反映投资者的投资从一开始就处于风险之中的事实——在退出之前总是处于风险之中。投资者退出前的权利将侧重于经济回报或在投资组合公司股票首次公开发行（IPO）前寻求资本回报的权利。然而，如果该公司真的能够上市，那么投资者就会想要首次公开发行的股票——届时，该公司将有权将其优先股转换为首次公开发行（IPO）的股票或普通股。

In practice, various mechanisms can be deployed under Cayman or BVI law to achieve the result of conversion with little trouble and potentially limited potential tax or other down side risk to the structure.

在实践中，可以根据开曼群岛或 BVI 的法律设立多种交易机制，且转变交易机制并不麻烦，也可潜在限制隐性税收或其他交易结构中的负面风险。

5.4 股份转让/转让限制（Transfer of Shares/Restrictions on Transfers）

The focus here is on stability and continuity. If an investor wants out, who will be the new investor or transferee? Existing investors will want a say and therefore would want to place restrictions on an investor's ability to transfer shares to a third party. Other than as provided for under the company's constitutional documents, Cayman or BVI law does not place additional constraints on the transferor's ability to transfer shares but does afford the parties the flexibility to manage those rights.

此处的重点在于（交易）稳定性和连续性。如果一个投资者想退出，谁将成为新的投资者或（股份）受让者。现有投资者希望对此有发言权，因此希望限制投资者向第三方转让股份的权利。除了公司章程文件的规定，开曼群岛或 BVI 的法律没有对转让人转让股份的施加额外的限制，但确实为当事人提供了管理这些权利的灵活性。

5.5 优先购买权（Right of First Refusal）

Aligned to restriction on transfer of shares is the right of an investor to have shares the subject of a transfer to be offered to existing investors first. There are no Cayman or BVI laws restricting the right to be offered shares ahead of anyone else.

与股份转让限制一致的是，投资者有权要求股份作为转让的标的，首先提供给现有投资者。在开曼群岛和 BVI，没有任何法律限制投资者对股份具有优先购买权。

5.6 优先认股权（Right of Pre-emption）

Similarly, subject to the discharge of its fiduciary duties, Cayman and BVI law does not seek to dictate to the parties to whom a company may issue shares to or what investors can be project partners.

同样，受限于信托义务的履行，开曼群岛和 BVI 的法律并无规定公司发行股票的对象，或规定哪些投资者可以成为项目伙伴。

5.7 股份回赎权/股份购回权（Redemption Rights/Repurchase Rights）

Shares may be purchased or redeemed by the company in such manner and upon such terms as may be authorised by or pursuant to the company's articles of association.

Accordingly, so long as the company would be able to pay its debts as they fall due following a redemption/repurchase, there is a great deal of flexibility as to the form or manner that purchase or redemption of shares could take.

公司可以按照公司授权或依照公司章程规定的方式和条件购买或赎回股份。

因此，只要公司能够偿还在赎回/回购之后到期的债务，购买或赎回股份的形式或方式就有很大的灵活性。

5.8 更改权利之条款（Variation of Rights Provisions）

The common law right that an investor's agreed position under the company's constitutional documents is not varied or amended unless otherwise agreed to, is well understood. Cayman and BVI law recognises this common law principle but also provides for its trademark common sense flexibility allowing the parties to determine how far and to what extent the arc of their understanding should extend–that's ultimately a matter for the parties to determine.

除非另有约定，投资者在公司章程文件下的约定立场不得更改或修改。开曼群岛和BVI的法律承认这一普通法原则，但同时也具有了其标志性的灵活性，允许各方确定他们的理解范围应该扩大到什么程度——这一问题最终由各方确定。

5.9 随售权（Tag Along Provisions）

Where an offer for the purchase of the shares of one shareholder is made, the company may afford the same right to other shareholders to be taken up on similar terms or in the jargon, for those other investors to tag along with that initial deal—there are no impediments to that under BVI and Cayman law.

在收购一个股东股份的要约作出时，公司可以赋予其他股东同样的权利，让他们以同等条件或用行业通行条件与初始交易一同出售——根据开曼群岛和BVI的法律对此随售并无限制。

5.10 拖售权（Drag Along Provisions）

Conversely, where there is the potential for one investor to hold up a buyout or sale, subject to the articles of association of the company, Cayman and BVI law affords the parties the flexibility to drag the hold out investor along.

相反，在一个投资者可能实施控制权收购或出售时，受限于公司章程，开曼群岛和BVI的法律给予当事方以灵活性，有权要求其他股东一同出售。

5.11 出售权（Put Option）

Subject to the lawful constraints on a repurchase or redemption of shares mentioned above, there are no statutory legal constraints on a right for an investor to sell shares back to the company.

受限于上述有关回购或赎回股份的法律限制，对于投资者向公司要求回购其股份的权利并无法律限制。

5.12 买入权（Call Option）

Subject to the terms of the allotment and issue of any shares, the company may make calls (or a request) upon shareholders in respect of any monies unpaid on their shares (whether in respect of par value or premium). This right is important, in particular where shares are issued as partly paid and a call is not met, when coupled with a right of forfeiture, such shares may be forfeited by the company.

受限于分配和发行任意股份的条款，公司可以就未支付的股份款项（不论是面值还是溢价）向股东提出缴款要求（或请求）。这项权利非常重要，特别是在以部分支付的方式发行股票而未满足赎回要求的情况下，当附加收回股票的权利时，该等股票可能会被公司收回。

5.13 保护/限制性条款（Protective/Restrictive Provisions）

The scope protective or restrictive provisions is often one of the most hotly contested provisions, These will vary in their scope and nature however, the key messaging as a matter of Cayman and BVI law is that the parties are afforded the flexibility to negotiate the scope and range of their commercial terms as one would expect experience investors to be afforded. It means Cayman and BVI law are light touch in their oversight of commercial terms.

保护性或限制性条款的范围往往是最受争议的条款之一，然而这些条款的范围和性质各不相同，开曼群岛和BVI法律的关键是，各交易参与方在谈判其商业条款范围时，被赋予与经验丰富的投资人相同的灵活度——开曼群岛和BVI法律对商业条款的监督较为宽松。

5.14 委任董事权（Appointment of Directors）

The investors usually want the right to be represented at board level or with respect to the day-to-day management of the company which board of directors undertake. For holding companies sitting under an investment fund, there is no onerous Cayman or BVI law regulatory oversight at the portfolio company level, or for instance, demands for local or independent directors to be appointed. The make-up and shape of the board of directors is a matter for the parties.

投资者通常希望在董事会层面或董事会负责的公司的日常管理方面拥有代表权。对于投资基金下的控股公司而言，在投资组合公司层面，开曼群岛或BVI没有繁琐的法律监管，例如没有任命本地或独立董事的要求。董事会的组成和形式取决于各方。

5.15 股息及分配 (Dividends and Distributions)

Under Cayman law, it is expected that dividends should be paid out of profits or assets legally available for distribution, and in any event subject to the company's ability to make such payments. As a matter of BVI law, a BVI company may only pay a dividend if its directors are satisfied on reasonable grounds that the BVI company will satisfy the solvency test immediately after the payment is made.

根据开曼群岛的法律，在公司有能力支付股息的任何情况下都应该从合法可分配的利润或资产中支付股息。根据BVI的法律，BVI的公司只有在其董事有合理理由认为在公司支付股息后能立即通过偿付能力检验，才可支付股息。

5.16 优先清算权/清盘 (Liquidation Preference/Winding Up)

Both Cayman and BVI law does make clear that there are rules of the road governing the rights of preferred, secured and unsecure creditors ranking ahead of investors or shareholders however, among themselves, the priority or order of distribution to shareholders where there are different classes of shares is a matter for the shareholders to determine. Therefore, there is somewhat of a free hand given to the shareholders to determine under its articles of association liquidation preference provisions among different classes of shareholders.

开曼群岛和BVI的法律确实明确规定了优先债权人、有担保债权人和无担保债权人相较于投资者和股东有优先权的规则，但是，股东之间，如果有不同类别的股份，向股东分红的优先顺序或次序应由股东决定。因此，在某种程度上，公司章程允许股东自由决定不同类别股东之间的清算优先权。

6. 开曼群岛和BVI投资结构构建"一带一路"倡议指引 (Cayman and BVI structures governing the rules of the Belt and Road)

In conclusion, what Cayman and BVI structures have to offer is a tried and tested product that is well suited for B&R projects. Whether structuring inbound China as seen through typical VIE structures, where Cayman and the BVI are used as an offshore holding company primed for listing on a Chinese or overseas stock exchange, or for outbound investments as a vehicle used to structure a B&R investment through an investment fund or otherwise to effectively deploy capital, Cayman and the BVI lead the way into and out of China.

综上所述，开曼群岛和 BVI 的投资结构久经考验且非常适合"一带一路"倡议项目。无论是通过典型的 VIE 结构来构建中国境内投资，此时开曼群岛和 BVI 被用作建立在中国或海外证券交易所上市的离岸控股公司；还是作为通过投资基金构建"一带一路"倡议投资或以其他方式有效配置资本的工具从而进行境外投资，开曼群岛和 BVI 都为中国境内外投资提供了指引。

— 作者简介 —

Everton Robertson is a partner of Maples and Calder's Finance team in the Maples Group's Hong Kong office. He is a private equity, finance and funds lawyer who has acted for major financial institutions, corporations, private equity firms and UHNWs throughout Asia. He focuses on venture capital and pre-IPO financing, mergers and acquisitions, IPOs and the establishment of open and close ended investment funds.

Everton Robertson 是 Maples 集团香港办公室 Maples and Calder's 金融团队的合伙人。他是一名专注于私募股权、金融和基金领域的律师，曾为亚洲各大金融机构、企业、私募股权公司和超高净值人士提供服务。他关注的领域包括风险投资、上市前融资、并购、IPO 以及开放式、封闭式投资基金的设立。